El Rancho Kid

El Rancho Kid

Copyright 1990 by Bill Adams

Copyright renewed 2015 by William Lee Adams

All rights reserved, including the right to reproduce this book, or portions thereof, in any form.

For sales inquiries and reprint permissions please contact:

TDLAD Publishing

2001 South Valley Drive, Las Cruces, NM 88005

www.tdlad.com   wla@tdlad.com

ISBN: 978-0-9817428-2-3 (pbk)

Printed in USA

Publishing history:

First Edition: 1990

25th Anniversary Edition: May 19, 2015

0 9 8 7 6 5 4 3 2

Dedication

I would like to dedicate my book to my posterity. My kids, Floyde, Sidney, Robert, and Bonnie, encouraged me to write my autobiography and my wife, Martha, encouraged me to stay with it after I started it. I started to write on a typewriter and soon decided that was for the birds. I was ready to give it up but Floyde got me into computer and word--processing and that was the boot I needed to go for it.

I have enjoyed memories seventy years back and I am thankful that I could write and pass them on to those who might be interested.

Contents

25th Anniversary Introduction		VI
1	Rafter G Ranch	1
2	Klondyke	7
3	Columbus	52
4	Barranca	64
5	Camp Sauz	90
6	Pajarito	100
7	Colonia Dublan	171
8	Duncan	196
9	Mangum	202
10	Martha Taylor	225
11	Morenci	240
12	San Luis Potosi	248
13	Dublan Second Time	270
14	U.S. Navy	285
15	Dublan Third Time	319
16	El Paso	343
17	Aftosa	348
18	Bell Ranch	375
19	Dublan Fourth Time	392
20	El Paso Second Time	402
21	Las Cruces	419
22	Fannie Ada Crabtree Adams	468

Introduction

Back in 1990, my stay-at-tiny-mobile-home-mom wife, Christina, grappled in turn with a Dell 386 computer, three kids and me. At least two of these five items were, at any given time, seemingly intent on mayhem. She ran Ventura Publisher on top of Windows 3.0 on top of DOS, one of which would playfully crash every few minutes. She learned quickly to save her work on the *El Rancho Kid* manuscript often. She put in an untold and unsung number of hours trying to force the files into some semblance of a book.

After printing almost a ream of pages on our spanking new HP Laserjet Series II (we still have it and it still prints if we could only find a computer with a parallel interface) we took our "camera ready" bundle to a local printer. What seemed like an eternity passed, but at long last 250 books finally arrived. Of course, we immediately spotted about a zillion errors that had inexplicably escaped our crack team of proofreaders.

My grandfather proceeded to sell them to everyone he could think of and put a "review copy" in the customer waiting area at our automotive repair shop. About once a week, for quite some time, a customer would ask how to buy the book after reading a bit while waiting for their vehicle to be fixed. We kept a few copies for this purpose and collected the cash for him - $17.50. He'd come in to pick up his "coffee" money every so often and replenish our stock. He'd cheerfully sign any that were sold, if asked (and sometimes without the asking). In a few years he sold all his books and we removed the worn out display copy.

I always knew we'd reprint it someday, though - it is simply too good not to. But it was a daunting task. Ever arose the question of what to do with the zillion errors. We toyed with the idea of cleaning it up some, but, as his daughter, my Aunt Bonnie pointed out recently, our collective heads would probably explode. So here is, warts and all, the absolutely original text, just as it fell from Wordperfect on my grandfathers computer 25 years ago. He sure did use "sure" a lot, but therein lies some of the cachet of his work. I'm not qualified nor could ever bear to change a bit of it.

He was and remains an amazing guy. His is a timeless story of a life well-lived. It may not be *The Old Man and the Sea*, but then again, Hemingway couldn't have written this book.

So here's to you, Willie Roy.

William Lee Adams ("little" Bill)   May, 2015

1
Rafter G Ranch

My great--grandfather Adams was among the Mormon families that moved to Mexico to escape the polygamy law of the US. That was in 1885. His name was Jerome Jefferson Adams. He was not a polygamist but his intentions were good. He took twelve children with him. My grandfather was one of them. His name was William, they called him Will. He married Domer Jones Johnson and also considered at one time of taking another wife but Domer wasn't that kind, so they settled down and had ten children. My Dad was the fifth. His name was Leroy Jefferson Adams. He liked to be called R J but was better known as Roy. I didn't know what the J stood for until I was grown. I didn't know his name was Leroy until I read the book, Heart Beats of Colonia Diaz. Colonia Diaz, Chihuahua, Mexico, was where they settled. My grandfather was very religious and a very strict Mormon, so much so that he didn't raise one church oriented child. The Adams' kids were known as part of the Colonia Diaz Wild Bunch. As soon as they were old enough to run they left home. Which means also that they all got very little schooling. The kids were mostly left--handed and that puts one in left field to start with. I've heard my dad tell how his left hand was sore because his teacher hit it with a ruler when she caught him using it to write. He said he finally had enough when he was in the fourth grade and he hit the trail. He went to work on cattle ranches and there finished his education. Some of it good and some of it not so good. He went to work on a ranch in Arizona. The owner's wife took a liking to him and taught him to read and write and numbers. He gave her credit for getting him on a better path in life. Dad was in his early twenties at that time.

In 1912, my grandmother Adams died in childbirth, number eleven. While they were getting the burial ready, my grandfather, Will Adams, was shot and killed in front of his home by some Mexican border official. His oldest daughter, Edith, had crossed the border at Columbus, NM, and was there for her mother's funeral. It seems the official had been drinking and was insisting on taking her back to Palomas and not let her stay for the funeral. There was a discrepancy with her border--crossing papers. My grandfather was insisting that he let her stay. They were quickly buried together in unmarked graves, because the Mormons panicked at that time and left all their belongings and went back to the US. At least the US officers wouldn't shoot them. It was not the first trouble in the Colonies. It's just the one that broke the straw. My Dad learned about his parents' death some time later when he was reading a newspaper. After he learned to read he said he would just pick up any old paper and read it. He was on some ranch in Arizona. Someone saw the article and asked Dad if he might know them. The fellow who shot my grandfather was Rojas. My father--in--law, Harvey Taylor, and Aunt Rhoda, my step--mother in law, spent some time at our home sometime in 1970. We were talking about those times in 1912, and the murder of my grandfather. I asked Harve if they had known the fellow who shot him. He said, "Oh yes, his name was Rojas, and we took care of him so that he would never shoot another man." That was his total explanation.

My mother's family, S P Crabtree, lived in the area of Vernon, Texas. Her father died, and soon after, her mother moved to Duncan, Az. That would have been in 1916. Mother worked in a restaurant at the Carlyle Mines near Duncan Az. The mines were near the ranch where Dad was working at that time. There were thirteen children in the Crabtree family. Mother was about in the middle. Her name was Fannie Ada. She and Dad got acquainted before long, and were married Dec. 6, 1917. Just as they had planned, I arrived on December 18, 1919. Now from here on I can tell it like it was. The above is just what I have been told. I was named Willie Roy. Good thing I wasn't very big or they wouldn't have gotten away with it. Dad had a favorite brother named Willie. Uncle Bill, I was named for him. There will be more about him later. He would never admit his name was Willie. I lived with it until my first year in high school. At that time we were living at Colonia Dublan, Chihuahua, Mexico. I went to live with the Foot family, Mother's sister, Mattie, in Duncan, Az. That was when I was determined to be known as Bill. Two or three friends I was raised with still call me Willie when we meet. That's OK if they smile.

I was born at York, Az, Dec. 18, 1919 on Thursday. I was someplace in my third year when we left there. Not much happens for a three year old to tell about. One of the very vivid events I remember well was when Floyd was born. June 26, 1923. I was down at the corral with Dad when a lady came driving up and said something to Dad then took her satchel and went up to the house. The ranch was at the foot of a hill and the house was uphill from the corrals. It was in the afternoon. After some time, she came back to where we were, said something to Dad and drove away. Then Dad and I went up to the house and there was a little baby boy. Well now there was only one road coming in from the canyon side and one trail coming off the hill. I sure hadn't seen any way of how that little kid could have gotten by me. I asked Dad just how did he get in. He said Mrs. Coan brought him in that satchel she was carrying. That made sense because that was the only thing I hadn't looked into that day. I learned the difference about the time I learned about Santa Claus. I told Floyd he wasn't even a brother because a lady didn't want him so she brought him in a satchel and gave him to the Mom and Dad. That broke his heart and he went straight to Mom, and the truth had to come out. I've been carrying a salt shaker ever since.

Our place was called Rafter G Ranch and still is. The brand was a G with a rafter over the top of it, thus the name. Dad bought it from a fellow by the name of Grady. In those days you bought a homestead or homesteaded yourself. In order to get a title on a homestead you had to do a certain amount of improvements. Sometimes it was better to buy one that was already improved on because in most places the easy water was already taken up. All the country around the homestead was called Taylor Grazing and anyone could run their cattle on it, called open range. On the ranch deal, Dad signed notes to Grady for payments on the ranch. Grady sold the notes to the bank in Clifton. Well, that was one of those deals that a man works his heart out and then loses the whole thing. Dad sold some cattle so he could get some payments made on the place and the bank took the whole thing. Dad always felt bitter over the deal because there was a gentleman's agreement that if things got tough, Grady would give him a chance to make it. He didn't know the notes would be sold. That was when we moved to Klondyke, Az.

I had a dog there at the ranch, and of course I've heard Mom and Dad talk about it, but I can remember the old dog. His name was Bishop. The thing that is vivid to me is a time that he saved my life. I had found a rattlesnake and was trying to catch it. The old dog had me by the seat of the pants and kept pulling me away until Mom heard the commotion and came out there and killed the snake. The thing I remember is that old snake was sure noisy and kept trying to climb the mesquite bush he was in. We had quite a few chickens and the coyotes would come around real regular. If those old hens went too far out in the bushes, they sure would run and call for help. Dad would run out and take a shot at the coyote even if he couldn't see it. One time the coyote got him a hen and she was sure squawking loud and Dad was shooting and the coyote was running. Old coyote had chicken for dinner that day.

Another time I remember Dad found a cat with some kittens in a cave up on the side of the hill. He decided to catch one and bring it down to the house. He had gloves on but that little cat bit him through the gloves and made a little spot of blood for each tooth. I don't know what happened to the little cat but I do know that was the last time I saw it.

At that time, Washington had made alcohol drinks illegal. The more they chased people the more it was worth and before long it seemed worth the risk to many people to get into the bootleg business. Some people got very rich. Now we have drugs in a big way. A fellow by the name of Bob Nichols showed up one day. I never knew from where. He had heard that Dad was from Mexico. He wanted Dad to help him go to Mexico and get some alcohol and make it into whiskey and make some quick easy money. Dad finally agreed to go with him one trip to show him how, because Dad knew the country by trail at night with no moon. Nichols told Dad that if he would show him and if they could do it then he would give Dad half. They each took a pack horse and away they went. Dad was riding Trigger. He took Toothpick for his pack horse. Both horses were from thoroughbred stock. They hit the border fence somewhere south of Hatchita, NM. That would be in the area known as The Corner. In those days they would just let the wires down, step the horses over and put the wires back up, brush the tracks and proceed per plan. They went to Ascension, about fifty miles south of Columbus, NM. They had no trouble getting the alcohol, enough to load the two pack horses. The alcohol was in rectangle five gallon cans. They were standard containers in Mexico for anything that was sealed. In later years I even bought gasoline that way. They rested for a few days and fed their horses good to get ready for the return trip. Ascension is across the river from Colonia Diaz where Dad was raised. Dad chose the time when there was no moon. They traveled at night. Bushed up and slept in the daytime. They made the trip with no trouble. Nichols took over from there. He made the whiskey and sold it just as he had promised and gave Dad his share for guiding him on the trip. It turned out so good that Nichols wanted Dad to go again. Dad told him no way. He said, "I took you once and I got enough to pay my bills and now I have a clean slate to start over." It wasn't very long after that when we moved to Klondyke, Az. Bob Nichols left then and never showed again.

I also had a horse when we lived at the Rafter G. Mom's brother, Tommy, gave him to me. He was a sorrel yearling colt. There was something wrong with him, they called it a thistletoe. It causes a swelling on top of the shoulder and the horse walks in short steps with his front feet. To cure it you take a running iron, which is a branding iron with a hook on one end. You brand a circle on each side of the shoulder then put a cross in each circle for good measure. Well he was a real pretty little colt with flax mane and tail. Dad didn't want to scar him up, so a clothes iron was used, in place of the running iron. The kind that was heated on top of a wood stove. The operation had to be done with the horse standing up because you have to do both sides right up to the top of the shoulder. One hind foot was tied up just far enough from the ground that he had to stand on one hind leg only. The reason for tying the hind leg rather than the front leg is because a horse gets up front feet first. With one hind foot tied off the ground he can't get the other one off the ground to kick or anything. OK, we had the colt ready for his cure. Before Dad left the house to go down to the corral, about a hundred yards, he told Mom to put two flat irons on the stove. When she heard him holler that he was ready, then to run one of them down to him. It took one iron for each side so while Dad was using the first one she ran back to the house then came running with the other one. There were actually two kinds of running irons. One with a hook on one end and Dad running it in circles on the animal and the other was a flat iron and Mother running it in a straight line from the house to the corral. The ironing procedure was to wet the hair then press until dry. I think that little horse decided right there that if he ever got away he would never come back, because when Dad turned him loose he left out of the corral and never came back. His name was Nestegg.

2

Klondyke

We moved to Klondyke in 1923. I would have been in the three year old bracket at that time. Floyd was born at the Rafter G Ranch June 26, 1923, and he was still little enough to put back in that satchel. The only thing I remember about the move over there is that Uncle Thad, Dad's brother, drove Dad's horses from York over to Klondyke. The Rafter G Ranch was at York, Az. I think he took them to Safford the first day then on to Klondyke the next day. I don't know how many horses there were, maybe three or four. Thad was riding Dad's favorite horse, called Trigger. Thad got to the ranch late at night so I heard what had happened the next morning. He was leading the other horses. About three miles from his ranch (we were staying at Thad's ranch) he met a car and the headlights blinded the horses. He couldn't get them out of the road before the river ran over him and broke one of Trigger's legs. In those times, cars mostly just had brakes on the rear wheels. The road was about a grader--blade wide and was laned with mesquite trees and brush. There was no place to get out of the way of the oncoming car. Thad always carried a pistol. He shot Trigger and changed his saddle to one of the other horses and went on to the ranch. I went with Dad and Thad back down the road where it happened. There laid Trigger in the ditch beside the road. Dad was very sad about it. Thad's ranch was on the north side of the road from Klondyke to Wilcox and about two miles west of the Safford road turn off. The ranch is still there and it's surprising how little change in over sixty years. We lived with Thad and his wife, Ruth, until we could get moved on up to the ranch that was in the deal for us going to Klondyke in the first place. The deal was thus: Some fellows in Safford had bought a ranch up in the Galiuro Mountains, but were about to lose it because they couldn't pay for it. The reason they couldn't pay for it was that the cattle were so wild they couldn't catch them. Those mountains were full of wild cattle. Many of them unbranded so they belonged to whomever could catch them. I think the fellow that owned the VAV Ranch was a Mr. Mitt Sims in Safford. I think Sims bought it from the Power fellows after they got into so much trouble. They told Thad that if he would work the ranch and could catch the cattle and get it paid for, they would give him half interest in the ranch. Thad went to Dad and asked him to go help him and when they got the place paid for, then he would let Dad have half of his half which would give them each a fourth and that sounded real good to Dad. Remember back where I told you that the Adams boys were known as the Colonia Diaz Wild Bunch. Well, that was where the wildness was about to pay off, because they were raised wild like those cows they planned to catch. The name of the ranch was VAV. That was also the brand. That is what we called it. It was really called Rattlesnake Spring. It is now called Power Garden. That spring being where we got our running water. Most of the cattle were not branded because the cowboys couldn't get close enough to put a hot iron on them. An unbranded animal that isn't still with the mother is called a maverick and he belongs to whomever can put his brand on him.

A ranch at that time was a homestead of one square mile that was proved up on and had the papers in order. The rest of the range was open range and anyone could run cattle there, free. That was before the government allotted land to the ranchers and let them fence it and pay lease. The rancher could never own it and still can't. The BLM program was started sometime in the early 1930's. Thad's ranch was on the Aravaipa Canyon and also part of the deal but those fellows couldn't legally hold it. They did some kind of paperwork so Thad could hold it for them. We went on up into the mountains to the VAV Ranch. We all went back and forth between the two places. It was about twelve miles. The only way to the VAV was by horse and pack mule. There were several ranches around in the mountains and the cowboys seemed to take a liking to me. One of them gave me a little black horse, called Chinate, and another cowboy gave me a little saddle and his worn--out chaps. Dad was an artist with leather and buckskin and I soon had a fine pair of chaps just my size. There were no stirrups on the saddle and that's the way I learned to ride.

By that time, I must have been getting close to four. On our first trip up to the VAV, Mom took Floyd on her horse, he was just a baby, and Raymon rode behind me. I think we were up there about a year. Mom never went back down to the canyon until we moved out of there. I went with Dad when he would take the mule train down to the canyon ranch for supplies. We always went down one day and back up the next day. One time we went down and back the same day. It was night on the way back and I was getting tired and sleepy. Dad turned my horse loose with the pack train and got me up behind him. I curled around under his jacket and went to sleep. Of course Mom was up waiting for us. When she saw my horse come in with an empty saddle she panicked before Dad could show her that he had me up there on his horse. He handed me down to her. I will never forget how she hugged and kissed me. We will never know what a fear she must have felt at that moment.

Farther on up the mountain was an abandoned gold mine called the Power Mine. I rode up there with Dad one day. A few miles sort of up and south from the VAV. He looked around the mine equipment and found some steel strap just right to make two stirrups to fit on my little saddle, and of course my little feet. I sure was proud of them. There was a blacksmith forge and tools under a big oak tree there at the VAV. I liked to turn the crank on the blower.

There was a large arroyo near the house. It was about ten feet deep and about thirty feet across at the top of the banks. It came off the mountain by the house, then flattened out into small channels before it joined the Rattlesnake Canyon, about three hundred yards from the house. I was riding Chinate and decided to cross over to the other side near where it joined the Rattlesnake. It was about a foot deep and maybe four feet across it. I thought my horse would step down into it then up the other side, but instead he jumped it. When he jumped I flew up in the air and landed on his neck right behind his ears. I got a good hand hold on his ears and clamped my legs around his throat. I lost my reins, they fell to the ground. Now you wonder just how smart an animal can be. That little horse turned around real easy and took me back across the ditch. However, that time he stepped down in it rather than jumping and took me back to the house where Dad was working. He kept his head high. Maybe because I was pulling on his ears. Dad was shoeing a horse under the big oak tree. Dad put me back in the saddle, picked up the reins for me, and I went on riding.

We had a visitor one day and Dad told him he could ride my horse. He was loose in the corral. The fellow tried to catch him to put the bridle on and Chinate was so silly the guy was afraid of him. He thought Dad was pulling a joke on him. Dad told me to catch him and ride him around a little to show the man he was safe. I did but I sure didn't like him to ride my little horse.

The Power Mine has quite a history. I will tell it the way I heard Dad tell it many times. It was owned by Mr. Power who had with him, his mother and two sons, young men, and a daughter. The mother was dead at the time of this story. They had made a road up there and used wagons to haul the ore down to the Aravaipa Canyon. We just called it the canyon. One of the wagons was still there at the VAV. When we were up there the road was completely gone, washed away. The mine had been abandoned since 1918. It was very rich in gold, about eighty-four ounces per ton. The Power boys had gone to Safford and they wanted to vote for something that was being voted on at the time. The town fathers would not let them vote because they could not read and write. They went back to their gold mine and worked away. Then came along World War I. Of course everyone must register for the Army. Word was sent up the mountain for them to go to Safford and register to go fight. They didn't go. Another message was sent to them that was a little stronger. Either go to Safford and register or officers will go after you. They sent word back that if they couldn't vote they would not fight. It seems it was the father's idea. Besides he needed the boys to help work the mine.

Safford sent four men up there to bring them in. One of the officers in Safford knew them real well and wanted to go along and talk to them and try to get them to give up peacefully, but the other officers would have none of that. So he didn't get to go. It seems the officers were drinking as they went up the mountain and wanted to handcuff them and bring them in like criminals, or better, have a good old western shoot out. Well it turned out to be a western shoot out, but not the way the plans had been set up. The officers were out among the pine trees and called for the Powers to come out with their hands up. Along with those three officers was a fellow from Klondyke. He was mainly for a guide, but for a little excitement also. The guide was a fellow named T.K. Wooten. I went to school with T.K., Jr. The father Power went to the door with his hands up. It was very early in the morning, still dark. They shot him dead right there. That was when things started to get western. The Power boys couldn't read and write but they could shoot. They declared open season on those men out there in the piney wood trees. They killed three of the officers and the other one got away. He went back to Safford and when he got his story told, every available man was out looking for the Power men. John was twenty--seven and Tom was twenty--five. He sure messed up on the details. The Powers didn't know there was a fourth man until later or they would surely have killed him also. Bill Wooten was my bus driver when I started to school. I think he was the father to the Wooten who was killed. There was also a Braz Wooten, and a Frank Wooten there at Klondyke. They were brothers to T.K. The hunted wandered around the state of Arizona among and with the hunters until they finally got tired of it and decided to give themselves up. They could evade all the hunters because no one knew what they looked like. When they left the mine after the shooting they went over the mountain to the west and crossed the Mexican border south of Hachita near a place called The Corner. It was about a month, however, when they gave themselves up. They were in Mexico but worn out and hungry. They got life in prison. When I was in the second grade, a rumor was started that the Powers had broken out of jail. Braz Wooten went to Safford and checked into the hospital until the rumor was verified. It was not a rumor, but they were only loose a few days. They got away a second time and then got all the way to Mexico City. They couldn't find work because they were tourists so it was illegal for them to work.

Dad said that people would ask him if he was looking for the Powers and he would tell them no, they sure hadn't done anything to him. Dad actually sympathized with them because he had also been hounded a lot about the draft. The draft board would call him in to Safford every so often to check him out again. He finally told the board to take him or leave him alone because that was the last time he would report. He was too tall and too skinny to pass the physical. The Power story is the way I heard Dad tell it many times. The rest of the story that Dad didn't live to know about is that they were finally paroled after forty--two years. Tom died in 1970 and John died in 1976. They are all buried at Klondyke.

One of the ways they would catch those wild cattle was with salt. No, you don't salt their tails. Roadrunners, yes, but not those wild cattle. One of the cowboys had sent me to the house to get some salt to put on a roadrunner's tail so I could catch him. I finally decided I was between a joke and a hard place, but I wasn't sure. When no one was looking I would get me a salt shaker and try again. The roadrunners even thought it was funny. In those mountains there were no salt licks. Salt was hauled in on mules in fifty pound blocks. The salt was put in the corrals at the various line camps, which there were several. The corrals had two gates. One a regular swinging gate, that opened to the outside, and the other was a trap gate. When the trap gate was set, a cow could go in and lick salt but not get out. To get a picture of the trap gate, hold your two hands about four inches apart, palms facing and fingers pointing away from you. Let the wrists be fastened to the gate posts, between the wrists being the opening or entrance to the corral. The fingers pointing to the inside of the corral, and representing about four--inch poles, eight feet long. Now imagine a tall post set on the outside of each set of fingers at the pointed end. A wire stretched at the top from one post to the other. The ends of the fingers are wired together and spaced about a foot apart and then suspended from the wire that runs overhead between the two tall posts. Now hold the wrists as they are but move the fingers to about half an inch from touching. You can see how an animal would or could go in but couldn't get out. But just to be sure, the ends of those poles were pointed real sharp. When the traps were set they were checked often to see how many cattle they had caught. Many times they would have deer in there, but when the cowboys went in the deer jumped out. They never did catch one. They would catch the cattle and brand them then turn them loose. Before long they had branded quite a few. Then as they would catch them again the brand would be haired over and they could take them to market. It takes about a month for one to hair over.

We built a holding pasture to put the cattle in as they would catch them. I say we built it because I pulled all the barb wire on my little Chinate horse. The barb wire was on a spool. One person put a crowbar through the center of the spool. He then rested each end of the crowbar on something so the spool of wire could turn as the wire was pulled. The person on the horse tied a rope to the end of the wire and rode off along the fence line unspooling the wire as he went. A spool of wire is a quarter of a mile long. In those mountains I didn't go far before I couldn't see the person on the spool or the person I was taking the end of the wire to. The person at the spool kept it from unwinding too fast by laying a stick on the spool of wire. When I was pulling wire they would put Dad's saddle on my horse. Mine would have come apart. Those barbs would dig in like a stalled buzz saw as I pulled it passed some of those trees. My little horse just pushed his chin out and pulled harder. He never did stall out but came close a few times.

Another way they would catch the cattle was with dogs. Each cowboy had his own dog and taught him to catch by command and turn loose by command also. Some of the dogs would catch and just stay on and not turn loose when first told. I have seen some of those dogs whipped like you wouldn't believe because they didn't obey. The dogs were taught to follow the owner right at the heels of his horse, and especially not to chase deer. The mountains were full of wild cattle so they could always find something for the dogs to catch. The terrain was so rough and steep with timber and smaller brush that they couldn't run and catch them on horseback unless they could run the cattle out over a mesa. Most of those cattle were too smart to do that. The dogs were each different in the way they would catch an animal. They always caught hold someplace on the head. The nose, an ear, the throat, but the dog that could really stop and hold a big bull was the one who caught by the tongue. Dad's dog Pat caught by the tongue. When the animal was running it would open its mouth and the tongue stuck out just far enough for a good bite. The dogs that caught other places got slung around and banged up badly but when a dog was on that old cow's tongue she just stood there and pawed the ground and talked to that old dog in bad cow language. The cowboy would ride up and put a rope on the cow and tie it to a tree. They tied them to trees in the area they were working at the time and would leave them tied for three days then go back after them. By that time it was hungry and thirsty and sure enough mad. When they went back after the tied up cows they would put a rope on the horns then get close enough to turn the rope loose that was tied to the tree, and the race was on. They took the animals to the holding pasture on the end of a rope. You have to let that cow get close enough to the horse to almost hook him but not quite, but she thinks the next jump she will for sure open him up. That would go on for about a quarter mile and after that you can just lead her home and put her in the holding pasture. When I would go with Dad to pick up one that he had tied to a tree he would tell me to stay way back and just follow him home. Sometimes my little old horse could hardly keep up, they would travel so fast.

I have told about how we followed trails everywhere we went. Those trails were the mountain highways. That was the way we went from ranch to ranch or wherever else we had to go. When they untied one of those cows from a tree, it was a race to keep out of her way, but all done on the trail. If the cowboy leading her got too far ahead of her she would quit the trail and fork a tree. That didn't happen very often. Dad was leading a cow over one of those trails and his horse could barely stay ahead of her horns. They were coming around the mountain, just like in the song. Maybe you think there wasn't much traffic on those trails. As trails go, there was. That day Dad met Joe Beachem. He was the fellow who gave me my first little saddle and chaps.

Today we think of pileups on freeways. That day there was a pileup on the VAV trail. Beachem didn't believe what he saw soon enough to turn and run back where he came from. Dad and the cow caught him. He couldn't quit the trail, he thought. Well, when that old cow got through with them, Joe and Dad had both quit the trail, rolling and tumbling. I was not there but when Dad came home he was sure skinned, mostly on his head. I didn't see Beachem but his story was that he met a wild man who damn--near killed him.

The dogs would get sore footed. The men would put shoes on them. They would put some pine gum in a wiener can and put the dog's foot in the can. By the time he wore the can out his foot would be healed and ready to go again.   When a dog had shoes on they would leave him home because he slipped around too much with those slick shoes. One day they left a couple of the dogs home with shoes on. They put them in the barn so the dogs wouldn't follow them. I had a little dog of my own and I wasn't allowed to play with the catch dogs at all. Those dogs were not allowed friends except their master and he wasn't friendly to them. Well, along about noon, I decided to look in on those two dogs. I opened the door and as I went in they came out. They circled the corral a couple of times with their noses to the ground and soon out the gate they went. The last time I saw them they were going up the mountain on the trail. Those dogs smelled the horse tracks and could tell which one his master was on. They were sure smart. This is not a joke. That was the first time I considered running away from home, and the first time I wasn't glad to see Dad when he came home that evening. The dogs found them alright, but they had worn out the shoes so it all had to be done over.

    The VAV Ranch had been there long enough that the easy wood was getting scarce. The buildings were near the bank of the Rattlesnake Canyon. When it rained the water would sure come falling out of the mountains and bring all kinds of logs with it. Dad and Thad would each get on a mule. When a log would come by they would ride out in the water and rope it and drag it to the high ground. Those mules would get all tangled up in the swift water and almost fall down and sometimes even buck a little if things didn't go to suit them.

    There was a spring up the canyon about a quarter mile. The reason for the name, Rattlesnake Spring. That was where we got all our house water from. Running water. You get a bucket and run to the spring. One evening after dark, Mom and Ruth decided to go after some water. Before long they came running back to the house without the water. They said they heard a noise and looked back and there was a bear rather close checking out their tracks. They sat the water down and made him some more tracks to look at. The guys went back down the trail and got the water and didn't see the bear. The next morning they found his tracks where he had sure been there.

On one of the trips down to the Aravaipa Ranch, we stopped by the Habey Ranch. Vivian Habey was my age. She had a new batch of pups just right to wean. She gave me one to take home, back up to the VAV. It was a little white spits dog. I called it Blanco. I carried him all the way home on my horse. The Habey Ranch was on the Aravaipa also, just a few miles below Thad's place. Blanco grew real fast and before long I had him with me every place I went. We had chickens and a few guinea hens. I think guineas were to serve sort of as watch dogs. They were sure noisy. The ranch house was on a slope and the back was off the ground about two feet. There was a setting hen had her nest under one corner. I would check her out regular and she would always peck me. Blanco was with me but always kept his distance from that old hen. Well, one day I was checking her out and I guess some eggs were starting to hatch. She came off from her nest and pecked me as she went by and after Blanco she went. Blanco ran around the house with that hen right on his tail. I was running fast as I could, because I just knew she was going to wipe out my little dog. Around the house we went but shortly they were around the corner out of sight but I could hear them and I ran fast as I could, thinking that I'd find her killing my dog any minute now. Shortly I heard them behind me and sure enough they passed me up. Blanco was sure yapping. I saw that I was going the wrong direction to catch them. About the time I turned around, there they came again. I scooped up my little dog and that chicken was going so fast she just slid on by. She pulled her wings in and went back to her nest. Just why did that old chicken slide? Like I said, "She was sure mad and my little dog was sure scared."

Guinea Hens. I don't know why they were there unless it was to warn the chickens when danger was somewhere near. They were always on the house or in a tree where they could see what was going on, or what was about to go on. I had been told that those guineas were too smart for the animals to catch them. Bears, wolves, coyotes, and maybe a skunk. We had them all. They didn't go in the chicken house at night. They roosted in the big oak tree there near the chicken house. I was playing in the front yard and one of the cow dogs came over to me, I guess to check me out. About the same time a pair of guinea hens walked by rather close, like maybe fifty feet. They were talking and pecking on the ground. We were on the side of the house where the arroyo was. Remember I told it was about ten feet deep and about thirty feet or more across the top. The sides were sloping. I knew that old dog couldn't catch them, but I couldn't resist the temptation to give it a try. My mind went into neutral and I said, "Sickum." Like I said, those birds were sure smart. The dog made a dash for them and they turned and flew across the arroyo. By the time the dog could go down and up the other side they flew back across, and there came the dog down and up again. I was sure laughing because I had a real game going there. However, after several flights across the arroyo those birds were showing to be getting tired. They were barely making it across. The dog was tired also but seemed to be gaining on them. I knew trouble was coming my way if I didn't get the dog stopped. I knew the command to get him to turn loose but I didn't know the command to stop him from the chasing those birds. Dad heard those guineas screeching and came out of the house to see what they were talking about. I don't remember the command he used to call the dog off. Those dogs minded very good. I'm sure he saved the guineas. I figured they would fly up into a tree or on the roof, but heck no. They just kept jumping that ditch until they were too tired to fly up onto anything.

The mountain ranch was hard work for men and animals alike, so it was important that they all had good feed and plenty of it. We hauled grain, mostly corn, up there by the trainload. Mule train that is. The grain bin was made from corrugated roofing tin, six feet long. That was how deep the bin was because the tins were standing vertical, about four by four feet square. It was under a large oak tree and there was no top on it. They poured the grain in over the top from the shipping sacks. There were lots of squirrels and they liked grain also. They would jump out of the tree down into the bin. When they were full they would jump back up into the tree, unless they had misjudged how far down the grain was, and they couldn't jump high enough to catch a limb. I would climb the tree and see them in there. They were sure wild. One day we had just arrived with a trainload of grain and Dad was pouring it in the bin. I had seen the squirrel in there but I couldn't get up there in Dad's way to watch him so I decided to turn him out the bottom. There was a little shoot with a sliding lid to get the grain out in the morales for the horses and mules. I don't know now how I thought that squirrel could come out there because he was on top of the grain. I guess I thought Dad was covering him up. Anyhow, I pulled the chute lid and out came the grain, and I couldn't get it shut. Dad came down with about a third of a sack of grain in his hand, and when that sack of grain hit the seat of my pants I went airborne, my first flying lesson. I have never seen so much corn come out of such a little chute.

As I have said, everything was moved up to the VAV by mule train. I think there were maybe about ten mules. Some of them real honest and some of them real dishonest. By that I mean some of them would just as soon try to get that pack off. If it didn't get tied on just right and should turn down under, then they would rather kick it to pieces than to wait for help from one of the drivers. On one trip, Thad decided he was tired of sleeping on a pine needle mattress (not a joke). He picked the most honest mule and along with the other things he put on that mule, he put the mattress over the top and tied it down good. He was very good at throwing a diamond hitch. We drove the train with flippers and rocks. Maybe today some would call them sling shots. What we called them then is unprintable today. That was the standard mule train tool. The train had to travel single file and if the front or any mule stopped on the trail you had to wake him up. Well the mule with the special cargo was about in the middle of the train, and that mattress stuck out to the side more than a regular load. The mule was coming to a tree that was real close to the trail and Thad could see he was going to hit the mattress and tear it. He quickly got a shot off at that old mule and hit him right behind the ear to draw his attention to the tree. Normally the mule would have understood but in this case his complete thoughts were on the tree and getting his pack by the tree like the good mule that he was. Well that rock behind his ear messed up his train of thoughts and he started doing a mule dance right there on the trail as he came to the tree. Now with the unusual cargo, the tree and the rock, he lost his footing, fell off the trail and rolled down the mountain to the bottom of the canyon. When he quit rolling he had the pack on his belly and a hind foot had gone all the way through the mattress. It was funny to all except Thad and the mule.

A new mule was always overloaded to keep him on the ground with all four feet, then he was tied to the tail of an honest mule so he didn't decide to blaze a new trail down the mountain someplace along the way. The pack saddle was tied to the mule in five places. A cinch under the belly, a cinch under the tail, and cinch called a brichen that was about halfway between the tail and the hock, a flank cinch, and a cinch under the neck called a breast strap. Now when all those seat belts were pulled tight, some of those mules just would not stand still, especially the tail holt. I have seen Dad put rocks on top of the pack if the cargo wasn't enough to hold the mule to the ground.

I told about the trap gates on the corrals. There was a trap gate on the corral at the ranch house. One day Dad had set it to see if something might go in there for some salt. Along in the afternoon I was playing down at the corrals. I looked in there and saw a big red bull. I couldn't see a brand on him so I ran to the house and told Dad we had a red bull maverick in the corral. Like three or four years old. The corrals were made with poles standing vertical, close together and held together with wire laced in and around them. They were about six feet tall. I had analyzed that bull from the outside looking through the spaces between the poles. Dad went down to the corral to check him out, and sure enough, I was right. He asked me how I knew he was a maverick, and I told him I couldn't see a brand. Well, how could I tell he was a bull? Right there I just figured that if he didn't know, I sure wasn't going to tell him, so I told him I could tell by the big horns. I never did think I had fooled him.

He sent me up to the house to get Mom to go and help him brand the bull. In the middle of the corral was a big oak tree. Dad got a couple of ropes and went into the corral with that bull. He told Mom to wait outside the gate until he had him caught and some dallys on the oak tree. Dad used the tree for a shield because the bull was on the fight right away. As he charged, Dad would get behind the tree until finally he got a good shot at him and put his rope on the horns. He took after Dad, and around the tree they went. Just as Dad had planned. The bull was winding up shorter and Dad was winding longer so shortly he had that bulls head tight against the tree. Now it was safe for Mom to go in there and hold the rope. Dad would take the other rope and get him by one hind foot so he couldn't shake the rope off. He would dally a post in the corral fence and they would just stretch him out and tail him down. Just as Dad got him by a hind foot, that old bull decided to chase Mom. She had the long rope and would have been OK but she got scared and ran, holding onto the rope, but guess what, she ran the wrong way and she was getting a shorter rope and the bull was getting a longer rope. Dad was going around with them trying to catch a post on the corral fence with his rope before it was too late. He was sure running out of time fast. About one more time around that oak tree and Mom and that bull would have been face--to--face. Dad finally got a dally on a post. They got the bull down and tied him good. Dad made a fire and put the iron to get hot. He and Mom sat down by the fence to rest up a little. They both thanked each other for not turning loose. It was sure close.

Dad branded him, trimmed his ears some and changed him from a bull to a steer. That was when that X--bull really got mad. Dad and Mom had a little meeting to decide how to turn him loose. Near the barn, which made up part of the corral, was a small gate just for cowboys to go through. The corral was maybe two hundred feet across. Mom would hold the small gate open and Dad would take the ropes off him, and run through the gate. Mom would shut it in that old bull's face. Dad would be going too fast to shut it himself. The gate was about four feet wide. The bull had plans also. Dad barely got the bull's feet untied when he got up and was closing the distance to Dad real fast. In fact, he was so close to Dad that Mom decided she couldn't shut the bull off, so she shut the gate before Dad got through. Dad was going so fast and was so scared that he went right over the top of the pole fence. Dad asked her why--in--the--hell she shut the gate on him, she said, "You told me not to let the bull out and he was sure getting close." The bull stayed in the corral until after dark, pawing the fire, butting the oak tree, shaking his head, and bellering. He finally left and Dad never saw him again. Dad sang a song that I loved. It always reminded me of the V A V Ranch and the red bull. This is a good place to put a copy.

Klondyke

It's way up high in the syree peaks where the yellow pines grow tall
Rusty Giggs and Sandy Bob had a round up there one fall
They took their horse and branding iron and maybe a dog or two
And allows they'd brand every long--eared calf that came into their view
So it's every little doggy that flops a long ear and don't bush up by day
Gets his long ears whittled and his old hide scorched in the most artistic way

Said Sandy Bob to Rusty Giggs as he throwed his seego down
I'm getting tired of this cow punch and allows I'm going into town
They saddled up and hit a lope for they wanted no sye to ride
For now was the time for the good cow poke to wet up his old inside
They started in at the Texas bar at the head of the whiskey row
And wound up down by the depot house some twenty drinks below

They sat right up and turned around and hit her the other way
To tell the God for sakes and truth those hands got stewed that day
As they were riding back to camp and carrying a pretty good load
Who should they meet but the devil himself came waltzing down that road
Said the devil you cowboy skunks had better to hunt your hole
Cause I've come up from hell's rim rock for to gather in your soul

Well devil be damned said Sandy Bob we cowboys are feeling tight
And if you gather any cowboy soul you've surely got to fight
He punched him a hole in his old seego and shot her straight and true
Yes he placed it around that devil's horns and he had it anchored too
It's Rusty Giggs a riatta man with his rope done up so neat
But he shook her out and built a loop and roped that devil's hind feet

They stretched him out and tailed him down while the irons were getting hot

They cropped and swallow forked his ears and burnt him up a lot
They trimmed him up with a dehorn saw and knotted his tail for a joke
And went off and left him necked up there to a great big black jack oak
So if ever you are in the Syree Peaks and hear one hell of a wail
You may know it's the devil himself howling about the knots in his tail

I was riding with Dad on the trail from the Huntington Ranch. It was at the foot of the mountain on the north side. It was a few miles south towards Wilcox. Not far as the crow traveled, but a long day with a mule herd. We took lots of the supplies over that trail because it was shorter, and there was a road from Wilcox to the Huntington Ranch. They would have supplies trucked in there, especially the heavy stuff like fifty pound salt blocks and grain, mostly corn for the horses and mules. As we were crossing a big canyon out jumped a yearling bull maverick. We didn't have a mule train that day. Dad told me to wait there, and he was gone. Dad carried his rope like a pistol fighter carried his gun, ready to shoot in seconds. He could take it off his saddle and build a loop in two swings. By that time his horse had better be on the target or he was in trouble. The race was on and they were shortly out of sight, but it wasn't long before Dad came riding back to me and told me to follow him. We went down the canyon a short distance and there he had that bull yearling tied to a tree and sure in bad humor. Dad took my rope that I always had on my saddle for those occasions, but I hadn't learned to use it yet from my horse, and roped one of the bull's hind feet, dallied a tree and soon had him well tied down. It was safe then for me to get off my horse. We tied our horses to a big old bush there close. Dad got the fire going, and while the iron was getting hot. Dad reshaped his ears a little and made a nice little steer out of him. Dad put the brand on him, and while all that was taking place, the bull's displeasure was being voiced loud and clear. When Dad was ready to turn him loose he told me to get behind a pine tree that was there close. He didn't want me to get on my horse because sometimes those unhappy animals would charge a horse and could sure cause a wreck. Dad turned him loose and got a tree between him and the bull. The bull saw right away there was something better than chasing Dad around the tree so he turned and came my way. Well I was peaking around the tree to see what was happening when I saw that bull coming towards my tree. I knew I was in trouble and it was coming fast. I took off running as fast as I could go. For some reason we'll never know, the bull decided to hook the horses instead of me, and hook them he did. They both broke loose and ran around until the bull had enough and went off up the mountain. In a few seconds it was all over and Dad came running over to me and said, "Why didn't you stay behind the tree like I told you?"

I said, "Papa, that tree was just too little."

Later after we had moved back down to the Aravaipa Canyon and after I had started to school, Dad and I were riding the same trail with a mule train. As we were crossing that same big canyon Dad said, "Willie, you see that tree right over there, it is the one you thought was too little to hide behind from that bull." I looked at it and I still have to laugh. I could have hidden behind it on my horse.

While we were at the VAV Ranch we got acquainted with an old prospector who worked gold mines someplace about a one day burro drive from our place. He always stopped for a day or so to eat Mom's cooking and rest his burros. He had about eight burros. He took the ore down to the road on the Aravaipa Canyon and there it went by truck. I think he sold it to someone, maybe the trucker, because he would return with supplies to last him until the next trip. I guess about every two months. He unpacked the burros behind the house and the burros would graze around close. When he was ready to go he would call them and they would come to him. One morning Mom was preparing breakfast and had boiled some potatoes. She drained the boiling water off and threw it out the window. The window was high and so she couldn't see what was under it. She didn't even try to look because it was common practice anyhow. Well that morning one of those burros was standing under the window and caught the full pan of boiling water. We heard a loud bray and running hoofs. That old burro was sure in a hurry to get up the side of the mountain because things had gotten too hot in the shade of the house. The prospector's name was Kenothe. We pronounced it Kanutey. He was a german and not a US citizen. He sure didn't want to be obvious to anyone. He wasn't about to speak up for the Power boys. After breakfast Kenothe went out and started calling his burros. They all came but one. He was still up on the side of the mountain. He just refused to come down. Kenothe went up after him and on the way he fell over a boulder and messed up one of his legs some. He got his burro down near the packs, but before he put the pack on him he picked up a big stick and hit that old burro right between the ears. His ears flopped, his eyes went funny, and all four legs buckled. There he sat trying to figure out just what he had done wrong. When he finally got to his feet, he went up to Kenothe and rubbed his nose on him. He would rather be friends. When Kenothe hit the burro he said, "That will to teach you, for hurting my leg."

Now that we are on the subject of burros, there were a few of them that belonged to the VAV Ranch. They were used to take the wild cattle down out of the mountains to a holding pasture that was at Thad's place on the Aravaipa Canyon. When they had caught enough cattle to make a drive down the mountain, they would neck two cows together so they couldn't run away. If they tried to run they would soon fork a tree. Then they would patiently wait for one of the cowboys to come along and help them back on the trail. The biggest and wildest cattle were the ones they necked to the burros. At first of course, the cows had in mind to just hook that old burro to death. They were tied too close together for that, so then they would decide to run up or down the mountain with him, and not on the trail. Those were not the first cattle those burros had taken down the trail to the valley below. They would let their cow buddy get up a little speed and then slide on all fours and spin. They would spin that old cow to the ground unless she gave up real quick. After a few spins they would become friends. Then it was just a little push and shove to see who got to put his feet on the trail. Usually the burro, because after all he was in charge.

I didn't ever get to ride with them when they were moving the cattle. I would watch them as they left to head down the mountain with the herd and it was hard to tell which was the wildest, the cattle or the cowboys. As far as I could watch them as they were leaving, it looked like the burros were the only ones that had things under control. We must have lived at the VAV Ranch for about a year because we went up there in the summer and spent a winter there. Then moved back down to the Aravaipa Canyon some time during the next summer. I have told about the deal that Thad and Dad had with the owners of the VAV. They were to get half the ranch when they could catch enough cattle to pay off the mortgage that was against it. The owners could see that Dad and Thad were sure enough going to get the job done. They found someway to back out on the deal. There was evidently too much handshaking and not enough contract. I also told how Thad was holding the homestead on the Aravaipa Canyon for those people. Thad told them that he would keep the homestead then, and he did. Then Dad homesteaded a section adjoining Thad's place.

   When we first moved out of the mountains we stayed at Thad's place for a while. Mom was doing the washing. Her only convenience was a real large mesquite tree near the house for shade. She had a boil tub with a fire under it, and in the water she put a little lye, a bluing tub and the final rinse tub. I was riding Chinate close to where she was working. He stepped on a shovel just right to stand it up under his belly and the handle poked a hole in him. The handle had been broken and had sort of a ragged point. He jumped a little at first then just stood there. There again, no way would he hurt his rider. Mom took me off from him and called Dad. He came out of the house and pulled the stick out of his belly. It had gone in about three inches. I sure thought I had ruined him. After about a week, however, he was good as new. With the excitement over the horse, Mom forgot to watch what Floyd was getting into. He had learned to walk and was into things he shouldn't. The lye came in a pint can with a press--on lid. Mom was in the process of putting lye in the boil tub when Chinate got the handle poked into him. She set the lye down on the wash bench. Floyd picked it up and got some in his mouth before Mom could stop him. All of a sudden the horse problem was nothing compared to Floyd. All they could think to do was rinse him with water. Ruth ran out to the road, about three hundred yards, where a car came along every day or so, and would you believe, she was barely in time to stop a car going by. We didn't have a car. Mom was running out there with Floyd in her arms and I was running after her. Near Klondyke there was a lady who was a nurse and that was where we went. She came out to the car to greet her visitors and saw Floyd. She ran back into her house and by the time we could get out of the car she was meeting Mom with a bottle of vinegar. She had seen that sort of thing before and didn't have to be told what was wrong. Floyd was a mess for a while. I'm sure the fellow in the car and the nurse lady saved his life. I have no idea who they were. When I took chemistry in high school I learned why the vinegar worked.

While I'm on Floyd's case, there is more. I have told, or will tell, about the first well we tried to dig and gave it up. Dad threw some mesquite limbs over the top of the well and piled them up so no one would walk into it. Well a skunk did and he fell to the bottom. About twenty feet. When the sun was overhead Dad held me over the well so I could see the skunk, and there he was walking around down there. Mom missed Floyd and she found him hanging over the well. He wanted to see the skunk also, but since he couldn't talk no one knew it. He had crawled out on the limbs that were over the well and fell through. He had a loose jacket on, called a cape, and it had hung up on a snag long enough for Mom to catch him. That was after the lye. Then after we had moved to the place where we found water, we had the house built and settled into doing some just living, Mom made some candy. The front of the house was about three feet off the ground, so three steps up to the door. The back of the house was sitting on the ground. Mom had the candy made and left it in the skillet. She gave it to Dad to whip until it cooled. He was sitting on the steps. There were three little boys sure excited over the candy and each one of us wanted to sit closest to Dad. Floyd slipped and when he put his hand out to catch himself it went right into the hot candy. Dad raked the candy off with his hand and blistered it also. Mom and Dad did some quick thinking. They had some linseed oil. They put some in a can that Floyd could put his hand into. They would soak it until the oil would get watery then get some new oil. Mom took him to Safford and the Doctor told her that the linseed oil had saved his hand. It didn't even leave a scar. I have heard Mom and Dad argue over which hand it was.

Thad helped Dad to get the homestead fenced and then we had to have water. Until we got a well dug, we carried our water from Thad's place. He had a windmill. Then Dad made a deal for a not--being--used goat camp. I suppose the homestead was abandoned probably because of no water. He tore it down and salvaged the lumber and nails and built a two room house. It was about a half mile from Thad's, so that was how far we carried water. Dad and Mom each carried two five gallon cans, I had two one gallon buckets that I carried. They had lids on so I wouldn't spill it. I carried most of mine on my horse because they would send me after drinking water when they were working away from the house. They built the house on that spot because there had been a well started by someone and not finished. It was down about twenty feet and that was a good start when you plan to find water at around fifty feet. After they dug on the well for about three weeks and another fifteen feet, they decided why the other fellow gave it up. It was real heavy clay and they decided they just couldn't go through it with a pick and shovel. They even drilled some single jack holes and did some blasting. That was the well the skunk was in that Floyd wanted to see. Dad moved down the ridge. A little closer to the canyon and went after it again. Dad sent me after some water after he started digging, and when he saw me returning he crouched down in the hole he had dug and hid from me. I thought maybe he had gone to the house and I was just ready to take a shortcut when out of the hole he came and drank nearly all my water. After digging about ten feet there he hit the same clay strata that was in the other well. So he abandoned it also.

Domer was born at the goat shed place, June 21, 1925. Grandma Crabtree was there to help Mom. She told Dad she had always heard that hackberry trees would only grow where they could reach water with their tap root. About a half mile up the canyon and right on the bank was a cluster of hackberry trees. We called that place, the goat shed, because that was where the materials came from to build it and besides that, cowboys hate goats. It was a neat place, at the side of a sloping hill, and I roamed all over the area on foot and on my horse.

On my roaming trips I was always looking for something new. I found a turtle. Now that was new. He was so interesting that I took him to the house to show Mom and see just what I had caught. She explained all about turtles to me. Mainly how tough they are, and that nothing can hurt them because they go into their shell, which is very hard and nothing can break it. Little did she realize that she had just handed me one real challenge. She told me to take him back where I got him and turn him loose. I took him back and turned him loose, and of course he just sat there in his shell. I decided to bounce a rock on him. He still didn't come out. I kept bouncing rocks on him and then I noticed he was coming apart. I left him there and went back to the house. I told Mom that he wasn't as tough as she thought. She told me I had hurt him very bad and that he would probably die. I checked on him every day to see if he had gone away. He hadn't, and finally one day I checked on him and only the broken shell was left. Something had eaten him. I felt bad and I have never busted another turtle.

The only way to get to our place from Thad's was to ride a horse or walk. There walked a fellow up the trail, and I knew right off he was no cowboy, and for sure not from our part of the bushes. I stayed out in the mesquites out of sight until I could sort of see what he was up to. That was just before Domer was born. He was selling Singer sewing machines. Dad bought one. Domer still has it. I learned right there that a mother with a baby must have a Singer sewing machine. So when it was getting about time for Floyde's arrival, I told Mart, "We must go to town in San Luis Potosi and get you a Singer sewing machine." I knew she would need it to make whatever our little kid was gong to wear. She still has it.

Little kids today don't have any idea what it is like to have never seen a book until they start school. I had seen one. I couldn't read it. I didn't even know I was suppose to. A fellow came up the same trail, all dressed up and fancy like. There again I knew he was no wild cow catcher. He was a preacher. When he left he gave Raymon and me each a little blue book. Since we didn't really have any use for those little books, we took them with us to the canyon to play. So how does one play with books? We covered them up with sand then we would find them and then hide them again. After a while we had made so many mounds and hid them so many times that we lost them. We never did find which mound of sand they were under. Many years later I asked Mom if she remembered. She said they were little Bibles, and when we took them to play, she had no idea we would loose them.

Dad took his pick and shovel and moved right up close to those hackberry trees and started to dig. It turned out to be mostly gravel. He had to curb the well as he went down for about the first twenty feet. When he had dug a few feet he hit moist digging and it got wetter as he went deeper, but didn't produce water until about sixty feet. That is a long ways down with a pick and shovel. Thad worked with him all the way through until they had water and had a windmill up pumping water.

Klondyke

The windmill was a used one Dad bought from a goat and sheep rancher, named Wetherby. He was the same man that later shot and killed Thad over some goats Thad had bought from him. That was a few years after we had moved to Mexico. They took turns going down in the well and digging. They built a scaffold over the well with a pulley on it and I pulled all the dirt out of the hole. I had a new saddle Dad bought for me in Safford. He tied the well rope to the saddlehorn so it wouldn't come off. Chinati and I would go away from the well until the bucket would come to the top, and whoever was on top would dump it. I would turn my horse around and let it back down to the man below. Chinate would work real slow, as if he knew just what we were doing. I was five at that time and I started to school that fall. Dad and Thad rode the bucket up and down also. I guess they trusted my horse.

When we finally had water, we could get down to building a more permanent type house. Dad got materials from someplace and we moved the goat shed over there. We made chicken coops and all the things to start to settle in. The next thing they made was a dirt tank for water storage for the cattle. Dad borrowed a scraper and harness and put two of those pack mules to work. First Mom was going to drive the mules and Dad would dump the scraper. That didn't work at all because Mom just didn't speak the right language to the mules, so Dad let her dump the scraper and he drove the mules. To build a dirt water tank, the idea is to take the dirt from the inside and pile or bank it around what will be the perimeter when finished. Dad had a good mule vocabulary, but I thought most of the time he was using it on Mom instead of those mules. They didn't stack much soil but they sure scattered a lot of it. After about three days of that, the mules settled down some, Mom got the hang of the fresno and Dad built a real nice water tank.

After the well was finished and the windmill doing its job of trying to keep water in the dirt tank, we noticed the water tasted bad. Each day it seemed to get worse. They had made a good enclosed top over the well so they could hardly believe anything had gotten in there. Dad took a mirror and looked down in the well. That was when I learned how to use a mirror to look into a hole or in that case, a well. It shined a beam of light to the bottom of the well and right to the bottom of the water.

Down there was the skeleton of a big rattlesnake. I can't remember of that water ever tasting good again.

A horse will learn to be a friendly general servant to man, but not a mule. He will be a pack mule, a riding mule, a wagon pulling mule, or a plow mule but never all those things in one mule. Never a pet mule. I have told how Mom and Dad built a water tank with a couple of pack mules. Now that we were living where a wagon could be used we needed something to pull it with. Dad and Thad would teach a couple of those pack mules to do the pulling. They knew there would be a problem so they were ready. Like I have told, the Adams boys were raised wild and they thought that way. They knew those two mules would try to run away with the wagon. A runaway wouldn't be bad if they would stay in the road, but for sure they would take to the bushes. They got those mules in the harness and hooked to the wagon. They tied a rope to a front foot of each mule, then ran it up through the line ring on the hames and back to the wagon. Dad and Thad got in the wagon. They let me go along. Dad held the lines to do the driving and Thad held the ropes that were tied to the front feet at the ankles. When the brake was released, those mules sure enough quit the road and they were gone but not in the road. As expected, Dad couldn't stop them or turn them. They went wild. Thad would pull on one rope then the other. Those mules were sure rubbing their noses in the dirt. Thad would let them get up and then jerk them down again when they would start to run. They settled down to wagon life and was a good team. The reason I got to go on the ride was because Dad and Thad both knew there would not be a runaway or even close. Maybe a skinned mule if he should fall down in front of the wagon but not a runaway.

When we moved our things to the new location we were just camped out until we could get some sort of shelter built. At first we had a tent. The cook stove was sitting out in the open and that was the way they used it for a while. The first day Mom was mixing a batch of biscuits. She asked Dad to build a fire in the stove. He did. Dad had a rawhide braided rope and he couldn't find it. He gave Mom a bad time for not remembering where she had put it. The fire was hot, the biscuits were ready and she opened the oven door. There she found one well done rope. Dad had put it there so nothing would happen to it. It wasn't his only rope but it was special because a Mexican friend that lived up the canyon a few miles had given it to him. The reason they made braided ropes from the cowhide was because no one could read the brand on a rope. Cattle rustling was common, and so was jerky and braided ropes. Those few Mexican families that lived there on the canyon were not the cattle rustlers.

I have told about Floyd burning his hand in the candy. The reason they had the linseed oil was to waterproof the tent. It rained a lot that summer and there was lots of lightning with it. Mom had been explaining to me about lightning and how it would kill people if it should hit them. We were all in our beds one night when it was sure raining hard and a bolt of lightning hit near our house. I thought it had hit the house and had killed everyone but me. I was real quiet for a few minutes then I called, "Mama did it kill you?" It seemed that she was the most important person right then. I got a relief like only a little kid could understand when she said, "Did what kill me?"

I told her, "The lightning that hit the house a while ago."

Then she explained to me some more. When it is close it makes lots of noise and sure makes the house light up. At the same time the lightning hit, the cat screeched and ran over the top of the roof. I didn't know it was the cat that exaggerated the lightning.

Not only did we find water near the hackberry trees, I think maybe six of them, but I found them very good to climb. They had thick and scratchy limbs but I managed to get to the top of them anyhow. One of them had a limb growing at right angles to the trunk, and about six feet above the ground. No, I said that wrong. It was not a growing limb but a dead limb about four inches in diameter, and about six feet long. It was so dead that the bark was gone. It was nice and smooth. I enjoyed climbing up there and just laying out on it and watching things underneath that didn't know I was there. Bugs, ants, and sometimes a lizard. The wood grain on those trees is twisted, like a cotton wood, maybe even more. The older it gets the more brittle, and it will almost break square. I knew better than to get on a small limb because it would just bend over, but that big one was just right. I know literally what the term means, to get out on a limb. One day there was something below that I needed to crawl out a little farther to see. I always laid on my belly when out on my special limb. I heard two sounds, one when the tree shed the limb, and one when that limb and I hit the ground. Actually I didn't hit the ground. I was still topside of the limb when it hit the ground. I was hurt from my head to my toes and everything in between, but none of that really mattered, I couldn't breath anyhow. As I grew older I heard of someone that was out on a limb, and I sure felt sorry for him.

I must tell here about Dad's dog, Pat. He was a medium--sized dog. Not pretty and maybe not ugly. Not a slick--haired dog but not a long--haired dog either. A mixed up type dog and sure too small to hold a wild cow even if he should catch one. Dad was in Safford and a little dog was looking for someone to pat it on the head. Dad did, then went about his business. When he returned to his car there sat the little dog. Dad went in a restaurant near by and returned with a biscuit for him. When Dad was ready to return to Klondyke the little dog was still there. Dad took him home. Maybe his kids would like him. At that time we were living at our ranch on the canyon. We were out of the VAV deal but still working the same country and the same cattle. Just not putting the VAV brand on them. When Dad saddled his horse the next morning to head into the mountains for a few days the little dog was close by him. Dad named him Pat. He was some kind of brownish in color. As Dad rode off, Pat went along. That little city dog had found a friend and sure planned to stay close to him. When Dad reached the Deer Creek Line Camp there were some of the cowboys there. "Roy, where did you get that little mutt and what in the world will you do with him? One of those old cows will get him on a horn and carry him off through the woods. Why, he doesn't even understand cow dog language."

A cow dog must understand and obey three commands: sickum, come here, and turn loose you son--of--a--bitch. They tried to get him close to their dogs so he would maybe get some idea of what a cow dog should act like, but he would only stay close to Dad. Early the next morning Dad and the other two men were saddled up and up the mountains they went to find some wild cattle. The dogs were trotting at the heals of his master's horse. Pat did that but he didn't know why. Before long they jumped a wild maverick and said sickum. Two dogs went into the timbers after it, but not Pat. He stayed put. Those dogs caught the maverick. Both of them had hold of him. Dad tried to get Pat to get in there and help them but no way. He didn't even pay close attention. That went on for some time. Several days, like maybe a dozen or so cow catches. Pat just didn't understand what he was suppose to do. Dad was sure getting the ribbing about his city dog. Then one day there were three men and Dad. They jumped a cow and said sickum. The three dogs went after it. When the men rode up to where the dogs were holding it there was a dog on each ear and one on the nose. Dad looked at Pat and said sickum. Pat looked at Dad then trotted over to the action and looked it over. He tried to find a place to get hold of but there was a dog on all the good places except the tail. For some reason he saw that old cows tongue hanging out and he bit onto it. He soon learned all the commands and was a top notch cow dog. Sometimes one of the men would want to barrow him. They even tried to steel him, but he would not follow anyone but Dad. He always caught by the tongue and could hold the biggest bull in the hills.

Dad was home for a few days. Pat was there with nothing to do. Cow dogs get restless if they get too much rest. They would go find a cow to catch on their own. I decided to take Pat for a walk. I put my rope on him then tied it to my waist because what I had in mind was what I shouldn't do. I went out into the corrals where some cattle were in for water. I chose a good sized calf, pointed to it and said sickum. Let me tell you now. He went after that calf pulling me in a run. I fell down and he drug me and still caught the calf. By the tongue. The calf was making so much noise I knew Dad would come out of the house any minute to see what was going on. I got to my feet and remembered the command to get him loose from that calf. I yelled, "Turn loose you son--of--a--bitch." I didn't know that Dad had already came running out of the house and was standing right behind me. He was as surprised that I knew how to talk to the dog as I was that he really turned loose. The only thing I knew about those words was that they were cowboy's dog language. It seemed that every time I messed with a catch dog he got me into trouble. Later in life I learned that command was used for other than dog commands.

After we were settled on our new ranch, Dad and Thad worked the same country they had been working before. They worked it the same way, with dogs and trap gates. When we left Klondyke we had a pretty good herd of cattle. Dad told me in later years what had happened. After the VAV owners threw them out, he and Thad kept on catching unbranded cattle, only then they put their own brands on them. He told me those fellows paid a high price for not staying with the agreement. That was when I learned what a dogie was. We were always raising lots of dogies. The VAV people knew they were being had but they couldn't send anyone up in those mountains to catch them. It was just too dangerous. That was when Dad had his .30--30 cut off on both ends. Easy to carry and for a quick draw if he should need it. Dad butchered and sold beef to the Johnson Brothers' store in Safford. They were brothers to his mother. Dad's mother was an orphan and the Johnsons raised her. One of the Johnsons would come after it. Mostly at night, but sometimes the whole family would come in the daytime and we would sure have fun. Their kids were the same age as we were.

There was a place down the canyon about four miles that grew mesquite trees rather than bushes. That was where we went to cut posts for the homestead section fencing and the posts to build the corrals. Those trees grew tall and slim. Two or three posts per tree. I have never seen mesquites like them any where else. We took the wagon and team. It would take all day to cut a load of posts. We made several trips. We took the dogs along. One of them being my little Blanco. One day while cutting posts we heard a noise and dogs barking. Mom and Dad knew the dogs were after something. It was in a hurry and coming our way. Mom started to gather in the kids, but Raymon was farther away. He was paying more attention to the noise coming than to Mom. The wait was short. There they came, Blanco in the lead. He was sure in a hurry to get back to the wagon. There was a havelina pig right on his tail, and the dog, Pat, right on the pig's tail. Threw the woods they came and went. As they went by the wagon, Blanco did a side step and quit the race, but Pat was determined to catch the pig. The pig got away and lucky for the dog. Now think back in my story and remember that Pat only caught by the tongue. The pig didn't stick his tongue out, so Pat couldn't get hold of him. Those pigs were death on dogs. I saw one dog that caught a pig. That old pig cut his throat wide open with his tusks.

Klondyke

The pig went right through our camp and missed Raymon by inches, and Mom was screaming for him to run. When it was all over Raymon said, "I sure did run." He was so scared, he never moved a foot.

I started to school when I was five. I would be six in December. I walked about half a mile to catch the bus, then about seven miles to Klondyke. At Klondyke there was a school and a store, and a forest-ranger station. The canyon was about two hundred yards from our house. It was about a hundred feet wide and about five feet deep at our crossing. One evening when I returned from school, there was water running in it. It had been raining up stream somewhere. Mom was waiting for me there on the house side. She finally got me to take off my shoes and wade to a small sand island. Not much water on my side, but the rest of the stream looked bad to me. About fifteen feet across and maybe six inches deep. My lunch box was a little shoe box with a red ribbon to hold it together. I sat it on the sand bar, while she was trying to get me to go on over. I was so scared because I had never been in running water before. After a lot of coaxing from her I made a try for it, and made it, but then I looked back and there sat my little lunch box on the sand bar. She tried to get me to go get it, but I wasn't about to play my luck twice the same day. While we were trying to get me brave enough to go after it, a head of water came down and covered the sand bar and my little box went floating down the canyon. I can still see the little box with the red ribbon.

I had a little wagon and I would tie it to his tail with a short rope and take Raymon and Floyd for a ride. Sometimes a little too fast and I would dump them out. One time I dumped them into a bush and skinned them up a little. I finally got them to stop crying and brushed them up as best I could but when we got home they got me in trouble anyhow. I had watched Dad tie a mule to another mule's tail so I was good at tying a rope to a tail. I tied a rope to Chinate's tail and the other end to the hitch rack. Just like where the cowboys tie their horses in the movies. I got on him and rode off to see if my knot would hold. It did and his tail was cracking and making so much noise Mom heard it. She came running out to see what was going on. I think she barely was in time to keep me from having a bobtailed horse. I guess he would have pulled his tail off if asked him to.

My little Chinate horse helped me earn my first dollar. Dad and Thad were in the mountains at the Deer Creek Ranch. A man rode up to our house and wanted to go up there where they were. He had left his car at Thad's place. Ruth had loaned him a horse and saddle. She told him to go to our place and maybe I could take him to Deer Creek. He talked to Mom and she said I could go. He said he would give me a dollar. That was my first time alone on those trails, but I had traveled them so much that I had no idea of getting lost. I could get lost in a big town like Safford but not in those mountains. I took him to Deer Creek. I liked to go there because there was a wire stretched between two oak trees and there was always jerky on it. I could only reach it from my horse. It was high so the coyotes and bears couldn't get it. He delivered a message or received one, I don't know which, and we went back down out of the mountains. He was a town man and rode a horse like one. He acted as though he had saddle sores when he got off his horse. I don't know what Mom did with the dollar, but I'm sure it was put to good use.

While I was in school my little black horse was turned out on the range for the winter. I was in the second grade and my horse was on the open range and I hadn't seen him for a while. One morning on the way to school the bus driver pulled off the road and said, "Willie, there is your little black horse." I looked and sure enough, there he was, dead. I was embarrassed because I cried before all those kids on the bus. That little horse is one of my most treasured memories.

Mom's brother, Tommy Crabtree, showed up at our place, and in the conversation, they decided to go see Grandma Crabtree. Tommy had a four door Star touring car. Grandma lived in Deming. Dad and Tommy were in the front seat. Mom and four kids, and Leona, Mom's youngest sister, in the back. By the time we got to Duncan it was late in the evening, and so was dark before we got to Lordsburg. There was no road from Duncan to Lordsburg. We just followed the best set of tracks. The coast to coast highway 80 was under construction. There was a graveled dump from Lordsburg to Deming. We could see the Lordsburg lights long before arrival. As we were nearing Lordsburg the car lights went out. They found a garage and had them repaired. Deming here we come and out went the lights again. Back to Lordsburg, another fix and we were gone again. Out went the lights, and back to

Klondyke

Lordsburg, another fix, and adios once more for Deming. Yea, out went the lights. Tommy said, "I'll guide by the telegraph pole line and we will go on to Deming."

It was moonlight. Every one was tired and sleepy. I don't know where we all got but I was on the floor under a bunch of feet. In those days the roads had dips on the water shed instead of bridges, but there was one bridge between Lordsburg and Deming, I know. Tommy misjudged the pole line and ran off the road. Where? Right on that one bridge. I guess he was going too fast to turn over because we sailed off into the ditch and landed, wheels down. I couldn't see what was happening, but there were sure a lot of feet kicking around where I was suppose to be. When the thing settled down, they got us all untangled and out of the car. There were no breaks or even skins. I don't know how I saved my face. It was too dark to do anything so we cuddled up until daylight. At daybreak we all got out and looked at what we had. Not even a flat tire. It was in soft ground, but with Tommy driving and the rest pushing that old Star climbed right up onto the highway. Tommy's wife and kids were at Grandma's. His daughter, Ola Pearl, was about my age. We became good friends. We saw each other often after that first meeting. Grandma and Tommy's family moved to Duncan soon after that trip. By the time the school year was out, Dad had found another horse for me. A bay streak face and larger size, mostly up. We tried to think of a real nice name for him, and after we had ridden him a few times, we did. I called him Crazy Horse. He was very gentle to handle and ride, but if I ever let him start to run, he would get faster and faster and before long I couldn't stop him. He would run back to the corrals full speed. The first time he ran away with me I was going to the mailbox, across the canyon about a half mile on the road near Thad's place. About halfway over there I decided to lope him and before I knew it, everything was turning to no good. I was bareback and I couldn't stay on him and pull the reins at the same time. I decided to hold onto his mane and hope I could stay on him. He was going too fast for me to get off proper. He made a circle and headed back to the corrals. He ran too close to a few bushes, but they went by me too fast to bother. All I could think of was the canyon crossing. I hadn't ever tried it at that speed before. Well we crossed the canyon and I was still topside. I had a good mane hold and legs locked tight so it looked like I was going to make it. I figured he would run into the corral, maybe circle it and give me a chance to get my balance and pull up on the reins. After crossing the canyon, the corral was close. We had to go along the side of it then a ninety--degree turn to the left and then another ninety--degree turn to the left again and into the corral. Those two turns slowed him down some, according to facts, but he was still full speed from where I was sitting when he hit the gate. It was closed and neither one of us had planned on that. He got stopped with no damage to the gate or himself but I went flying in the air and landed inside the corral. Mom saw us come up the bank out of the canyon. She knew I was in trouble so she came running out there. The horse just stood there because he thought he had done just what I wanted since I never did pull on the reins. Mom picked me up and brushed me off and I guess she was checking me over for broken pieces. That was when I named him Crazy Horse. I rode him a lot but I sure never let him get out of control again.

I told about the Johnsons from Safford came to see us a few times. Two of the boys sure had to go horse back riding. I let them ride Crazy Horse but I told them not to lope him or he would bring them back to the corral in a hurry. Sure enough they rode across the canyon and decided to sweat him out a little. I was down by the canyon watching them, and when I saw them lope him I knew they wouldn't be gone much longer. They made it about halfway across the canyon before they fell off. I have told that the canyon at that crossing was about five feet deep at the banks and about a hundred feet across. It was clean sand so they didn't get dirty like I did when I landed in the corral.

Dad had a horse that I rode sometimes if we were going for some distance. He called him Toothpick. He was a race horse and too tall for me to get on by my self. He was very gentle and very honest. We were in the mountains at a line camp called Deer Creek. I was riding Toothpick and Raymon was riding Crazy Horse. We were with Dad and Thad. We had rounded up some horses to brand some colts. The buildings and corrals were down in the bottom of the canyon, but up out of the canyon was a mesa that sloped away from the mountain. We had turned the horses loose and they had gone up on the mesa. They were headed back to their grazing ground. When we started to leave for home, Raymon and I climbed on out of the canyon in front of Dad and

Thad. As we topped out on the mesa, there were the horses just grazing along. Crazy Horse loved to run and when he saw those horses he did a little dance and instead of Raymon pulling him up, he grabbed the saddlehorn with both hands and started to yell because the race was on. Dad and Thad were back far enough that they couldn't catch him and right away he was running in among the horses and across the mesa they were going. I rode Toothpick up in the lead of the runaway and I turned the whole bunch back. I circled them around the mesa and as they went by Thad he was able to catch Raymon's horse. Raymon had been telling me that we should come up with a better name. After that race, Crazy Horse it was.

A farmer in Safford named Dick Layton made a deal with Dad to take his farm horses and turn them loose on our ranch during the winter so he didn't have to feed them hay. They were big farm horses and they had a big appetite. Those big old horses would get to running with some of the wilder horses and get real hard to catch. When we would go after them to take them back to the farm in Safford, they would be real silly and didn't want to go to the corrals. They would run around over the hills. They stayed in the foothills between the mountain and the Aravaipa. That was where Crazy Horse showed pleasure for running. Dad would tell me to run those horses around the hills for a while until they would start to wind then he would get into the race on a fresh horse. Then he could take them on in to the corral without much trouble. When I would do that, Crazy Horse was fast enough to run right in among them and over the hills we would go. Dad would pick out a high point where he could watch and decide when to get in the race. I also would sometimes do that on Toothpick but I could handle him and turn the horses where I wanted them to go. On Crazy Horse I just got in the bunch and went where they went until they got tired of running.

Dad came home one day and told Mom that we have a car. It was the summer of 1924. He had been up to the Huntington Ranch and some smart guy from Safford had driven up there in his little model T. I guess the cowboys were having some fun with him. He was proud of how fast his little car would go. Dad told him he could out run him on his horse. The fellow took him up on it. They set the distance, I think about a mile. The bet was that the winner would get the car or the horse. Dad was riding Toothpick and evidently had no trouble outrunning the little car. Thad had a car and he took Dad back up there to get it. Dad got it home, and trouble started right then and never quit as long as we had it. Our driveway was very sandy, which hadn't ever bothered the horses, but that little car got stuck right away. It was so light that with Dad driving and Mom pushing they got it on harder ground. The next thing was to run down the canyon a few miles to see some neighbors. The top was so low Dad had to take the seat cushion out from his side to sit up in it. It was a coupe with a hole in the back about two feet square. The three boys sat around the hole with our feet hanging inside, and Domer on Mom's lap. The canyon crossing had a gentle slope on the going away side, but a steeper bank on the coming home side. When we would leave home we all would ride. When we came back home Dad would stop and let us all out and Mom would then run after the little Ford to help it get up the bank and home again. Every time we took it for a ride we had some flat tires. Dad would patch them and pump them up and take off again.

We had a wire gate between our place and Thad's that was hard to open and close. On returning from one of our trips Dad told Mom that he would open the gate and for her to drive through. The gate was about twenty feet wide. Would you believe she missed the opening and hit a gate post and knocked down the fence? She about ran over Dad. She finally got the little T car stopped out in the mesquite bushes. She never did drive again until we moved to Columbus, NM. Then if she saw a car coming, she would pull over and stop until it got by because she was afraid she might hit it.

About the model T. It had three foot--pedals in the floor. Left was low gear forward, middle was reverse gear and the right was the brake on rear wheels only. On the left side between the driver and the door was a long lever coming straight up out of the floor. With the long lever back you only had low gear if you pressed the left pedal, but once you were moving you would push the long lever forward and then you were in high gear. Now let's think about the possibilities here. You had to crank the car to get it started. There was no self starter in those days. You had a wire poking out the front near the radiator and that was the choke. Up on the steering wheel you had two levers, one on each side.

Klondyke

The left one was spark control, the right one was the throttle. There was no foot throttle. Those cars used magnetos, no battery. The little engines were bad to try to run backwards. To be sure the engine didn't backfire when you turned the crank, you put the spark lever all the way up and the throttle lever down just a poquito, and never forget to pull the high gear lever all the way back. That lever had a squeeze handle to release it or hold it back so it stayed where you put it. Dad was all dressed up to go to Safford and I was going with him. He went out to start the car and did all the things just right, but forgot to pull the high gear lever back. That little Ford started on the first pull of the crank and began to move forward. There was Dad out in front of it pushing with all he had. It was backing him up and he was speaking to it in model T talk. Mom was there close. He told her to pull the lever. She did. She pulled the throttle lever all the way down. That caused him to back up a little faster so he told her to come and help him hold it. The two of them slowed it down a little. Dad jumped around and pulled the long lever back and pushed the throttle up. It was in our front yard sand was why they could hold it, almost.

Dad and I went on to Safford. On that trip I saw my first movie. Sure was noisy. The old boy at the piano sure banged it hard. They were called silent movies. It has been on my mind ever since and I still can't describe it. I didn't know what I was seeing but it was sure funny. There was a spring on the divide we had to cross on the road to Safford. It was at the west end of Mt. Graham. From Klondyke it was quite a climb up to the pass, a beautiful drive, then down the north side to Safford. We stopped there to drink water and cool the car off some. The radiator would sure be boiling by the time we topped out in the pass. The spring is still there and running water. In Safford we stayed at the Adams Hotel. Three Adams ranches adjoined. Dad, Thad, and Jimmy. The hotel belonged to Jimmy's mother. They were no relation that we ever knew, but very good friends. The next morning Dad and I walked a few blocks to the Johnson store and back to the hotel. Later in the day he ran out of smoking. He sent me to the store to get him a sack of Bull Durham. I got to the store all right and got the Bull Durham but on the way back I got lost. I could get along fine in the canyons and mountains and trails, but all those houses and streets sure got me messed up. Before long I knew for sure I was lost and I started to run. I would run up one street and down another and I was more confused as I went. I was going the wrong way and couldn't find a familiar landmark. I didn't know about street signs. I couldn't read them anyhow. I was running down a street and saw a big house at the end. I ran to it and right up the steps, inside and down the hall. A big one--armed man was coming towards me and grabbed me by the arm. I was sure patinando but he held on to me and asked me where I was going. I told him I was looking for my Dad.

He asked, "What does your Dad look like?"

"He is real tall." That was all the description I could think of. Then he asked, "What is his name?"

Even in my excitement I could remember that, "Roy Adams."

Still holding me with his one arm he said, "Come with me."

He took me to his car. It turned out I was about three blocks from the hotel. The big house I ran into was and is the courthouse. I never go through Safford that I don't think about what a scary town it used to be. That was the last trip in the little Ford. Dad traded it to George Adams, Jimmy's brother.

Back to the farm horses that Dick Layton sent over to our ranch. Among them was a little black streak faced mare. She was very gentle. Dick told Dad to let me ride her. She was running in the hills with the rest of the horses. Dad and I had been up in the mountains at the Willow Creek Line Camp and were on our way home when we ran onto a bunch of horses. There was the mare among them, and already as wild as the rest of them. Her name was Maud. Dad took after her but she was too fast for his horse and she got away, so we went on our way. As we were arriving home we passed along outside the fence of the horse pasture, where we kept the horses we were using. There he saw his top horse he called Jack. He was white with a little blue mixed in. He was one of those horses that when you showed him a target he would go to it. When we got to the house Dad told me to go get Jack. I did. We ate a good lunch Mom fixed for us then we went back up there in the hills to get that little Maud mare. The cowboys were always bragging on their horses and their dogs, and of course I was sure Jack must be one real horse because I had heard Dad say so many times. Dad got on Jack and we went back up in the hills where we had seen the bunch of horses last.

Klondyke

Sure enough they hadn't gone far after we quit chasing them. They were grazing on a ridge about halfway down the side. We were on top of the ridge on the trail. Dad was a master on horseback with a rope, and in later years I saw him do some beautiful roping, but that day will always stand out as the best. Dad told me to wait for him on the ridge, and I heard him say, "Let's go Jack." He ran down the side of the ridge and right into the middle of those horses. He showed Jack which one he wanted and roped her before they got to the top of the ridge.

Let me tell you that little horse had a fit like I hadn't ever seen on a horse that I was fixing to ride. She just couldn't believe she had been caught like that. Dad led her around some and we found a place to change my saddle onto her. By that time the other horses had gone over the next hill out of sight. Dad told me to get on, that she was all right. I knew Dad wouldn't tell me wrong, so I climbed on, and she turned out to be a real pleasure. She had a good mouth, good gate, and was a real pet.

One of the things Dad did to supplement income while he was building a cow herd, was breaking broncos. A bronco is a wild untamed horse that would much rather kill a man than carry him around. There was a ranch down the canyon below Klondyke called the T Rail. They raised good horses. Dad said he would break them for $30.00 per head. He would teach them to let him get on and off and ride around the corral without them bucking. In other words he would take the hump out of their back. Dad would go down to the T Rail Ranch and bring back ten head at a time. In about two weeks he would take a broke bunch back and get some more. I don't know how many he broke, but it seemed like a lot of them. I think maybe around fifty head. I helped him bring them to the corral everyday and he would ride each horse every day. He would get on one and go around the corral a few times and tell me to open the gate and let him out. The pasture where he rode them was mesquite, almost like trees. We worked at Jimmy Adams' place. He had better corrals. When I opened the gate to let him out I would get on Maud and go after him. Sometimes those horses wouldn't turn too good at first and I would run along in the lead of them. The bronco would follow me until Dad could teach him to handle. After about three rides he could ride them where he wanted to go.

The reason he could turn those horses out of the corral so soon was because he used a draw rein bridle on them. Dad never let one of them buck. A horse can buck only if his head is free and he can get it down to the ground. If he can't get a free head then he can jump around a little and that is all. The draw rein was a special bridle Dad made. The bit was a farm horse bit. He put a two inch ring on each side of his saddle, fastened just under the fork. The rein was a rope with a snap on each end and just the right length to snap one end to the left saddle ring, go to the bit, which was in the horses mouth, and through the bit ring, up the left side of the neck, then over the saddlehorn then down the right side of the neck to the bit and through the bit ring, and back up to the ring on the saddle and snapped on. Now you can see that gave him double leverage on the bronco's mouth. If he tried to buck his head was pulled up tight and if he wanted to run, his head got pulled real tight to one side.

There was a real pretty black horse in one of the bronco bunches. He was a stallion and he was sure mean. He would try to buck and Dad would hold him up, he would try to run and Dad would spin him, then he would fall down. At this point you might ask, how come the black horse didn't get up and jerk loose from Dad and run away. You know that was what he had in mind to do. What surprised the horse was that when he would fall down, Dad would hold him down until he quit thrashing his feet and head, then Dad would let him get up onto his feet. When the horse got to his feet the rider was still on him. A horse can be held down real easy by just pushing down on the saddlehorn and let him thrash until he gives up. When he fell down the third time Dad took his rope from his saddle. While holding him down with the saddlehorn, he tied that old horses feet, took his saddle off and castrated him right there, and turned him loose. I got Dad and his saddle on my horse with me and took them back to the corrals to get another bronco. Dad let the black horse heal up for a few days and tried him again. That old pony didn't want to buck, he didn't want to run, and he never fell down again. He already decided not to fight that cowboy no more.

After a few days with a bunch of those horses, they would be easy to take to the corral from the pasture. Dad would send Maud and me out to round them up and bring them in. Another reason they would go to the corral without much trouble was because the only water was in the corral. They always ran a lot when I went after them, but I would follow them close and they would go to the corral. One day I was taking them in fast and Maud ran under a mesquite limb and knocked me off. I grabbed the horn to try to stay on but the saddle turned down on her belly. When I quit rolling all I could see was her and the broncos leaving and she was trying to kick my saddle to pieces. I walked home that day, about a mile. The pasture was real thick with mesquite trees and we didn't find her for two days. She had gotten the reins tied around a bush and there she stood. She would not break a rein. My saddle wasn't hurt at all.

When Dad finished the bronco busting and delivered the last bunch back to the T Rail Ranch the fellow was very pleased. There was a one--eyed white horse in the large holding corral. He was about eight years old and broke but not gentle. Anyhow, he was not a bronco. He was almost impossible to catch. The fellow told Dad he could have him if he could catch him. That white horse hadn't had a rope on for a long long time and he had no intention of sticking his head into one then. In the large corral was a large oak tree. Dad climbed up in the tree. Tied his rope to a big limb and told the fellow to drive the bunch of horses around the tree and sooner or later that old white horse would get close enough to catch him. Sure enough after a while old whitey walked under the tree and Dad put a loop on his neck. That old horse had such a fit that he about shook Dad out of the tree. Dad took him home and used him a lot. He was a good horse. I don't know what Dad did to the horse to catch him later. I don't remember having any trouble with him.

The range we worked was on the south side of the Aravaipa towards Tucson. One day Dad and I went up in the mountains on the north side of the canyon. That was the big mountains west of Mt. Graham. Dad was riding his one--eyed white horse. We were going up to a line camp. There were line camps in several places in all those mountains. No one lived there but they were kept stocked with food and bedding by the cowboys themselves for whoever might be riding that way. The sign on the door said, "Don't leave dirty dishes." On our way up to the camp we were riding in the bed of a canyon. The walls were about three hundred feet high and about straight up. Somewhere towards the head was the line camp we were going to. I don't remember seeing any rain but somewhere up in the mountain it had rained. We rounded a bend and there came a head or wall of water like I have not seen before or since. We did a quick about face and spurred our ponies to full speed. The canyon we were in was not very wide, like just a few feet. The water seemed to be squirting it was coming so fast. We ran back down the canyon looking for a place to climb out. Dad had me running in the lead so he could keep track of me. I heard a noise and looked back just in time to see that one eyed horse standing on his head. I turned and went back to Dad. I was laughing. He said, "What's so damned funny? The water is about to get us and my horse stands on his head." He quickly remounted and we were gone again. I didn't realize the danger we were in at the time. We soon found a place that looked like we could climb out. Then was where the real danger came in. It was too steep for the horses to carry us. We dismounted to lead them up the mountain, but that was also dangerous because of when they lunge to get up a bad place. Dad tied a lead rope to his horse so he couldn't run away. He tied my reins to my saddlehorn and turned my horse loose to find his way as best he could. I found my way also, staying out of the way and behind the horses. As we were going up the side of the canyon we saw the water go by. It was roaring and looked mean. We topped out on the ridge and went on up to the line camp. Those were sure some good groceries we found there. That was where I ate my first and only wild grapes. The oak trees we rode under that day were covered with grape vines.

Our house was built at the foot of a steep hill, about a hundred feet high. The back of the house was on the ground, and the front was off the ground about three feet. That hill turned out to be a perfect place to develop a slide. We could climb up the hill from the side where it was not so steep then slide down right behind the house. We barely had the slide going good and Mom told us no more of that. It was too hard on the pants and we didn't have any spares. I tried it once more however to see if she meant it, and she did. I decided my pants were too thin. We still liked to play up there. One day I gave Raymon a little shove and he slid down the hill. That time my pants seemed thinner than before. We still played up there. It was such a good place. I accidentally started a rock to rolling. I think she heard the rock coming before it hit the house, because she was out so quick. That time it felt like I didn't have any pants on at all. I stayed clear of the slide, but I thought of it a lot. One day we were playing along the edge of the canyon and we ran onto a little goat that had strayed from the herd. There were some Mexican people up the canyon about four miles. They had a few goats. I told Raymon and Floyd to let's take the little goat up on the hill and put him on the slide. Surely Mom wouldn't care if a goat came down. We pushed and pulled and carried, and finally got to the top of the hill with our goat. We gave him a big shove off the hill onto the slide. He didn't slide. He would climb right back up on top, and we would shove him off again. I think the goat was playing games with us, and we got tired of playing before he did. Mom was watching us. She decided to fix us some old and patched pants to slide on and we really enjoyed our slide after that. When I have been back there years later, I look at that spot and think what a great place it was to play. My brother, Louie Jack, was born there Aug. 4, 1927.

Mom's brother, Tommy Crabtree, was quite a horse trader. He bought some horses from the Klondyke area. He brought his brother, Bill, to help him to gather and move them to wherever they were going. They came in a car with their saddles, and mounted up on horses they had traded for. Tommy brought his family along. He had a son younger than me, named Mike. I took Mike for a walk up one of the canyons near the house. We climbed a steep hill to get out of the canyon. I played there all the time, but Mike couldn't get all the way to the top so I told him to go to one side and I would show him how to roll rocks. He did and I rolled a rock. He saw the rock coming, but instead of staying put, he ran back down the hill. He ran to the rock path instead of away from it. The rock got faster and jumped higher, and caught up with Mike. The rock jumped over him, but as it went over him it didn't quite clear his head, and cut a gash right on top. He went down right there. I came off the mountain like that rock did, running and jumping. I got to Mike and found him still alive, but he was screaming so loud I thought he was dying. I threw him over my shoulder and ran to the house with him. His mother thought he was dying also. We put him in the car and hurried to where his dad was working horses. His dad came over to the car. He picked him up and told him little men don't cry that way. He shut up, and then was the first time anyone had looked to see how much damage there was. Very little. It had just scared him, and I think me more than him, otherwise I could never have carried him off that hill and home.

As the men were driving the horses to the corral, Bill Crabtree, Mom's brother, saw a Gila Monster and decided to rope it and take it to the house to show it off. He arrived at the corrals a little late. He told that his horse didn't like the idea of leading that monster, huffing and puffing and jumping, so he bucked him off. It took a few minutes to get his rope off the monster because by then he was mad also.

When I graduated from the first grade we had a school picnic on the canyon below Klondyke. The water was always running there. The kids waded and splashed in the water and had a great time. There were no swim suits. We went in clothes and all. It was a hot day so no problem drying out. Now the important memory of the picnic is not the water fun, but the fact that it was where and when I was introduced to PORK--n--BEANS. Today I am still a Porky fan.

In November 1927, Dad's oldest brother, Bill, came to Klondyke to get Dad to go to Mexico and run his ranch because he had gotten into some trouble and couldn't go back to Mexico. He was living at Columbus, NM. It wasn't safe for him to go back for a while. He offered Dad a salary. Groceries at the ranch and let him build a herd of his own. Dad and Mom talked it over and decided to go. That move changed the future of them and their posterity forever. I go back to Klondyke once in a while now and try to imagine, what if we had stayed there. Sixty years have gone by and the people who still live there just aren't prosperous at all. The move took us to the Mormon colonies where the Adams' were raised. There we found a hard working, well educated, and prosperous in everything but money, group of people. Of course those were depression years and we actually made it through the depression better than had we stayed at Klondyke. My allegiance is to the Mormon colonies and not Klondyke. Because of the schooling and association I grew up with there I have had a very prosperous and rewarding life. Dad sold everything we had, which was the homestead of one section, the house and cattle. Thad and other men there helped him round up all his cattle, and we drove them to Wilcox, Az. From there they were shipped someplace by train.

As they rounded up the cattle they were put in a holding pasture until they were all gathered. When they were ready for the drive, the cattle were all put in the corrals, in order to get an early start. That evening Dad and the buyer were in the corrals among the cattle, and ever once in a while Dad would catch a cow's tail and cut the bush off. I always paid close attention to how Dad did things. He wrapped the bush around his pocketknife blade and as the cow took off, the bush stayed in his hand. That was another first for me. After supper, it was dark, I decided to go to the corrals and see just how that was done. I tried one, and sure enough the bush came off in my hand. I don't know how many I cut off, but enough to prove that I could do it. Dad never new about it. I have wondered since if I caused him to get more money or less money. I'm sure now that the bobtails were a different price. I never knew and I sure didn't ask.

December 1927. I was just turning eight. When we left the corral with the cattle Dad let me go along and help drive them for a short distance. I had Raymon on behind me. We had driven the herd about three miles, early in the morning. I saw Dad coming my way and I knew he would tell me I had better go back. I sure did want to go with him. He said, "Willie how would you like to help us drive these cattle to Wilcox?" I sure did get tall in the saddle. He told me to take Raymon back home and ask Mom to fix me a bundle of clothes then catch up with the herd. The only thing I remember about that bundle was the sox. I didn't have any but on that ride it would be cold and I needed sox to help keep my feet warm. She had some of Dad's sox that needed mending. She put a pair on my feet and turned the extra length under and put my shoes on. They just fit and were warmer also. We followed the Aravaipa up stream all the way to where it widened out to be the Wilcox valley. Thad's wife Ruth drove the chuck wagon. It was a van type truck. The sides were wire mesh and there were curtains to roll up or down for enclosing. The first night we camped near a big sacaton draw that we had to cross the next morning with the herd. The sacaton grass was so high that we couldn't see the cattle or even the men across the herd. It was about half a mile through it and we counted the herd to see if any had been lost in the grass.

After following the herd about four days I was getting sort of tired of it. Thad always watched me real close. He would tell me to ride up the side of the herd, not too close, then some times he would send me up to ride with the lead man. After a day of driving there will be some animal take the lead and the herd will follow it. The lead animal will follow the lead man. The rest of the cowboys come along to see that none of the cattle decide to shade up along the way. You always have some stragglers that didn't want to go in the first place. I think we were seven days on the drive. One day I guess I was looking pretty tired. Thad came over to me and told me to rope one of those calves and maybe they would keep up a little better. They must have been tired also. I had never roped anything from a horse before but I sure knew how. I threw a few loops to sort of get the hang of it. There in front of me was a calf just my size and I threw my loop at him. That little rascal jumped out of the way and I caught his mama by a hind foot. My rope was tied to my saddlehorn so I couldn't turn it loose. That old cow went silly and pulled my saddle down on the side of my horse and I was sure hanging on. My horse had his feet braced good. She was sure trying to get away. Thad was close and saw me catch the cow. He knew I would need help quick. He jumped off his horse and got to my horse before we had a wreck. He pushed me and my saddle back up on my horse, then tightened my cinch. By that time we had some help and got the cow turned loose. I went on roping, and caught a few calves. When I would catch a calf one of the men would turn him loose for me. I think it sort of relaxed the whole crew for me to be roping those calves for them to turn loose. I was careful not to catch another cow.

As we were driving the herd one morning, it sure was cold. A skunk came bouncing out from the back end of the herd. One of the fellows saw it and called to me to come over there and rope it. I went over where it was and followed it until it found a hole. I didn't try to rope it. I knew better than that. I knew what they smelled like. I did wonder at the time why it let all those cows almost step on it, then I chased it until it could find a hole to get into and never did shoot. Its tail was up and looked like it may pull the trigger at any moment but it didn't. Many years later I learned why it didn't fire. It was too cold. When a skunk is cold he can be picked up by the tail and carried. You must hold him at arms' length because he will sure bite. A skunk cannot shoot if you carry him by the tail even if he isn't cold. However he may not behave while you get hold of his tail. Unless he is cold.

We delivered the herd to the stock pens in Wilcox and Dad got his money. We went to the barber shop. That was my first barber shop hair cut. Mom did our hair cutting. One wall of the shop was a large mirror. I was sitting facing the mirror and thought I saw Raymon sitting there, but as I jumped up to go over to him I noticed he jumped up at the same time. I slumped back to my seat but not before Dad and the barber noticed.

Thad and the rest of the men took the horses back to the ranch. Dad and I caught a ride on the mail truck to return home. Dad got in our car and went back to Wilcox and traded it in on a new 1927 Chevy. The car we had was a Durant. A real nice car. The new Chevy had a trunk box on the back that opened to about five by four feet. We loaded it with the things it would hold and left the rest there. About all we took was Mom's machine, and bedding and clothes. Columbus here we come.

It was thirty years before I went back to Klondyke to look around to see if it was as I remembered it. I have been back to Klondyke several times over the years and each time I look up to the mountains where the VAV Ranch should be but I had no way to get up there. March 21, 1988, Mart and I went to Klondyke and I was showing her some of the places I remembered, when a rancher drove up, and was real friendly. We were at the Jimmy Adams place, which now is only a windmill and watering for cattle. He told me where to find the road that goes up to the Park boundary. The VAV area is now a wilderness park, and only for foot folks or horseback. We drove up to the boundary. The road is on the trail where we drove the mules, and I can see why a mule would fall off once in a while. Mart wouldn't look down at some of those saddles we crossed. It was four wheel drive terrain, but we were in our Blazer. I enjoyed getting that close. We could drive up to where the big mountains are and I was surprised at how familiar they seemed. The trail goes off the ridge and down into the big canyon just as it did when I was there.

3

Columbus

We arrived in Columbus in December 1927. I was in the third grade. We rented a house on the first street north of the railroad, and a block west of the arroyo. The house is still there. I checked it out in May of 1987. We got a big tricycle for Christmas that year and the house was so big that we rode it in the house. We didn't have any furniture so there was plenty of room. There were three old sewing machines in the house. At that time Columbus was quite a large town in terms of houses, but no one lived in them. The few people who lived there went to the vacant houses and got anything there that they could use. We furnished our house that way. The houses were built for the Army after Pancho Villa raided Columbus. There were a few soldiers there at that time. As the Army was moved out, it seems about all they took with them was their clothes and bedding. Our silver was even stamped US. Each house had a basement or a cellar and that was where the fruit was stored. It was still there. It was in bottles, like home done. The houses were so close together that we played cowboys and Indians on the roofs and would jump from one house to the other. The houses we played in and on were between our place and the railroad. One of them must have been marked some way because that was where the hobos would hang out as they came through town, and there were many of them. Many times I would go in where they were and they would give me something to eat. Maybe they had just gotten it from Mom. She was handing them food all the time. They would build a little campfire to cook on and

Columbus

keep warm if it was cold. They were good people out of a job and going west. Now as I think of them, I suppose to California, but at that time I hadn't ever heard of that place.

All these houses had chicken runs and chicken houses also. We had a dog called Bounce. On a weekend, out of school, and three boys needing something to do, Mom would say, "Why don't you boys take Bounce and go out and see if you can catch a rabbit and I'll cook it." The first rabbit we caught that way was unplanned, but after that we knew what to do. There were lots of rabbits at the edge of town and even some in town. We would take Bounce and head west to the last of the houses. It wouldn't be long before he would jump a big jack rabbit and the race was on. Now Bounce couldn't out run those rabbits but they didn't know it. For some reason, when Bounce would get after a rabbit and get to crowding him close that old rabbit would swing around and head for town. I guess to get under the houses. They were lumber and sitting on pillars. Almost every time, the rabbit would wind up in one of those chicken runs. Mom sure made good fried rabbit.

School there was a new experience. At Klondyke we had the first six grades in one room and the seventh and eighth grades in another room about a hundred yards away. There at Columbus there were two grades per room and lots of kids. It seemed like most of them would whip me sooner or later. I finally decided the easy life was over and I had better figure out how to handle such bully kids. There were about ten swings, and such a dangerous thing for a school ground. I could run fast so I could always get a swing at recess but I couldn't keep it. A big kid would come along and take it away from me. One day I was in a swing and there came one of the kids who had taken my swing away from me before. Usually he grabbed the swing and shook me out then hoped on. That day I was ready. When he got close I jumped out and threw it to him but he wasn't ready and didn't catch it. It hit him on the head. I had intended to hit him with it but not on the head. The way he fell I thought I had killed him. Someone ran and got the teacher, Miss Massy, and she wasn't very nice to me. She had several pets and that kid on the ground was one of them. They got him in a car and took him home. He lived near the school. Miss Massy told me to go to his house and apologize to his mother. I did. He came to the door but stood behind his mother. His head was all bandaged up and his eyes still looked funny. I told his mother I was sorry that he took my swing from me. That didn't stop my swing losses however. I found a rock, round and long as the width of my hand and carried it in my pocket. I didn't have to carry it many days before there came a kid to get my swing. He grabbed the swing and shook me out. I landed on him with that rock in my hand and bruised him up real quick. Then I put the rock back in my pocket. He said, "Willie, how come you are so mad with me?" He gave the swing back to me. He never did know what I hit him with, but he got the word out that Willie sure gets mad when you take his swing.

One of the tragedies I think of when we lived in Columbus was the Passage family. They lived near our place. The Passage kids and we were good friends. Two of the girls were my age. They ran around on the house roofs right along with the boys. Their dad was in charge of selling coal and wood and he ran the water pump for the city water tank. The water tank is on legs and is maybe about a hundred and fifty feet up in the air. It always looked high to me and still does. It seemed Mr. Passage got himself into some kind of trouble. One night he climbed up the water tank tower and jumped off. I sure felt sorry for those kids. They were never the same after that.

The ranch Dad was running for Bill was at Colonia Diaz. That was the place where they were raised. It was fifty miles south of the border in Mexico. There was a kid rode me down the school steps real often at noon and in the evening. One day at noon Dad drove to the school house to pick me up. Usually we walked home for lunch. He had just arrived from the ranch. He noticed I was having trouble and asked me about it. When we had finished dinner and was ready to go back to school, Dad went out to the tool house and fixed me an equalizer. It was a nut about one inch square with a four inch leather strap tied to it with a loop in the other end to fit my finger. He said, "Remember that the head is where to get their attention." That same day and that same kid rode me down the steps. What he didn't know was that he was enjoying his last ride. I got my finger in the loop and came out of my pocket with that thing and swung it over my shoulder. It caught him right between the eyes. He jumped off my back and put his hand over the hole in his head and ran back into the school house. I knew I was in big trouble again because he was another of Miss Massy's pets. She came running out. She got me by the arm and took me in and sat me down very rough. She wanted to know what I had hit him with. I told her with my fist and she said to me, "I know you are lying because you can't make a gash like that with your fist, now tell me how you did it." I pulled it slowly from my pocket and I thought that old gal was going to use it on me. I was on her stink list from then on. She was the only teacher I ever had that I couldn't get to like me just a little. She was my fourth grade teacher. I think I gave her some gray hair. I went to school there until Christmas 1928. Then I went to school about three months in Colonia Dublan. I went about three weeks in Hachita, then to Columbus again and Miss Massy to finish the fourth grade. That was sure a tough school year. That time she showed me who was in charge and it was not me. She didn't pass me to the fifth grade. I was back in Dublan for the next year. They put me in the fifth grade anyhow and I didn't have any trouble.

Grandma Crabtree lived at Duncan Az and always had a lot of nice chickens. On one of our trips to see her she gave mom a dozen red young chicks. They were Rhode Island Reds. They grew fast and were sure pretty and were about ready to start to lay. Every evening Mom counted them into the roost pen and shut the gate so no skunk or whatever could get them. In my rounds of the unused houses I have mentioned, I found a very large rat trap. I knew where there was a rat den. I thought I would set the trap and catch him. I didn't know what rats ate but I assumed they would eat about like a chicken. I put some corn on the trap trigger. I watched it all day and no rat. In the evening when Mom counted her red chickens there was one short. She looked and called and no chicken. She started to question me because she knew I had the trap and planned to catch the rat. She asked what did I use for bate, and I told her I put just a little bit of corn on the trigger. "Where is that trap?" she demanded. On the way to show her, I was sure hoping it had my rat in it and not her red chicken. We had chicken dumplings for dinner the next day, but I had to stand up to eat them. She tenderized that chicken on the seat of my pants. With the trap still on its head.

I enjoyed going upstairs where the big kids went to school. The seventh and eighth grades. They did some real neat things. On one of my trips up there a kid asked me if I had a penny. I had a penny and that was all I had. He wanted it, and he would make a dime out of it. Now that I had to see, and maybe learn how to do it. That was my first experience with quicksilver. He put a little ball on some paper and asked me to pick it up for him to put on my penny. If you have ever tried that little trick then you know I didn't pick it up. He quick--silvered my penny and sure enough it looked like a dime, almost. I carried it for several days waiting for the stuff to wear off so I could buy some candy. I went into Mrs. Power's drug store and chose the candies I wanted and gave her my penny. She gave me back change for a dime. I tried to tell her it was a penny, but instead of listening to me she threw me out of the store. All the kids were afraid of her anyhow. She told me no little kid was going to get the best of her.

Mom made great cookies and before long my friends learned about them. I would give them a bite sometimes. Now mom didn't care how many cookies I ate but she didn't have enough for me to give my friends. I soon learned that I could sell them. Mom thought I was sure eating lots of cookies. They were large like maybe five inches. I would get a nickel for them.

I also shined shoes in the only barber shop. There were still some soldiers there and they would let me shine their boots all the way to the top. I charged a dime but they mostly gave me a quarter. Also I carried my axe from door to door and chopped wood. Most people would pay me then maybe a little extra. I went to the hotel with my axe to chop some wood. It was run by a big lady. I had chopped wood for her before. One day when I went to chop wood for her she was doing chickens for her restaurant. She told me to chop the chickens' heads off. She would catch the chicken from the pen and hold him on the chopping block. I would chop off his head then she would put him on the ground to jump around while she got another one. I guess I chopped off about twelve heads that day and I never went back to chop wood for her again. I learned later that it is important to bleed a butchered animal in order for the meat to be good. Butchering wasn't new to me but so many chickens at one time was. We spent some of the weekends at the ranch at Colonia Diaz. When school was out we spent the summer there, and what a great summer it was. 1928. We had a lot of fun with Bounce. There was lots of wild game, and Bounce liked to catch them. There were lots of road runners. Bounce would hear one talking and if I didn't pay any attention, he would come to me and do a roadrunner dance so I would go with him to catch it. He would chase it up in a mesquite bush then I would shake it out. We would do that until we would catch it. He would never kill the roadrunners or the coyotes. He would catch it and hold it until I would get to them then he would turn it loose. If it ran he would catch it again unless I called him back. He minded very good. There was a sacaton draw close by. Sacaton is a tall course grass that grows in the wide and flat water flood plains. I liked to ride my horse and take Bounce over there. I would ride around in the grass for a while and I could always jump a coyote. As I think back now, there must have been two or three coyotes because Bounce would chase one and when he would almost catch it, it would run back into the sacaton grass and out the other side. He must have been getting a fresh coyote each time they took him through the grass. Bounce would finally get so tired he would stop. When he stopped the coyote would stop also and wait for him.

During one of those hunts in the tall sacaton grass I lost my saddle blanket. I didn't know I had lost it until I found it.

I was riding back and forth through the grass helping Bounce to flush out the coyotes when I came across a nice blanket lying on top of the grass. I could reach down and get it from my horse or I would have just left it there. I was not about to get off my horse in that grass that I knew was full of coyotes. I felt safe on my horse. I carried it out of the tall grass then dismounted and removed my saddle and replaced the blanket, and it sure didn't take very long.

Sam Hinton, who lived at Geronimo, Az. gave Bounce to us. He was a little weaner pup. His mother was a wild dog Sam had caught on his ranch. Sam kept her tied up for two reasons. She would run away and she was mean. She was so mean Sam had to throw the food to her. She was collie type and the daddy was bulldog.

The Colonia Diaz ranch had lots of mesquite and lots of brush of many kinds, and so there were nesting birds also of many kinds. The horse I rode was gentle. I would ride him up to a mesquite with a bird nest in it. I would stand up in my saddle and take a look to see what was in there. There were lots of crows and hawks. I wanted to get a crow or a hawk and tame it.

We always had a chicken setting on a nest, so I brought home some chicken hawk eggs, about four, and put them under the hen. Hawk eggs are white and the same size as a hen egg. One day Mom said, "If you go find me some eggs I'll make some cookies." Those old hens would make a nest and lay eggs out in the bushes so we had to hunt for them. When we would find the nest and get the eggs the hens would make another one someplace else, so we were constantly looking for the hidden nests. That day I scouted all the nests I knew about and didn't find one egg. Mom said, "I'll go get your hawk eggs and use them." I didn't like the idea because I had worked hard to get those eggs home without breaking them, but more than that I just couldn't bring myself to eat hawk--egg cookies. She made the cookies and they sure looked good and they smelled good but there was no way I was going to taste one. Dad ate them and the other kids ate them and even Mom ate them. They all bragged about how good they were, but Mom and I had our little secret, and even though she ate them, I was not about to. I think that was the largest batch of cookies she ever made, because she used all of my eggs. I sure wanted them to all get eaten and gone so she would make some more, with chicken eggs. Dad and I had ridden to the very farthest part of the ranch one day. Mom had made a good lunch for us, and of course included some cookies. There was a stream of water running across the part of the ranch where we stopped for lunch. There near the water was a big cottonwood tree. We always stopped under the tree for lunch and while Dad would take a nap, I would try to catch a killdeer. They were clever, I never did catch one. That day Dad broke out the lunch. We ate the sandwiches. There were those cookies looking so good, and Dad was eating them but I wouldn't eat one. He asked how come. I told him that mom had used my hawk eggs in them. That was when I thought he would have a real fit and probably throw them up. He started to laugh and said, "Did Mom tell you that?" Then he told me she was kidding and my hawk eggs were still under that old chicken. He told me that he watched her make the cookies. By that time he had about eaten all of them, but he gave me what was left. I have never eaten more delicious cookies before or since. When I got home I looked under the chicken to be sure and my hawk eggs were there. They never did hatch. I guess I ruined them carrying them home.

I told back about when Mom and Dad were married that she said she would not ever go to Mexico with him. As you can see she did. Our home at Klondyke wasn't much but the house did have windows and a wooden floor. At the Diaz Ranch the house was adobe with dirt floors and shutters on the windows and doors made from 1x12 boards. I called the door a shutter also because Dad was always saying, "Shut the door." The roof beams were cottonwood logs from the river with branches over them and then a mud mix over the branches then a dirt layer on top of that. It made a very cool shade but if it rained very hard we had muddy things inside. It was better to go outside in the rain. The most exciting to me was watching the swallows build nests hanging to those log rafters. There were no screen doors so when Dad said shut the door I never knew if he wanted to shut the swallows inside or shut them outside. That was Mom's fist experience in Mexico. She made almost no effort to learn Spanish. We would go to Ascension to visit Mexican friends Dad had known when he was a kid. Mom would sit and smile while Dad and they talked Spanish. I know she learned to love her life in Mexico after we moved to Dublan. No one could not like those people.

I always wanted to tame a bird. I was watching the nests to find a bird that looked about right for a weaner, and I would take him home. One day I found a hawk's nest. From a short distance I could see the birds. They looked about right. Summer was getting away, so if I was going to tame a bird I had to get started. They were chicken hawks. The nest was so high that I couldn't see in it when I stood up on my horse, but by standing on the saddlehorn and tip toes I could get my hand in the nest. I moved my hand around in the nest and I got hold of what I thought was one of those birds. I brought it out over the top of the nest. I had a hand full of rattlesnake. I yelled and jumped down to my saddle, but when I got there it was gone. I had thrown that snake right over my horses head and he didn't want it either. He didn't run away so I didn't have to walk home. When I got myself put back together and started normal breathing again I took a look at the snake. It hadn't moved from where I threw it. The head was gone. I looked up at the nest, and there sat two young hawks on the very edge of the nest and on the opposite side. I decided to forget the birds and turn to rabbits, but Bounce refused to have any live rabbits around.

Since my life up to that time had been with pack mules, I decided that I would teach Bounce to be a pack mule. I made a pack saddle, and made a bridle for him. He seemed to like the saddle alright, but he never learned to like the bit in his mouth so I had to use a hackamore. I had a can of water and Mom fixed me a sandwich. I tied them on Bounce real good and headed down one of the cow trails (I still thought of trails also) to find a good shade to have dinner. I hadn't gone far when one of those darned roadrunners snapped his beak. The roadrunner went over the fence and Bounce went under. My pack outfit was left hanging on the barbs of the bottom wire. The roadrunner got away because I didn't go shake it out of the bush. Bounce came back and I could tell by his eyes that he had fully intended to be a good mule, he just forgot that mules don't chase birds. I gave him the sandwich, and I carried the pack back to the house.

I spent a lot of time on my horse and one day for some reason I was riding around the yard under the large cottonwood trees. I had seen bronco riding all my life. When the rider had things under control and wanted to show off, he would take off his hat and fan that old pony's ears. That day I thought I would fan my horse a little. I took my hat off and hit his ears one time. Now let me tell you, that complete horse just flat disappeared. All I could see was cottonwood tree limbs and blue sky and they were spinning. Dad came running out and dusted me off, I thought a little rough since I had just been thrown off. Instead of asking me what had happened, he said, "You are too damn little to be fanning horses." I agreed with him. He sure messed up the story I had in mind to tell him. I was going to tell him how mean that horse was.

I rode with Dad to a ranch across the river. The river didn't run through our ranch there at Diaz but was real close. It was the same river I will tell about later at the Corralitos. It is called Rio Verde. He was on a deal to buy some cows from a Mexican rancher near by. The river was dry most of the year but during rainy season it would flood from up in the mountains. They were about a hundred miles away. After a lot of rain in the mountains and the skies were all clear, and about two weeks later the water would reach our part of the country. That was one of those days. When we got to the river on our way home, it was running full, bank to bank. I was riding a horse called Pig. I had never been on a swimming horse before, so Dad told me what to do, or maybe what not to do. Don't ever try to guide him with the bridle. He will turn upside down. He must have his head free in order to swim. Dad told me to guide him by splashing water on his face. If I should ever fall off a swimming horse, to get him by the tail and hold on because he will try to put his front feet on anything he can find. Pig swam high and with my feet pulled up I didn't get wet. Some horses swim with their nose barely out of the water.

Main Street in Diaz was still pretty, even though it had been abandoned since the exodus in 1912 when my grandfather was killed. It was a wide street. Lined with cottonwood trees that about touched at the tops. It was a mile long, and always a thrill to drive through it. We went through it each time we went to Ascension for groceries. The river ran between Colonia Diaz and Ascension. Diaz being the Mormon colony. On those trips we went to a garden and bought some vegetables. When we got home Mom found a beet about the size of a golf ball in among them. I thought it was pretty so she gave it to me. Now just what does a kid do with one little purple beet? I'll tell you so that you won't ever do it yourself. I found an old rusty can and put some water and my beet in it. I made a little fire under one of those cottonwood trees and cooked it. When it started to boil I thought it should be done and I didn't want it to get too hot anyhow. I had sharpened a stick to get it out of the can with, and I ate it. It tasted bad but I ate it anyhow. Now let me tell you, that little beet made me sick, and I mean the kind of sick that kills people. Many years later I read about how poison beets are if they aren't cooked properly. Tin cans in those days also could be very hazardous to one's health. I eat beets now, but with very little gusto.

The summer was getting near to the end and we would soon be going back to Columbus to school. A fellow showed up driving a remuda of paint horses. Maybe fifteen head. I learned later that he was on his way to the Hunt Ranch on the Corralitos. From there he moved to a ranch in the mountains, up the river from Colonia Juarez. He spent a few days at our place to rest himself and his horses. He was a loner. He had a sister somewhere, his only relative. His name was Bob Cook. He was a very likeable person. I thought that if I had one of those paint horses, there just wouldn't be anything better to wish for. I tried to get Dad to trade for one or buy one or maybe just take one. Mr. Cook seemed like a nice fellow, but he wouldn't even discuss parting with one of his paints horses. Finally the day came when he left and I stood there waving adios to him, thinking, some day we would meet again and maybe then he would let me have a paint horse. Dad said, "Looks like Mr. Cook left the corral gate open, you better go shut it." Right then I would just as soon be shutting gates as anything else, so out to the corral I went, no hurry, and there tied back in a corner out of sight was a pretty little paint horse. It was a yearling filly. She had a large white spot on each side so we named her Antelope. She was not a sorrel, or black, or bay paint, she was an orange paint. She was a bronco with no schooling. Dad let the Mexican cowboy ride her, until she would behave, then he turned her over to me, and of course, Raymon and Floyd. She was given to the three of us, not just me. We had her for about two years. The worst thing you can have in a bunch of saddle horses is a mare, and she was guilty of causing a lot of sore backed horses.

After we moved to Barranca, Bill was coming to the ranch quite often. He would spend a few days and go back to the US. One day he told Dad to get rid of that damn mare. I thought he was a little too heavy, but he was the boss. Dad traded her for a paint horse we called Hereford. He gave Hereford to Raymon. I already had my own horse. A black horse Dad got from Flay Peterson. He traded a pistol for him. His name, one guess, Chinate.

Bill was leasing a ranch on the Corralitos when he got into trouble and had to leave Mexico in a hurry. He got Flay Peterson to take care of his cattle. Flay moved them to his own ranch at Colonia Diaz. When Dad went there to run the ranch for Bill they decided to move the cattle back to the Corralitos. Dad moved them back in December 1928, then went to Columbus to spend Christmas. After Christmas we would move to Colonia Dublan. A few days before Christmas, my little brother, Louie, took sick and couldn't get better. It went into pneumonia. There was no cure for pneumonia then and he died the day after Christmas, 1928. He was born at Klondyke in 1927. We loaded what we could, in and on our 1927 Chevy and went to the ranch at the Corralitos. There were no buildings. Just a chuck wagon and campfire. It was called Barranca. It was on the bank of the river and there was a big, permanent water hole about twelve feet deep. I said there were no buildings there. Barranca was a smelter ghost town. The only evidence was the adobe walls still there and the slag dump. It was a good place for diamondback rattlesnakes to hide. I think back and think how lucky that I never got bit by one of them. My dog Bounce did.

Dad had rented a house in Dublan, so we took our things there and sort of got settled in and ready to start school. I was in the fourth grade. Columbus was a rat race from start to finish, and if that was a sample of town life, I sure didn't like it. When I went to school in Dublan, I was ready for some more of the same. I had my guard up. Dublan was the first decent place, and decent people I had ever lived in and with. It wasn't very long before I learned to love it and still do. It was a Mormon Church school so most of the kids were more my type. My teacher was Mrs. Eva Taylor. She took an interest in me, and helped me get some feeling of belonging, and I never had a teacher I didn't like after Miss Massy. I had some that I liked better, but never another Miss Massy.

4

Barranca

We arrived at the Barranca Camp in the evening and that night it snowed. Not much but it was cold. Barranca means bank. The camp was on a high bank on the bend of the Rio Casas Grandes. When I say camp I mean a chuck wagon and plenty of space to roll out the beds. There was a large permanent water hole there in the river bend. It was twelve to fifteen feet deep and about three hundred feet long. The camp fire and hot grub was sure good. I received a thousand shot BB gun that Christmas. I could see right away that I had arrived at a real hunting ground. Lizards running in the bushes, the trees full of birds, ducks on the water, and fish in the water. Bill Holmes gave me the BB gun for Christmas. He was Bill Adams' partner in the ranch. He worked for the AS&R mining in Chihuahua City. He would come to the ranch every few months. We spent the rest of the Christmas holidays there in camp. When school started we went to Dublan. Dad had a ranch house built soon and we spent the weekends at the ranch. The camp was a chuck wagon and camp fire. I liked that kind of living. It was part of the Corralitos Land and Cattle Co.

I started midyear in the fourth grade in Dublan. I was in for a new experience. There were no swings there. A little girl was hit in the head and killed a short time before I arrived there. They took all the swings away. Since I was a swinger, I didn't know how to play the games those kids played. Hop scotch, marbles, leap frog, and johnny ride the pony, to mention some of the main ones. I was a fast learner however, and the kids were good to teach me. I soon learned that as I got leaped over, I also got a spat, so I took that up right away. What they forgot to tell me, was that you don't spat the girls as you go over them. The thing that took more instruction was marbles. Those kids were good and they played for keeps. I didn't even have any marbles to loose. A kid by the name of Ray Thayne was sort of sidelined from the crowd so he took me in tow. He lent me some marbles and taught me how to hold and shoot them. It wasn't long before I could out shoot him. I was able to get a few marbles on credit to get started. I was never again without marbles. I Think. By the time I finished the eighth grade in 1933, I had a gallon can full. I decided to bury them and some day go back there and dig them up with my kids. In 1953, I did just that. I had Floyde and Sid. The burial place was at the Pajarito Line Camp, where we lived for several years. I buried the marbles near a larigoncillo bush, which was on the edge of a montezuma, in 1933. When I went back there twenty years later, the montezuma had been dug in so much, I could hardly recognize it. I buried a five gallon can with my marbles and some other treasures I wouldn't need any more. Some artifact hunter sure got my treasure. I still wonder what museum my marbles are in.

The original Corralitos was a very large ranch. It was cut into several pieces and then leased to the various ranchers. At the headquarter ranch was George Houghton. He was also in charge of the leasing. There was Bradefoot, joined us on the north, and Morris north of him. On our east was Cox. To the west was Stewart Hunt. West of Hunt was the Jeffery Ranch. The Jeffery headquarters was Ramos. The south line was all ejido. The river ran between us and Hunt. The fence ran zig zag across the river in order to give water holes to both ranches. The water table was near the surface so those holes were never dry. There was much trouble with stealing on the south fence line. A man rode that fence every day to see if any cattle had been taken during the night. If he found where a cow had been taken through the fence he would get Dad and they would trail it until they found it or lost the trail. Usually they would find the meat and get the thief.

We spent the summer of 1929 at Barranca. That summer I learned to swim and to fish. The first time in my life I had been around water. The ranch was so big and the rides so long that I didn't get very far from the house that summer. We started school in the new school house in the fifth grade in Dublan. I started to school in Colonia Dublan with intentions of finishing the fourth grade there. It just wasn't to be. About three months and there was some kind of revolution. Groups of would be soldiers running around over the country. Taking what they wanted as they went. Some soldiers went through our ranch and ate a few cattle on the way. Dad got nervous and took us to Hachita, NM. He remembered how his father was murdered by the same type of Revolucionarios. Those bands of fighters would take horses and cars. Dad took all the horses, about forty head, the car and his family to the US. He kept a horse for himself and each of his cowboys. We stayed a month with Lorin Adams, Dad's brother. Lorin worked for the Diamond A Ranch near Hachita. Then back to Columbus. Miss Massy didn't like me that time around any better than before. As I said in the Columbus chapter, she left me in the fourth grade. We stayed there until school was out then back to Dublan. That time Dublan was home for many years.

The summer of 1930 was spent at Barranca and it was lots of fun. I was ten then and able to make a hand on the roundups and cattle drives. I mentioned that I had another black horse and I named him Chinate. That Chinate had a different disposition from the one I had at Klondyke. He would throw me off every time he caught me loose in the saddle. He would buck in a spin. After a few falls I learned to ride him, but I didn't learn to like it. I learned to tell when he was going to buck. I would lean into the spin and pull him up. I could tell by his ears. Just before he bucked, his ears would stand straight up. He always grunted when he bucked. Raymon and Floyd never could ride him so I had him all to myself. We had another little horse at that time, belonged to Elsie, Bill's daughter. His name was Little Man. He didn't buck but when she would try to ride him out in the pasture, he would go out about a half mile, then take her back to the house. She just couldn't handle him. Bill would take him for a spin then put her back on him and the same thing. One day he got tired of it and asked me if I would like to have him. I did. I took him out in the mesquite bushes away from the house and me and Little Man came to an understanding. Sometimes he would almost forget but my spurs would improve his memory. He was a great little horse and a real little pet and a very good cow pony. Sometimes I would rope something bigger than he was but he would sit down on all fours and hold on. I have had him jerked up in the air but never had him jerked down. He always landed on his feet. My sons, Floyde and Sid, learned to ride him. He was old and gray headed and sassy with them.

We returned from riding the range one day and there sat a fellow in the shade by the side of the house. Mom knew he was there. She and Dad had known him in Arizona. His name was Jack Wright. He lived in Duncan, a bachelor, and loner. In the corral was a sorrel horse with very pretty flax mane and tail. You might say he was a blond horse. Dad told me that he was Nestegg. My thoughts quickly went back to the Rafter G Ranch. The first and last and only time I had ever seen him was when Dad put those hot irons on the top of his shoulder. He was a little colt horse then. There he stands in the corral, a full grown, ten year old horse. He had white spots where Dad had ironed him that day at the Rafter G. Nestegg was drawn from such a long journey. We let him rest a few days before riding him in order to get his waist back in shape. Dad gave Jack another horse that was fat and rested. He spent a few days with us then went on. I guess back to Duncan.

Dad rode Nestegg a few times to see how his character was. Then turned him over to me. He was the nicest riding horse I ever had to just go over the range. He had a real fast running walk, and he never pulled on the bridle. What ever direction I pointed him, he liked it and gave it his best gait, but that was all he was good for. He was afraid of a rope. Dad told me to never try to rope on him. He didn't know anything about working cattle, but he was sure nice to ride and I enjoyed him. When he had gotten his fat back he was a real pretty horse. There are some events that I have never figured out. One was, how come Jack rode Nestegg to our ranch in Mexico. The other was the day we came in off the range, towards the end of that same summer, and there sat Jack Wright in the same shade as the time he brought Nestegg to us. That time there was a big gray brown horse in the corral. I didn't hear any of the conversation, but after Jack had been there a few days, I saw him put his saddle on Nestegg and ride off. That was the last time I saw or heard of them. Jack I didn't care, but Nestegg I missed. Dad had traded him a fresh horse again for the used up one. I wouldn't even look at what I had wound up with. Dad assured me that he was a better horse for me. I knew Dad worried when I rode Nestegg because he was nothing but a good gaited horse, and he had a white ring around his eyes. Cowboys do not trust horses with white rings on the eyes.

We let the new brown horse rest up a few days and Dad told me to catch him for that days ride and we would try him out. He said Jack told him that he was a good horse. I called him Jack. He had no gait at all. He was a trotter. Usually a very rough gait, but Jack was unusual. His trot was softer than most gaits. He could trot forwards, backwards, side ways, or just stand there and trot in one spot. He was a big horse so was hard for me to get on, but he would stand still as long as it took me to climb up. He was the best cow horse I ever had, and when I roped something, no matter how big he could handle it. He would catch anything I pointed him to except a coyote. He just wasn't interested in chasing coyotes. It turned out that he was trained by Dad's brother, Lorin, one of the best. Jack wasn't just a horse. He was a real cow horse.

I said that was the last time I saw Jack Wright, and that was what I hoped at that time. After we moved to Pajarito in 1932, we came in from riding and would you believe, there sat Jack Wright. Dad had already traded my horse Jack for a Corralitos horse, so I knew Jack couldn't get him. Now think back in my story at Klondyke. I told about Toothpick. That was the horse Jack was riding that time. Dad traded him another fat horse and he went on. This was really the last time I saw him but not the last time he got in my way. Toothpick, even at his age was still fast and just a real pleasure to ride. I never rode him that I didn't think about when I had run horses on him at Klondyke when I was about five years old. We had Toothpick only a few months when he injured one of his hind legs at the hock. He could still outrun anything on the ranch on three legs. Well mas o menos.

There were lots of antelope in the foot hills on the east side of the ranch. When Bill Holmes came to the ranch, he would stay about a week. Of course his main thing was to see the ranch and how it was being run by Dad, but the highlight of his stay was the antelope hunt. He always got some good shooting but never killed one. On one hunt we jumped a buck out of a canyon. He was close, like fifty yards. Bill and Dad jumped off their horses, Dad was standing there with his gun waiting for Bill to shoot. The buck was so excited that he ran a circle around us then ran across the canyon and stopped broad side. At that time maybe two hundred yards, looked us over for a few minutes then went on his way. There was not a shot fired. Dad was waiting for Bill to shoot, and Bill was so excited he stood there and threw all the bullets out of his rifle. There he was with an empty gun and a buck looking him over. Dad had his short .30--30. For it, two hundred yards was out of sight.

The next day Dad gave his sawed--off .30--30 to Manuel Quintana, one of the cowboys, and told him to bring back an antelope, and sent me with Manuel. We had no trouble finding a herd, there were lots of them. He shot one and broke a hind leg. I ran after it to rope it. I was riding Chinate, and he ran right over the top of it, but Manuel was close behind me and he roped it. He put it on my horse, and I sure was proud that evening to ride in with an antelope on behind me. I sure watched Chinate's ears that day because he didn't like where that antelope was at all.

Dad took Holmes for a ride to see things down the river. Floyd got the turn to go with them that time. During the ride they decided to lope their horses for a change in pace since Holmes wasn't used to riding. It is restful to lope a short distance. Floyd's horse got too close to one of the other riders and somehow pulled his bridle off. The faster they ran to catch Floyd's horse the faster he ran, so by the time Dad caught him, it had turned into a real race, and Floyd just about got away. As they were running Floyd was calling to Dad to come and get me, and kept saying that until Dad caught him. When I saw Bill Holmes during the years, he always mentioned that race and he would say, "Come and get me."

The Barranca Ranch horse pasture was about five square miles, and was full of mesquite brush as high as maybe twelve feet, and thick. Every morning someone had to go out in that stuff and find where the remuda was hiding and bring them in to the corrals. Each man would get his mount for the day and then turn them back to hide in the bushes again. Each man had five or six horses because a roundup takes a lot of horsepower. We kept a horse in the corral at night, called a wrangler to ride in the morning to find the remuda. The wrangling deal fell to me more often than I liked. To make the job easy we put a bell on a yellow mule. That was about all that mule was good for, was to carry the bell.

He was suppose to shake his head about day light, and keep it up until he was located. That was what that mule was suppose to do. For some reason, all the horses stayed close to the bell. There was always a bell on one of the horses out on the open range. We had a humpbacked mare that carried a bell all her life.

When I would leave the house in the morning to go after the remuda, Bounce would always go with me. He was good to help bring the horses in once I found them. One morning I called and he didn't come so I had to go with out him. He was good company and I missed not having him trotting along my side. There was a hill in the pasture, maybe two hundred feet high. I would climb the hill, and keep going up until I could spot the horses, that is if I didn't hear the bell first. Mostly I didn't hear the bell first, because that mule had big ears and could hear me before I heard him and would stand still and not make a sound with the bell. The reason I know this, is that I caught him at it. I was up on the hill and located the mule, so I went down and rode to the area where I had spotted him. I would stop and listen for the bell, but never could hear it. I arrived at the place where the mule was suppose to be, but he wasn't there. I found his tracks so I knew he had been there, and the tracks were fresh. I listened more for the bell and no sound. I decided to follow the tracks, I just knew he couldn't have gone far unless he ran. If he ran I would have heard the bell. I followed the tracks for a while and I soon noticed there were horse tracks with the mule tracks, so I kept going and the trail was getting plainer and easier to follow and more horse tracks along with the mule's. That was fine because that dumb mule was leading me to the rest of the horses. Then it finally came to me that all those horse tracks were made by the same horse and I was riding him. I took a short cut through the brush and there was that mule tip toeing along the trail we had made. The reason he hadn't done that to me before was that Bounce would flush him out, but this morning Bounce hadn't gone with me. I got after that mule with all I could think of to call him. I was moving him through the mesquites so fast he had to ring the bell and the horses soon came to him. When they heard the bell traveling they came to it.

About the time I had the remuda together I came to a clearing and there was a bunch of coyotes running in a circle. The clearing was about three hundred feet across. There were too many for me to count, but I guessed eight or ten. They were running so fast and having so much fun that they didn't notice me watching them and that was the reason I couldn't count them. Then it dawned on me that there was Bounce running in that circle with them. About that time one of them saw me, and with some kind of a signal they scattered. One of them stopped at the edge of the clearing, turned around and gave that coyote bark. Of all the coyotes I had heard bark, that was the first and only one I ever saw do it. He didn't put his foot in his mouth to make those funny sounds, but he did sit down. Bounce came over to me but didn't offer any explanation. About that time he noticed a badger hole there close. He went over and smelled it. He knew I liked for him to catch badgers. I watched his ears and tail and figured there must be one in there. I said, "Sickum," and that was all it took. He went to work digging the hole to fit him while I sat there and watched. I had seen him do that before, and he always came out with an animal of some kind. The ground was sandy, so it was easy to dig. About the time he had dug in where I could just see his tail I heard him make a different sound and his tail went straight. I knew he had something or something had him. He started trying to get back out of the hole and couldn't. He would try to get out then rest then try some more. Finally he came dragging a badger out of there. The badger had him by the throat and he had the badger by a front leg. When he got the badger out of the hole he sat there and rested. The badger wouldn't turn loose and neither would Bounce. I looked around and found a stick and laid it on the badger's head and he turned loose and ran for the hole. He didn't make it. Bounce held him and I finished him off with the stick. A badger is very easy to kill if you hit him on the head. The reason Bounce couldn't pull him out of the hole, was because they are very strong in the legs and have real long digging claws, and he still had three free legs. All that caused me to be a little late getting the remuda in that morning. My story didn't keep me out of trouble.

Barranca means bank. I need to give some history at this point. The town of Barranca was a mining ghost town. It was a smelter town. The way I heard the story was; In late 1800, a mining company in New York bought the San Pedro mines. In order to get the mines, they had to buy the range also. The range was about three thousand sections, or square miles. That was lots of ranch land even for those days. They called it Corralitos Land and Cattle Company. I don't know where the name came from. It means little corrals. There was also a smelter at the hacienda. The ranch was stocked with Red Durham cattle and thoroughbred horses. During the Villa revolution, the ranch was fairly well destroyed. Most of the fences were torn down and the buildings were run down. The Corralitos Land and Cattle Company never tried to go back into the cattle business. Instead they leased large parcels to various cattle men. Uncle Bill was one of them. Dad replaced the fence on the country we had. It had been open range since the Villa days. George Houghton was manager of the Corralitos. He was raised there. His father was with the company in its hay days. After the revolution the government took a ten mile strip from the south side. It was made into an ejido and given to the people. In the 1940's the ejido that joined us took about half of our west pasture. Then the other ejidos started to push for some of the range land. The Company decided to sell what they had left before they lost it all. They sold it to the cattle men who were leasing at the time. By that time Bill had bought the Benton Ranch farther west and we leased our ranch then from the ejido people. That was the Pajarito. We just stayed where we had been for several years.

In the bend of the river near our house was a high vertical bank, like maybe six feet. We were playing in that area. Bounce was smelling all the holes he could find. He smelled one and kept smelling it. It was at the bottom of the bank. He would put his nose in the hole real tight trying to figure out what was in there. The hole fit his nose right up to his eyes. He looked at me to see if I wanted him to dig. I told him to go ahead. It was still in the morning. Raymon and Floyd were there with me. The bank was loose gravel and sand so it was easy to dig. The hole was at the bottom of the bank. He would dig a while then come out for water and rest then back to digging. At noon time, I sent Raymon to the house to get Mom to make us a lunch, and also one for Bounce. We all had a good lunch and we sure kept a lookout on the hole. If there was something in there we didn't want it to sneak by us. Along in the afternoon he had dug in so far that we could barely see him. We would take turns crawling in behind him to see how he was doing. The one that crawled into the hole had to be pulled out by the two kids on the outside. It was my turn to go in there and see how Bounce was doing and all of a sudden his tail went straight and he let out a whine. I called to Raymon and Floyd to pull me out because I thought Bounce was coming out too. As soon as I was out of his way he came out of there, whining. There was a very big rat fastened onto his nose. He sat there and looked at the rat and the rat looked at him. The rat knew if he turned loose to run Bounce would get him, and Bounce knew that also. Bounce looked up at me to see if I would do something about that rat. I looked around but there were no sticks close but plenty of rocks. I didn't dare throw a rock for fear of hitting the wrong one. Bounce would push on the rat with his paws, but real easy like, and that old rat just stayed on there. That went on for several minutes. We were all real quiet and thinking, including Bounce, when the rat turned loose and ran. That was when he committed suicide.

On one of Holmes' trips to the ranch, he brought an army canteen. He always brought things he thought we could use on the ranch. Of course we all wanted to drink from the canteen. Raymon wanted it but I was a little bigger so I had it and was drinking first. While I was drinking he hit it on the bottom and broke my front tooth. That was in 1930. I have had the gold patch on my front tooth for many years.

Harve Taylor and Lorin Taylor were very good friends of Dad and Bill. They had put some cattle on the ranch with permission from Bill. They would go to the ranch to see how their cattle were doing, and just to be good friends. They lived in Dublan, and were farmers. Harve later became my father--in--law. Lorin came to the ranch more often and would bring his son, LaSelle, my age. LaSelle and I became very good friends, we were together so much, we were like brothers. We had a very small pasture in the bend of the river. To get to it we had to cross the river, which was dry at that point most of the time, but during rainy season it would be flooded. It would swim a horse to cross it to or from the little pasture. When the flood was up the cattle would not cross in or out. There was high sacaton grass in there and there was always a few cattle in there to partake of it. When the river was in flood stage, we had to go in there and make the cattle swim out. LaSelle was visiting us, the river was about five and a half feet deep at the crossing, and there were some cattle in there that we had to get out.

LaSelle could not swim so we showed him how to jump up and down as he went across, and to take in air each time he came up. He was about halfway across when he was still taking in air after he went down. That worked for about two jumps, and I could see he was a goner. The river current was washing him towards a fence that crossed the river. I went in after him, grabbed his hands and started jumping with him and got him back in tune. He sat on the bank and watched as Raymon, Floyd, and I would run the cows up to the water one or two at a time. As they would jump into the water, we would go right in after them and hang onto their tails until they reached the other side. It was really a great sport. I don't think Mom ever knew. When we had crossed all the cattle, we had to get LaSelle back to the other side. That time we decided to all jump together, and he made it across OK. Before we put our clothes on we went to shallower water and that day he learned to swim.

When school started that same year, we moved to town, 1931. Harve and Lorin went to the ranch with Dad. They were riding the range on the west side of the river. Bill had bought Stuart Hunt out by then. We had the range on both sides of the river. That made a big cow ranch. It was about forty miles east and west, and about twelve miles north and south. Dad was riding a horse he called Bashful. He had been telling them how he could rope coyotes on Bashful. That he would take to a coyote as if it was a calf. As they were riding along, out jumped a coyote, and Dad said, "Let's rope him." They all got their ropes down and away they went. Dad was in the lead and got the first throw at the coyote, but he missed and the coyote turned back. Bashful turned back with him, but at that point Lorin was running right behind Dad ready for his turn if Dad missed. As the coyote turned back he ran in front of Lorin and Lorin caught him. Everyone was traveling so fast and erratic that no one could stop. Bashful ran over Lorin's rope and fell, rolling over on top of Dad. When Bashful got up he ran for about a hundred yards, then stopped. He turned and looked to see what had been roped. Dad had been training him for calf roping and tying. What had been roped was Dad. When Bashful got to his feet, he took of, but then his training came to him and he stopped and turned around. He stood there just long enough for Harve to run over with his pocketknife and cut Dad's rope. At that time Bashful panicked and ran about four miles back to the ranch house. The loop of Dad's rope had tightened up on both his arms just above the wrists and he was drug that hundred yards by his horse. His mouth was full of dirt and Harve dug it out with his finger and got Dad to breathing again, but he was unconscious. Harve stayed with Dad. Lorin went back to the house, about four miles, and got Dad's car, a 1927 Chevy two door. They took him back to the ranch house then to Dublan, about fifteen miles. There were no roads at all. You just followed the best ruts and wound through the mesquite. That was what we called a road.

That same day a man came to our house in Dublan looking for Dad. I think he wanted to buy some cattle. I went with him to the ranch to show him the road, or the way. We met Dad's car about halfway returning to Dublan and Harve was driving. I knew Harve and Lorin had gone to the ranch with Dad and would bring the car back to town to Mom. Never in the world did I ever think Dad was in the back seat unconscious. We went on to the ranch. The ranch hand told me that they had all gone to town. He didn't tell me Dad was hurt, but I had some sort of feeling all the way back to town. Dad always did his own driving, and how come I didn't see him as we passed. It was just getting dark when we met them and I allowed for that, but I was still bothered.

The fellow and I arrived back in town in time to see the hotel burning. It burned to the ground that night. Mom met me at the door and told me Dad was hurt bad. She took me in to see him. I thought he was dead and she wasn't telling me. That is one of the indelible times of my life. A telegram was sent to Bill in Columbus. He arrived the next night. Wilford Farnsworth had a new four door Chevy and he loaned it to Bill to take Dad to Deming to the hospital. Mom went with Dad to Deming and stayed there until Bill brought them home. I think about four weeks. He was unconscious, I think for three weeks.

When Bill took Dad and Mom home he could barely walk by himself. I will never forget, when he came home he didn't know me. While they were gone to Deming, I had Raymon, Floyd and Domer to look after. We worked things out together and I don't recall any problems. We ate most of our meals at Lorin Taylor's home. LaSelle called his step--mother Aunt Lillian, and we did also. She was a very special person to me. As I have said, "LaSelle was like a brother to me." That time in our lives was part of what created that feeling. I think of all the men I was raised with and that I really liked in many ways, Lorin Taylor was number one. He was always a pleasure to have around or to be around. We spent lots of time at each other's homes.

The doctors in Deming said Dad had a broken neck. About fifty years later Harve talked to me about the fall. He told me about digging the dirt from Dad's mouth so he could breath. Now when I think how Dad was, I think maybe most of his problem was being so long without breathing, and there was brain damage. I had never heard about the dirt until Harve told me. If it had been discussed I would have known. Dad walked and acted like brain damage. Besides, if his neck had been broken, the way he was handled would have finished him off. The first thing was, Harve and Lorin had to stuff him into the back seat of a two door car. There was no way to do that without folding Dad in various shapes. Then transport him over the roughest of terrain. Not even any ruts to follow from the accident sight to the ranch house. Then, ruts and chug holes from the ranch to Dublan. Then a hundred and forty miles to Deming over the same kind of ruts and bumps. I just don't see how he could have survived all that with a broken neck. Now here is the clincher. Besides all the above, a chiropractor, Clarence Turley, came to our house once a week for over a year and gave Dad neck adjustments. Dad kept improving and his memory was getting better and his walk was also getting better. I think not because of the treatments but in spite of them. After about two years he was able to pretty well take up where he left off after the coyote chase. He never tried to rope anymore coyotes and didn't want me to. I never had a horse that could catch one, anyhow. I tried many times. I caught a few young ones. They would never get tame, and it was hard to keep them in rabbits for breakfast so I would turn them loose.

In 1930, there was an outbreak of the scab on some of the ranches. Since the cattle market was the US, it was important that we didn't get quarantined. That would close the border to all shipping. When that happens it is much harder to get it open again. There has always been US ranchers who would like to see it closed and stay that way. The scab is caused by a little mite, on the order of a flee. Usually noticed first on the neck and then spreads to the rest of the cow. The ranchers were told that if they would dip all their cattle, they could probably get rid of it and keep the US border from being closed.

That was one busy summer. We first rounded up all the cattle from the east side of the river and put them on the west side. Corrals had to be built, and a dipping vat. There was a US man there to see that the operation met the specs. Most dipping vats are long and just wide enough for cattle to go through single file, and deep enough for them to swim, so that they get wet all over. The solution was a creosote and sulfur mixture. It had to be heated. The vat we built was round and about twenty feet diameter, and eight feet deep. A slide on the entering side and steps on the other side to climb out. There was a lift gate at the steps to control the swimming time. Men were placed around the vat with poles to make sure that all the cattle got a good ducking. The cattle were kept in there for a few minutes then let up the steps into the drain pen. One bunch, about ten head, draining while the next bunch was swimming. That took most of the summer. Bill was there, overseeing, but hadn't moved back to the ranch yet.

As the cattle were dipped they were put in the pasture on the east side of the river. After it was all over, we had to split up the herd again so that we had about even amounts of cattle in each pasture. The pastures were one large pasture on each side of the river. The cattle could rome where ever they wanted in that pasture, and some did. We would find a cow at one water place one time and at another later on. Mostly, however, they were dependable to stay put, or what we called locate.

After the dipping was over we were always on the watch for cattle we might have missed and that might have scab. We found a few and Dad would shoot it on the spot and we would gather wood and cremate it. It must have been a year before we felt completely safe.

During the dipping operation we would fill the corrals with cattle for the day's work. After we got the cattle in the corral was when the show really started. Those cattle had always been rounded up and branded and worked on the range in the roundup, but had never seen the inside of a corral before. In those days we hadn't started dehorning yet. Those old cows still had their defence system intact. It didn't take long for the men to learn to keep the corral fence close by. There were three corrals and lanes to move the cows to the vat single file. One of the Mexican cowboys became a little careless one day. An old cow was sure about to mess up his hip pockets. He was near the center of the corral when the race started. He was running so fast that he went up over the fence and into the adjoining corral. That corral was full of mad cows also. One of them saw him coming, and as he was falling into the other corral that old cow just pitched him right back up on the fence top. He was not hurt, but he was looking down at two unfriendly cows. Help arrived and sent the cows to the vat for their swim. It took two men to pry him loose and get him off the corral fence. He was no good in the corrals after that so they put him to opening and closing the drain pen gate. After the swim those cows were not looking for someone to hook, but just a chance to escape. That gate let them go back to freedom.

    Along about that time was when Thad was killed. Dad's brother at Klondyke. After we left Klondyke he decided to go into the goat business. He bought the goats from a Mr. Wetherby, also a Klondyke rancher. That was the same man Dad bought the windmill from. Thad bought the goats on credit, and when the notes came due the man wanted his money. That was the way he did business. Thad couldn't pay for them so he took them back to Mr. Wetherby. Then he talked to a friend who advised him that if he had the goats in his possession, Wetherby couldn't take them away from him. It seems Thad had already paid some money on them. That sounded like good advice. Thad watched for a day when Wetherby had gone to Safford. He had to pass by Thad's ranch. Sure enough, one day there he goes. Thad got on his horse and down to the Wetherby Ranch he went after his goats. Wetherby didn't go to Safford, and wherever he went, he returned too soon for Thad to get the goats back to his place. He was still driving them out of the Wetherby Ranch when Wetherby drove up. Thad was told to leave the goats and ride off but he refused. Wetherby fired a shot over Thad's head, he testified in court, to scare the goats. Thad went for his gun. Wetherby already had a bead on him and shot him through the middle. Thad ran his horse to the Sole house which was behind the Klondyke store, and fell off his horse there. They didn't find Thad's pistol, and reported he didn't have one with him. Dad always said he believed Thad had his gun because he never went anyplace without it, especially when he expected trouble. I never saw him after we moved from Klondyke. I liked him, he was a good uncle. Mr. Sole was a forest ranger.

Barranca

When Bill bought Stewart Hunt out, he got the cattle also. What Bill bought from Stuart Hunt was his Corralitos lease and cattle and horses. Hunt bought and sold two and three year old steers. No mama cows for him. In those days cattle were not sold as weaners. That came into play a few years later. The bigger the cattle the better the buyer liked them. Some of those Hunt steers were big and ready for market. They were three and four year old Mexican Sonora types. We were shipping a train load of them at the Corralitos Stock Pens. They were being crowded up the shoot and into the cattle cars. They were real tight in the shoot, when one of them jumped up on the backs of the others. He walked on their backs up to the door of the train car, but instead of going into the car he jumped upon top of the car. I was sure I was witnessing something unusual there. He walked around on top of the car while the loading continued. Jose Terrasas was the buyer and he was there. He was part of the Don Luis Terrasas family, who at one time owned most of the state of Chihuahua. He told the cowboys to get him down, which meant, make him jump off. If he breaks a leg you can eat him. That old steer must have heard, because he jumped off the back side of the car, did not break a leg, and if they caught him I never did hear. The brush was thick and he got in it. At Barranca, cattle stealing or rustling was the most talked about, and the biggest problem with running the ranch. We heard a lot about it. We would hear about catching the rustler and hanging him to a cottonwood tree. I was still too young to be in on any of those trips. There was a Rural Police and Segundo who did the dirty work. Raymon, Floyd, and I liked to play rancher. Now if there was a rancher there had to be a rustler, and Floyd was him. Raymon and I had adjoining ranches, and we sure tried to catch the rustler. Well, one day I caught him, and Raymon and I decided we would hang him. Before that we had let him get away. The car shade was made from cottonwood poles. We tied his hands behind him and put a rope on his neck and threw it up and over one of those vigas. I took the slack out of the rope and tied it to a post there close. Now this is how quick fun can turn to tragedy. I was going to leave him tied there for a while. I was going into the house and get me a drink of water. As I started to go I noticed Floyd moving a rock with his toes. The rock was about six inches high. He maneuvered the rock under him and stepped up on it. I took that slack out and tied the rope again. Just as I had the rope tied good, the rock rolled out from under him and there he was, really hanging. He couldn't reach the ground, and I couldn't get the rope untied. When he fell he had pulled my knot tight. I have carried a pocketknife all my life, and I'm sure my knife saved his life that day. I cut the rope and he fell to the ground choking for breath. It took a while to get him up and around again. I sure had a time convincing him that I was just playing. He said his rustling days were over.

Another fun thing we did when the folks went to town was rope the chickens. When Dad bought us those special little ropes, I'm sure he never thought what all we would rope with them. Mom had about two dozen hens. We sure needed the eggs. We actually started our roping career on chickens. The object was to see if we could catch all those old hens and get them tied down before the folks returned from town. The chickens roamed the range like the cattle. They just didn't go as far from the house. There was a gate about a hundred yards from the house. Dad would always honk for one of us to run and open the gate. That one day, we had most of the chickens tied down. We put them in the shade of the carport. There was also mesquite bushes blocking the view to the gate. I sent Raymon to open the gate. I told him not to run too fast, because Floyd and I had to get all those chickens on their feet and acting normal. Now, the way you tie a chicken. First you must rope it, and that was the most fun. Put its head under a wing, hold it between your hands out in front of you, and whirl it around about four times and sit it on the ground. It will sit there and not move until it is tipped over with a foot or hand. We managed to get them all tipped over and walking around, but instead of going on about their business, they were still walking around in a stupor in the carport when Dad and Mom drove up. If Dad would have asked me how come all the chickens were in the carport, I would have told him. For sure, I would not lie to him. He always told me that lying was much more dangerous than whatever I had been up to. He said, "Get out of the way, chickens, you have been in the shade long enough."

The close call behind me, I was in good shape because I had gone to a lot of effort to have dinner ready when they returned. I had cooked macaroni, my first and last. I filled a pan with macaroni then added some water and set it on the fire. When Mom saw that all of the pots and pans were full of macaroni, and some on the floor that got away from me, she began to laugh. I also made biscuits, again my first. I didn't use a cutter, I don't think there was one. I had watched Mom squeeze off just the right amount of dough and pat it into a biscuit. I noticed mine were not the same size as hers but I thought nothing of it. At dinner I just had to ask how they liked my biscuits. Dad said, "They look like little elk turds, but they taste all right." The first time I was around elk, many years later, I could see why he said that. I didn't see any elk, but from Dad's description I knew they had been there. I said the pans were full macaroni, all but one. I had hail stones in it. The day was bright sunshine, but from someplace there fell about a dozen hail stones larger than hen eggs. As each one would fall I would run and get it. Never entered my mind that one might hit me.

Our neighbor to the west was Stuart Hunt. His ranch was about the same size as ours. About two hundred thousand acres. In 1931, Bill bought him out, cattle and lease. In the deal he got about sixty head of horses. In the bunch there were two that were gentle, and they were both pacers. The pacers were sure good to travel on, but no good for working cattle. I don't think there was a good cow horse in the whole bunch. One pacer was called Piojo, and the other, after a few rides was called Bonehead. Bill had legal papers by that time to permit him to go back to Mexico, and not be captured. As soon as school was out in Columbus he moved his family to the ranch. He took the Barranca Ranch, and we moved to the Hunt Ranch, which was on the north west side.

That place was called Sauz. There was a spring near the house, and that was where we got our running water. Like the VAV Ranch. Run to the spring and help yourself. Only that spring was close to the house, like maybe two hundred feet. Real cool and good tasting. It formed a marsh for about a hundred yards wide and a half mile long. There were lots of ducks there. They nested there in the summer. Back at the Diaz Ranch it was hawk eggs. At Sauz it was duck eggs and I didn't need a horse to find the nest or to get the eggs when I did find it. I was able to hatch some mallards. I clipped the very tip joint of one wing on each duck that I hatched and then turned them in the marshes. We only lived there one summer, then to Dublan to school. We lived there the summer of 1931.

In 1943, I was back over there looking for a cow we thought was watering there. I was riding around the marshes, thinking back to that summer of 1931, and how much I had enjoyed living there. I saw a duck with about twelve little ducks. When a mother duck is disturbed, she will fake being crippled until the intruder follows her away from the little ones then she will stay just out of reach unless the intruder gets too close then she will fly. I played her game because I knew the rules as good as she did. As I got closer to her she still put on the same act, and then I decided she couldn't fly. I caught her and she was short the tip of one wing. I turned her towards her little troops, and went on looking for the cow. I didn't find her but the duck made my day.

In the east pasture there were three windmills. San Pedro, which was east on the Cox fence line, Buena Vista, and the Huerfano, both on the Bradefoot fence line. Bradefoot took care of the Buena Vista. We took care of the Huerfano. Cox took care of the San Pedro, until we ran water from there to the Palma Alta. There was an old pipeline there about four miles long and we put it back into operation. We agreed to run the pump jack if the wind didn't pump enough water. The San Pedro was in the pass and I think we ran the pump jack one time. The wind blew most of the time. There was always wind there. We pumped a couple of days and the wind came up again. We hooked the mill back up and went home. While we were there we sat in the shade and listened to the pump motor, not much else to do. The motor had a water hopper to be filled about once an hour. The water would boil off. My job was to keep the hopper full of water. On TV, I'm sure you have seen those movies of the wild sheep. They step off about thirty paces and then but heads at full speed. You heard the sound. Well I heard that sound before they caught it on TV. On the Cox side of the water trough we heard a bang and stood up from our shade to see what it was. Among the cattle at the water was a big old ram, big horns and all. The ram took a disliking to a bull. The bull was minding his business, checking out the cows as they arrived for water. The ram stepped off about thirty feet and hit the bull head on. The bull just stood there and watched as the ram got ready for another charge. The bull stood and let that ram hit him about six times. As the ram was setting up his next charge, the bull decided he had enough and turned tail and ran. The ram charged anyhow. He just hit the other end of El Toro.

The Huerfano was our windmill and cattle water to maintain. Those wells were drilled before metal windmills. They had large wooden wheels. As they needed repairs, it finally became cheaper to replace them with the new windmills. We used the Aeromotor. The Huerfano well was about three hundred and fifty feet deep so it took a large mill to pull it. We put an eighteen foot wheel on it. The tower was a good wooden strong tower so we only replaced the stub where the gears sit on top of the tower. We also got a new pump engine and pump jack. We pumped water there often because there were many cattle watered there. Bradefoot's and ours. There was a large cement and rock tank, about thirty thousand gallons. Deer and Antelope watered there also. The windmill is at the foot hills of a large mountain range. The Corralitos paid for the windmill but Bill paid for the pump engine and pump jack. Dad sent a man with the wagon and team to Columbus to haul them back. It was about a two week's trip. When he got back to the ranch, and was taking the load on up to the windmill Dad let Raymon and me go along for the ride. Along the way we were jumping in and out of the wagon from the rear. For some reason Raymon decided to get in on the side of the wagon. All the time the wagon was traveling on up the road. He slipped and fell under the wagon. The rear wheel ran over his toes of one foot. The driver stopped and gave him first aid. Pulled his shoe off and checked each toe. Not even mashed much. The road was sandy and his foot mostly mashed into the sand. We stayed in the wagon the rest of the trip, about three miles. The Mexican fellow was afraid we would tell Dad that he had ran over Raymon, but we told him, "Senor, we are more afraid than you, no tengas quidado."

The pump engine sat about thirty feet from the pump jack. The jack was driven with a flat belt. We put a twist in the belt because the jack had to turn the opposite of the engine. It was the old one lunger type engine. A large heavy fly wheel on each side attached to the crank shaft. Once the flywheels were up to the speed, preset by a governor, then the exhaust valve was held open and the engine floated, or free wheeled, until the inertia of the fly wheels was slowing down. The governor would let the valve close. It would fire two or three times to pick up speed then the free wheeling again. The floating was usually four to five exhaust strokes. It was a very beautiful and different engine sound. The old John Deere tractor was that type.

I have been scared a few times and that windmill did me one of them. Once a year it is recommended to check the oil in the windmill gears. Those gears that sit on the very top that the wheel and tail are fastened to. The very top. A hat type cover sits over the gears that had to be removed to look inside where the oil was. It took about a quart a year for one of those big ones. There was no wind so Dad took his quart of oil and up the ladder he went with me right behind. If there was wind he would put the whole thing off until another day. That day he took me up there with him to hold the wheel while he climbed on to the top to check it out. It was an eighteen--foot wheel and it took very little wind to turn it. Dad was on top with the gear hat in one hand and the oil in the other and I was holding the wheel. There came a very little breeze, and it wanted to do two things, change the tail direction and turn the wheel. The tail I had to follow, as we went around on the platform, but the wheel I had to hold onto. The platform wasn't very big so I sure had to watch my step, but when that wheel lifted me off the platform I was scared. There wasn't quite enough breeze to turn the wheel all the way over with me holding onto it. The wheel would pick me up about a foot then let me down. I didn't turn it loose because I thought it would knock Dad off the top. It would not have, but I was too busy to figure all that out right then. Dad was so busy with what he was doing and holding onto his seat that he didn't see what was happening to me. We climbed down to the ground and he said, "I'm glad that is over for another year."

I said, "So am I." The windmill had a break lever to shut it off when we were pumping with the pump jack. I don't know why Dad didn't use it at that time.

The other windmill was Buena Vista. Bradefoot took care of it. I was there often to get a drink but never worked on it. That was where I learned about mule colts and cattle. They raised paint horses and mules. The paint horses watered at Huerfano, and the mares with mule colts watered at Buena Vista. Those mules would go to water early and spend the whole day chasing the cows from the water. The cows could not water until those mule colts got tired of playing and left for the range. Surely Bradefoot didn't know about it, but a little kid doesn't tell a big cowman anything. I knew Bill or Dad wouldn't put up with something like that. The cattle of the ranchers did not mix at those waters. Each ranch was fenced to keep them on their respective rancho.

The north side of the ranch was at the Corralitos Hacienda. We stopped in there regular when we were riding that part of the range. Bradefoot lived there. The Hacienda buildings were built with a patio inside, about a quarter mile square. There they had the rodeos and any other fiesta that came along. It was Cinco De Mayo fiesta time and they had a big parade around the patio. All the Mexican cowboys and families lived there. There was a school and church. Wayne Bradefoot rode one of his paint horses. I thought he would never quit bucking, and Wayne rode him until he did. Before the rodeo there was a parade and everyone got into the march. For some reason, a goat decided to join the parade and got under one of the wagons to march in the shade. Dad and I, and George Houghton were sitting under a large cottonwood tree watching the show. George's bull dog was sitting there with us. When that old goat came by the second time, the dog jumped out there and got hold of him. We couldn't get him to turn loose. He hadn't been taught the cow dog command to turn loose. It was used, but he paid no attention. Dad got hold of the goat and George got hold of his dog. They were going to pull them a part but that was about to pull a piece off from the goat. They held the goat and started stomping the bull dog. I thought they were going to kill the dog before he finally turned loose. I don't ever want a bulldog.

I enjoyed touring the corrals when we were at the Corralitos Hacienda. I could always find a few deer in the barn eating hay. They had been raised there so were quite tame. Sometimes they would wander out in the patio and dogs would take after them. In the back of the barns were windows, about three feet square and about four feet from the ground. Those deer would run and jump through those windows into the barn. That was far enough for the dogs.

About the barns, there was a large corral enclosed by adobe. Everything was made with adobe. In the large corral was where they broke the horses. Dad and I were watching them handle a horse one day. The vaqueros had to throw him down to get the hackamore on him, then tie a foot up to saddle him. He wasn't really a bucker but he was scared to death of a man. He was the last colt from the Corralitos remuda. The

Corralitos, at one time, raised horses and good ones. He belonged to Houghton, then Bradefoot, then Wilbur Stevens. Dad wanted the horse, but they wouldn't let Dad have him. The horse finally outlawed. They couldn't do anything with him at all. He was a high--strung thoroughbred and he fought like tiger a when a man got near him. Wilbur was not a bronc fighter, so he had no use for the horse at all. Actually he traded for him for Dad because they would not let Dad trade for him. Back to my horse, Jack. Dad traded him to Wilbur for that outlaw horse, and called him Ultimo.

Dad was good at training bad horses. The first thing he had to teach that one was how good the bridle bit tasted when he took it nice like. After a few days of lessons he would come up to Dad with his head down and his mouth open. All he wanted was the bridle before that cowboy got mad again. Then came the lessons to behave while the saddle was put in place. He learned that, but then he was suppose to enjoy carrying the man that made him glad to do all that. The thoroughbred breed itself is very temperamental, and Ultimo was true to the breed. Dad rode and trained him for about two years then turned him over to me. He never got over being nervous, but he was not mean, just afraid. He was one very good horse.

To handle a horse, you kick him to go forward, push the reins for left or right turns, and pull the reins for the stop, and pull harder for reverse. As you start any of those maneuvers, there is the signal as the movement starts. Ultimo could sense the signal and respond before you could actually give the command. That made him a little hard to sit on some times. He was so fast that when I was going to rope on him, I would get my rope ready before I gave him the forward signal. The forward signal was a knee squeeze, for sure no kicks.

To rope on the range was an art, because we had to do it and not spook the cattle and make them wild. Our biggest job in the summer was checking the cattle for screwworms. Especially after the spring branding roundup and the brands started to peal. We carried medicine on our saddle and range doctored. When we found one with screwworms, we would ride among the cattle until we could cut him off to himself. Then rope him. When I did that and showed Ultimo the one I wanted, he went to it. Through bushes, over bushes, around bushes, and sometimes under part of those bushes to give me a good throw. If I should miss, which was seldom, I had to stop and start over because he followed the calf so exact and close that I couldn't stay on him and build a new loop. He could catch a coyote but he ran just as twisty as that coyote, and I couldn't stay on him and rope at the same time, so I would give old coyote a chase and let him go.

Dad had three horses that were tops. He got them young and trained them himself. He was a very good horse trainer. They were Bashful, Ultimo, and Diamond. Jim Raynolds came by and wanted to buy them. Dad sure needed the money. He got $150.00 per horse. Jim bought them for resale. He had some friends who wanted some good cow horses. Bashful was a pet and they got along fine with him. Diamond was mean and a bad bucker. They got along fine with him. Ultimo was nervous, but gentle, and he outlawed. He was a cowboy's horse. He was my favorite of the three.

I have to tell about Blue Rocket. A tall blue pacing horse. Fast, but not a real trained cow horse. I liked to ride him because of his gait. We were gathering the remuda for one of the roundups. I was sent to take some horses to the Barranca corrals. When the horses had been loose in the big pasture for a while they didn't like to go to the corrals. It took a good fast horse to take them in. I was driving the bunch of horses and they were running fast. They liked to run and try to get away. They came to the fence line on the river and were suppose to turn right, but instead they turned left and shifted into high gear. I turned Blue Rocket on and to my surprise he outran them. They were running parallel to the fence, and I was running parallel to them. I mean Old Blue was stretched out, when all of a sudden they saw they were losing the race, and turned back. I mean they did a 180--degree turn. Old Blue did a 180 at the same time just as he should, but I didn't. I didn't land on my head or my feet, I landed stretched out and rolled like a barrel. It didn't even knock the wind out of me. Another surprise, Old Blue came back to get me, but he was sure antsy for me to get on so we could get back in the race. He stood still for me to get one foot in the stirrup, and he was gone. I was still getting on him when he caught up with the remuda. The reason he came back to get me was because he knew he could never handle those horses without a rider in the saddle. I was sure glad he thought that way because most horses would have left me there.

I must tell here of three men who worked for us while we were at Barranca. They were Manuel Quintana, Rafael Macias, and Antonio Zamora. Antonio had worked for us when we were at Colonia Diaz. Manuel was from Colonia Juarez. He had worked for the Mormon people there and had learned some English. He was working for Miles Romney when Dad hired him. He was recommended to Dad by Juan Pavela, who was caporal for one of the Palomas divisions, just south of Columbus. The Pavela family lived next to us in Columbus. Juan Pavela was the man who gave the word to the Army at Columbus that Pancho Villa was coming. Villa's men were camped on the ranch Juan was running. Manuel helped me to start learning Spanish. I rode with him a lot and he was always good to me. Rafael was from Colonia Dublan, and also worked for the Mormon people there and knew some English, but was not as good to help me as Manuel. Sonon was a younger fellow from the Colonia Diaz area, but too young to have worked for the Mormons there, so he didn't know English at all. None of them stayed long when Bill moved back to the ranch. Manuel went with Quevedo, and I heard he fell off a windmill and was killed. I never saw him after we left Barranca. Rafael went with Harve Taylor and was there many years. I saw him regular as time went by. Sonon worked for us at the Buena Fe Ranch. My sons, Floyde and Sid, knew him well. They were all good men.

I have told how so many things were new to me when we moved to the Barranca Ranch. The river with water holes at every bend. Fish in all of them, turtles, water snakes, and frogs, a kid's delight for sure. I have told that at first we didn't have a well, so we carried water from the river. It was about a hundred and fifty feet to the edge of the water, and of course it was dangerous for us because none of us could swim except Dad, and the water hole there was about twelve to fifteen feet deep. We strained the water through a cloth to get out the largest little animals, sure was good water. As we rode the river we would wade our horse out in one of those water holes so he could drink. We would ride him in deep enough so we could reach the water also for ourselves, and we would both water out. We wore felt hats. Dad showed me how to get a drink with it. Roll up the brim, dip it in the water and drink from one end of the roll. It would hold about a cup. You don't just dip up the water, you swish it around some to get rid of what's floating on top and that will also scare most of the little animals away so you can get a nice hat brim full of cool good water. I had done this many times. Most always there would be a water snake or two come in close to check things out. One day I was sure thirsty and was going back in for the second dip with my hat, when up popped a water snake and bit me on the hand. At that time I thought all snakes were poison. I had seen Bounce when a rattlesnake bit him and he about died. I kept watching my hand for it to swell up like Bounce did. It didn't, and if I hadn't watched that old snake bite me, I would never have known about it. His teeth made very small blood spots on my hand. It didn't swell at all. I had been told they were not poison and then was when I sure hoped it was right.

5
Camp Sauz

Uncle Bill was allowed to return to Mexico some time during the school year of 1931--32. He took the Barranca ranch house for his headquarters because it was centrally located for the entire operation of the ranch. Even though he had his papers in order giving him permission to be in Mexico again and not be captured and put in jail or worse maybe shot, he was very nervous. He practiced shooting a lot. He was a good shot. I have seen him empty his pistol and roll a can every shot. I have been told a drunk Mexican fellow was going to kill him, was what got him in the trouble in the first place. Bill claimed he didn't kill the fellow but he was found dead and Bill was the one the law went after. Dad thought Bill had been set up by someone. When the papers were finally ready to pardon him and let him back to Mexico in peace, he was told to go to the courthouse in Old Town, Casas Grandes. Go before a judge he knew, and sign them. Then he would be free to come and go. Bill lived in Columbus, and would slip in at night to the ranch, but not very often. When Bill had to leave Mexico in a hurry, Harve Taylor, my to be father--in--law, loaned him a race horse. It was barely fast enough to get him to the US border before the officers caught him. After about five years of exile from Mexico, all he had to do was go to the courthouse and sign some papers. Here is a secret that I hope is safe to tell after all these years. He was afraid to go sign those papers. He talked Dad into doing it for him. They looked very much alike, except Dad was 6'6" standing in a hole, and Bill was about 5'9" from the ground up. Harve told Dad he was making a big mistake. If the judge caught on, he would land in jail and they would throw away the key. Dad did it anyhow, and Bill never treated him the same after that. The judge looked at Dad when he walked in and said, "No me requerdo que eres tan alto." I'm sure the mordida was enough that the height didn't make so much difference. As far as I know, it was never questioned again. When Bill could return to Mexico and run his ranch himself, the whole picture for Dad was changed. Some of the original agreement seemed to have been misplaced. Of course there was never more than a handshake in the first place. He cut off Dad's salary of $100.00 US per month, and let me tell you, things got tough for us. By that time, Dad had built up a pretty nice herd of cows and Bill told him he had to buy enough bulls for his amount of cows. One bull for twenty--five cows. When he hired Dad to leave Arizona and go to Mexico, the deal was $100.00 US per month, and permission to build himself a herd of his own. By that time Dad had built up a sizeable herd. He was branding over two hundred calves a year. That sounds good, but in those days they weren't worth very many pesos.

Now I want to look at this from Bill's side. In the beginning of this century and on up into the thirties, there were many opportunities for a little cowman to build himself a herd and some would become big cowmen. Bill had done this, and a good job. There were some very large ranches in Chihuahua and Sonora. One of the ways they ran them was to hire a good man and let him run cattle along with a small salary. The Boyd Ranch, Carretas, was one of those. Howard Alley, and Jim Laferty, both built up nice herds while on the Carretas. Bill Bedford, Wilbur Stevens, and Bob Cook built cattle herds on the Stuart Hunt Ranch. George Houghten on the Corralitos, and now we are talking about Roy Adams on the Bill Adams Ranch. Bill had all the expense of running the ranch. To help compensate for stopping the salary, was to give Dad ten heifer calves at branding time each year. He even let Dad choose which ones. Dad never topped the herd. He chose the off color, but the herd was so good that even the off color was good calves. Bill also let the Mexican vaqueros run a few cows. They were Manuel Quintana, and Rafael Macias. Harve and Loren Taylor ran some cattle on Bill's ranch also. Money was a very scarce item, but he had more grass than he needed at that time and he had to pay the same, so he was liberal, without having to spend more cash. I know there were times he had to barrow to meet expenses, and times that he had trouble getting money. I have said that the Adams boys left school at about the fourth grade, but don't ever think they couldn't hold their own in the world of cattle ranching. Bill was a pro, I think the best. He was highly educated in his profession. He didn't know algebra or geometry, but he could sure calculate cattle. He could calculate one head or he could calculate a thousand head. He could do it on foot, horseback, or in later years, from his airplane. When Bill sold out to the Jefferys, Dad had built up a comfortable herd by then, and that was because of the opportunity he had with Bill. Dad was not a quitter, and of course a wife and seven kids will sure make a man think twice before quitting. Bill was not the sort of man I could talk to and ask questions, so I watched him like a hawk. If he did something I liked, I made a mental note of it to be used later in my life. If he did something I didn't like, I tried to figure out why he did it. He usually had a good reason and it worked for what he was doing. One of the things he was good at was making money, and I sure tried to learn from him. I never made much in cattle, but using his methods of buying and selling works with other commodities, and I have been successful at it.

Sometime in the 1960's, Bill sold all his ranching interests. He had bought a home in El Paso in the Upper Valley Country Club area, with enough space to build a private airfield. He loved his airplane, a Beech Bonanza. The R O Ranch at Cananea Sonora was in trouble. He was asked to take it over and put it in order. He did. He made some sore toes, but did what he was hired to do. Put it on a paying basis. The large ranches were being chopped up or plain taken over by politicos with inside pull, and money. The Boyd Ranch, Carretas was no exception. Boyd decided to sell it while he still could. Bill knew the right people all the way to Mexico City. Boyd got him to handle the deal. Bill sold it to a dairy man in Ciudad Juarez, name of Oscar Rodriguez. In the deal with Oscar, Bill was to run the ranch for, I think, three years. Bill flew his own plane from El Paso to Carretas, but his age was starting to slow him. He couldn't pass the flight physical because of his eyes. He started hiring a pilot to fly for him. Sometimes the pilot couldn't go when Bill wanted to. Bill and I had kept in touch through the years, and he knew I had a good business and also that I had a good airplane, a Comanche 250. He called me one morning and asked if I would fly him to Carretas. I said, "Yes." I was to pick him up at his house in El Paso. I knew his field was short, but that didn't bother me, because I had a short field on my ranch. (That was in 1972, and I had a ranch in New Mexico I will tell about later.) I could handle that part. Now what I didn't know was whether I could fly to suit him, because he was a very good pilot. He saw right away that I could handle my plane, and I saw right away that he wasn't going to mess with me. We got acquainted in a different setting, and I loved every bit of it. He called me about each week. My son, Floyde, would take him sometimes. The only time Bill ever criticized my flying, he said, "Your son is a better flyer than you are." I knew that. Floyde was an instructor.

When school was out in 1931, we moved from Barranca to the Sauz Line Camp. It was the Stuart Hunt Ranch house. After Bill bought Hunt out, he made it into a line camp. It was on the north west side of the ranch. There were about five miles of fence line that joined the Janos ejido. Those ejidos were usually trouble areas however we never had trouble with the Janos side. My job that summer was riding that fence, and taking care of it. The road from Janos to Dublan went by our house. The people from the Janos ejido never gave us any trouble. When we acquired the Hunt Ranch, it gave us about thirty--five miles of what we called outside fence. That included what we already had, all but the five miles of Janos was on the south east side. We didn't have much stealing on the east side, but on the west side of the ranch that we got from Hunt, cattle rustling was a continuous problem. The west fence was close, like a mile, from the ejido farms, and some of those people liked to eat meat rather regular. The river divided the east and west pastures. The ranch was about 200,000 acres in each pasture. The river ran through the middle dividing it in about even acres on each side. There was no cross fencing, just two large pasture open ranges with the river dividing them. The cattle could roam as they wished. Mostly they liked to water on the river. They liked to wade out into the river, fill up with good cool water then go sit in the shade of a large cottonwood tree until sundown. The river was almost solid shade with cottonwood and blackwillow trees.

Sauz was in the north west corner of the west pasture and on the Cieniga. A Cieniga is an area where the water table is near the surface and swampy. The Cieniga covered about five square miles and had two large springs, one at Sauz and the other near the center. Nothing grew there but salt grass. The cattle ate it in the first part of the summer if the rains came late or not at all. It was fenced off for that very purpose. If we had a dry year we would throw the poorest cattle in there. Three reasons for having it fenced. To hold the grass for when we needed it, to keep the cows out of the bog holes, and because that salt grass wore out their teeth. A cow only has front teeth on the bottom to start with. That is the reason when a cow eats, she always throws her head forward and up. That causes the feed lots and the dairy people a lot of extra work. A horse has teeth both top and bottom and he pulls his feed back towards him. Knowing these facts, and when you are trailing an animal Indian style, you can tell if it is a cow or a horse by the way it is feeding as it goes along.

When we lived there I thought it was where the mosquito was invented. My arms and face looked and felt like there were BB's just under the skin. The horses looked the same on their necks. LaSelle came to see us there and he got malaria and he sure had a tough time with it. We were on a roundup at the time and sleeping at the chuck wagon. He didn't cover his head at night like we did. As I mentioned before, my summer job was riding the fence from our house to the north west corner of the ranch. That took me into and over the Chilicote Mountains. A small but very interesting range. There were blacktail deer and wild hogs. I was never able to rope a deer but I would catch a hog once in a while. Those hogs were tame hogs that had gone to the hills and turned wild. They were harder to turn loose than they were to catch. The area was overpopulated with rattlesnakes. I rode the north fence, which ran east and west, and over the Chilicote hills, which were about half in our ranch, and half in the Janos ejido. On the west side of the hills, the fence line turned south for about twelve miles. I rode about three miles of it then I turned east and headed for home. At that point, there was a large canyon that drained that country. It headed on the Jeffery side of the fence, but came into our side and went out onto the flats and played out.

I liked to follow the canyon out of the hills because I could usually see the deer or the hogs, and sometimes both. I liked to ride down in the bottom of the canyon. I would be sort of hidden as I rode along. The banks were about four to five feet high. As I was riding down it one day I heard a rabbit squeal. I looked all around to find a coyote that had caught a rabbit. Then came the squeal again. I decided it wasn't coming from the ground where rabbits belong but from a tree that was on the bank of the canyon. I had just ridden under it, so I turned back to investigate. Rabbits just do not climb trees, so what was I looking for? I found it. A rattlesnake had caught a rabbit and took it up in the tree. He was sitting up there on a limb, with a coil around the rabbit, and squeezing it to death. The bank was steep at that point and I couldn't get out of the canyon to fight that snake from topside and I sure wasn't going to bother him from underneath. I was afraid he might drop his rabbit on me and scare my horse. I have killed as many as six rattlers in one day while making my fence round. They were the big diamondback type, green, the color of the grass. Sure ready to bite at the least disturbance. I learned to pop them with my rope, from on my horse. It was too dangerous to hunt them on foot. They sometimes used the buddy system. Like two of them someplace there in the grass. One to get your attention and one to bite you.

There was one old rattler, however, that gave me a challenge. I told about the road went by our house, from Janos to Dublan. Where the road came into our ranch was a cattle guard and a gate. The way we made our cattle guards was to dig a hole, two feet deep, six feet wide, and ten feet long. Frame it with two by twelves, then put a center divider, also of two by twelves running length wise and on edge for strength. Then we put two by twelve runners cross wise, or the direction the car travels. There was one runner for each wheel. If you missed the runner with a wheel, you fell in the hole. Most drivers would hit it so fast that if they missed the runners, they would jump the whole thing. Please don't ask how I know. Now back to my snakes. There was a very large rattler lived in the cattle guard. In the mornings as I was approaching the cattle guard, he would see me and I would see him then he was gone. He would dive into the cattle guard. He had a way of getting in behind the frame. I couldn't get to him. I didn't know where he was except that he was in there someplace. We played games all summer. I tried to sneak up on him, I tried to rush him, I tried different schedules, but I never caught him. I would see him running towards the cattle guard but before I could cut him off, he would go down into the hole, and shake his rattles for me as he disappeared. I think he missed me when I left for school.

The ranch country on the west side had many Indian pueblos' mounds. There was plenty of water for them. The river, two springs on the Cieniga, and a large spring at Ramos. It was only six to ten feet down to water any place they wanted to dig. In their day, whenever that was, there were many Indians there. On my fence route, I crossed a low hill. On top was like a big flat rock, and in that rock was, and I'm sure still are, some holes they used for grinding grain. They are shaped like a funnel. About ten inches at the top, and about a foot deep. I also found some of the same type holes in the south west corner of the ranch, near the Pajarito. I have always enjoyed looking for artifacts.

When we acquired the Hunt Ranch, we also received along with the deal, a fellow and his small herd, named Wilbur Stevens. He was an old bachelor, and real nice person. I told that there were about sixty head of horses in the deal. Of those horses, there was about six head that we hadn't caught yet, because they ran wild there on the Cieniga and up in the Chilicote hills. Mostly they weren't worth catching anyhow. Among them was a blue horse that belonged to Wilbur. He was an outlaw and a bucker. Wilbur told Dad if he could catch him he could have him. Dad and a ranch hand, Francisco Quesada, and I were riding on the Cieniga. We were at the Sauz Line Camp. Sauz means blackwillow. The Quesada cowboy was living or stationed there at that time. We saw the bunch of horses coming out of the hills onto the Cieniga for water. We stopped. We sat and watched them until they had drank all the water they could hold. A horse can't run as fast if he is carrying a lot of water. Dad told me his plan. It was like we were back at Klondyke. I knew just what to do, only then I was older and had flat ground to run on. I was to run those horses and try to keep them on the Cieniga and out of the hills. They saw me coming. Since I was between them and the hills, they ran for the open Cieniga. They could circle back when they were ready, they thought. They hadn't planned on getting relayed by three riders. I took them for a big circle, and ran them by Quesada.

He took them for a big circle, and when they came by me again they still were not ready to go into the corral. For good measure, I took them for another VUELTA. The idea being that if we couldn't pen them, we could wind them enough so Dad could rope the blue horse, since he would be on a fresh horse that sure wanted to get in the race. When I came around with them the third time they were ready to be driven into the corral.

Dad caught the blue, his name was Hungaro. He didn't like the rope and he didn't like the saddle, but he knew what to do as soon as the vaquero got aboard. By the way, Quesada was the rider. Dad told him to use his spurs all he could. Dad would run along and whip him (the horse) with his rope and they would keep it up until he quit bucking. I was to lead the Quesada horse home to Barranca and go along behind them. We still lived at Barranca. Dad snubbed Hungaro to his saddlehorn while Quesada mounted, then turned him loose, and the show was on. Quesada was a good rider, I guess, he stayed on. He had both hands on the horn and locked his spurs into whatever was down there. That old horse bucked and squalled, and then he saw the open gate. He left the corral. Hungaro had one thing on his mind, "Throw the cowboy off and go back up in the hills. Shouldn't have come down out of the hills for water today anyhow." That kind of thinking was his second mistake. He ran and bucked for about a mile. I have never seen a horse take so much spurring and whipping as he was getting. All of a sudden, he had enough. He never put himself in such a position again.

He made a very good horse, and a choice to ride. His gait was a single foot. One day, he threw Dad off, however. Dad roped a cow and forgot to tighten his cinch. His saddle was pulled up on Hungaro's neck. He hadn't agreed to behave that much. He threw his head down and his front feet up. In a few jumps he came right out from under Dad and his saddle. Of course the cow was pulling on the rope which was tied to the saddlehorn. Dad was sitting on the ground but still straddle his saddle. The cow was dragging him through the grass. Hungaro didn't run off, he just moved to one side and watched. He seemed to be cheering for the cow. I quickly had my rope at the ready. Dad wanted me to get that old cow by a hind leg, but the more I tried to get close enough to put it on her, the faster she pulled Dad over the grass. It seemed maybe I should get in front of her so she would stop dragging him. I did, and that old cow turned back and almost ran over Dad going the other way. That gave the wild cow two lengths of Dad's rope to get up speed. When she hit the end of the rope, Dad turned a flip in the air, but he held on. He sure didn't want that old cow to run off with his saddle. I got her to going in a circle. Dad kept turning his saddle to face the cow. He didn't want her to wind him up like the bull on the oak tree at the VAV. She didn't get on the fight so he was lucky. She just wanted to get away from there. I was good with a rope, but it took me about three throws to catch a leg of the old cow. Dad told me he was sure glad he hadn't roped her where there was some cactus.

Sauz had good corrals, and one of them was large, like maybe three hundred feet square. A rancher from beyond Janos was driving a herd through our ranch on his way to the Corralitos Shipping Pens. That was where all the ranchers shipped their cattle from. He arrived at our place in the late evening. He asked Dad to let him put the herd in the corral for the night so he wouldn't have to night herd. Sure why not. Yet, Dad knew better. Tired cattle should always be bedded down loose. Not tight like in a corral. Not only did they put the herd in the corral but they hung a saddle blanket on the gate to be sure none of the cattle would try to leave during the night. They were well made corrals, about five feet high. Lots of wire and poles close together. Not only did they hang a blanket on the gate, but they bedded down in front of the gate. Another dumb thing. Just before daylight a little wind caused the blanket to wave at those sleeping steers. About three hundred head. When a herd stampedes, it moves as a unit. When it was light enough to see, they had two steers left, one inside the corral and one outside. Both dead. The rest were gone, and it was obvious they had left in a hurry. One side of the corral was flat on the ground. It was the side next to the horse pasture, which was about a square mile. All of those steers were still in the horse pasture, and sure nervous to handle. We rounded them up and settled them down some. We pointed them in the right direction with their cowboys, and saw them no more.

Summer was about over and time to go to Dublan to school. The seventh grade, 1931--32. Dad rented a house in Dublan from Eva Taylor. My last job at Sauz was to drive a milk cow to town, about twenty--five miles. When you drive a cow that far you sure have to be careful. You must take her slow, really at her own pace or she will find a shade and bush up for a nap. I drove her slow and when I came to a shade big enough for both of us I would let her stop for a while. It took us all day, and I was sure tired. My chore was the care of that cow. We took a cow to town each year for school. Then would sell her to be butchered in the spring. The reason for selling the cow was because they would get full of bailing wire and die. No use to take them back to the ranch. The wire ends would stick out through the stomach. Looks like a porcupine. We used bailed hay. For some reason the bailers liked to cut little pieces of wire as they were bailing, and let them be bailed in the hay. That was in the days when two men rode the hay bailer. One on each side of the bail being made, to feed the wire to the machine. Now the feed lots use large magnets to catch metal objects in the cattle feed.

6

Pajarito

While we were in school in the fall of 1931, Dad had a ranch house built near the foot of the Pajarito Mountain. I should say it was about four miles out in the flat from where the mountain started up. We lived there for about twelve years. It was in the southwest corner of the west pasture. Only ten miles from Dublan. We went to town often. That area was interesting. It was a large open flat, lots of grass but no trees or mesquite at all. The horse pasture was a square mile and we could see the horses from the house. Sure beat the Barranca horse pasture. The open area was only about half in our ranch. The rest being in the ejido. It was pretty much a circle, about two miles across. In the circle and on its perimeter were many mounds of soil. They were about a hundred feet diameter and about four to five feet high. Indians had at one time lived there. We called them Montezumas. I have told that the west side of the river pasture had many Montezumas. This one small area had most of them. The mesquite and hackberry trees stopped growing in this circle as if there was something wrong with the soil. Grass grew there so thick and high that we could have cut and baled it. I think, when it was inhabited by the Indians, they used the timber for fire wood, but mainly I think it was probably farmed. I don't see any other way they could have so completely wiped out the timber. Today it is all being farmed, and raising some abundant crops. When we were ranching there the water was only down about ten feet.

During the summer, friends from Dublan would come out and ride with me for a few days. By then, Lorn Taylor had moved his cattle to the Jeffery Ranch at Ramos. The Jefferys joined us on the west. Also part of the Corralitos Land and Cattle Co. In the summer LaSelle Taylor went with his dad, like I did mine. As they went from Dublan to Ramos, or the other way, they always stopped at our place, and sometimes spent the night. LaSelle rode a little sorrel pacing horse he called Sarco. He was a very good pony. LaSelle could do anything on him. Bill gave LaSelle a horse he called Bawly. He also gave Lorn a horse he called Chavel. LaSelle didn't need two horses so he gave me Sarco.

The real reason he gave me Sarco was because he was about to loose his eyes. Sarco means glass eye. He didn't only have glass eyes but was bawled faced also. He was kept in a barn most of the time and the flies literally tried to eat his eyes out. He was so bad that LaSelle told me I could have him and try to cure him. All I had to do was put some medicine on his face that we used in our screwworm doctoring. The flies would still get on his tail but they sure stayed away from his head. He had a very good pacing gait so he was especially good for long rides. LaSelle was on a roundup with me one summer. We were working the west pasture. At that time we were camped on the Cieniga. I know now, that is where the mosquitos migrate from to go to Alaska. I forgot to tell him to sleep with his head under the cover, he didn't. I also forgot to tell him that the daytime mosquito is just a scout for the nighttime hoards. Mostly they roost in the daytime. They got all his blood that night and just made a meathead out of him. He was taken to Dublan and sure had a bad time with malaria. I don't know how we worked there so many years without getting it.

LaSelle and I always rode and roped at the rodeos, every Dies y Seis de Septiembre. We had been riding bulls. He asked me to ride one with him. Sure, why not. We wanted to entertain the crowd. The rodeo was at Casas Grandes on the polo ground. We called for them to put a big bull in the chute to ride double. We put his saddle on El Toro. That put me in the back seat. We got on him and that old bull wanted out of the chute so they opened the gate. Now, when they put the saddle on him he became a little upset, then when LaSelle got on, he got mad, and when I got on he decided to put an end to such goings on. The only thing I had to hold onto was the back saddle strings, which were good ones. I didn't want to hold onto LaSelle, because he might fall off and take me with him, or the other way around. He got the saddlehorn and I got the saddle strings. Well I never did see that old bull's horns because LaSelle was in the way, but I saw tails and feet flying all around me. I stayed in among those tails and feet for about four jumps then I went up in the sky and watched LaSelle finish the ride from there. Both of those saddle strings broke at the same time, and I went so high, I was able to get my feet down and in motion so that I hit the ground running. I passed that bucking bull, and LaSelle called to me, "Why did you get off?" After it was over I gave him his saddle strings which I had carried with me. We got the prize for riding a bull double. We were the only ones dumb enough to do that. Riding a bull with a saddle is very dangerous because there just is no way to step off gracefully.

I also rode a horse bareback. They put a white horse in the chute. He had such a fit that no one would ride him. They turned him back into the corral and put another horse in the chute. That horse belonged to Kelton Alley, a rancher from Carretas. At the end of the rodeo no one had ridden his horse. He started looking for someone to ride him. They started working on me to ride him, but I was like the others. I figured that old horse had too much experience for me. I talked to Kelton about him. He told me that he was a good horse, but the reason he was hard to ride was because he threw the man off before he could get on. I asked, "If I can ride him, can I have him?" Kelton jumped at that so quick, I thought, what have I got myself into? They put the surcingle on him, and I climbed in the chute and got aboard. He just stood there in a squat, like a cat about to spring on a mouse. I sure felt like the mouse. They opened the chute gate, and we put on the best show of the rodeo. I had sharp spurs, and I made him think he was carrying a lion. When he quit bucking, Dad picked me up and took me back to the chute. We didn't ride for eight seconds by the clock like the rodeos you see today. We rode until he quits bucking, or we didn't ride until he quits bucking, whichever came first. I decided to give the crowd their money's worth. I took my saddle from Boogers and put it on Rodeo. I had already given him a name. When I got on him, he just stood there. Kelton said he didn't believe it. I rode him home to the ranch and used him a lot.

He never bucked with me again until I had been gone for a few months and when I came home I put my saddle on Rodeo. Floyd and I were going out in the pasture. I put my foot in the stirrup, and I didn't see that old white horse again until Floyd caught him and brought him back to me. I was sure glad for plenty of room because he threw me so far. Floyd was a good rider and he sure wanted to uncock him for me. I told him no way. I have never had anyone to uncock my horses yet, and this was no time to start. I moved up to him again and that time I was doing all the right things like a good tight left rein with a good leverage swing hold on his mane and my knee solid in his shoulder. I knew I would have to get on quick and find the right stirrup quick or he would unload me again. I got on and dug in. That old white horse came out of there sunfishing. I mean he was going up north and down south at the same time. I gave him a good reminder of my spurs, and he soon had enough. That was the last time he tried to throw me, but when I left home the next time, Dad traded him for a mule. He was throwing Dad's cowboy off. That was the first and last mule I ever owned. I never did see my mule. Dad traded him for a cow and calf. Dad was afraid that old horse would someday hurt someone because he was sure spoiled.

About a mile from the house was a brush thicket, which was different from any other on the ranch, and that is the only place I have ever seen that type of bush. It is called largoncillo. It grows in bunches like ocotillos, only twice as tall. No limbs, just a straight trunk, about one inch in diameter. No thorns and ten to fifteen feet tall. The thicket was about a half mile square, and that was all there were anyplace. We used them for stays or floaters in the fence. They grew back about as fast as we cut them down so we never had a shortage. For the yard fence, we put up a lower and upper wire then tied those largoncillos vertically to them as close together as we could. Four feet high. The cats and dogs could jump it but they sure couldn't go through it at first. After about four years the yard fence seemed to be sort of you might say, going away. There was some type of worm termite eating the wood from inside the bark. Then with a wind or any movement the hollow bark would fall off the fence. The fence line up to the Pajarito had been stayed with this same stuff. Three stays between each two posts. When I rode this fence there were no stays left. Just some pieces hanging on the wires here and there. Not until our yard fence was eaten, did I realize what had happened to all those stays on the fence line. The fence posts were desert willow and nothing ate them.

Rollo Pratt came to spend a few days with me. We enjoyed riding the range. He was our baseball pitcher and his ambition was to kill a jackrabbit with a rock. We had lots of rabbits and he threw lots of rocks but was never able to hit one. We were riding on the river at Barranca, and I challenged him to a race across the river. When I lived at Barranca, I knew just how the water holes were, and how deep, and anything else important about them. The crossing I challenged him to had a high bank on our side sloping down to the water. I figured when he saw how high the bank was he would slow down and I would win the race. I had run my horse across there many times, so I knew what I was doing. I enjoyed fooling my friends, anyhow. We started to race and his horse was outrunning mine. I was trying to get more speed as we approached the bank and sure enough, he pulled his horse up and I won the race. We were each riding a red roan horse. His he called Canelo. I called mine Corbata. My horse jumped right into the water. Well now, let me tell you, instead of the water being about knee deep, I didn't find out how deep it was. My horse went under and I went under. We finally came to the surface, both of us blowing water and grabbing for air. My horse swam to the bank on the other side. Rollo sat on his horse and yelled across to me, "That is the best race I ever lost." It was a hot day so it didn't take me long to dry out. During a flood stage since I had lived there, the river had washed out a deep hole where it was shallow before.

Rollo had two fingers gone from his right hand. He made an aspirin bomb and it went off in his hand as he was about to throw it. Now, just what is an aspirin bomb? You mash up about three aspirins, then put the powder between two flat rocks, wrap the rocks with paper into a nice package and tie it with some string so it stays together, then throw it high in the air and as far out as you can. When it hits the ground it will explode and blow pieces of rocks like a hand grenade. When I take an aspirin I sure am careful not to bite it.

About my little red roan Corbata horse. He was one fine cow pony. Dad and I were riding along the road one day and we met Blas, a Mexican cowboy who had worked for Stewart Hunt before Bill bought him out. He was riding this little red roan horse that Dad knew. Bill Bedford had trained him. He was good but he was mean. When Bedford left he gave him to Blas. Dad asked me if I liked the looks of that pony, and of coarse I did. By then a bucking horse didn't bother me too much. Dad bought him and gave him to me. I had him for years, until I left home. He knew more than I did, so I learned a lot from him. He bucked a lot, so I got lots of practice. He was mean to shoe so I learned to shoe a horse with his feet tied and upside down. I learned never to walk close behind him. He refused to carry anything but me, and didn't want to do that. He had a very good mouth, so when he bucked, he was easy to hold, but when his head came up, it had to be turned loose quick or he came right on over backwards. I pulled him over on me one time. Like I say, he taught me a lot. His hind feet were white so I had to keep shoes on them all the time. Corbata and I went to school at the same time. I taught him to let me put shoes on his hind feet with only hobbles on his front feet. I roped and drug broom weeds by the hour. He would kick and stomp like he had ants climbing his legs. He even learned to help me with my trapping. Carried coyotes, or whatever I wanted him to. He and I became such good friends that he would only buck when I would give him a certain signal.

When I would ride him to Dublan and be among those smart farm kids, I needed something to get their attention. I would give Corbata the buck signal and he would put on a nice show. He learned to buck real nice, however. The buck signal was, spin him to the left, and hook him with my right spur. He would quit when I pulled him up. He was easy to ride because he bucked soft--legged like a mule.

He always had to be uncocked in the mornings as long as I had him. As a horse gets old, say around fifteen and older, his ears stand almost straight up. A young horse's ears stand up when his mind is on getting rid of his cowboy. You can tell what a horse is thinking by just watching his ears, even if you aren't riding him. Shoeing horses was one of the chores that had to be done. When I was about twelve, Dad decided it was time for me to learn to shoe my own horses. I started out on Little Man. He was nice and had gentle feet. A horseshoe nail has a right and wrong way to use it. The right way, it will come out of the hoof about three--quarters of an inch up, but the wrong way, it turns to the inside and quicks the foot. Even a nice horse isn't about to stand still for that. Well that was the first thing I did to Little Man. He flinched but didn't kick me down. When I pulled the nail out blood came out the hole in the shoe. He was very patient while I was trying to learn.

About those horseshoes. They were made in Mexico, in fact a blacksmith in Casas Grandes made them. They were made with a forge and a hammer, so were very uneven. We had to shape them and cut them to fit the horse we were shoeing. We let the horse wear the shoes for a while until his feet grew some then we would pull them off. The fitting was so important, that when we pulled the shoes off we tied them together and put the horses name on them. Sometimes we would put the same shoes on the same horse three times. Iron was a scarce item in those days, so guess what was the main source to get horseshoe iron. Railroad spikes. The railroad folks didn't like that.

Here is a good time to describe a horse's gaits. How he moves. His natural gait is walk, pace, trot, and gallop. Horseback riders say gallop, but the cowboys say LOPE. The gait is determined by the way the horse moves his feet. In a walk, slow or fast, he will step over or past the front track with his hind foot, but the two feet are not off the ground at the same time. A rider can teach a horse to take a fast walking gait for covering long rides. This can be a fast walk, which is the slowest, or a single foot, or a fox trot, all very comfortable. The pace is the silliest movement a horse makes, and if he is a natural pacer it is even more silly. A natural pacer is one who paces when he is loose on the range. Other pacers will take the gait when the rider puts them into it. A pacer is the most worthless cow horse, because he changes feet so often, and especially if he is in a hurry, like a cutting horse. He moves his feet on the same side at the same time. His hind track goes far past the front track, and both feet on the same side will be off the ground at the same time. This is why a pacer swings. A camel is a pacer. Then we have the trot, a very useful and very maneuverable gait, but also the roughest. Most horses trot stiff--legged. It is the most jarring gait. In a trot his feet move together, left rear with right front, no swing here, just up and down. Last, but not least, is the lope. All the other gaits are limited in producing top speed, but not the lope. The horse can be taught to lope slow, or fast, or any speed in between, and with good control of his feet. A horse that is slow--loped for a while will change feet sometimes. In a lope, he moves his front feet at the same time and his hind feet at the same time, and they will be off the ground at the same time. At high speed, all four feet can be off the ground at the same time. In a lope, one of the feet leads the other, so he leans to the side of the not--leading foot. When he changes lead feet, you can feel him also lean to the other side. If he doesn't change feet, you will never know he is leaning. In a lope, a horse's top speed depends on his ability, and that sure varies.

Now, here is one I think is a favorite. We brought the remuda in each morning to catch our mount for the day and then turn the rest back out to pasture. We had about four horses each. One morning I caught Little Man for the day's ride. When I started to saddle him I noticed he favored his left hind leg. I looked him over and found two holes through the skin just in front of the hock. Looked like a bullet hole maybe. At breakfast I was telling Dad, and Mom said, "Oh my goodness." We had butchered a beef two days before and the only way we had to keep the meat was to make jerky. It was hung on the clothesline during the day and brought inside at night so the coyotes wouldn't get it. Takes about six sunny days to cure, and then it is put into gunnysacks to finish drying. We usually would all work on it at night. Then it was ready to hang out the next morning to start the drying process. That time Mom got in a hurry. She cut some jerky and hung it out on the clothesline. Some crows spotted it and were stealing it off the line. She took the .22 pistol out there and took some shots at a crow but he just sat there. She went back in the house and got the sawed--off .30--30. She fired two shots with it and the crow still sat there. She said she could never see where the bullets were hitting, so she went out there and just scared him away. Little Man was drinking water at a forty--five--degree angle from the crow, and about the same distance. She said after a few shots with the pistol, Little Man left the water in a hurry. We started looking around and found two .30--30 holes through the hood of the car. I didn't ride Little Man that day, but he soon healed, good as new.

At the foot of the Pajarito Mountain was a very special cliff, or a very large boulder outcropping. This is where the mountain started to be a steep climb. That is how far we rode the fence then turned down towards the windmill, which was about a mile. This rock was about thirty feet high and maybe a hundred feet across the face, straight up and down on the downhill side, but sloping up towards the big Pajarito Mountain on the upper side. The rock was cracked at about the center. The crack was two to three feet wide and went from the bottom to the top. A trick we enjoyed was to put our hands and feet on each side and climb up to the top. We never tried to go down it. We would go out the top then go around it to come down.

From that rock to the windmill was about a mile, and that was always an interesting mile. Coyotes played there a lot. I think they looked forward to us giving them a chase. Now Tio (Floyd) and I rode that area together a lot, but sometimes only by ourselves. He was always looking for something to get into and usually could find it. In that mile he had seen a very large lizard, and seems that the lizard would be in the same place and run into the mesquites. Tio began to plan how he could catch the lizard. Each day he would watch and study how it ran and the direction it would go when he would jump his horse at it. He had it all planned and now he is ready to pounce on that lizard and teach it a lesson. Sure enough, the lizard was there waiting for him to give chase. He jumped from his horse and caught the lizard, almost. As he grabbed for the lizard, and mind you they are both at full speed forward, the lizard turned back and ran up his pants leg. He said, "I have had ants in my pants but that was the first lizard. Wouldn't have been so bad if he just ran up there and would be still, but he just kept climbing." When he got home, Mom asked him what in the world happened to his pants. He told her about the lizard and he had to get out of them fast like. He said he never saw the big lizard again, but if he had it would sure be safe from him.

All our heating and cooking was done with a wood fire. We kept a large stack of wood and of course it was a big job to keep it cut into lengths to fit the stove, or the fireplace. The boys tried to keep the wood box full so Mom didn't have to carry her wood, but sometimes she ran out of wood and had to go to the woodpile herself. She wore an apron most of the time. She would put a few sticks in it to carry back to the house. I was home that day and I don't know why she didn't send me for the wood. I was in the yard and didn't even offer. She was out there at the woodpile picking up sticks, when all of a sudden she let out a yell and stampeded. She dropped her sticks and grabbed the hem of her dress and threw it over her head, and threw it on the ground. I ran out there to see what had happened. I was sure a rattlesnake was after her. Turned out she had shook a little lizard out of the wood and he ran up her dress. The last time I saw that little fellow he was headed for the big pasture.

I have told that we burned wood for all fires. At night and about bedtime in the winter, I had a special rock of my own. I would warm it up on the campfire, then wrap papers around it, then wrap it up in a towel, and to bed we would go. Sure felt good to the feet in a cold bed. Tio and Raymon and I all slept together and sometimes if I dozed off before them, they would get my rock.

I have told that our horse pasture here was open and about a square mile. No trees, only a few bushes. Dad told me to take the pickup, Ford A model, some posts and wire, and shovel. Go around the fence and repair where some horses had jumped in from the ejido side. I had Domer in front with me. Raymon and Floyd rode in the back. We had the little truck fixed up for a family car. The two folding front seats from the '27 Chevy had been put in just back of the cab. That was many years before Suburu thought of the idea. Raymon and Floyd let the tailgate down and sat there with their feet dangling. Away we went. We found where the fence was down and repaired it. We were ready to continue the inspection of more fence line.

I thought then was a good time and place to teach Domer to drive. She was at least seven years old. Only those who have driven a Model A will know how the gas feed was. A little rod comes out of the floor with a hat on it about the size of a quarter. That was so it didn't poke a hole in the shoe sole. The throttle was very responsive, so it was easy to get the car to bouncing. In other words, the driver gets out of phase with the machine. Raymon and Floyd were seated and holding onto the sides of the pickup bed with their feet almost reaching the ground. Domer was in the control seat, and I was giving her instructions. I told her to give it lots of gas and let the clutch out. She did and we were gone. She was driving, or maybe I should say she was holding the steering wheel. Nothing in the way but wide--open space. All she had to do was to not turn short and turn it over. She leaped it forward alright, then came off the throttle, then back on the throttle, and I mean she really gave us a good demonstration of the Model A bounce. It was getting out of control and I was trying to get her stopped so we could start over. She lost her direction and ran over a large rat mound, which not only stopped us but we were stuck on top of it. I was just going to let her get it off since she put it there. She killed the engine each time she tried to drive it off the mound. I gave her some more instructions. I told her to get the gas feed all the way to the floor and hold it there and get this thing off the rat mound. We couldn't go forward so this was all taking place trying to go backwards off the mound. She did what I told her. That little A truck leaped backwards off the mound just like it leaped forwards onto it, but she also held her foot on the throttle just like I told her. Well, sir, she backed over the fence, knocked down some posts and Raymon and Floyd thought they were already no--legged. The wire held, however, until I could get her foot off the gas. Then the stretched wire treated the little car like a spitball on a rubber band, and we were back onto the rat mound again.

We repaired the fence and went on. I still thought I could teach this little sister to drive. Raymon and Floyd stood up behind the cab. They decided it was safer than sitting down in the back. On the floor behind the cab and between those two seats was a two--gallon canteen of water. For emergency use, which was not unusual. Raymon was standing with his feet straddle of the canteen, and Floyd was sitting in one of the seats. We were speeding along maybe about twenty MPH. We were driving along the fence so we could check it out. She was sure getting the hang of it when I realized she was just before running over a big mesquite bush. I calmly told her to quickly turn left to miss the bush. She did. Then I told her to stop, as we had lost Raymon. He was in the bush and sure enough mad. He had locked his feet onto the canteen and they were both there in the mesquite bush. He didn't get scratched much going in, but we scratched him up a little getting him out. He said, "Willie, I think you better drive. Domer is going to kill us." We were getting back close to the ranch house, anyhow, and I couldn't take any chances with her near the house and the corrals.

I have told about the little A Ford. The rear fenders had been cut off by the Helms rancher. Dad got it from Jack Helms. He used it to pump water from the Buena Vista windmill in a pipeline out over the range to make the water places closer for his cattle. That is the same ranch that was run by the Bradefoot folks when we first moved to Barranca. The fenders were cut off so they could put a belt on the rear wheel to turn the pump. That was about all they used it for, so it didn't have many miles, but lots of use. Not only were the fenders gone but the paint was gone also. Dad thought maybe we should dress it up a little. He bought some paint in quart cans, and a brush and told me when I had time to give it a paint job.

My folks were living in Dublan and I was in my senior year in high school. We had a cowboy that stayed at the ranch. I went to the ranch to check on things and see how the cowboy was doing. While I was waiting for the cowboy to come in from the range and report to me, I thought that was a good time to paint the little feller. No thinner, and the paint was thick. I thinned it some with gasoline. I stirred it good and went to work. About the time I got it painted the ranch hand came in with news of some sort of a problem at the Pajarito Windmill. I didn't wash it or sand it or anything, just brushed the paint on, nice and thick so it would last a long time. I took some tools and left for the windmill. I put my fingers to the paint in a few places and it was pretty dry, I thought. No matter, I had to go. The road to the windmill wound through the mesquites and the limbs reached out into the road. Those bushes had a lot of the old paint on them from so many trips to the windmill in the little truck. I tried to miss all the limbs I could because my worry was that they would take off my new paint. When I dismounted the little truck at the windmill, I had to laugh, and I sure hoped Dad would think it was funny also. Instead of the mesquites taking the paint off the truck, the paint took the leaves off the mesquites, and there just isn't any way to describe how funny it looked. I went to town the next day, and Dad didn't think the paint job helped its looks any. The paint job took place after Bill had sold his cattle on the Corralitos and bought the Benton Ranch. We had our own cowboy at that time and we lived in town.

Bill and three Mexican cowboys ran the east side of the ranch, and Dad and I ran the west side. Remember the river divided the east and west pastures. Each of those pastures was about 200,000 acres. Raymon and Floyd took turns going with Dad or me. Dad and I would ride the fence then check cattle and waters on the range. The whole south fence was an outside line so we had to ride it daily, and that wasn't always enough. By outside line, I mean we didn't have rancher neighbors on that side. From our house east to Barranca was about ten miles, and west to the foot of the Pajarito was about five miles. I rode to the mountain most of the time, and sometimes all the way to the top. The idea was to ride the fence in the morning, then zig zag over the range looking for cattle to check them out and see if they were OK.

In the summer we had lots of screwworms. We rounded up and branded about the first of June. After that, the worms were busy. There are two kinds of flesh eating worms that come from blowfly eggs. The maggot and the screwworm. The maggot eats a large area but the screwworm eats straight in and goes deep. The only roping I got to do was when I could find a critter that needed doctoring. I was raised all those years on the ranch and was never let in the roundup. I never cut cattle and I never drug calves. I sure helped hold many herds, however, while they were worked. Bill was finally so against me roping that he gave orders for me to bring anything I found with worms to Barranca, and he would rope it so I could doctor it. I did that one time, and that's when I quit finding worms. He would ask me about the worms. I just hadn't found any. One day he told me I'd better just go ahead and doctor them where I found them, if I did happen to see any. I never roped the cattle for the fun of it, and if I wasn't suppose to doctor them on the range, I'll tell you for sure, I didn't. He rode the range in a little Model A Ford, and he would find a high place. With his field glasses, he knew what was going on.

I was in the eighth grade the school year of 1932--33. That was the first year we went to school from the ranch. Dad bought a one--horse buggy from O.P. Brown. Brown was from Colonia Diaz also, and about the age of my grandfather. He would always stop me on the street to tell me about him, and what a fine and fearless man he was. That is what got my grandfather killed. He didn't have his gun on, but still stood up to a drunk man that did. That was in 1912.

Dad went down on the river among the ejido farmers and found a bay work horse he thought would make a good buggy horse. He did. We called him School Boy. The horse needed a little schooling for his new role in life. He learned fast, and was a real good, gentle and honest buggy horse. We got him in the summer, and since all those people's work animals are poor, the first thing we had to do was get some fat on him so he would be ready for school. We fed him all the corn he could eat without getting foundered. We soaked it in water overnight so he could eat it without wearing his teeth. His breakfast was one gallon of corn, and that is a bunch for one horse. A saddle horse you lope, or gallop for speed, a wagon horse you walk, no speed, but a buggy horse you trot, and the faster the better. A trotter will go so fast, then break into a lope, so he has to be trained not to break the trot. School Boy learned to trot those ten miles in one hour, and would seldom break it. When the weather was good we rode two horses and let School Boy rest. Floyd behind me, and Domer behind Raymon.

Bill gave us a yellow mule to take turns with School Boy. I used him the summer before to pump water at the Pajarito Windmill. Now a mule is not the same as a horse. He looks like a burro and thinks like one. No speed is fast enough for him. When we got the mule, we called him Old Yeller so we could tell him from School Boy. He didn't like to move faster than standing still, and it didn't matter what gait he was in. We loped him a lot. Dad made a real nice buggy whip like you see in the movies. He was good at braiding. It was made from rawhide. With School Boy, we just tapped him and he was gone, but not that mule. His old hide was too thick for the buggy whip. We couldn't get enough speed out of him to make the trip in one hour. We had to leave earlier or come up with a better whip. Dad made what we called the mule whip. A three--foot stick with a two--foot chain on the end of it. The mule got all the corn he could eat also.

The first day we used the mule whip we cut some time from the usual hour. I laid the whip on him, and there was one surprised mule. I mean he had energy he didn't know about. He went from stopped to a high lope in one jump. We soon learned that if we hit him once in the morning and once in the evening, then just rattled the chain, the results were good. He kept his ears tuned to the chain. We rattled the chain right handed. I didn't like mules anyhow, so I had tried to knock him out of the harness a few times, and he never forgot. When he heard the chain, he would panic. Since the whip was right handed, he was hit on the right side. He would go full speed, but he would quit the road to the left and run over whatever was there. Mesquites mostly. The driver would just circle him back to the road, keeping him headed in the right direction. Sometimes he would get mad and have a runaway but we could always circle him back to the road at full speed.

The winter before, Elmer Thayne had trapped coyotes on the ranch for half the hides. He caught lots of them, but the price dropped to nothing. Dad took his to the tannery and had them tanned with the hair on. Mom made a quilt with them for us to use in our buggy. We looked like Eskimos all wrapped up in that coyote quilt. It sure was warm.

One morning it sure was cold, and we had Old Yeller in high gear. I didn't know about overdrive or I would have had him in that. Raymon was driving. I was handling the whip and Floyd and Domer were under the seat trying to stay warm. The coyote quilt was large enough to cover the front seat and wrap around to protect the two under the seat. The last half of the trip to school was in the lane with farms on either side. As we entered the lane, Old Yeller slowed a little to catch his breath and that was when I gave the chain a good rattle. That mule had no business breathing, anyhow. The lane was about a hundred and fifty feet wide.

He ran sideways to the left and went clear to the fence. There was a post in the fence with a fork on the bottom about a foot high. The left front wheel caught on that fork. Now, Old Yeller was moving on, and when the left front wheel hit the fork it jerked him into the fence. That barb wire fence made him wild. He made a ninety--degree turn to the right. The buggy was hooked on the post so it didn't turn, but the shafts did. They broke off and stayed with the mule. It threw Raymon and me out, almost on top of the mule. The mule was running up the lane and Raymon was holding onto the lines and being drug until he had to let go. The first turn in the lane was about a mile and Old Yeller was still in a hurry when he went around it and out of sight.

We looked things over and pushed the buggy off the fence. The most damage was that the shafts were gone so no way to pull it. Floyd and Domer were still under the seat, just wedged in a little tighter. A fellow came along, looked us over, then said, "Faltan macho (you need a mule)." We agreed and asked if he had seen one. He had and told us that the mule was standing in the lane around the corner about half a mile. I mean a half mile after he rounded the corner. It was one mile from where I was standing to the corner. I went after the mule and drove him back to the buggy dragging the shafts. Old Yeller was also gentle to ride but he was so nervous and spooky I didn't dare get on him with only the harness to hold onto. We took the shafts off and put them on top of the buggy and tied the mule to the back. We had five miles to go back to the ranch. We pushed the buggy and pulled the mule. I think the mule was more work than the buggy. We had to guide or steer the wheels by hand.

Now at this point, you might think we were in trouble. Yes, but the real trouble was still to come. We knew Dad was going to town that day and would be coming along anytime now. We were about halfway back to the ranch when we saw dust coming, it was him. We had just pulled through some big mesquites and were out in the open. He couldn't believe what he was seeing. We told him what happened. He looked us over, then the buggy, then the mule. The barbs had scratched the mule some, but hadn't opened him up so he was OK. Dad was pretty upset at first, then he started to laugh. I thought he was laughing because of the mess we were in. Negative. He already had a mental picture of how he would repair the buggy. I also found out at that time, that he liked that mule better than his four kids. He didn't say a word to the mule, about it being his fault.

Dad went on to town and we spent the rest of the day getting home. We called this a buggy, it was actually a very light wagon. Instead of getting parts or repairing the shafts, Dad decided to cut the buggy in half. He took the rear wheels and fastened the shafts solid to the bottom. The box was large enough for a seat for two and two under the seat and that is the way we used it after that. If you have never ridden a two--wheeled cart behind a trotting horse, then you should try it someday. After you try to focus your eyes for ten miles to the tune of the trot, then you get out onto solid ground, it takes a few minutes to go normal again. Could be called trot lag.

We boarded the school horses and mule in the barn at LaSelle's. They ate hay all day. In the evening while I was hitching the horse, Raymon would go to the garden. He would dig up a big onion and eat it on the way home, like an apple. It was terrible, and I couldn't get him to quit. We were on our way home one evening, and for some reason, we stopped and he got out of the buggy. I decided to teach him not to eat onions. I left him there to walk home. He could run fast enough to catch onto the buggy but not fast enough to get in. He finally gave up and promised not to eat any more onions in the buggy. He didn't, but he stayed mad at me for a long time.

One of the hazards we had to be careful of was crossing the river. We had to cross it just before entering town. In those days, there was water in the river all the time, a nice clear stream. Sometimes it would flood and would swim a horse at our crossing. I had crossed it enough to know when it was safe to cross. It was about a hundred yards across. One time I thought it was safe and drove into it, but the water was rising and before we got across it was getting into the bottom of the buggy. School Boy didn't pay it any mind. He didn't panic. We never took the mule when the river was up. He would probably have stopped for a rollover. If it was raining in the mountains, and we anticipated flooding, we would ride our horses. It took several days for the mountain rain to flood the river out in the flat country.

I have told about how we, Raymon, Floyd, and I, liked to rope the chickens when we lived at Barranca. Now there at Pajarito, we were older and we were into riding cows, horses, burros, or just whatever came along that we could catch. If I haven't already told you, I'm telling you now. We pumped all the water by hand with a pitcher pump. A horse or cow will drink about five gallons, twice a day. The only way we had of collecting the water--fee for letting stray animals drink was to capture them while they were drinking. Shut the corral gate. The water was inside the corral. This made the animals easy to catch. Then we would put a surcingle on them and ride them out of the corral until they quit bucking or threw us off, whichever came first. It was about half a mile from the corral to the edge of the mesquites, and sometimes we would ride one that far. Sometimes after we had ridden a horse a few times, he would run rather than buck, and that was very dangerous. You could sure get skinned--up trying to land. When that happened, we would spur him on one shoulder to make him spin to slow him down. The surcingle was a loose rope through a loop and folded back, so when the rider turned loose of the fold, the rope fell off the animal. The rider picked up his rope and walked back to the corral, and the animal went to pasture, until he became thirsty again. The smart ones found another place to get water; Ramos, or the Pajarito Windmill.

We became good riders, and as time went by and the strays quit coming to water often enough, we had to find a replacement. Now I have told how we kept several cows in the summer for milking and raising dogies. Two things we didn't do; run your horse, unless you want to catch something, and don't trot the milk cows when bringing them in from the pasture for the evening milking. Dad watched for sweat signs on the horses and milk shortage with the cows. Raymon, Floyd, and I were alone at the ranch and I was in charge because I was the oldest. We made ourselves lunch. We had just run completely out of something to do. The water trough was full. There came all those milk cows for their noon drink. Comes to mind, why don't we just ride one of them? If we ride a dogie cow, Dad wouldn't know if the calves were getting the same amount of milk. The way we would get on these animals, was to rope them and snug them up to a post we had planted in the center of the corral. The post was there to snug up an animal for branding, or doctoring, or dehorning, or for milking a wild cow when her calf couldn't take all her milk. The milk cows were gentle so we didn't have any trouble getting on them.

We closed the gate while they were watering and picked out a suspect for the first ride. Raymon got on and we opened the gate and let her go. What a ride. Floyd wanted to ride one. I consented, knowing better. Sure enough, what a ride. I couldn't let that pass me by. I wanted to ride one. I chose a brown cow. She was part jersey, and was the cream cow for Dad's coffee and pie, and just whatever else should have cream on it. She was my special cow to take care of. Her milk was kept separate because it was so good. I got all set on Brownie and they opened the gate and out we went. She went out the gate and just threw me off right there. That little brown cow sure put on a show while I lasted.

We always milked with the calf, and would give the calf half. That evening I shorted the calf so my milk bucket looked OK when I delivered it to Mom. I made a deal with Raymon and Floyd that we would keep that secret the rest of our lives, and that we would never make that mistake again. After about a week the pressure was getting to me. I knew that being dishonest with Dad was worse than riding the milk cows, and would sure get me into more trouble. I was riding with him in the tall mesquites somewhere between Barranca and Pajarito. I rode up along side of him and said, "Papa, I just have to tell you something I did that I knew better, and I sure won't do it again." We rode along there in silence. I could hear my horse's heart pounding. I said, "You know the other day when you and Mom went to town, well I rode one of the milk cows." Silence. By now, I could hear the hearts of both horses.

He looked over at me and gave me a surprise I shall always remember. He said, "Did she buck?"

"She threw me off."

"Which one?"

"Brownie."

"She didn't fall off in her milk."

"I cheated the calf."

By that time, my heart was beating so loud I couldn't hear the horse's hearts anymore, and he said, "This evening when we get the milking all done, let's just ride those old cows and have some fun." As we rode on home I told him how it happened, and how many of them we rode. I was the only one bucked off.

The rest of that summer we had our own little rodeo each evening after chores. We rode the cows and roped the calves. Dad had done some rodeoing in his younger days and was pretty good. By the end of the summer he had three kids that were pretty good. At the rodeo in Casas Grandes, on the Dies y Seis De Septiembre, we took all the first places. I think the first money was twenty pesos. I won four of them, but they would only pay me for three, because I got the horse I rode. The judges said it wasn't fair for me to win so much, anyhow.

I had worked all those years and had never received one peso. I was out of mischief and got lots of experience, but I could have sure used a peso once in a while. I finally got my chance. The summer of 1936, Bill ask me to go to Barranca and work for him. I was sixteen at that time. I didn't ask any questions. I sure wanted to make some money and I knew he would treat me as good as his other men. He had three men and fired them all. One chopped wood and milked the cows. One fed the young bulls and wrangled the remuda. The other one rode the fence and checked the range. I got the three jobs all into one. I was tough and not afraid of work. Then he turned all the horses the fence--rider had been using out in the big range. He got up six of the spoile-dest and buckingest no--good horses I have ever tried to do anything with. One horse, a blue, didn't buck, but he didn't do anything else either. If he was stopped, he was hard to get started, and if he was started he was hard to stop. I thought if I just ran him towards a fence I could set him up, and teach him to stop that way. I was wrong, he just ran over the fence. Knocked down four posts. Needless to say who put them back in place. I decided to spur him in the same place, so he would get tender, and maybe wake up. He got tender but he was dead all the way through his hide. Bill threatened to take my spurs. He didn't.

I rode the fence line east, and a vaquero from the San Pedro Line Camp rode west on the same fence line. My part was about ten miles and his about seven. We had a meeting point on the trail at a right angle to the Huerfano Windmill which was to the north. We would then ride together north to Huerfano, then he would ride out the east part and I would ride out the west part of the east pasture. In the evening, I would arrive back at Barranca. I would usually arrive at the meeting point on the fence line first so I would wait for him. I would lay down under a bush and do some very needed resting while I was waiting. One day, I had ridden Old Blue and tied him to a fence post there at our meeting place. Those horses he gave me to ride were all bad to break loose and run off. I had a big rope on their neck and used that to tie them up. Old Blue was standing there half asleep, when all of sudden, he looked up the fence and saw the rider coming. Now I don't know what was on that horse's mind, or if he even had one, but he threw a fit and pulled the post I had him tied to out of the ground, off from the fence wires, and he was gone, post and all. I saw at that moment what will make Old Blue run. The rope was tied to the post good, and as he ran the post got between his hind legs. The faster he ran the more the post whipped him. He was running and kicking. That old post just skinned him all to hell. I wished it would have killed him so I wouldn't have to take him home and explain how I skinned him without killing him first. The rider finally caught him and brought him back to me. He was sure one skinned horse.

Bill was sure upset over the Blue horse. He told me to never tie a horse to a fence post. I learned my lesson and listened good. One of the horses was a real spoiled black. He bucked, he tried to get away when I dismounted, and spun like a top when I was mounting. When I tied him up he would sure try to break my big rope. I was at the Huerfano and tied him while I went for a drink from the windmill. Don't tie him to the fence I thought, tie him to that big limb on that old mesquite tree there. I did. The limb was over his head. Now while I was drinking he decided to leave me on foot. He gave a hard tug on the rope, but instead of the rope breaking as he planned, the limb whacked him on the head. He jumped forward and then pulled back and each time that limb whacked him again. It reminded me of a boxer punching a bag, his head being the bag. Now I had this damn horse with a skinned head. How the hell would I explain that? After he settled down I was afraid he would get away from me when I untied the rope, so I talked to him for a while and he promised to behave. He did. My next stop or check point was the Buena Vista Windmill. About four miles on north.

A couple of miles along the way and there came a dust devil. Just what I needed. With all the open range for that dust devil to go, I have never understood why it had to hit me. It blew my chaps to flopping towards that Papoose horse's face and he had a fit. I rode him, but my hat came off and hit him on the rump, which he didn't like. I finally settled him down, but there was my hat on the ground. That was the only time I ever lost my hat that I considered just leaving it there. I knew I couldn't trust him, but after talking to him for a few minutes, I wrapped the reins around my hands and stepped off. Just as I picked up my hat, that black pony had one of his best or worst fits. I wasn't sure which. My bridle pulled out of his mouth and up the side of his head. I thought the next thing my reins or the head stall would break, but I was sure hanging on. He was having such a fit and was in such a hurry to get loose from me that he got his feet tangled up and fell down.

At Klondyke, I told how Dad held that horse down by pressing down on the saddlehorn. My memory flashed back and I jumped on the saddlehorn. Can you imagine what it is like, holding a horse down, and all his feet flying and his head beating on the ground? When he quit fighting so much, I put the bridle back in his mouth and put a rein on each side of his neck. I had to hold him down with one hand while I arranged those things with the other. Each time he squirmed I would quickly get both hands on the saddlehorn. I decided that the only chance of me and him returning to the ranch house together, was for me to be on him when I let him get up. That isn't as difficult as it sounds since he has to get up on his front feet first, but when he gets all four feet under him, you don't have long to find the stirrups, take the slack out of the reins, and get a good hold on the horn. We each got things together about the same time. After that day he became a good friend and turned into a real nice horse. He belonged to Elsie and she rode him for a long time. His name was Papoose.

Another horse Bill had me ride was a paint that belonged to Alice. She was Bill's youngest daughter. That paint was the most spoiled horse I ever tried to do anything with. He was a real bucker, and he would run over anything in his way. Rather than go around a mesquite, he would go through it. He bucked all the time, Bill would only let me ride him on short trips there near the house. There was no chance to put some miles on him and teach him some manners. When he bucked he would run away. He was so mean, he finally got into some kind of mess and killed himself. Lorn Adams called him, "Now one good paint horse."

I have got to give, at this time, honorable mention to the mule team. Bill had his personal horses in a separate pasture from the regular remuda. Moso, Jerry, and Paint. They were three of the finest horses I have ever known. He fed them grain whether they were hungry or not. Now, he had those two black mules taken care of the same as those special horses. He rode the horses once in a while, but those mules would go months without seeing a harness. They were big black army mules. When the cavalry was abolished at Ft. Bliss, Bill bought that pair of mules. A male and a female. Big mules. The male was nice to bridle and harness and put to the wagon. Big mules. The female was hard to bridle. She had what we called touchy ears, quite common with mules. A mule never forgets, and if his ears ever get abused, he is a problem the rest of his life, usually.

It took two men to bridle the she mule. They used a twister. A two--foot stick with a hole in one end, a rope ring about six inches diameter in the hole. The ring is passed over the lower lip and twisted, and by twisting and pulling by one man, the other man can carefully put the bridle over the ears.

Someone had missed the runners on the cattle guard up on the Pershing highway and messed it up. The Pershing road went through the east pasture, running north and south. General John J. Pershing built it when he was trying to catch, or trying to not catch, Pancho Villa. Bill told me to put some lumber in the wagon, hitch the mules, and go up to the damaged cattle guard to repair it. He would be up later in his car. He left to check out someplace else before arriving at the cattle guard.

I had seen that mule bridled many times and I knew how to do it, but I wasn't sure if I could do it alone. It had always taken two men to bridle her. I put the twister on her, but I couldn't twist and pull hard enough to make her be still, and still reach her ears to put the bridle on. Big mule, and those ears were way up out of my reach. I had to do some fast thinking. I put my rope on her lower lip and tied it to a corral post. I expected her to set back some. Did you ever see a twelve--inch lip on a mule? I was looking at one. I was scared, like you don't even know what I mean. She stepped back and started pulling and stretched that old lip. She just sat back on it, and brayed, and peed. I don't know how long that took, but when she quit pulling, she moved close to the post and just stood there trembling. That was the only time I ever saw a mule tremble, and the sweat just poured off her. I wanted to try to bridle her but I was afraid she would hang back again. I took a chance and as I approached her with the bridle, she put her head down and helped me get her ears in the head stall. She sure had a long face after that, but she didn't need a twister anymore. Bill commented that her lip seemed a little long. He was glad the men had finally got her where they could bridle her without much trouble.

This is the first time that secret has been shared with anyone, and I might still be taking a chance. I didn't even tell Dad. I hooked those mules to the wagon and climbed up onto the spring seat. I got me a good hold on the lines, braced my feet on the front of the wagon, and tried to release the brake easy and quiet, because they had already scratched little holes to put their feet in for the take off. The road up through the pasture was like a pole bending course, only there, we used mesquite bushes. When I say road, I'm talking about two trails about five feet apart that run around and among the bushes in the general direction you want to go. Those mules only did one thing right, they stayed in the road. I had ridden bucking horses, bucking cows, wild burros, but this was the worst ride I ever had. I couldn't stay in the seat and I couldn't get out. They ran for about a half mile full throttle, then after having their fun, they settled down to business. Those mules were an exceptionally good team. They just liked to play. I had seen them do that before, so I knew what to expect. I pulled a car out of a mud hole with them one time, and they literally got on their bellies, and never quit until the car was on dry ground. The last time I saw that old mule she looked to see if I was carrying a bridle to put on her. Mules have good memories.

I was there about two months that summer and I think it was the toughest summer I ever spent. I chopped the wood, fed the bulls, milked the cows, wrangled the remuda, and rode the fence and checked the waters and range in between. I must say here how much I have always liked Elsie. She was always dear to me when we were kids, and to this day I think the world of her. She is Bill's oldest daughter and my special cousin. We had a lot of fun growing up on the ranch.

The next morning after the cattle guard repair, Bill came up to me with a check in his hand. I was smiling clear to my toes, because I knew I had sure earned it. However, I wasn't ready for what he said to me, "Here is your check, you can go home now, I over paid you but that is alright, I have a good man now." The check was for sixty pesos. A peso a day for a day that started when I couldn't see in the morning and ended when I couldn't see at night. He had fired three two--peso--a--day men to give me their three jobs at one peso a day. That was my first man's lesson in a man's world, and I was determined to learn something from it.

When Bill moved back to Mexico and the ranch, he took from us the horses we had been riding. They were his, so he was right. We had to start putting a remuda together of our own. A horse Dad traded for, and gave him to me was a sorrel with silver mane and tail, much on the order of Nestegg. Only that horse turned out to be good for less than nothing. As a cow horse he didn't know, and didn't want to learn. He fell down with me so often I was afraid to rope on him. We called him Silver Mane. The day we got him, we just turned him in the horse pasture with the rest of the remuda. The next morning when I went after the horses, they all went into the corral but the new one. When he got near the corral he would turn and run. I would circle him and as he would get close to the corral he would do the same thing, run away. Dad, Raymon, and Floyd saddled up and came to help me. All of us, together, could not pen that flaxy horse, so Dad roped him. Dad tied a two--foot chain to a front foot. A good run with the chain banging his legs and he would be hunting for a gate to go through. No way. He quickly learned to swing the chain and hop over it with the other front foot, so it still took a good horse to pen him after a race. Dad went back to the drawing board, and came up with a long chain, like six feet. When Silver Mane went out of the corral that morning, he stumbled and fell a few times, and Dad sort of smiled. Some of those spoiled ponies just have to learn the hard way. We went on about our range riding for that day. Now that horse, Silver Mane, went way to the far side of the pasture where no one would see, and started practicing with the new chain. The next morning, I brought the remuda to the corrals and they all went in but Silver Mane, he was gone again. No problem I would run him a little and make him wish he hadn't ran that time. Wrong again, he was swinging the long chain and jumping it with the other three feet, and giving one good race. Dad said he would find a place for him. He was starting to spoil our other horses which we could pen on foot.

In good time, along came a fellow on the road that was near our house. He was on a poor horse, and a very good Sonora saddle. Dad traded him that fat and pretty Silver Mane and my saddle for his horse and saddle. The horse was no good and I don't know what happened to him, but the saddle was the best saddle I ever owned. It had a good seat that sloped down to the back, a high cantle, a wide fork, saddle pockets for my lunch and canteen, but best of all a brass horn that just exactly fit my hand. When I got hold of that brass horn and my knees squeezed under the fork and my spurs dug in, I was sure hard to unseat. I was never bucked out of that saddle. It is the saddle I had when I worked for Bill or I could have never ridden those horses he put me on. I have told about when I worked for Bill. Actually I worked for him all my years of growing up on the ranch but that one summer was the only time I was on the payroll.

Dad had a horse he called Diamond, Bill gave him to Dad. He was one of the best cow horses I ever saw, and for sure, one of the meanest. If he was working, he was good and he was honest, but if Dad was just riding along, and a wind blew his chaps a little, Diamond would have a fit and throw Dad off. Dad was a good rider, but he couldn't ride Diamond.

Dad had recently traded for a horse he gave to Raymon. We called him Foolhen. A tall long legged, bald faced, pretty horse. Ran fast, but handled very badly. His mouth was messed up. I mean he didn't respond to the bit as he should. Raymon liked him anyhow. One evening Dad was arriving home from riding all day. He was on Diamond. I was in the front yard and saw him coming, when all of a sudden, all hell broke loose. Diamond was bucking and spinning, and holding on to one of Dads boots was a dog. That old dog was flying straight out as Diamond was spinning and determined to get rid of him and Dad at the same time. Dad said the only reason Diamond didn't throw him that time was because he sure didn't want to get down there with that mad dog. The spin got so fast that the dog was thrown off and Dad came on to the house. I had my horse in the corral. Dad got his sawed--off .30--30 and we went after the dog. The dog's teeth had not gone though Dad's boot.

When the dog was thrown loose from Dad's foot he took out into the horse pasture. We could see him running the horses. He was a mad dog and lucky he didn't come to the house or Bounce would have tangled with him. Dad and I went on out where he was and killed him. We didn't see if he was able to bite any of the horses, but we were watching for any signs for the nine day danger period to be sure. We sure didn't want to ride a mad horse. I was bringing in the horses about the ninth morning. As they were nearing the corral, Foolhen started to run, then buck then just went into a real fit spinning and jumping. He jumped the fence out of the horse pasture, then jumped back in. It was hard to believe what I was seeing, and after a few minutes of that, he gave a real high jump up and fell over backwards. We watched him lying there, dying. A large pile of foam came out of each nostril. It was real weird. Raymon had planned to ride him that day.

The head of our river is at Colonia Pacheco, a Mormon colony high in the mountains. It seemed to always rain a lot in the mountains, because the river would run in flood stage every summer. I have said how the fence crossed the river zig zag in order to leave water holes for each pasture. The reason there were water holes on the river was because the water table was near the surface. Where the river washed out a hole in the channel bends there would be water the year around. We had two water holes on our part of the river that were about fifteen feet deep. One of them was at Barranca. The hole at Barranca was also about three hundred feet long. It was a great swimming place. Where the fence crossed the river, we called water gaps. When the river flooded it washed out the fence or water gap. The way we built the gaps was, we set a strong post in the center of the river, and a strong post on either bank. The fence was tied solid to the bank posts, then not so solid to the center post. That allowed the center to break loose first when there was pressure. The fence then would wash or swing down stream to its corresponding bank. When the flood went down to less than belly deep to our horse, we would tie a rope onto the fence and pull it back into place. Many times logs would get tangled in it and we would have to rebuild, taking each wire loose and starting over. If it was a rainy year in the mountains, we would spend the summer repairing water gaps. We made play out of it, however. When the water was too deep to repair the gap, we would take our horses in for a swim. We would get them out in the water then fall off and get hold of their tails. We took our clothes and saddles off. We would also watch for a log to come floating down. We would ride it downstream then swim to the bank. Run upstream again and catch another. Those logs were the real gap breakers, so they owed us a ride. They would hang up on the first gap and when it would break loose, they floated on to the next, until all the gaps were washed out. There were six of them.

There were ducks on this river all year. There was a sharp bend with a vertical bank about six feet high above the water, and there were always a few ducks swimming there. On top of the bank was heavy sacaton grass. Sacaton is a bunch grass. Grows in flood plains and can sometimes hide a man on horseback. That grass wasn't quite so tall or I would have walked instead of crawled to find those ducks. I had planned for some time, how someday I would bring along my .22 pistol, crawl through the grass to the edge of the bank and get one of those ducks. That was the day and the time. I tied my horse well back and started crawling. I could hear them talking, so I was sure they were there. I was doing such a good job making my way through the grass that my thoughts were making more noise than my crawling was. When I got to the edge of the bank I parted the grass to look over. I wanted to see exactly where they were. I moved my eyeballs over the bank. I was still well hidden in the grass, and there they were under me, about six feet away. They were so close and straight down that no way could I get a sight on them. I made a guess and fired. They all flew away but one. I tossed rocks in the pond until he floated to the shore. I tied him on the back of my saddle by the neck and headed for home, about ten miles.

A cowboy is usually wide awake and sees lots of things, and one reason is because he learns to watch his horse. The horse will see and hear things sooner than his rider. Some he pays attention to and some he doesn't. But he will always give a signal with his ears. I was on my way home with my duck. I saw my horse throw his ears forward, and sure enough there was a coyote not far away. I gave him a chase since he was going in my direction, anyhow. Through the mesquites, over and under and around, what a chase. I knew I couldn't catch him and so did he, but we had fun anyhow.

I was getting pretty close to home and I thought again about eating my duck, and wondered just how Mom would cook it. I was sure she could make him good. I looked on the back of my saddle to check him out and admire him once more. He was gone. It was too far back to go look for him, but I knew right then why that coyote was grinning so big when I quit chasing him. He was after my duck all the time.

Dad and Lorn Taylor were always arguing about something. Lorn spent lots of time at our ranch. They were the greatest of friends. One of the things they argued about was roping. Lorn used a very large loop and many times the calf would go through his loop before he could take up the slack. Lorn says, "I caught him but he went through my loop." We used a smaller loop but still some calves would go on through. When that happened, we called it "Lorn Taylored." There were some large Tabosa draws below Ramos. Tabosa grows best where there is a flood plain. Where there is a Tabosa flood plane there is also sink holes. In the winter when the grass is dry and thinned out, the holes can be seen, but in the summer when the grass is green, they are covered over and out of sight. One winter Dad roped a calf in one of those draws and Lorn said, "Roy, you sure are brave to run so fast in all those holes, your horse could fall down and kill you." Dad said, "I could see them so I figured my horse could also." The next summer we had lots of rain and lots of grass. Dad and Lorn were riding in that same area and there was a calf with screwworms. They each took down their ropes.

Lorn jumped his horse in front of Dad and caught the calf. As they were doctoring it, Dad said, "Lorn, you remember how you thought I was so brave to rope that calf last fall? Do you realize this is the same place with all those holes? They are just covered up, I believe you are the brave one."

Lorn walked around a little and when he saw all those holes, he said, "Brave is not the word for me."

We were moving some cattle in the same area. The grass was dry and I could see the holes. I expected my horse to see them also. I was riding Chinate. There was a calf out there running the wrong direction. Chinate and I would head him off before he got away. I have told already how, when Chinate ran hard and quick, he grunted with every jump. Now we were about to overtake the runaway calf and his grunts were coming real fast, when all of a sudden he let out one big and last grunt. He had stuck both front feet into one of those holes. I was lying on my back on the ground looking up at a very rare sight. Chinate was standing on his head and balanced there long enough for me to rollover and get out of the way when he came on over. He went straight over and landed on my saddle, but now we were both on the ground upside down and lying side by side. He had two ways to roll, on me, or the other way. He rolled the other way, or I wouldn't be telling about it now.

The east pasture was watered by windmills, except for the river. The west pasture was all natural water except for one windmill. It was at the foot of the Pajarito Mountain. The water was about a hundred feet deep so the windmill was an eight--foot wheel. The drought summer of 1934 was also a summer of no wind to pump water. The windmills in the east pasture all had pump jacks and were used regularly. They were the Buena Vista, Huerfano, and San Pedro. Water was piped down hill from the San Pedro to the Palma Alta. In early days there had been two windmills at the Palma Alta, but the wells went dry. The wells in the east pasture were over three hundred feet deep.

Dad heard of a Malacate pump jack at the Bass Ranch near the town of San Pedro. It later became the Cox Ranch. We went to the Bass Ranch and looked over the contraption, then sent the wagon for it and moved it to the Pajarito, a four day trip. I will try to tell you a picture of the Malacate pump jack.

Its power source was a yellow mule. The same Old Yeller that took us to school. A heavy three foot diameter iron wheel on the outside of a fifteen foot circle. A two inch iron shaft tied to it solidly. The mule was hitched near the wheel and as he went around the circle the wheel rolled along behind him turning the shaft because it was solid to the wheel. In the center of the circle was another heavy coged wheel that the shaft went through and about a one foot crank near the cogwheel, where it passed through. A vertical two by six board fastened to the crank which gave about a two--foot stroke. The vertical cogwheel traveled on a horizontal cogwheel laying flat on the ground. I will let you make your own picture of how they were fastened together. As the mule traveled, he turned the crank and developed a two--foot stroke at the Malacate. A five foot vertical connector was fastened to the crank by a hole in the bottom end. It was made from two by six lumber. The top of the connector was fastened with some sort of pivot to the end of the walking beam. The walking beam was two by eights nailed together for strength and about thirty feet long. It reached from the connector of the malacate to the sucker rod on the windmill. There was a fulcrum post just outside the circle the mule traveled in. You see, he had to go under the walking beam each time around. How Dad figured the distance to put the fulcrum post, I never knew. I hadn't heard of geometry yet and he only went to the fourth grade. It worked because I spent one summer pumping water with it. To keep the mule in the circle there was a lead rope tied to an arm that extended from the center out to the mule's bridle. I have told that I usually rode the fence from the house to the Pajarito Mountain, then to the windmill, which was at the foot of the mountain, checking the range and cattle and returning back to the house. I was home in time for noon meal, unless I went on up to Ramos to check that area and that would take all day.

Now back to that dry summer, with no wind. When I rode that five mile fence I took the yellow mule with me and spent the rest of the day pumping water. You don't lead a mule, you drag him. The mule would not pull the malacate if he could see where I was so I had to blindfold him, then he would travel. After a few days, the wheel the mule pulled made a rut or ditch, and was getting heavy to pull. We made a path for it with two by twelve lumber, and I had that worn out by the time summer was over.

I spent the entire summer trying to outsmart that yellow mule. First the blind fold, then I would tap him with a stick each time he came around, and talk to him the rest of the circle, but he would stop 180--degrees from me. I would go around and sneak up behind him with my stick. I think he had eyes back there because he would move on just before I could hit him. I would never hit him if he was moving. I came up with a winner, however. I made a flipper. The same like we drove the mules with at the VAV. That way I could stay in the shade of the windmill, and shoot him at any point in the circle. That worked so well that I would take a nap. I soon found out that when I napped so did the mule. How he could tell I never found out, but as long as I sat there awake, he pumped water. The flipper allowed me to move around as long as I could reach him with a rock once in a while. Me and that yellow mule became great friends that summer. I hated him.

There was lots of game on the ranch, lots of rabbits and rats, so lots of coyotes. I was riding on the south edge of the Cieniga and spotted a coyote. Floyd was with me. The area was a good place to rope a coyote, so we went after him. We caught him, and then found out why. Usually our horses couldn't outrun one, but this one they could, and we caught him. Gave us a real chase. He was three--legged. One hind leg cut off just below the hock. We looked him over pretty good. He was grown. We knew he would never get tame if we took him home, so we cut his ears and tail off and turned him loose. He didn't even look like a coyote. George Houghton was in charge of all the Corralitos properties in Mexico. He lived at the Hacienda, and ran a ranch of his own besides. Dad was at the Hacienda to get some well--working tools. The tools were kept there so that all the ranchers would have access to them. He was chatting with George when he said, "Roy, I shot the damnedest looking animal a few days ago, no ears, no tail and only three legs."

Dad said, "George, you shot my boys' coyote."

I was riding Little Man and as I rode up to the Pajarito Windmill I saw a coyote. He didn't look very big or very smart, so down came my rope and I built a loop to just fit him if Little Man would get me close enough to put it on him. Through and around the mesquites we went and sure enough it looked like I was about to get close enough to gather him up. He ran around a bush then seemed to shift gears and get out of reach. I coaxed Little Man for a little more speed, and we got up close again, and around a bush, and he speeded up again. Now this went on until Little Man ran out of desire to catch him. I pulled up and sat there thinking how close I was to roping that coyote a few times. While I was sitting there wishing my horse could have held on just a little longer, I saw three coyotes come out in the open, their tongues hanging out, and a big grin on their faces. They had been relaying me and caused me to almost kill my little horse.

Another day I saw some coyotes do that to a jackrabbit. If the rabbit would have ran straight he could have outrun them, but he ran in circles and those coyotes had rabbit for dinner.

I had been riding all day and I was tired and about three miles from home when I heard a swishing and then a thud. From the corner of my eye I saw an eagle with wings folded and diving. I was in high mesquites so couldn't see what it was all about. I changed my course to the left to check it out. By that time the eagle was back in the air. There was a small clearing about a hundred yards across and a jackrabbit made the mistake of trying to cross it instead of going around. The eagle paid no attention to me so I had a grandstand seat. He would dive and grab the rabbit with his claws. The eagle picked him up about twenty feet, then dropped him. Each time the rabbit was a little more drunk. When the eagle dropped him the third time he didn't get up. He just squirmed with his feet. That time the eagle landed and had dinner.

While we are on rabbits, I'm reminded of the time I roped a jackrabbit. Again I was on Little Man. I rode him a lot. The summers were hot and the rabbits would shade up and some of them wouldn't move out of the shade until I was right on them. Then they would jump out and startle my horse. The rabbit had been asleep, my horse was not ready for spooks, and I about lost my seat. That old rabbit jumped out from under a bush but instead of running, he was bucking, just like a mean horse. By the time I had given a thought of what to do, I already had a loop built to fit him, and sure enough, I roped him. He jumped and squealed. I thought maybe I made a mistake, he was so crazy. Maybe he had hydrophobia, then I saw why he was so loco. He was covered with ticks of all sizes and he was trying to buck them off. I took a stick and scraped the biggest ones off and turned him loose. A few days later I had an earache, not bad so I didn't pay much attention to it. Then pretty soon I could feel something walking around in there, and he wasn't headed to the outside. I decided I'd better tell Mom. She said, "You probably have a tick in there." She was raised in East Texas where they have lots of ticks. She melted some butter and poured it in my ear and had me lay still with that ear up. Sure enough, in a few minutes a tick came walking out for some fresh air. My pay for helping that rabbit.

You can see by now that I spent lots of time trying to catch a coyote, one way or another. Most of my horses weren't really interested in chasing them, anyhow. I had made the Pajarito fence ride to the foot of the mountain, and that is where I usually turned back, unless I was going to the top. As I rode down to the windmill I saw a coyote there getting a drink. I was riding the Hungaro horse, and he was definitely too slow to catch the coyote, but I was carrying my .22 pistol automatic. Now Hungaro was that outlaw horse we caught on the Cieniga that day a few years back. He never bucked anymore unless something unusual happened, then he would forget he was a gentle horse and he would throw a fit. He had a way of bucking that he would put his head right down between his front feet and come right out from under the rider and saddle at the same time. He would jump forward then jump straight backwards and the rider and saddle would go over his head.

Now, I knew all of that, but by the time I remembered I knew all that, it was too late. You see, a coyote doesn't stand around and wait while you think about the best way to catch him, so I made a snap decision. Run up on him and shoot him. I hadn't ever tried that before. Hungaro surprised me and got me so close to the coyote I could barely see him over Hungaro's head. We were running full speed and I fired a shot right between Hungaro's ears. I missed the coyote, but I thought maybe I had hit my horse the way he acted. He threw his head so low I couldn't see it, and I mean he intended to get out from under me and my saddle. Now, think a minute about the mess I was in. I had the reins in my left hand, my pistol in my right hand, and that old horse trying to throw me off. The only way I could stay on was to lock my spurs into him. I was trying to keep the pistol over my head so if it should go off it would be in the air. Each time his feet hit the ground he jarred me and I would pull the trigger. I was too busy to take my finger off the trigger.

I think the shots scared him, because after a few jumps he quit bucking and tried to run away. That was good, now I could loosen up on the spurs, holster my pistol and get him back under control. I was by myself, and that is one I never told anyone. I was afraid Dad would not let me carry the pistol if he knew. I had seen Dad shoot at coyotes from his horse, and after I got things settled down and could think, I knew what I had done wrong. Dad would run the coyote until he turned then shoot out to the side, not over the horse's head.

I have told how I rode the fence from our place to Barranca. Elsie liked to ride, so she would have her horse saddled and be ready to ride out on the range a short distance with me then return home. She never went far with me, but we usually went down the river. The river had lots of cottonwoods and blackwillows. It was a nice place to ride. There was about a mile of river on my ride just before arriving at Barranca. There were bobcats most any place on the ranch but they were hard to see. Mostly they sleep in the daytime and hunt at night. There were lots of them on the river. I was always looking up in the branches and quite often I would spot one. They would run down the tree and into the grass, to hide from me. Sometimes I would jump them again, but no way could I catch one. Lucky for me.

One day I was riding along the river as I was arriving at Barranca. The bank there was about four feet above the river channel then flattened out for about thirty feet then another bank about ten feet high. The trees were growing on the flat place below the high bank which means that you could look down into a good portion of the trees. Since the trees were growing down in the channel, some of the older trees had large limbs that sagged and laid over onto the high bank. That morning I rode along looking for whatever there was to see. There on one of those limbs were two bobcats. It was a large part of the tree trunk that was laying out over the high bank. I was close enough to see that they were sleeping with their eyes open. I kept riding as if I hadn't seen them. I knew I hadn't fooled them, but I had a plan anyhow.

I knew Elsie would be waiting for me so I went on to Barranca. I told her about the bobcats and my plan. Floyd was with me, he didn't see them, and Alice was with Elsie. We would all ride back up the river to a spot about a hundred yards from them, dismount, and tie the horses.

Each of us would pick up two rocks, then run and yell, and maybe scare them up higher in the tree. If it worked, we could then make plans of how to maybe get one of them with a rock, but we knew the odds were for the cats. All those plans, assuming they were still there. We made lots of noise, and I was running in the lead. They were still there. As I approached the tree where they were I threw my rock at them as we had planned. A real windmill underhand softball pitch. Now would you believe, that rock hit one of those cats right between the eyes. He fell out of the tree and I was there to hit him again. No need, he was dead. The other cat ran the limb out to the ground and disappeared in the brush. We were all so excited, we could hardly believe we had that cat in our hands. I carried him on my horse across my saddle in front of me. I was riding Little Man. As we were going back to the house at Barranca, we saw the other cat following us. It would run in and out of the bushes, and pretty soon that cat came at us and ran under my horse. Now, Little Man wasn't enjoying carrying that dead cat, but when the other cat ran around among his legs, he decided that was going too far, and he tried to get rid of the cat that was on him. I skinned the cat, had the hide tanned and kept it near my bed until I was married. That was one of the things I couldn't take with me. I left it at home in a trunk with other treasures. The hair came off and so that was the end of the bobcat story.

    Roundup time was always interesting and lots of work but lots of fun. The one I will tell about, we started at the Huerfano Windmill. The first thing was to get the cocinero and his helper. He would get the chuck wagon fitted out with groceries and get the cooking tools cleaned and ready. Then the cocinero would take the chuck wagon to the starting point. Next get the cowboys hired and send them to the chuck wagon. About fifteen men. Those were temporary men for the roundup time only. We had a spring roundup and a fall roundup. Keep in mind that I am talking about maybe 400,000 acres divided in the middle by the river. I am also talking about four to six thousand head of cattle. It took about ten days if we worked the whole ranch. The roundup is the time for branding the new calves and gathering cattle for selling.

We put the remuda together that was on the open range. About sixty head of horses. In other words, we had to round up the roundup remuda. Those are mounts for the new cowboys. We had a humpbacked mare with a bell on. For some reason horses will stay close to a bell, and especially if it is on a mare. When we found her most of the horses would be close. On that roundup, however, there were several horses missing. We found them in the Buena Vista area, and they were running with three wild and crazy mares. Dad put me on Canario, a long--legged sorrel with flax mane and tail. He was a thoroughbred and loved to run. That was what we were getting ready to do. The Buena Vista area was just what the name says. Big flat open country. No mesquites. Just grass for miles. I was to run those horses in a big circle, and Dad would wait on a small rise where he could watch me. At the right time we would turn them towards Huerfano and the rest of the remuda. He could do that because he would still be on a fresh horse.

Now that I was on the Canario horse, I could outrun those wild horses at anytime. I had no trouble pointing them in the direction we wanted. So all Dad had to do was try and keep up with me and those horses I was running. I was about twelve at that time. The evening shadows were getting long by the time we hazed them close enough for them to see the main remuda at Huerfano. They joined the herd. Dad had his sawed--off .30--30. He rode into the middle of those horses and dismounted. The horse wrangler and I got the horses to going in a circle around Dad. As one of those wild mares was clear, Dad would shoot her. A few minutes and three dead mares. That was in about 1932. Wild mares can sure raise hell with a remuda.

More about the roundup time. It was always exciting and I thought lots of fun. One man herded the remuda day and night. He followed each day to where the herd would be put together. He brought the horses in at daylight. The men would catch their mount for the morning drive. He then met the herd at noon for changing horses. We rode one horse on the drive, then a fresh horse to work the herd. Dad and Bill used two horses each to work the herd. A cutting horse or a roping horse will quit if he gets too tired. A roping horse drags the calves from the herd to the fire and that is a lot of work. The remudero must keep the remuda on good grass and water, because they are worked hard. Each cowboy had about five horses to change off.

When it was time to catch the horses, each cowboy walked out to where the remuda was being held. He took along his bridle and rope. His rope is not to catch his horse but to make a corral. Dad or Bill always roped the remounts. He tossed one end of his rope to the man on his right. Each man does that until the horses are in a corral. A little shaking of those ropes will keep the horses from trying to escape. Sometimes a spoiled horse would jump the rope, and whoever he belonged to was told to get him out and keep him out. The roundup cowboys ride their own horses to the starting camp then were furnished horses for the work. Some of them ride in on some spoiled horses. Those are the ones we would have trouble with. Once all the men have their mounts the ropes were pulled back to the owner and the wrangler took over once more.

I have told that the chuck wagon has a cocinero and helper. He did like the horse wrangler. He moved to where the next herd would be held. We had regular roundup spots that we used each day and of course each roundup. We were camped on the river at Stell's gate. The gate was between the west and east pastures. The reason it was Stell's gate was because, as I have told, that country was abandoned during Pancho Villa's time and Dad was the one to put the fences back in their place. It was open range in all those years. Stell had a herd of sheep there. Stell was our Dublan Doctor. I guess he saved my life once because he sure gave me lots of little pills.

Now about that camp on the river. The chuck wagon was pulled under a very large blackwillow tree. It was summer and the locusts were sure singing. The trees were full of them, and other bugs also. We got the herd together and it was time for lunch. The cowboys took turns leaving the herd for lunch. The ones eating would hurry so they could get back to the herd and change off with someone else. You can be sure, roundup folks sure get hungry. That day I was in the first bunch sent to eat. Beans were cooked in a large pot. Maybe about five gallons. That old cocinero was not real pronto about keeping lids on things. Those beans were boiling and sure looked and smelled good and I went after them with my tin plate. All eating tools were tin. They lasted good but got a little hot with those boiling beans sometimes. Those cowpokes might bend them a little but no break. If you have never had boiling beans in a tin plate, then you probably have never inspected a hot horse shoe either. The same rules apply.

I got a big old dutch oven biscuit and a plate of beans and instead of looking, I was eating when I realized the taste was sure good but the chewing seemed a little crunchy. I found several big red bugs in my plate, well done. I scooped the bugs out that I hadn't already eaten, ate the beans and went back to the herd.

Mexico has a country judicial system and the man is called Juez De Campo. That means country judge, and he has in his charge a certain amount of the area where he lives. When we worked cattle, for whatever reason, we had to advise the Juez De Campo so he could inspect and OK the thing we were doing. Even to move cattle from one pasture to another. In reality, the ranchers did to suit themselves, but they helped the Juez with some pesos once in a while. The Juez was put on the payroll during roundup time and when the herd was together he was asked to go into the roundup and look the cattle over. That made him feel important, and that was very important. The one we used the most was Apolinar Nunez. He was tall and skinny, and rode a little skinny horse. He used long tapaderos that almost reached the ground. His legs were so long that he never kicked his little skinny horse, but his tapaderos were swinging all the time to the tune of his pony's gait, which was a pacer. We went right by his ranchito on our way to school in our buggy. He was always friendly.

As time went on there at Pajarito, we acquired more horses. I bought Boogers for twenty--five pesos. A very good, gentle and honest horse. He was a tall dark brown horse. The kind I put my favorite girl on when we were on an outing. The first time I saw Boogers, a fellow was on him bareback with a nose loop and working some cattle. The horse was sure trying. Dad told me there is a good horse, let's buy him. That was the winter I trapped coyotes, and I had a few pesos. After the eighth grade, I stayed out of school for a year. With Dad's help I got the horse for my hard earned trapping money. He was poor so I let him rest up for about a month then I started riding him to see what I had. He was better than I had hoped for. He had a single foot gait, and that is one of the best for long rides. He turned out to be very good and very special.

I taught him to jump fences, cattle guards, rodeo calf roping, and even to showing off with him at a rodeo. I pulled my bridle off and roped and tied a calf with everyone seeing but not believing they had seen me do it. It was the first time I had actually taken my bridle off, however. I knew it would work because I had practiced him at home without using the reins. I made a special bridle for him. I used Mom's bridle bit that she used at the VAV, and which I still have. It is a very light bit and only good for a very good mouthed horse. I split a regular bridle rein of three--quarters of an inch. That gave me about a three--eighths inch rein. That will give you an idea of what a good mouth Boogers had.

I was riding in the largoncillos and spotted a yearling. I thought, I'll jump Boogers onto it and give it a pat on the tail. I did, and then I set down on the reins too hard and broke both of them at the bit. Boogers immediately went after the yearling again, but I didn't want to pat him again. I had to do some thinking of how to stop the runaway. I had been practicing for the rodeo, but never without a bridle. We were at full speed. I threw my rope with no loop. I sure didn't want to catch that yearling. I jumped off holding to the horn as if I had roped a calf, also I held the horn so I wouldn't fall down. He slid his hind feet to a stop. He was, by far, the best horse I ever owned. That is when I knew I could pull my bridle off and rope a calf. I also had taught him to guide by pressing my knee the way I wanted him to turn. Where from the name Boogers? When I bought him he was very snotty nosed.

Raymon had Socks, a horse we raised from Antelope before we had to get rid of her. She was the mare Bob Cook gave us when we were at Ascension. Socks was one of those pets that everyone loved, especially Raymon. Floyd had a black horse he called Indian. We had lots of horses through the years, but those were the ones we started with, and that stayed with us all those years. Floyd has had some real good and well--trained horses as he got older but none could ever take the place of Indian in his memory. Well maybe, but in a different way.

I'm going to tell you about Battling Sicky (the horse). A guy came down the road with a colt to trade or sell whichever came first. Dad got him and right there and then gave him to Floyd. I named him for a Tarahumara Indian that had worked for us. We turned him on the range for a few months so he could grow, then it came time to get him in and start teaching him some manners. He was the ugliest, most out of proportion of any horse I had seen then or since. The reason we turned him loose on the range for a while was to see if his body would grow to fit his head and feet. It didn't. He was long headed, long necked, long tailed, and the biggest feet I had seen on a horse. Floyd started to ride him, and he bucked all the time. Floyd had no trouble riding him at first, but the horse got better, because he practiced every time Floyd got on him. When we would come to a gate, I would open it because Floyd had trouble getting on and off him. All the fence gates were wire, and while I would be trying to open the gate, this horse having a fit, would jump the gate. The first time he did that, it sure scared Floyd, but he got used to it. In fact, he thought it was funny to ride up to the gate and jump it. I thought it was pretty neat also. I taught Boogers to jump, and he got real good. Mostly we jumped mesquite, it was safer than fences.

The way I understand some of the history of Mexico is that Pancho Villa was the man for the campesino, and his idea was to break up the big Haciendas and form ejidos, which would belong to the government, but be worked by the people. At the time of the revolution, the Corralitos south border was at the Dublan north border before Pancho Villa's time. The Dublan Shipping Pens were on the Corralitos. Our south fence was the Corralitos south border at the time we were there. The Corralitos lost a ten to fifteen mile strip on the south side and about thirty--five miles east and west when the country was refenced in 1927. In about 1936, the ejido joining us decided to expand. They surveyed and cut a brecha through the mesquites straight from the river to Ramos in the west pasture. They wanted the south half of that pasture and eventually got it. That cut the west pasture in about half. The Jefferys leased what was left of the Corralitos and Dad leased part of what the ejido took. He leased it from the ejido. All those years we had been friendly to those people and now we needed them. That meant we didn't have to move, and we leased our ranch from the ejido until the summer of 1943.

In late 1937, or early 1938, Bill bought the Benton Ranch and then sold his hereford cattle on the Corralitos to the Jeffery ranchers who joined us on the west. That was a sample of his ability to think and get things done. I was paying close attention. Those are lessons they don't teach in school. The Benton Ranch was stocked with black cattle rather than hereford like we were used to. Dad was then on his own. Dad had built up a herd of a few hundred head and things just got better and better for us from then on.

Dad sent Floyd and me for a load of wood. We had lots of mesquite, and there was an area east of Ramos where the wood was best. I took the team and wagon, and Floyd rode the fence around to where I would be cutting wood, then he was to help me. We had two axes. After a sandwich lunch, we got hot and tired from those axe handles and ran out of water besides. I told Floyd to go on up to Ramos, about two miles and get a bucket of water. All we had was an open bucket. There was a lid to start with but he lost it somewhere in the bushes and was afraid to get off and get it. He was riding Battling Sicky. When he got back to where I was cutting wood, he didn't have a drop of water left in that bucket. He told me the horse wouldn't behave and shook it all out. I told him to get off and cut wood. I would teach that bronco how to carry water. He asked me to let him try one more time. I told him OK, and when I saw him returning, his horse was sure silly but he was holding the water bucket out with his arm and it was swinging all over but when he got to me it was full of water, well almost. We drank the water, and he and I still laugh about that silly horse. He never did let me ride his silly horse. I don't know what he thought I would do to him.

The reason he had a little trouble carrying the water was because his memory was turned on. A few days before, he was on that same horse. We were riding in the horse pasture and the wind was howling right in our faces. Floyd always had a habit of riding his horse just behind me. We would talk back and forth, but I had to look back at him, and with the wind I couldn't hear him anyhow, so I just jogged along trying to keep my hat on. I thought of something to tell him. I glanced back over my shoulder, and there is Battling Sicky with an empty saddle. Not far behind was Floyd trying to make me hear that he needed a little help. I tried to get him to let me show him how to ride that horse, but no way. His horse had bucked him off and I missed the show.

I wasn't home much after that summer, but each time I was home and saw that horse, his head was longer, and his feet were bigger. The one and only good thing about him was his gait. He had a running walk that was sure nice on a long ride.

About the Indian the horse was named for. He was a Tarahumara from up in the Sierra Madre Mountains. When we moved to town, which was Dublan, in 1937, we needed someone to watch the ranch house while we were gone. I spent a lot of time on the ranch, but I also went to town a lot. There was a girl there that I didn't want to forget me. The ranch could not be left alone because of stealing. The Tarahumara Indian was working for Oscar Bluth in Dublan. Bluth knew Dad was looking for someone lazy enough to sit around and watch the ranch. This guy had spent some time in Los Angeles, and he spoke very good English and had as pretty a handwriting as I have seen. He told us he was a lightweight champion boxer.

I have told that we kept a large pile of wood at the ranch and the watchman chopped it, then we hauled it to town as we needed it. That Indian didn't wear out any axes, but what he did do was practice fighting on a punch bag he rigged up. I was going from town to the ranch to check things and as I was approaching the ranch house one day, I saw a man sitting on top of the woodpile. Then I saw a man sitting on the corral fence, then there was one sitting on the roof, then one just sort of leaning on a post. I was about to get spooked. I decided I had better circle the place and see if I could figure what was going on. It looked like the place had been taken over by some banditos, and I planned to be hard to catch. I was in the little Model A truck. As I got closer, I kept looking for at least the one on the woodpile to report someone coming, but he just sat there. I finally got close enough to see there was sure something odd going on, and then I saw my Indian come into view. I went on in. The Indian called himself Battling Sicky. He had made all those dummies to be his audience, while he was fighting the punch bag. Since those little A trucks didn't hold much gas, we kept a fifty gallon drum of gas at the ranch. Many times after our running around buying calves we would need gas to get to town. That was one of those days. I siphoned the gas out of the drum with a hose, into a bucket and then to the truck. That time out came water, and of course very rusty and dirty. I asked him what he did with the gasoline. He said, "I just took the lid of and looked in."

I said, "It must have sure been a dirty look." He had been selling the gas and then putting water in the barrel so it would stay full.

I have told how I always carried my .22 pistol when on the ranch, and that day it was on my side. I made a quick decision. Decrease the Indian population by one, and do it right now. I told him to put his pack together and hit the road towards Sonora and don't come back. I expected trouble. I knew I couldn't whip him with my fist, so I kept him at a safe distance. I was afraid of him by then and I knew I had to make him afraid of me. He threw his pack over his shoulder and took off. I watched him. About a half mile away, and sure enough, as he was going through a cattail draw he laid down there and hid. I don't know what he had on his mind, but I sure wasn't going to take a chance. I got on my horse and rode out to where I had seen him lay down. He wasn't there. The cat claws were thick and I had to hunt for several minutes to find him. I had my pistol in my hand, I just didn't know what he was up to. When I found him, I fired a couple of shots into the bush real close to him. That was the only time I ever saw that Indian move fast. He didn't even pick up his pack. I told him to get his pack and start to trot. That I would follow him and watch from a distance. If I had to shake him out of the bushes again I would just kill him right there. He hit a trot and I went back to the house. I sure hoped I had convinced him, and that he wouldn't double back in the night. I didn't sleep where I was suppose to, just in case. The next day I had to clean the place up and get rid of his trash. I found letters he had written to Lucy Bluth, and to his fight promoter in L.A.

About halfway on the fence from Pajarito to Barranca was a place we called Cook's Camp. The same Bob Cook that gave us the paint mare when we were at Colonia Diaz. When Hunt had this west pasture he had three fellows with him. They each had a few head of cattle, and all were bachelors, including Hunt. Bill Bedford, Wilbur Stevens, and Bob Cook. Cook had the paint horses. When Bill bought Hunt out, he let Wilbur Stevens stay with his few cattle. Cook took his paints and went up in the mountains near Pacheco. Bill Bedford had a reputation like the Adams'. If he rode a horse very long it learned something. He made some good cow horses, I had one of them, his name was Corbata. The area at Cook's Camp was heavy with mesquite, catclaw, and hackberry. The wood haulers liked to get in there to cut wood. They were the ejido people who joined us on the fence line. The wood haulers took the wood to Dublan and Casas Grandes to sell. We did not allow wood cutting on our ranch because stealing was so bad. They would kill an animal and put it under the load and haul it out. As much as we watched, they would still get in and cut wood. When we found a wagon track we would follow it and find where they cut wood. Many times where they had butchered a cow. As we rode this fence, many mornings we would see cutters just outside working away. As soon as we went by they would go inside and cut the better and larger trees. Throw it over the fence to the wagon.

One morning I was riding along the Cook area, when I spotted one of those cutters, but as I was even with him I noticed a little boy coming my way, as if he wanted to talk to me. I stopped and waited for him to approach the fence. That was one of those days a person always remembers. He was one--legged. His leg was cut off just below the knee. His artificial leg was made from a mesquite fork. One side cut short, and the other side left long to reach to his belt and tied there. Padded to put his knee in. Rope wrapped around his leg to hold it in place. He asked if he could come to my house and live with me. I looked him over and we talked for some time. He was born in Morenci, Az. His parents were dead. During the depression years of the twenties, the mining towns were closed down. There were many Mexican people put out of work. The US sent them all back to Mexico. In the late twenties, they went to Casas Grandes by the trainload. Most of the ejido people near our ranch were of those repatriados. I told him I would talk to Dad, and if he would meet me there the next morning I would let him know. Dad gave me the go ahead. He was there waiting for me and when I told him to go on over to my place his smile and white teeth covered his whole face. I had to finish my day's range riding. When I got home he was there. He lived with us about four years.

Parjarito

He didn't go to school, but we taught him. He learned English, numbers, reading, and writing. He was smart and learned easy. His name was Alfredo Santian. We called him Peggy. He was soon helping with horse wrangling, milking, wood chopping, and whatever was needed. After Mom moved to town, he did the cooking for us. He could sure make good beans and tortillas. We would have a contest to see who could make the roundest and best tortilla. I was good but he would never admit I was better.

I finished the eighth grade in 1933. I missed school year 33--34. That put me behind my crowd a year. I tried to catch up and finish high school in three years so I could graduate with my best girl, but I didn't make it. It took me three and a half years. The year I stayed out, I trapped coyotes. I would ride the fence and check my traps on the way home. I had them all set about a mile from the house. By the time the winter was over, all my horses had consented to carry live coyotes. I would put a stick in his mouth and tie it shut so he could breath but not bite. One day I didn't get the mouth tied good. The stick came out and the tie fell off. That time the horse and I both didn't like that coyote to ride with us. With the help of my horse I dumped him to the ground. My horse kept him shook so he didn't get to bite me. What I mean is my horse was sure jumping around. I carried those coyotes with front feet tied together and the hind feet tied together. He was no trouble to catch and start over. I caught bobcats but I didn't take them home alive. They were very dangerous to handle. The bobcat didn't have long enough nose to tie his face shut. I caught badgers. They were real easy to handle, they didn't jump around like the cats. I carried a .22 automatic pistol to shoot them. The things I hated to find in my traps were the skunks. I skinned one just to prove I could, and what I really proved was that I would never skin another one. I about ruined my horse just carrying the hide home.

I caught an eagle in one of my traps. I took him home to see if I could tame him. I had a large pen that I put him in. Three feet wide, six feet long, and four feet high. I made this pen for some rabbits but they didn't survive. At first he wanted to fight when I took feed to him. Before long he would hop down from his perch and take his food like a gentleman. I would bring him a rabbit each day. I thought I would have no trouble shooting a rabbit for him, but with my fence riding, and trapping, and of course the normal chores such as milking, horse wrangling, and wood chopping, that eagle turned out to be more than I expected. I opened the door and let him out. Instead of flying away he hopped up to me for his rabbit. I didn't have one for him. He checked back inside the pen and still no rabbit. When he came out again I shut the door then waved my arms to get him to fly away. He couldn't fly, he had been confined too long. He would fly a short distance then rest and try it again. After several tries he finally rose up and was gone. He had become completely dependent on me.

I'll try to tell here about the tools it takes to get in the fur business. First some traps. I had about twenty #3's. A .22 pistol, a good skinning knife, a gallows frame to hang them on while removing the hide, and stretchers to put the hide on once you take the coyote out of it. The stretcher is made from two one by two boards, pointed on one end at about sixty--degrees. The boards are laid down with the straight sides together with the points in the same direction. A leather strap is nailed over the pointed end to give a hinge effect. The other ends can be moved together or apart to form an angle. The hide is removed like a sweater. You start at the bottom and peel it off at the nose. The coyote is hanging upside down on the gallows. The hide is cut from one hind foot along the back of the leg, across just under the tail then to the other side to the foot. The four feet stay on the carcass. Now you start to peel the hide down towards the head. No more openings. The tail gets the bone pulled right out of the hide. The ears and nose stay on the hide. The hide is now pulled over the stretcher. A nail driven into the nose to hold it in place right on the point. The hide is pulled full length. The stretcher now pulled apart tight to the hide and a board nailed there to hold the established angle. It is called an A frame. In about six days the hide is cured and the stretcher removed. Now the hide must be stored properly and watched closely because there are bugs that can ruin it in one night.

Of course, to get the hide you must first catch the coyote, and he is very smart. You have to make him think he is smarter than he really is. The .22 pistol captured a couple of nice fat jackrabbits. One was used for a drag. If you just set a trap the coyote can't find it, so you drag the

Parjarito

rabbit around through the brush, until you find a good place for a trap. A good place is a bush with open branches on one side, and not hanging low. A coyote travels a lot on cow trails, so the drag must cross the trails. When he is trotting along and smells where the drag crossed, he will quit the trail and follow the drag. What a smelling ability those animals have. Not only will he follow the drag, but I did also. I didn't follow it by smell, however. The drag sign was the only way I had of finding my traps. About once a week I would drag a new rabbit.

The traps had about a three--foot chain tied to one of the springs. That got tied to a limb of the bush. Put the trap in the set position, sit it on the ground and mark around it. Dig a hole the size and deep enough for the trap to be flush with the ground. I carried a Sears catalog with me. A sheet was the right size to cover the jaws of the trap. I used a piece of screen wire to sift dirt over the paper, just enough to cover it, but not enough to trip the trigger. I put a piece of rabbit near the limb where the chain was tied so the coyote had to step on the trap to get the meat. A coyote will not step on sticks. When the trap is all ready, you line some sticks on each side in a V shape to give him a nice clean place to put his feet when he goes in there for the meat. That gives him a nice clean trail to go in there and grab the meat. When a coyote is caught in a spot, he will sure tear the bush up, but for some reason that becomes a good place for a trap. I would catch several in the same place. I suppose the scent left on the bush. I made stretchers of different sizes to fit the hides.

Among the important things to do on the ranch was keeping boots, saddles and bridles well oiled, and the saddle blankets washed to get the sweat out. We used rendered beef tallow to oil the leather. It was the cowboy stand by. It was good, but messy. I noticed the badgers had a layer of fat about a half inch thick over the entire back. I decided to fry the oil out and try it on my saddle. Mom and Dad were gone to town that day and they wished they had stayed there. That badger cooking left the most terrible smell in the house. It took days for it to go away, or maybe we just got used to it. Even so, I still lubed my saddle and boots real good. I mean they sucked in that badger oil like an old cow at the watering trough. I will say this, I never had to oil that saddle again, and it never quit stinking. No one would ride down wind from me. Mom made me keep my boots outside and almost to the corrals.

I caught bobcats, badgers, skunks, foxes, eagles, and coyotes. That winter sure made me ready to go back to school. In the spring a hide buyer showed up in town. Someone told him that I had been trapping and had some hides. He sent word to me of when he would be by the ranch to look at my hides. I was expecting him, but I was not ready for who it was. He was Jose Terrazas. It had been several years since I had seen him. He had been a big cow buyer. Always came to the ranch in a new car and a pretty girl. He would deal for the cattle and help us ship them then head back to El Paso. The last time I had seen him, we shipped a train of cattle at the Corralitos Shipping Pens.

Besides the girl he also had a .22 pistol. Dad had gone to town to get some final shipping papers. Jose was supervising the loading. They got through before Dad returned and the cowboys were all sitting on the corral fence. Jose pulled the gun on them and fired a few shots over their heads, then took the rest of the bullets out and handed it to me with the scabbard. He told me to give it to Dad when he got back. He hopped in his car with his pretty girl and made dust towards the border. When Dad drove up and saw the pistol on my belt, he wanted to say something, but I didn't wait. I told him that Jose gave it to him. Dad gave it to me when I graduated from the eighth grade, and that is what I was using to shoot my animals with.

Jose drove up in an old worn--out pickup, and he was dressed accordingly. We didn't haggle over prices. He looked my hides over, graded them and made me an offer. I took it. He had gone broke in money but not in spirit. I haven't seen him since, but have heard of him in later years. He made millions in the real estate business in Chihuahua City. He is part of the Terrazas family, who at one time owned most of the state of Chihuahua.

The summer of 1934 was the driest year I can remember. There was a total of about six thousand head of cattle on the ranch. No grass and no rain. The combination means catastrophe. We rode the water places everyday to drag the dead ones away so the live ones could get a drink. Bill fenced the Cieniga and we put cattle in there until it looked like a day herd. The water there was shallow, so the grass grew green without rain. However, it was a salt grass. The cattle that stayed on it for very long would die later, anyhow, because it would wear out their teeth. We dug a well, about three feet to water, and made a frame over it with a pulley. A rope through the pulley and a five gallon can on each end of the rope. A man camped there to do nothing but pull water. His groceries were delivered to him. We made water troughs from 2x12x16 lumber, nailed and wired together. The ends of them were close to the well so that as he pulled a bucket up he hardly had to shift his feet in order to pour it in the trough. The cattle became so tame that some of them would try to catch the water from the can as it was being poured. We figured an average of five gallons per cow, some would drink more. Some of them were so poor and so weak, when they drank their five gallons or more, would move out from the water and lie down. Then couldn't get up with all that water.

Since a cow gets up with her hind legs first, to help her, you get her by the tail, wrap it around your neck and, as she tries, you lift. If she gets the hind legs up then you hold her while she rests before she tries for the front end. She has to do the front end on her own, because if you get hold of her head, she has a fit and down she goes. Rest a while and when she wants to try again, you stay close to that tail and hope this time she will make it. A poor cow is the dumbest thing, she never gets in the shade. On the Cieniga there was no shade anyhow. That summer all my shirts had permanent off--color collars.

As the summer was coming to an end and too late for rain to make feed even if it came, Bill leased a ranch in the Santa Rosa area of New Mexico. We rounded up all the cattle that was left that was strong enough to make the trip and shipped them to that ranch in NM. Those cattle were sold in N.M. After expenses, we received $1.00 US per head. The cattle that were too poor to ship was the foundation herd to start over. They mostly all lived. Dad always said he could still see the train smoke when it started to rain. We didn't save the herd by shipping.

I had a cow Dad gave me when she was born in 1930. At that time in 1934, she was a good milk cow, and the best dogie cow we ever had. I trained her from the time Dad gave her to me. I taught her to lead, to ride, and I could catch her anyplace. I would go after the milk cows on foot and ride her back, driving the others. We called her Roney. Most cows will fight a strange calf, but not Roney. We always gave her three calves to raise besides her own. That summer of 1934 was when there were more dogies than we could handle. Roney raised twelve calves that year. When we would find a dead cow with a calf, we would put the calf up in front in the saddle and carry it home. Dogies are not worth the cost if you have to hire them cared for, but with three boys, that labor was cheap. It was sure worth it for us.

The milk cows were in the pasture in the daytime and the calves in the corral. Then at night, just the reverse. We built a corral just large enough to hold those dogies, about a hundred yards from the main corrals and in the evenings after we were finished milking and taking care of the dogies, we would drive all the calves to this corral. Dad would then let them out one at a time and Raymon, Floyd, and I would rope and tie them. We got good and so did our horses. Bill tried to put a stop to our play house as he called it, but they were our cattle and our horses, and we kept right on playing.

There were some big herds that came through our ranch at times. Anyone from the ranches west of us that shipped at the Corralitos railroad pens had to come through our ranch. They would spend one night on our ranch. They would come in at Ramos and bed down about halfway through our ranch then on out the next day. We always followed those herds as they moved on our ranch, and checked them out the gate as they left, to be sure none of our cattle were mixed into their herd. Most of them were from Sonora. Quite often, cows would have calves on the drive, and if it happened on our ranch they would give the calf to us kids. We would take it home and put it on one of the cows. Howard Alley gave us one. It was from a registered hereford cow and it sure did grow to a beautiful cow. Another one we got from a Sonora long horn cow. I told how we roped the dogies in the evening after work. That little long horn calf could out run our horses from our holding corral to the main corral. It was all legs.

Dad and I were checking a herd out the gate. He told me to watch them go through and he would ride around and talk to the men to find out who they belonged to and who was in charge. It turned out to be a fellow with very much beard and rough clothes. He was not only the boss but the owner. He and Dad sat on their horses and talked while the herd was filing through the gate. Pretty soon they both stepped off their mounts and I hadn't ever seen such hand--shaking as went on there. The man was Bob Nichols. Yes, the one I told about at the Rafter G Ranch and the bootlegging.

He shipped his cattle then went to town and got new clothes and a shave and hair cut then came to our home and spent about a week there. He and Dad sure had a lot of talking to catch up on. He told Dad that he kept on bootlegging. It was just too good to quit. He was caught and put in jail for a while and when he got out he took his money and went to Mexico. He had built up this herd, a large herd in the Sonora Mountains. He decided to sell out and go back to the US. He gave Dad a pearl handle, chrome, .44 pistol. He said he didn't need it where he was going. He was going back to the US. My brother, Floyd, still has it.

Anytime there is a large cattle ranch, and hungry people nearby, there will be cattle rustling. Those people did not steal to build up a herd, they stole to eat for the time being. It was really quite a game. They tried to cover their tracks and we tried to find them and track them down. There was what was called the Cordada. That is a Mexican rural policeman and a Segundo. He got his authority from Mexico City. He took orders from no one. He was the judge and the jury. He was on twenty--four hour call, and I never knew him not to come pronto when needed. Dad would never try to make an arrest or catch a rustler, but would trail them until it was pretty clear of the hide out, then go for the Cordada and they would trail together until they lost or found what they were after. Some tracks were so plain that they could follow them horseback, and others they had to walk. The Cordada man was not left in one place but maybe a year, so he wouldn't make too many friends. He had too much depending on his right judgement. All the ranchers helped him financially, but the only favors he did was to be there when they needed him. He would only act on what he saw with his own eyes. When he caught a man with the goods it was adios. He never caught the same thief twice. The first thing he would do was draw a crowd to show what happens when he caught a thief. Sometimes he cut their head off with his sword, other times he had them hung to tree and told how many days before taking them down. Other times he would tell them to run. Then shoot them at a nice pistol range. Like I said, he never caught the same thief twice. One time they were trailing two men in the Casa De Janos area and they found them. One man had the meat, and he told on the other, but the other didn't have any meat, or at least they couldn't find it. He told the one with the meat to run and he shot him before all the crowd. He turned to the other man and said, "I didn't find any meat with you, all I have is the man's word that you were his helper. You can go. Run and don't ever come back." That poor fellow was so scared that he would be shot, he started running, but just stayed in one spot. He finally got some forward motion, and was never heard of again. He probably couldn't stop when he got to the Baja, and drowned.

There was a nest of rustlers in a large canyon on the Pajarito Mountain. It was about maybe ten families. It was a vinata where they made pulque from the sotol plants, which there were plenty of them there in the foothills. I think they lived on pulque and meat. We even got to know their horse tracks, and could tell who it was. They were so clever we never caught them. We found where they took the beef out the fence and where they butchered it up one of the canyons on the mountain near our fence but we never caught them with the meat. As I say the Cordada man had to see to believe. I always felt that those guys were up in the rocks on the side of the canyon with guns on us. I think really all we were doing was to let them know that we knew, so they wouldn't get too bold, and take too many. They would take the animal up the Pajarito Mountain and butcher it in a big canyon then carry the meat out on their horses. One of the horses had funny feet. That horse helped to steal a cow about every four months. I never saw him but I'm sure he saw me. And his rider probably had a .30--30 pointed our direction. Me, Dad, and the Cordada.

The name of the ranchito was El Gato. The people lived in caves in the bank of the canyon. I went through there once on my way to hunt a horse that had been seen on the Tenaja, a ranch around the south end of the Pajarito Mountain from our place. I knew that ranchito was in the area but I didn't know just where until all of a sudden I was there. I was alone and I was sure nervous. I was going to ride on through their little round the tub on the outside. They had some pigs inside the tub and ran them around to soften up the stumps. Then they put the stumps in the squeezer. The juice came down a little trough to the outside of the tub and they caught it in containers. The thing they were doing, however, was each of them had some sort of a can for a cup and they would catch some and drink it. That is what they invited me to do. I had no thirst for pulque before and for sure not since I saw them making it. As soon as I could get away I hit the trail and went on to where I was headed. But I had to come back this way because the trail went in the bottom of the canyon between their caves. I was through there after that and they would come out of their caves and wave to me as I rode by.

    I was riding the ranch checking cattle, and I thought I saw a movement in the brush down in the draw about a mile away. I was higher up on the Pajarito slope. I rode down there but the brush was so thick I couldn't find what I thought I had seen. I hunted around and looked for tracks. I was sure I had seen something like a man riding. Whoever it was had no business there. Anyone going through our ranch must stay on the road, or he got checked out. I always carried my .22 pistol as a backup if a coyote should charge me. I kept looking and found a fellow hiding in some real thick brush. He had seen me coming off the slope in his direction. He was riding a burro and carrying a small calf. If he had been on the road I would never have stopped him. I made him go to the ranch house and sit by the corrals. I sent word to Dad who was in town to bring the Cordada. We always kept a watchman at the ranch. That old boy had cut the burro's ears off almost down to his head. Along in the afternoon the old boy decided he had been there long enough and left towards town on foot. I called for him to come back but he couldn't hear me, I called louder, the same thing. By now, he was farther away and walking faster. I went in the house and got the sawed--off .30--30 and put a shot over his head. He didn't hear that either. The next shot was almost too close to his feet. His hearing got better and here he came, not walking but running. He said, "Senor, ya mero me mataba." I told him the next shot would have broke a leg. It was night when Dad and the Cordada arrived. The old boy was still sitting in the shade where I told him to stay even though the sun had been gone for some time. He had stolen the burro from around Janos and picked up the calf as he came through the Jeffery Ranch. He cut the burros ears off to disguise him. The Cordada took him to jail, I think, and gave the burro to us, unless someone should ever claim her. They didn't. Martin Jeffery picked up his calf the next day. Years later my sons, Floyde and Sid, learned to ride the burro after we bought the Buena Fe Ranch. She started biting at them so I got rid of her. A biting burro is worse than a biting dog. She had a little colt was the reason she got mean.

We had lots of good summer rains there at the Pajarito Ranch. Our ranch house was out in the flat area and it sometimes looked like a lake. Our house would be on a very small island. The water ran off the mountain and would flood the low country. Those summer rains seemed to bring lots of thunder and lightning. I was told not to ride near the fence when it was raining. I have learned since that a wet horse is very dangerous, and so is getting under a tree, so I spent most of the rainstorms in a lot of danger. I was almost knocked off my horse twice, and it was sure scary. I didn't worry too much about lightning running down the fence until I was just ready to get off my horse to open a wire gate, and a bolt jumped to ground right there in front of me. I didn't open that gate. I made my horse jump the cattle guard.

We were in the house during one of those heavy rains and heard about six cracks, sounded like my .22 pistol, doing some quick shots. Mom said, "That was lightning and it hit close." When it quit raining we went out to see what happened. Out in the corral in the calf pen were three dead calves and two just standing there looking silly. The bolt had come down the fence and what we heard was when it jumped off. The calves were fat. We went back to the house for the skinning knives. Lotta Jerky coming up. When we returned to the corral those calves were all standing up. They looked sort of stupid but they were alive. That was how close they came to getting skinned alive.

There were a few head of cattle we could see from the house and they were milling around sort of different. I got in the A truck and drove out to look them over. There laid a fat cow the lightning had just killed. This time when I returned with the skinning knife the cow was still dead. Sure made a lot of jerky. The cow belonged to Floyd, and he still thinks the reason his herd didn't multiply faster was because we ate them while he was away.

Another time Dad was sitting on the bed and the lightning bolt came in the door, hit the ceiling, then the bed, and out the window. It knocked Dad flat. The bed was one of those old iron head and foot types. That may be what saved him. Mom was in the kitchen and ran in to see what happened. When lightning hits close you can smell it. She smelled it and there lay Dad. He was stunned but not hurt. It took splinters from the door and window. Every time Dad went through that door he looked up and said thanks.

The Pajarito Mountain is a large landmark. It can be seen from sixty miles and maybe farther. We ranched the east side of it and Jefferys ranched the west side. The south end was ejido after it was taken from the Corralitos Land and Cattle Company during the Villa revolution. The east side sloped off into a valley about thirty--five miles wide to the next mountains, with the river running north in between. That is where our ranch was. On the west side, on the Jeffery ranch were low rolling hills. Lots of good grass and lots of antelope. I asked Martin Jeffery if I could go onto his ranch and hunt antelope. It was OK. Then I asked Dad if I could take the sawed--off .30--30 and go try to get an antelope. It was OK. I asked Raymon if he would like to go with me. He said OK. Then I got hold of Boogers and said, "Old horse, you want to carry me to the other side of the Pajarito to get an antelope?" It was OK. Mom said she would sure enjoy a good antelope steak.

The next morning, early, we were gone. We let the fence down at the north end of the mountain and crossed into Jeffery's ranch. We soon topped a ridge and in the draw below was a herd of about ten head. Antelope run single file and when they saw us, they formed their line and ran upstream in front of us, about a hundred and fifty yards. I was so excited I hoped I could get enough shots off to get one of them before they were out of sight. Fifty yards was out of range for that little gun. I pulled the trigger. Then waited to see the dust so I would know how to sight for the next shot. No dust, all I could see was a tumbling antelope. I leaped on Boogers like a TV cowboy, and down the hill I went. When I was about halfway to the antelope, he got up and took off. I was traveling fast and I could see he was about to get away so I took my rope down on the run. Boogers went to him like he was a calf and I roped him. His hind leg was broken, and it was still a good race. I told Raymon to jump off and get him down and hold him then I would get down and we would dress him out. Raymon did get down, but by then that antelope was mad and he almost reached Raymon with his horns before I could take up the rope slack. Since he wanted to fight we decided to treat him like he was a calf. Raymon roped his good hind leg and we stretched him out. We dressed him out and I put him on Boogers. At first Boogers didn't like him up there and wished he had stayed home. Boogers had never been hard to get along with so I was a little surprised that he was silly then. He settled down and I started to get on when I noticed the rifle scabbard was empty. I mean the sawed-off .30--30 was not there. The first thing I thought was, "Boogers I sure hope you made deep tracks, because I have to look at every one of them until I find that gun, or we won't go home tonight." I had lots of experience tracking, so I knew I could backtrack, but in that case I had to find the tracks and the gun also. It turned out I had run the antelope farther than I thought at first. I was following the tracks, as if the horse was running in reverse. Backtracking. I still hadn't found the gun, and I was getting back close to where it all started. There was tall grass and I guessed I had missed it, but I was still puzzled of how it jumped out of the scabbard. I had carried it many times and chased coyotes and never lost it before. As I topped the ridge where I shot from, there laid the gun. I had kneeled down when I shot, and when I saw the antelope go down, I threw the gun down and took off. That was when I remembered Bill Holmes ejecting all the bullets from his gun as the antelope circled him. Antelope fever.

I have told about my Chinate horse and how he enjoyed throwing me off, or at leased trying every once in a while. Mostly I could ride him, but he sure got out from under me one day. I was on him bareback and coming out of the river up a steep bank. He went under a tree limb and knocked me off.

As Raymon, Floyd, and I were riding the range we saw a nest not very high on a soapweed. We rode over to check it out. There was a chicken hawk about ready to learn to fly. Let's just give him a flying lesson. I rode up to the nest and he just sat there looking me right in the eye. The nest was low enough that I could stay tight in the saddle and still reach the young hawk. When on Chinate, you stayed tight in the saddle or he would get rid of you. As I reached for the little hawk he still just sat there and looked at me. I got him by the legs and pulled him out of the nest. His wings began flopping and he was trying to bite me, and Chinate had gone crazy. Now I couldn't ride a bucking horse and hold onto a flopping bird at the same time. I tossed the bird, planning for him to fly at least a little ways. He didn't. He grabbed his claws onto a coil of my rope as he was falling and held on. I had a bird upside down holding on to my rope flopping his wings, and one spinning horse. Chinate was spinning so fast he had that bird standing straight out. I knew something had to give, and it looked like it would be me. If he threw the bird first I could ride him out, but if he threw me first, well, I just couldn't let that happen. I got a better hold, and pretty soon the hawk had enough and turned loose. He catapulted out about a hundred yards and made a bad landing. Being his first landing and dizzy besides. I don't know what that hawk thought, but I thought he would just have to learn to fly by himself.

One thing we were alert for as we rode the range was for stray animals or riders that were not on the road. At the Pajarito Ranch we pumped the water with a pitcher pump. It was only about twelve feet to water which was real cool and good. We had quite a few cattle come in the corrals for water, but most of them went to the windmill up near the mountain. Since we had to make this water by hand we sure didn't like to have any strays come in. When they did we would take them to the gate about a mile away and turn them back to the ejido side. I think most of the time the owners would put them in our ranch because we had good feed. After we would put them out a few times, then we would tie some tin cans to their tail and never see them again. They were mostly just broom tails anyhow.

A couple of two year old colts came in for water one day. A bay and a black. They were obviously of good stock. Dad told us to let them water and he would try to find the owner and trade for them. He knew pretty well who they belonged to. Pete Saenz was our ejido neighbor and they were his. Dad bought the colts. He gave me the black one and Raymon the bay one. The next time they came in for water we shut the gate on them and looked them over pretty good. Dad told us that was as good a time as any to break them. We each caught our colt and after sacking them out good we put our saddles on and rode them in the corral for a while, until we could turn and stop them. Mas o menos. Dad opened the gate for us to ride out. He got on his horse and rode along with us in case we should have a runaway. My colt handled good for a bronco, and we got along fine, but about a hundred yards from the corral, Raymon's colt threw him off. Dad was there to catch the horse. Raymon got on him again and pretty soon he was on the ground again. Raymon got bucked off so much that the colt was about to outlaw. He had a bicycle that I sure wanted. I traded my colt for his bicycle and the bay colt. We called the black one Warlock, and the bay, Spooks. That was a trade he always regretted, because I could ride the colt and I made a good horse out of him.

Each time he would buck with me I would put him into a long lope and keep that up for a couple of miles, then put him back in his gait as long as he would behave. At first he didn't behave very long at a time. He didn't buck stiff--legged but he bucked crooked, and that made him hard to keep track of. If I moved, he bucked; if the wind shook my chaps he bucked; if he saw a rabbit, he bucked; if a kangaroo rat jumped across the trail, he bucked; and when he bucked I spurred, and when he quit bucking I loped him. I rode him everyday, and after about a month of that, I put my saddle on him one morning for some more of the same. As I put my foot in the stirrup to mount, he looked around at me and wiggled his lips. In horse language that means let's be friends.

That was my last summer at home, but I sure made a good horse out of him while I was there. He was fast and could catch anything, anyplace. He is the only horse I ever had that I could outrun wild horses like they were cows. I took Floyd with me on one of my rounds. I had seen a wild horse on the north side of the ranch. I told Floyd to get on Spooks and I would ride Boogers. We would go find and rope that old horse and put him off the ranch. I had it all planned just how to catch the horse. We found the horse where I had seen him before. I knew Spooks could outrun the wild horse. I told Floyd to run him about a mile. Bring him back by me, and I would rope him. I waited while Floyd did just that, but when he brought the old horse by me he had his rope ready, and he was right on the old pony's heels. As he went by me he yelled, "Let me rope him, Bill." By that time, I was running alongside him and I said, "Put it on him," and he did. The Spooks horse was still in second gear. That wild horse couldn't run fast enough to open Spooks up.

I have told how Demar Cardon went to the ranch with me at times, and I always had a horse to show off to him. I had my Spooks horse doing everything just right. Demar was riding with me in the vicinity of the Pajarito Windmill, when I saw a calf that needed doctoring. Down came my rope and Spooks put me on him quick and I caught him. At the same time I think to myself, my my, I forgot to tighten my cinch, and while I was thinking my my, the calf hit the end of my rope, my saddle went up on Spooks' neck, and Spooks threw me and the saddle both off right there in the dirt. That was the last time he ever bucked with me.

The summer of 1937, I worked in Bisbee, Arizona. I met a fellow, Earl Peterson. We became good friends, and then became partners in the cow business. He had some money saved and wanted to invest it. He furnished the money. I would buy steers and we would split any profit. He gave me five hundred dollars, when I left to go back to school. I bought calves as I could, but I decided to go to the mountains and see if I could find more to buy. With five hundred dollars changed into pesos, I was in the buyer's market. Floyd wanted to go with me and of course I wanted him to go. We put a packsaddle on School Boy with our bedroll and a little chuck, and headed up hill to the mountains. School Boy was retired from his buggy days. That was the last thing I used him for. Those three years of school had wiped him out. He was stiff--legged and slow motion. He drug his hind feet so bad we had to keep shoes on him so he wouldn't wear the toes off. Instead of making tracks with his hind feet, he made lines on the ground.

We were three days to the little town of our destination. It was a ranchito type town of about twelve houses up in the high mountain country, on the same river as Colonia Juarez. Also the same river that ran through our ranch. Everything went in and out of the place by pack animal. We went by the Howard Alley Ranch, and that was the end of the road for wheels. Howard's ranch was on the river about fifteen miles above Colonia Juarez. By the time we got that far, School Boy had the hang of what he was suppose to do. Instead of leading him we turned him loose and he followed us. That way he could graze as we traveled. The next ranch we came to was Bob Cook's place. Yes, the same man that gave us Antelope in 1927. That was in the fall of 1938, and he was still raising paint horses. He told us that the lions ate one once in a while. He had cattle there also. We spent the night at his place. He had just returned from Casas Grandes with a mule train full of groceries. From Cook's place the terrain really got rough. Bob filled us in on the trails, so we wouldn't get lost. He had been to the ranchito we were looking for.

Next morning Floyd and I were bushy tailed and ready to go. The high fresh air smelled real good. I was on Boogers, Floyd was on Tuffy, and School Boy was on his own. Up the trail we went. We were in the mountains, but a long distance from the top. We climbed from Cook's ranch house, and topped onto a large mesa. It was the mesa where the Mormon people hid their teams and saddle horses during Pancho Villa times. It is completely surrounded by bluffs, hundreds of feet high, except the trail we were climbing up on. There is one trail down to the river for the cattle to water, and one on the west side that we were hoping to find in order to get off. We found the trail and started down. About halfway we came to a fork that Cook told us about. The left fork follows the river and on up Colonia Pacheco way. The Colonias are Mormon colonies that were established in the 1880's. We took the right fork.

Now those trails don't just go off down the mountain. It is too steep. They rim around with a downhill grade that is nice to ride on. We were looking down in a canyon and couldn't see the bottom. There were large pine trees and many of them. It was at least a mile across at the top. By the time we had crossed that canyon it was evening. We were about halfway up the other side when we jumped a flock of turkeys. I gave Boogers the spurs and did a quick draw with my pistol. I was sure gaining on those turks, when all of sudden they turned around and flew right over my head. No time to aim, but I pulled off several shots. They flew back across the canyon where we had been about two hours before. We saw several deer on this trip. They would stand and look us over but too far away for my .22 Woodsman.

We topped out on more level ground, and in the evening we arrived at the ranchito. It wasn't far from the big canyon. We left home planning to eat at the ranches we would be seeing. Then we would sure find food where we planned to buy calves. We took very little food with us and it was already gone. When we arrived at our ranchito destination we found about a dozen houses. We rode among them trying to size the place up. People came out of all of them trying to size us up. Visitors came there very few. There was a group of men near the large corral. We rode over to them, to say howdy. One came up to me and held out his hand for the shake, and of course I shook hands with him. Instead of turning my hand loose, he tried to pull me off my horse. I gave Boogers a get--the--hell--back signal and was able to jerk loose. Some of the men got hold of the guy then asked me to get down. They told me not to worry about this fellow, he is poco loco. They were all friendly and we shook hands with all of them. I told them I was looking to buy some calves. They told me to come to the corral the next day and they would round up some cattle for me to buy. I told them that we were hungry and asked which house could we buy some food, like tortillas and beans. They pointed out one of the houses and we went over to it.

Now, you have never seen hospitality like is found with those people in Mexico. They don't have much, but they will sure give what they have. They cooked and ate in the same room, which was not very large. The ladies sat us down at the table and fixed us up something. We couldn't eat it. They had just butchered a pig and they had him scattered all over the house, and it was part of him they fed us. We nibbled a little but just couldn't go it. We bought all the corn tortillas they had made, which was about a dozen and asked where we could camp for the night.

We camped away from the houses, about half a mile, at the foot of a high mountain. There were lots of large pines. We tied a rope between two trees and hung our bed tarp over it for a wind break. We cleared a place off for a fire. The pine needles were thick, so we cleared a little extra. There was plenty of wood and the fire sure felt good. With our heads towards the fire, we were sacked out and enjoying the view of the stars through the trees. We hobbled the horses to discourage them from going back home without us. Seemed like we had just fallen into that sound sleep when a whirlwind picked up our fire and set it down in those pine needles. We put our boots on and grabbed our saddle blankets, and after that fire we went. It was spinning and going up the mountain so fast we could hardly catch the front of it. We didn't have any clothes on, but I'll tell you for sure we were not cold. When we got the front stopped, it was easy to put out the rest.

The next morning we made a small fire and warmed a couple of tortillas for breakfast. Our horses were nowhere around. We got on their tracks and found them about a half mile from camp. We loaded our gear, mostly bedroll, onto School Boy, threw a diamond hitch on it and headed down the mountain to the corrals to see what those people had for sale. It didn't take long to buy about ten calves, and we headed them out on the trail. Most of them were still on the cows, but I had handled weaners before. Move them in a hurry so they don't have time to think about their mamas. About half a mile on the trail and they all decided to go back to the corrals, and in ten different groups. Like maybe one calf in each group. We were two busy cowboys for about thirty minutes. Finally we got them pushed off the small mesa, out of sight of the ranchito, and started down the trail into the big canyon. When they went over the rim, they fell in line single file on the trail. Now we just needed to keep them thinking about going forward.

They settled down and traveled along fine. We finally hit the bottom of the big canyon and were going up the other side. There was no place for them to go, except stay on the trail until we got climbed out to the trail fork. The same trail fork we saw the day before. We wanted them to take the left fork, but it was still going uphill, so for sure they would turn right because the other one went downhill. It went down into the river just above the big box. No way to get ahead of them to turn them to the left trail. We yelled instructions at them in both English and Spanish. The lead calf was almost to the fork and if they turned right, we would have to follow them for about two hours to the bottom at the river before we could turn them back. I pulled my pistol and put a shot on the right hand trail just as they were approaching it. They didn't spook or miss a step, they turned left and we later topped out on the big mesa of Cook's Ranch. There we let them slow down and graze as they went along. They were no trouble now, their mamas already forgotten.

We went off the mesa, and into Cook's place late in the evening. We had put our tortillas in our chaps' pockets. We nibbled them as we drove our little herd along the trail. By now, two cowboys were sure starting to get hungry. Bob Cook had figured that out and prepared a fiesta for us. We had told him when we would be back to his place. He cooked over the fire in the fireplace. Hanging on a hook there was a large kettle. We soon learned it was full of chicken soup. Two chickens in there including head, feet and most of the feathers. We were never sure about the guts. It was soon dark and his only light was from the fireplace. He had about six dogs. He made the biscuits after we arrived so they would be nice and hot to go with the soup. He tossed in a few potatoes, whole, unpeeled. His flour was in a hundred pound sack, sitting in a corner. He made the biscuits in the top of the sack, pinched off a few hunks and tossed them in the soup for dumplings. Floyd and I could see we had a problem. We sure weren't hungry enough to eat that chicken soup, so we came up with a plan. His plates were the chuck wagon type, tin and about one inch deep. They held lots of food. He got a spoon and sampled the soup, and smacked his lips, "Yep she's ready boys." He filled us each a full plate. Now hear this, I was glad for only the fireplace light for two reasons. One, I couldn't see what was in my plate, and two he couldn't see what I was going to do with it.

Floyd and I sat ourselves in the door leading to the outside of the room. The door threshold was about a foot off the ground. Just right for a good place to sit. A dirt floor and only one room. We fished out the potatoes, and were glad they had the skins on. We messed with them and ate them slowly, and when Mr. Cook wasn't watching, we would hold a plate out the door behind our backs. Those dogs would clean it up in a hurry. He would see a plate empty and fill it up again. He said, "I knew you boys would sure be hungry." He was eating a plate full himself about as fast as we could feed ours to the dogs, and we got rid of the whole thing. I mean all of his chicken soup. He was so pleased that we liked it. We almost got caught, however. Those damn dogs got to fighting when we would stick a plate out there behind our backs and he wondered what had come over his dogs. Never saw them act that way before.

The next morning he took a biscuit outside and divided it with those six dogs. They were so pleased, they all jumped on him for more and knocked him down. He got on his feet and looked at all those dogs, and said, "Damned unappreciative sons--of--bitches." We didn't stay for breakfast. We told him the chicken soup was about all we could handle. He understood, because it was sure a big pot. We went to the corrals to get our cattle and all the calves were up, but one. He just laid there and wouldn't move. One day and one sick calf. I wondered how many I could get home with. I told Cook we would head on down the trail and if I never came back for the sick one, he could have it, if it lived. He said, "It has blackleg, wait and help me and we'll operate on him and you can take him with you." I knew about blackleg and I knew they die when they get it. We always vaccinated all the calves at branding time, so I had never seen a sick one before. He tied all four feet together and made a small hook from a piece of wire. His pocketknife was sharp. He cut the foot just above the hoof fork, and in there he found a main blood vessel that goes down the leg, then forks to each toe. With the wire hook he got hold of the vessels where the three come together and pulled them out of the skin, gave them a twist and cut them off. Each foot got the same treatment. We removed the rope from the feet and that little old calf got up and joined the others. Mr. Cook opened the gate and told us adios and to come back.

Now, we were two hard day's drive from home, and about to run out of tortillas. We had planned to make Howard Alley's ranch and spend the night there. We were sure of some good food there. Late in the evening we pushed our little herd into Alley's corral and went to the house. There was no one there but the Chinaman cook. He had orders to not feed anyone. We had known the Alleys for years, but that Chinaman wouldn't listen to us at all. Floyd and I looked at each other and we thought the same thing. Can we find our way home at night on those trails? Let's try. We each had a tortilla left, but they were so hard we had to break small pieces off and soak it in our mouth until we could chew it, and besides, it went farther that way.

We drove those cattle all night and the only problem we had was finding the trail to cross a deep arroyo. One of the calves fell in. It was so dark we had trouble finding him. When we got them on the other side and counted them there was one short. We had to go back and find the one that fell into the arroyo. That arroyo was only a few miles from our ranch. I had crossed it many times in the daytime, but never at night and driving cattle besides. It was about ten feet wide and about six feet deep and straight banks. It could only be crossed on the trail.

We arrived at our ranch just before daybreak. We didn't put the calves in the corral, we just quit driving them and they quit traveling at the same time. We turned our horses in the horse pasture and went into the house. Dad was there and when he heard us he got out of bed. He said, "You are a day early but I cooked a pot of beans because I knew you would be hungry." We ate them. He said, "But I sure didn't think you would be that hungry." I have never been that hungry before or since. We told Dad about the trip and how Cook cured the blackleg. He had seen cattle with blackleg and they always die. There is no cure once they have it. More about that part later on.

When Floyd and I left on that trip, he had a very bad boil on his back. Seems boils were common in those days. Mom made a poultice from soap and sugar and put it on the boil to draw out the core. That was the only thing she knew to do. She wrapped him in sheet strips to keep it in place. It hurt him all the time and as we were riding he would beg me to stop and take a look at it to see if it was ready to get the core out. When we camped at night he would beg me with tears to check it out. I wouldn't because I knew when I took the bandage off I could not put it back on. I also knew that if I took it off too soon he would be in more trouble. One evening when we made camp I decided to take it off. It seemed he had about all he could stand. When I took the poultice off, the core was sticking out about a quarter of an inch. I tried to pull it out with my fingers but it was too slick. I tied a string to it and started pulling it out. It was about an inch long and about the size of a cigarette. He went into shock and it took me a while to get him settled down. At the time I sure didn't know anything about shock, but I knew I had a problem with him. When he finally quit shaking he was OK and the hurt got well. He was in good shape except for hunger when we got home with those little steers.

I have told that the ejido took part of the Corralitos, and we were then leasing part of that land from the ejido. We lived in the same place. A fellow from the ejido came riding into our place and he had a problem. All the ejido people's cattle were dying. Blackleg. Would we come quick and vaccinate them? Dad had to leave to buy some cattle, but he told me to do it for them if I wanted to. I told the fellow I would charge them one peso per head. He liked that. I told him to tell all the people to round up their cattle the next day and I would start at the north end and work south. The ejido town was one street about two miles long.

When I arrived there the next morning, horseback, they had rounded up most of the cattle into one corral, and that sure made it easy for me. The first thing they showed me was one of the best cows, dying. She hadn't been on her feet for two days. Then was my chance to see if I had watched Cook close enough. I told them to tie all her feet together and I would cure her. The audience got bigger and bigger. The little things I was saying to myself was what no one ever knew. I sure needed to be right. I made a little wire hook and cut in the toe fork to find the blood veins. Would you believe, they were there! I did each foot and they took the rope off. We had to hurry and get out of the way, because that cow jumped up and went to the feed trough. That was the most abrazos and handshakes I ever got in one place. There were so many vaqueros that as soon as I vaccinated one, another was ready. I worked hard that day and I went home with my pockets full of pesos. Even Boogers stepped happy. Of course, he always stepped happy when I turned him towards home.

That was a very wet summer and the cows gave more milk than the calves could use. We rounded up some of the best cows to milk and make cheese. Now those cows had never been milked before. Some of them tamed with very little trouble, and some didn't tame with a lot of trouble. I have told about a post in the center of the corral. What you do is rope the cow and snub her up to the post then get a hind foot, just one, so she won't fall down, and it must be the foot on the milker's side so she can't kick. One old cow never gave up. She had long horns and wanted to try them out on someone. She finally got to wanting to fight when we would just go into the corral.

We were milking a cow and Dad was walking around in the corral. That old cow threw some dirt on her back, bellered, and charged him. He ran for the fence and jumped it before she caught him. She backed off and stood there watching him, shaking her horns to let him know she meant business. What she didn't know, was that when he jumped the fence, he landed on a pile of lumber. He was then in the process of finding a two by four the right size for what he had in mind. He found one and climbed back over the fence and into the face of that old cow. She came up to him shaking her head and he knocked a horn off. She backed off a few steps and came at him again and he knocked the other horn off. His next shot would have been in the middle of the horns, and we would have had steaks for supper, but the old cow backed into a corner and never charged again. We were tired of the cheese thing, anyhow, so in a short time we turned the herd back to the open range. I say he knocked the horns off. They were still fastened to her head but not where she could use them on him. We snubbed her to the post in the center of the corral and with the dehorn saw made a nice muley out of her. She sure didn't like her new arrangement.

The last roundup I was on, was at the Jeffery Ranch, in the summer of 1938. They were our neighbors to the west. They had the Ramos Ranch, also part of the Corralitos. The roundup lasted about two weeks. We branded close to four thousand calves. All I had ever done on a roundup was hold the herd. The first day at camp I got a surprise. I knew it was going to be different from any roundup I had ever been on, and I was raised on roundups. We got the herd together and we all caught fresh horses. We were at the chuck wagon eating dinner and Martin Jeffery told Dad to cut him off a rope. He told me to get one also and I would trade off with Dad roping calves. Martin had brought a complete roll of the best catch rope from El Paso and we used most of it on that roundup. I had never been in a herd before, much less drug calves. Those little calves sure didn't like to leave their mamas and be taken to the fireside. It is hard for me to believe that I was raised on the ranch and went on most of the roundups but had never been in a herd to cut cattle or rope calves. There were lots of brands so it was important to call out the right brand for the calf as he was drug up to the fire. I had to be sure of the calves mama when I roped him. Those calves were fat and husky and we broke a rope once in a while. We just went to the coil and cut off another. I hadn't ever been treated like that before. In fact I hadn't seen a good rope for a long time. We used the chavinda, made in Mexico.

Two men were in the herd at the same time to drag calves. Dad and I teamed or took turns with each other and Martin and Bill Jeffery took turns. When Dad roped, I earmarked and the other way around. I used Boogers. He was nice and quiet in the herd. The reason we broke so many ropes was because as we drug the calf near the branding fire, we put the rope over the fork of a post set there for that purpose and drug the rope through it until the calf was standing on his hind feet as he was pulled up to the forked post. The post was just high enough to lift the calf's front feet off the ground. That way the flankers just had lay him down and take the rope off so the roper could go after another. Two men, was a set of flankers, and we had four sets to keep up with the ropers and the branders. You can see how a rope got worn fast, being drug through that fork each time.

About the fourth morning, Martin came up to me and asked if I would like to go to town and get some supplies for the chuck wagon. I stood real tall and said, "Si senor." He gave me a list of what he needed and the keys to his pickup. He told me to just give the list to Gandara and he would put it all together for me. Gandara owned the largest mercantile in Casas Grandes. I made two trips during the roundup, and it sure felt good to be something besides a herd holder.

One night was very special. It rained all night, so we couldn't go to bed. We huddled under the wagon, not much good. No stars to put our bedroll under that night. I worked hard and made a good hand, but that was not new for me. What was new for me was getting paid for it. When the roundup was over Martin gave Dad a check for four hundred pesos and me one for three hundred pesos. That was the first I knew I would get paid. He also told Dad and me to each cut off a new rope to take home with us. We used a thirty--five--foot rope.

Parjarito

Bill stopped by the roundup one day on his way from his ranch to town, and saw me in there dragging calves. I don't know what he thought, but one thing he was sure of, I damn sure didn't learn that in his roundup. I'll let the secret out now. I learned it roping Old Bounce, my dog. At that time, Bill had sold his cattle to the Jeffery people and bought the Benton Ranch at the Cerro En Medio. We were not with him anymore. We were on our own and Dad was finally making some good money buying and selling cattle.

I will tell a little here about ropes so you will understand why I was so pleased to be given a new rope when I left the Jeffery roundup. In my life I had very few American--made ropes. The ones I did get hold of were already worn out or had been rained on or drug threw the river water a few times. Water takes the life out of a rope and it becomes limber like a rag. Some of them had been broken and had a splice in the middle. We used the Mexican--made rope called a chavinda. They were pretty good but not very stout. Then there was the riata which was a braided rawhide rope usually made in Sonora. It was not very stout and was used with the dally only. I never learned or wanted to learn to dally. A riata stretches like rubber. I roped a wild burro one time with my riata tied and the burro broke it. That was when I learned why not to tie a riata. The thing broke close to the burro. It came back at me and whipped me from head to foot and also whipped my horse. I knew what I had done wrong, but my horse wouldn't listen to my excuse for him getting whipped when he was behaving himself.

Now the rope we used that I really hated was a hair rope. We collected hair from horses tails and mane. The tail hair was used to make ropes for the cavresto. The mane was used to make smaller rope to make the saddle cinches. We roached our saddle horses to get mane hair. We roached the tails of the wild horses that we caught. The wild horses were the strays that got into our ranch or were put in there because we had lots of grass.

Now to make a horse hair rope, after you have removed the horse. We had a twister made from a stick about one inch diameter and about fourteen inches long. Cut a notch or head on one end to fasten the cord to then drill a three--eighth inch hole, just under the head to put the handle through, in order to spin or whirl the stick. If you want a right-hand rope you spin the first strand to the left.

As we collected hair it was tied in bundles. To prepare the hair for twisting we used a saddle blanket laid on the ground, or in the house on the floor if Mom was in good humor. Dad and Raymon, Tio, and I would sit cross--legged around the blanket and pull hair. You pull a few hairs at a time from the bundle and toss them onto the blanket in every which direction. The pile of hair was then rolled into a loose roll. Dad sat cross--legged with the roll of hair in his lap. I held the spinner close to the hair and he put a loop of hair around the head and I started the twister to whirling. Dad feeds the hair to me a few inches at time so that the twist is kept tight. My memory is good about those hair ropes. It was summertime. Dad sat in the shade of a cottonwood tree and even though I started there in the shade with him I didn't stay there long. As he pulled the hair and as I twisted I was moving backwards right out into the sun. The first strand was about a hundred and fifty feet long. When the first strand was ready we called Raymon and Tio into play. I quit twirling and kept the strand pulled very tight while Raymon and Tio chose spots at about one--third distances. They each had a stick in their hand to loop the strand over then let the strand slide between their fingers until we had folded it in exact thirds. One of them put his loop over the head of my twister and the other loop went to Dad. Then I started the whirl again in the opposite direction. While all this was taking place the strand must be kept very tight or it would sure make a bird's nest on the ground. By now I'm sure you would like to ask if the finished rope didn't have lots of whiskers. It did until it was passed over the campfire.

7

Colonia Dublan

We moved from Columbus to Dublan right after Christmas, 1928. I had just turned nine in December. Louie Jack, my youngest brother, at that time was about two. He got pneumonia, and died, I think on Christmas day. He was buried there in Columbus. We left for Dublan the next day. We don't know where his grave is. The Columbus graveyard has not been cared for at all.

Colonia Dublan was, is, and will be home base for the rest of my life. Even though I haven't lived there for many years it is still home because that is where I was raised and learned to love it very much. Colonia Dublan was the second closest colony to the US border. We called it a hundred miles to Columbus, NM. The Mexico colonies were established by the Mormon church after the US government passed a law against plural wives and was trying to enforce it. That caused lots of hardship on those with more than one wife and lots of kids. My great-grandfather, Jerome Jefferson Adams, was among some of the first settlers. He was at the first colony, Colonia Diaz, which was also nearest the US border. It was about fifty miles from Columbus. Dad was raised in the Mormon colonies so he was actually taking his family back to his stomping grounds.

Dad had already rented the Will Walser house, so we had a place when we arrived in Dublan. Longhurst was on the east, and Memmott on the west across the street. My first Dublan lesson was at Memmott's.

Dad arranged to buy milk from him. In Columbus it was delivered in nice bottles. In those days everyone in Dublan had a milk herd. There was a real good cheese factory there. I had a gallon bucket with a lid and I was the one to go after the milk each morning. I would go to the corrals where they were milking and one of the men would fill my bucket and back home I went. As they milked, they filled ten gallon milk cans for transporting the milk to the cheese factory. They would fill my bucket from one of those cans. Memmott also raised lots of pigs. He picked up the swill from the cheese factory to feed them.

 I skipped over to get my milk one morning, sure was cold, and one of the fellows called to me that he would pour my milk. I was surprised they had started putting the milk in large drums. I was new at being a milkman, so no questions. I held my bucket like he told me and he poured it full of swill. The workmen sure thought it was funny. I couldn't understand what they were saying, but I knew I had to learn Spanish, and soon. I went back home and Mom washed the bucket. I went for my milk once more. I couldn't understand them but I knew they were apologizing. They hadn't realized how dumb I was.

 I spent lots of my early Dublan days at the Longhurst home. Everything was so new to me. I had never been around farming before. Brandon was the youngest. He and I were good friends through the years. Brandon and I were sitting in the shade of a tree in front of his house. I had already found out that those Dublan kids knew a lot of things that I had never heard of. He said," Willie, did you ever see a turpentined cat?" I told him no we just had common old cats. He told me to follow him. We went into the barn and found a cat. There seemed to be plenty of cats. He picked up a corn cob while we were in the barn, and on the way back to our shade tree, he went in his house and came out with a bottle of something. He poured a little of whatever was in the bottle just under the cat's tail then rubbed it with the corn cob, then sat the old cat there on the grass. The cat just sat there, and I was thinking, so that is a turpentined cat, how exciting. All of a sudden his eyes got big and he let out a meow and he was gone. But instead of running to the barn, he ran up the tree. There was a row of trees all the way down the sidewalk. They were about twenty feet high. That cat was going so fast when he reached the top of the tree, he jumped out, hit the ground running, and up the next tree, up to the top and jumped out, and on to the next one. He was still doing that as far as we could see him. Brandon said the cat didn't hunt rats in his barn anymore. I learned later that this terps thing was a way they used to discourage stray dogs and cats from continuing to come around.

Another thing they did was tie tin cans to a horse's tail. I never tried the terps, but I did try the cans on a stray horse that we couldn't keep out of our ranch. I was tired already of hand--pumping water for him. I don't know where he went but I didn't have to pump anymore water for him. The cans don't hurt them, but it sure scares them.

I also got some good trading lessons. One of my first was a Mexican jumping bean. Those beans came from the mountains and every so often some would show up in school. I sure did want one of those beans. I finally traded something for one but when I got it, it wouldn't jump. The beans the other kids had would all jump but mine would just sit there. I carried that bean in my pocket for several days. I said the words they told me, but it was too lazy to jump. They could say the words to their beans and they would jump. Finally one of the kids told me to rub it real fast on my pants leg before I talked to it. I did and it jumped. There is a bug of some kind in there, and when he gets warmed up he jumps around making the bean act alive. It was fun until everyone learned how to make them jump. Then the bean season was over and I haven't seen one since.

My first problem encounter was with Demar Cardon, so I will write about him first. As I have told; I moved to Colonia Dublan, Chihuahua, Mexico the 1st of January, 1929. At that time, school was in what we called the old school house, and we were in the fourth grade. I had to walk over a mile to get there. That was where and when I met Demar Cardon. That first day I went to school, I was checked out and tested by the full group of boys from the school, seems about ten of them.

Now to bring in some background to that first meeting with Demar, let me say; my Dad was from the Colonia Diaz colony and it seems the Adams boys were problem church goers. Up to that time I had lived on a ranch in Arizona and been taught no religion at all. I had no idea what a Mormon was, but Demar taught me that. Now back to the group.

They kept asking me if I was a Mormon and if not, why not, and I sure didn't want to be dumb before all those obviously smart kids. I had no idea what the Mormon thing was they kept asking me about, but I decided that whatever it was I didn't like it. I finally said, "I'd rather be anything but a damn Mormon." That was when Mac Bluth decided that I should be whipped and Demar should do it. He quickly gave Demar a shove towards me. Demar put up a hand to catch himself against me. We were close and in the process he hit me on the throat which sure did me in for a few moments. As soon as I got my wind back, I came in for the fight and expected all those kids would sure tear me up. Well they didn't do that at all. Maybe they just wanted to see if I would fight. Demar had not intended to hit me in the first place. Mac Bluth was the boy in charge, I was soon to learn.

I had just moved from Columbus, NM, and had really had to fight my way in that school and I thought here it goes again. As a group those kids explained to me what was or is a Mormon and I have never forgotten it, mainly they stick together. Mac Bluth, I soon learned, was better to have as a friend than as an enemy. While I was learning that, however, he sure dealt me some misery. The only water at school was a pitcher pump in the school yard. You hold your hand over the spout and some one pumps the handle for you then you do that for him. We could only drink water at recess, and that was when Mac took charge of the pump. I was one he wouldn't let drink.

At that time, I started planning to someday remind him of those days and make him wish he had been kinder to me. I wasn't the only one he was ornery with. He was much bigger than any of the kids his age. I must say that the bigger I got the more friendly Mac was. I always admired his horse. He got it from my cousin, Hugh Adams, when he left Dublan. Hugh's dad (Lorin) had been running Bill's ranch but he stayed drunk so much that Bill had to get someone else and that is where Dad came into the picture. In later years when we were on a scout hike my bedroll was lost from the wagon. It was raining and sure no time to sleep with only my saddle blanket. Mac took me in with him in his bed. That made me forgive him of our first meeting times. Mac was not a fighter, he was a teaser, and he only teased those who could be teased.

When I think of him I always remember how good he treated me on that scout hike.

That first meeting was the start of a lifelong friendship with Demar. However, since we didn't really fight that first day, there was always a question of who would have won. Sooner or later we would surely find out because maybe a year later we were becoming good friends, but still didn't know which one was the leader or boss or whatever the term. One day a bunch of us were at the Leon Pratt place. Rollo had some boxing gloves. After some of the kids had a few rounds, it was decided that Demar and I should put them on. Well, I think each of us had enough at about the same time because our friendship grew rapidly from that day on. We would have been about ten at the time.

Demar had a white mare and everyplace he went he rode her and of course as time went by he would come by my house and up behind I would go. We hardly ever used a saddle so there was a trick to getting on behind him. He would hold a stiff foot and give me a hand, and up I'd go. The stiff foot took the place of a stirrup. Demar also taught me about my first halloween. He came to my house at night on that white mare. He called me out of my house, which was no problem, because by then I sure thought I had a good friend. As I approached him as he sat on his white horse he threw flour all over me and took off. He had gotten me again. He made a small circle and came back and sure thought it was funny. I guess it was, because he invited me up behind him and gave me some flour to put in my pocket and we would go call someone out. We did, and as each one joined us we had all our age group or crowd together and ended up at one of the homes for a little party. He had taken me into a real fun crowd. My future wife was one of that crowd.

Because of Demar, I was accepted and became a Dublanite and sure one of the crowd. Our friendship continued into high school and after we were grown, and went our separate ways. There was a problem during high school, however, that sometimes happens to the best of friends. We both wanted to date the same girl. I soon decided that just wouldn't work because it seemed I was losing the girl and my best friend also. I decided to back off and let him date her all to himself. I would just date around until they would have a fight then I would step in, if she would let me. I knew that would happen, because that was the only time I would get to date her was when they were on the fight. Then she would go with me until she and Demar would make up. Then I'd be sidelined again. He had a very good personality, and besides that, he was in town all the time and I was in town part of the time. Girls need lots of attention.

Sure enough, after a while they had a big fight. We didn't call it a lovers' quarrel. I watched for the right time, then one day I said to him, "How are you and our girl getting along?" He told me that this fight was for real and that they would never make up. I told him I didn't believe him but he assured me it was true. We talked about it for some time, then I told him what I had in mind. I told him that I had left him and her alone and if this fight was for real and final, then I would ask him for a promise. That he would not date her again as long as she was my girl. He promised, and he kept his promise, and I married the girl. He always told me how lucky I was, and I sure agreed. I'm on my way to his funeral now, that girl driving while I'm reminiscing and writing some of it down. She never knew about our arrangement until now, and she sure whopped me a good one. I always thought Demar was such a lucky guy to have all those sisters. His memory will always be with me. He was a great friend.

I visited him not long before he died, when I was in Las Vegas, Nevada. He was on a kidney machine and we both knew we were having our last friendship abrazos. We laughed and talked about our growing up in Dublan. I hadn't seen him for several years. Mart and I were staying at the home of our friends, the Henrys, in Las Vegas. I called Demar and said, "Surdo, venga en su caballo, cola mocha y dame un jaloncito a mi foringo." (Lefty, come over on your bobtailed horse and give my little Ford a pull). Demar was left handed.

He said, "Bill, where the hell are you." He knew and I knew that only he and I knew about that episode.

I was trying to start Dad's model A pickup. It was in our yard near the street. Along came Demar on his black bobtailed horse, and stopped to see if I needed some help. The battery was dead and the crank wasn't turning so good. I told him to tie on to my foringo and give me a pull up the street. He did, and up the street we went. I let him get into a fast trot and I dropped it into first gear. That was the wrong gear for starting a car I learned later, but it was too late for that time. The rear wheels just locked up and my model A came to a sudden stop. The bobtail kept going. Now you think the rope broke. Wrong. The cinch broke, and there sat Demar on the saddle on the ground right in front of the bumper. The horse was putting out so much effort that it took him a short distance to get stopped. We pushed the A model back in the yard, fastened the saddle on the horse and the two of us rode off. I think we were both headed to see Mart anyhow.

The school bus stopped sometimes in the Station (Nuevo Casas Grandes) in the evening. We would all go into the stores, look around, mostly because money was short. On one of those stops, Demar and I were looking at some red and white cloth with large flowers. He said he would buy enough material for two shirts if I'd get my mother to make them for us. My mother was a very good seamstress and she not only made my shirts but also made my pants. I was well dressed, and they fit good. We had lots of fun with those shirts.

Another time we were in the same store. In those days, they kept the eggs in a tub sitting on the counter. Demar picked one up and tossed it to me. I caught it and tossed it back to him. Instead of catching it, he stepped aside. I have never seen an egg make such a mess. Everyone saw me toss it to him, but no one had seen him toss it to me. Guess who was in deep trouble.

Later in the same store, on another day, we bought some sodas and for some reason he put his in his back pocket. The egg episode flashed in my mind and I hit his soda with mine. For some reason my soda didn't break. His did. Friends don't get mad, they get even.

Speaking of eggs, the reason the stores displayed them in tubs was because they buy them as they were brought in from the ranchitos. Everyone had a few chickens. One day we were riding in a car with a friend from the Station. Jeronimo Rodriguez. Demar and I both liked to drive when we had a chance. The friend was crudo (drunk) and he got in the back seat. Demar drove from his house down the back street to the Spencer store then let me drive back. About a mile. The street had ruts in it, where most everyone traveled, and lots of potholes. The Dublan streets were dirt and no grading at all.

I was traveling at high speed, like maybe thirty-five MPH, and there was a buggy in my path with a man and woman sitting on the spring seat, enjoying their ride. I started to steer out of the ruts to pass the buggy and the car got sort of silly on the steering, so I hit the brakes. The left front wheel locked up and turned me at right angles to that buggy. I mean broadside, and I was still at high speed. I was passing on the right side. Things sure got out of control in the next few minutes. I hit that buggy broadside. The man flew through the air and over the car and landed on his feet going full speed. The lady landed where he had been sitting. The horses ran away with the buggy and the lady. The lines were dragging on the ground. The man had been driving. As I said, the man landed running and he never slowed down. He just made a left turn and fell right in behind the wagon. I had sure given him a running start but the team was too fast. He couldn't catch the wagon.

That was on a Sunday, and that doubled our problem. That day I sure wished I had gone to church. Dave Haws was on his way home from church. He was crossing the street in front of his house, about four blocks from where the mess got started, and he saw the runaway coming towards him. He jumped out in front of the horses. He was able to catch them and get them settled down until the man could get there and take his seat again. That was before seat belts.

Demar and I didn't stay around for the drawing. The show took place on the back street and everything from there to the river was farms. We left our drunk friend with his wrecked car, leaped the fence, and took to the fields. The wheat was about waist-high, so it was easy to hide. We hid for a while until we could sort out just what had happened and the best way to handle it. We decided to give ourselves up to our dads. Demar's dad gave the buggy folks a piece of harness that got broken and my dad paid the fine of a hundred pesos. As it turned out, those people were friends of my Dad. They lived near our ranch and we had been in their home several times. In all the excitement, I hadn't recognized them. Now guess what they had come to town for. They had two tubs of eggs in that buggy and all they asked for was; to pay for the eggs. There was no market for scrambled eggs in a tub.

It seemed that every time Demar would go to the ranch with me I would have to show off my horse a little. I would get thrown off and my horse would run away. Demar would go catch him for me. The last time he told me he sure enjoyed the way I entertained him. That was after we had returned from the war. He was in the Air Corps and I was in the Navy.

Another horse story; Demar, in later years like in high school, had a little bay horse that could hardly carry the two of us. The horse came up lame in one of his front legs. We analyzed the trouble and decided he had a sweeny. I had heard Dad talk and describe the symptom and also the cure. You throw the horse down and tie all his feet good then cut a hole in his hide just at the top of his shoulder on the lame side and put a silver peso in there. That we did and sewed it up because we sure didn't want that peso to fall out. A sweeny is where the hide grows to the meat on the shoulder blade and hurts when he moves the leg. The idea is that the peso will move down as he travels and cut the skin loose after a while and he will be OK again. We watched the peso as it did exactly that. We could feel it through the hide. The peso was in there several months, and sure enough, the horse got well and the peso was right down to the bottom of his shoulder blade. One day we were riding that little horse. We were at Romney's store, and short of money. You guessed it. Right there, with everybody wondering just what we were up to, we threw that little horse down and got our money back. He had used it long enough.

After we were in high school we got together for a goose hunt one weekend. He took Mary Farnsworth and I took Mart. We went to the Dublan Lakes. There were always lots of geese wintered there. There was a large flock on the edge of the water, but we had no cover to hide behind so we had to crawl on our bellies. I drove the car up as close as I thought was safe for them not to fly. We each had a .30--30 rifle. We left the girls at the car, and we must have crawled for an hour, very slowly, so as not to spook the geese. As we were almost in position to get a good shot, those girls jumped out of the car and started running and hollering at the geese. We already had our guns cocked, we were so close. The girls ran to where we were and sure thought it was funny. I grabbed Mart around the waist and gave her a good swinging, when a gun went off. I thought it was Demar's and I was sure giving him hell when he said, "Bill, it was your gun." Sure enough, I threw an empty shell from the chamber. Then, I did get scared. It hit the ground by Mart's foot, and as we checked, it had nicked the sole of her shoe. I have always said that was sure close, I almost had to marry her.

Tom Jones had good farm horses, but he raised one horse that was too small for a plow horse, but just right for a saddle horse. When he was a yearling, the Jones kids rode him all over town. They called him Smokey. He looked like the Smokey in the story. As the colt grew, he turned out to be a pacer. He paced stiff--legged and was almost impossible to ride. The Joneses gave him to Demar. I tried all the good words I knew to get Demar to give him to me. I couldn't buy him, no money. Demar didn't like him because he was so rough. He gave him to his cousin, Elone Farnsworth. When he was a colt, I was in the 7th grade. Elone used him for some time and also got tired of his rough movement. In 1937, the horse would have been about six years old. I was walking up the street and there came Elone on Smokey, bareback, and in that intolerable gait. We met and chatted for a few minutes when he said, "Bill, you have wanted this Smokey horse since he was a colt, do you still want him?" I sure did, and Elone slid off and handed me the reins. He said, "Just take the bridle with him." He told me he had ridden that rough thing for the last time. After about six years I finally got the horse, and that was my last year in school, so I didn't have much time to enjoy him.

I took him to the ranch and worked with him in all my spare time. In those days we had a school hike at the end of the school year. I wanted him to be ready to show off at that time. I made him afraid to even think of falling into that stiff--legged pace, and I put a running walk on him that was out of this world. I could slack the reins and he would hold that running walk all day long. I made a rope horse out of him, and he was so honest I could rope a calf and tie it without any cheaters on him at all. For the school hike I put Mart on Boogers and I rode Smokey. All the Dublan kids knew him and they couldn't believe they were seeing the same horse. I told them the horse was there all the time, it's the difference in farmer kids and cowboy kids.

I left home to work in the mines at Bisbee and while I was gone he was stolen. I didn't get to enjoy him very long. Some years later I saw him pulling a wagon. He was in that stiff-- legged pace. He was very, very poor. Just skin and bones. I turned my head and wiped away a tear.

During the school year of 1931, a fellow came to see us. An old man, white headed, with a heavy mustache. The mustache was brown from straining coffee and whatever through it. In order to eat he held it up with a finger, but to drink coffee he just let it flow through. He stayed with us for several days. His name was Kabe Adams. Dad had known him years before, no kin that they knew of. He said, "Roy, you are the closest kin I have, and while I'm here I'm going to will you my ranch and cattle." About two years later, Pancho Villa (not the bandit) stopped by our house in Dublan and told Dad that Kabe Adams was dead. The Villa Ranch was in the same area as Kabe's. Very high in the mountains of the Sierra Madres. Kabe had also told Villa that he was going to leave his outfit to Dad. Dad told Harve Taylor, later my daddy--in--law. They went to Casas Grandes, and sure enough, there was the Will. Dad told Harve that if he would help with the legal end and help get the cattle out of the mountains, he could have half what they got out of it. Kabe's ranch was in the top of the Sierra Madres, then down in a hole. It was called The Hole because of mountains on all sides and no way out except to climb to the top by trail only. It was on the Chihuahua and Sonora border, but on the Sonora side.

I was in school so missed that trip. I always wished Dad would have let me miss school to go along. Lynn, Mart's brother, got to go. Dad and Harve put a pack outfit together and some cowboys and headed for the mountains. About a week on the trail to get there. It was in Tarahumara Indian country. Turned out the ranch was in Sonora, and the Indians would not accept the papers from Chihuahua. Dad and Harve returned to Dublan. Harve had a little Model A pick up and they headed for Sonora. They had to go to Huachinera, then to Cumpas to get permits to move the cattle. That is the road that goes through the Carretas Ranch, which I became acquainted with many years later. The Cumpas town was not far from the Kabe ranch, but the mountains were so rough that only a Tarahumara Indian could go straight through. It took Dad and Harve a week to go around the mountain by car to go in from the north side. Mennell, Harve's son, went with them to drive and to repair the A truck should it give trouble. Mennell was the town auto fixer, and he was good.

With what they hoped were the right papers in their pocket, they went back to their pack outfit and up the trail they went once more. I still didn't get to go. Lynn did and I still thought how lucky he was until they returned with the cattle, and I found out how they were almost all murdered by those Tarahumara folks. Dad and Harve knew it was risky so they went well--armed with rifles and pistols. They also took the Cordada of two men which was the rural police. Traveling was by trail, and single file after they got into the mountains.

On the first trip up there they took a wrong fork in the trail. When they saw they were on the wrong side of the canyon, it was a day's ride to go back to the fork and start over. They talked it over and looked the mountain over and decided they would just go straight across to the other side of the canyon to the trail they should be on. That was a mistake. They were soon in a place where they couldn't go on down and couldn't go back up to the trail they had just left. They sure wished they had gone back to the fork to catch the right trail. They had to think and find some way to get out of their mess. The horses couldn't go down the mountain without rolling. Rolling would get them down, but horses with broken legs are no good. They tied their ropes to the saddlehorn and dallied a pine tree. One man led the horse and one gave slack with the rope as was needed. When the horse would fall down the man on the tree would hold until he was on his feet again. Then some more slack. They had to move the whole pack outfit down that way. That was half the job. Now they had to climb the other side up to the trail they should be on. They went up the mountain in reverse of going down. Tied the rope to the saddlehorn and dallied a tree uphill. As the horse took a step uphill the slack was taken up and when he fell, he was held from rolling back down the hill until he could get back on his feet. Dad and Harve never got together that they didn't reminisce about crossing that canyon. I sure wished I was there.

They made the second trip in there and they were ready to round up the cattle and head up the trail with them. About three hundred head, and single file. They still had trouble with the Indians. Those Tarahumara men had planned to keep the cattle. Dad thought maybe they had killed Kabe with that in mind. The Indians had no idea that anyone would know about Kabe's ranch and try to go after the cattle.

The cattle were in the corrals ready to start up the trail with them early the next morning. Dad made a deal with the Indians to leave a few head in the corral for them and take the rest. At daylight they turned the cattle up the trail. Dad and Harve in the lead so they could be sure and turn the herd on the right trail as they came to forks. Lynn was to bring up the rear with the Cordada. Everyone was carrying a pistol and a rifle. Dad and Harve were raised during tough times and so were armed and ready, but hoping they had satisfied those Indians. As the cattle were lined out up the trail and looked like they had things going as it should, up popped a Tarahumara in the middle of the trail and told them to hold the herd. He had a rifle and it looked like he might know how to use it. He hadn't checked the corrals to see if any cattle had been left there, but just assumed that these white men were leaving so early to try to get all the cattle. Stopping a herd of cattle on a mountain trail is like stopping traffic on the freeway in L.A. They tend to pile up.

Dad and Harve tried to tell him that the cattle were down there but he didn't believe them. They considered shooting him and going on, when they noticed that he had not come alone. There was an Indian behind every rock with a gun pointing at them. When I heard that part of the story I was sure glad I wasn't there. The only way to get from one end of the herd to the other was on foot, like those Indians traveled. The Cordada was in the rear and the trouble was in the lead. They finally convinced the Indian to send a runner back down the mountain to the corrals and count the cows left there then come back and report. That took some time. Meanwhile, they had a nervous herd on a dangerous trail. The runner returned with the right count and the Tarahumara fellows backed off. Dad said he and Harve had already chosen their targets if it had come to shooting their way out.

The rest of the drive was standard. Harve took his cows and Dad took his cows. The brand was Circle A. Dad gave one of the horses to Danny, Mart's brother. He kept two horses but they were no good. Those old mountain horses were slow and lazy. A bay and a white horse. I got the white horse, called him Chivo. For some reason that old white horse was always full of air, and every time I spurred him he would backfire. You can imagine what it sounded like when I was trying to rope a calf on him. Usually the calf outran him, and Raymon or Floyd would catch it.

A lot of things modern we didn't have while growing up in Colonia Dublan, but something we did have was good environment. We had lots of parties at the homes. Parents were good to entertain us. Every Friday night was entertainment of some kind at the church house, mostly a dance. Many of the dances were for fund raising, and they were the most fun. The ladies would bring a box lunch to be auctioned off to the highest bidder. One fellow who always made it exciting was Owen Skousen. He watched the young fellows. When he saw some one really after a box he would run the price up and wind up with the box. I was one he took after. Mart would put a mark on her lunch so I could tell it. When Owen saw me bidding, he ran my price up and he knew the young kids didn't have much finances. He would maybe run the bid up to ten pesos. He would carry Mart's lunch around for a while then come over to me and see if I would give him a peso for it. Sometimes, however, he would carry it so long I would think, that rascal is going to eat with Mart for sure this time. He never did. He was killed by lightning while hunting cows on Harve Taylor's ranch. Dublan lost a good man.

The house parties were lots of fun, especially when a new kid had joined the crowd. We always tried to break him in right. Pin a glass of water on the wall, and of course the great snipe hunt. One we played was called run sheepy run. No jokes with the sheep game, just plain kids dumb enough to run in the dark. I don't know how come we didn't have some broken legs or arms.

At grade school the thing was hockey, marbles, basketball, baseball, tops, and hopscotch. When in the eighth grade, in the spring, I organized a new game. We called it Cowboys. There was a vacant block across the street north from the school and it was a perfect place. You might say, "I took my rope to town." All the kids joined in, boys only. My top horse was Bud Taylor, a good kid. He was a fast runner and for sure my top rope horse. One of the wildest and hard to catch, was Gustavo Brown. He liked to be a wild horse, and of course I had to rope him. He was sure wild. Gustavo is the Brown that owns Rocky Point in Mexico. Not a poor boy. The game got a little too rough, however, and some of the kids went home with rope burns on their necks and the mamas didn't like that. I was told to don't bring my rope to town.

Gustavo Brown reminds me of a dog story. The dog belonged to his aunt. She was named Williams. She had a very mean dog who spent his waking hours trying and planning on how to get hold of one of my legs. She lived in a large house that I had to pass going to and from school. The Williams' yard had lots of trees and the yard fence had a very thick hedge. That old dog would sneak along inside the hedge as I was walking on the sidewalk going home. The cow barns and corrals were in behind the house. To get to them with the cows or farm equipment, there was a lane with a large lumber gate, about twenty feet wide. The old dog liked to sneak along on the inside of the thick hedge and just as we would arrive at the lumber gate he would let out with his worst growl and jump at me. The gate was between us but he always gave me a good scare. He would just scare me out of my shoes every time and that was every day. I just knew he would chew me up if he could get through the gate. The gate was always shut, but I worried anyhow.

Well, one evening I was going home and by that time I had watched the dog and had him figured out. Each time I thought I wouldn't be so scared, but every time he jumped at me at the gate I would panic. But I had also learned that the gate was always closed so there really wasn't anything to fear. The gate was not visible until I was there. It was hidden behind the hedge, but like I said, it was always kept closed. I noticed that old dog stalking me. When we got to the gate I planned to jump at him and see what he did and sure hoped he didn't jump the gate, which I was sure he could. So there sneaks the dog and I had a stupid grin on my face, because I planned on showing him that I wasn't a bit scared of him. I came to the end of the hedge and I yelled and gave a big jump to the gate. At the same exact time the dog jumped and gave his bloody growl. THE GATE WAS WIDE OPEN. That old dog was in the air and couldn't stop and I had jumped forward and couldn't stop. We didn't quite touch. That dog literally fell over backwards howling and crying and running. I never saw him again. We each pulled a bluff and I was the winner.

I have always liked wild animals. I have told how I have tried to tame them. I would catch coyotes, rabbits, birds of many kinds, but never had much luck teaching them to like me. I did raise some mallard ducks by putting the eggs under a chicken. I also put some quail eggs under a chicken, but as soon as they hatched they would run away. I think they jumped out of the shell running.

We were at the garage where Dad had work done on the car. I was paying close attention to the mechanic to see how he did the fixing. Someday, I thought, I would sure like to be that smart. One day when we were at the garage and I was sure watching El Senor Maguiness work, in came a coon and got in his way. He moved it away but it hopped up on his shoulder and checked his ears to see how well they were fastened. I was so excited about that coon that he took it off his back and handed it to me and said I could have him and take him home.

Me and that coon were friends right away. Dad didn't like the idea but finally consented to let me have him. What a mistake that was. I think the only thing that can get into more trouble than a coon is a monkey. In those days, the town put on a fair each year. I entered my coon. He drew lots of attention and won the blue ribbon. He was the only coon. He sure liked piloncillo candy and the crowd fed him a lot. As he got older he would leave and then come back after a few days but finally I guess he went to the river and found some coon friends. He left and I never saw him again. He stayed with me for several months. He sure liked to play. He would climb up a tree there in the yard to watch for me coming from school. As I would walk under the limb he was on, he would jump onto my shoulder then down and into my pockets looking for candy. I had to go without candy to feed that coon.

Most mornings Mom made mush for breakfast. Cracked wheat we got from the flour mill. There were two flour mills in Dublan. Wheat was the main crop on the farms. After she served up all the mush, she would take the kettle outside to the pump and fill it with water to soak until she had time to wash it. Our water system was a pitcher pump in the front yard. While it was soaking the coon would reach in and get the mush that was left. Scrapings, we called it. One morning I heard my coon calling for help. I don't know how he did it, but he was sitting on top of the rim of the kettle, his hands, or front feet on the rim and the bail on top of them, and his hind feet were on top of the bail. The harder he pushed to get loose, the more he pushed the bail down onto his hands. He didn't do that again.

    The first music we had at home was a record player Dad got from Mart's Dad. Harve got a radio and gave the record player to us. That has to be one of the nicest gifts a person ever gave. We enjoyed it no end. He gave us some records with it, then Bill Holmes brought us a lot of records from Chihuahua. When radio came out, the record players were no more in demand. We didn't call it a record player. We called it a Victorolla. That was not my first musical instrument, however. My first was a bugle. I made it from a cow horn. I guess I got pretty good with it. When I played it the dogs howled.

    When school was out in the spring of 1938, I went to El Paso. I stayed with Bud Taylor. His folks lived at White Spur in the Upper Valley. Bud's mother was my dad's cousin, and his dad was Mart's dad's cousin. Bud went to school at the JSA and we became very good friends. I lived with his folks while I was trying to find a job. I mowed the lawn and hoed cotton, and worked along with them. They sure treated me good. We were in the field hoeing cotton, Virgil Taylor and I working together. Virge took his shirt off and hung it on a tree at the end of the field. The next time I came to that end, I took off my shirt and hung it on the same tree. When I got my hoe, I watched Verge to see how he did it and then I came along behind chopping away. He looked back at my row after a while and quickly gave me another lesson. When they told me to chop cotton, I thought that was what they meant, and I was getting most of it. Some I missed, trying to keep up with Verge. At noon, there came Aunt Hazel with lunch and cold lemonade. When she saw me she just came unwound. Where was my shirt and why did I take it off and didn't I know any better and it was too late now anyway because you are just cooked. I said, "Virge took his shirt off so I thought that was the way to do it." She said, "Verge has skin like a Mexican and he can do that, but you don't and you can't." She took me to her house right then and doctored me. She was right. It was too late, and by night, I was well aware of it. I had been burned a little before but never like that time. My entire back was a solid blister, then a solid scab.

I watched the paper for jobs and made lots of calls. The first thing I was asked was what did I know how to do. I could ride mean horses, but no one needed a mean horse rider. I called on a help wanted add in the paper and the fellow didn't ask me anything, he just told me to come on over. Aunt Hazel rubbed my back once more and gave me the stuff she was putting on it and away I went to take on my new job. I had no idea what it was but that was no matter, I could sure do it. The man was Mr. J.V. Harris. He was in the trucking business. He had about four trucks. They were all two ton bobtails with high sides, like about five feet. In those days there was a market place in south El Paso. He had a store and warehouse there. He trucked in produce and wholesaled it from the warehouse. His home was at the foot of the Franklin Mountain, with large trees and a bunk house. The men who worked for him also got board and room when they were in El Paso. When on the road, we ate at restaurants and slept where and when we got tired. We carried a bedroll.

Now under one of those big trees was the biggest stack of onions I had ever seen. They were in sacks. Mr. Harris was walking towards those onions as he was telling me, "Now here is what your job is." He fed me then showed me how and what he wanted done with those onions. I was to dump them a sack at a time, into a hopper and sort out the rotten ones and resack the good ones. I got started that day and got the hang of it. Then the next day he left after breakfast. I didn't see him until in the evening. When he came in I was about finished with the onion job and was afraid he wouldn't give me anything else to do. He was so pleased at how fast I had done that stack of stinking things, that he called his delivery truck to come and get them. I helped load them then went to the warehouse to help unload. He took me back to his house in his car, a Terraplane. On the way, he started to ask me some questions. Now I was nervous because I knew I didn't have experience on anything. I must be truthful. He said, "Have you ever driven a truck?"

I had to think fast and be honest, "No sir, but I have driven a school bus." That was the clincher. He didn't question me anymore. I didn't tell him that I had only driven it once, and then only a few blocks. There is a very good Mexican saying; Con la boca cerrada no entra la mosca. (Keep your mouth shut and the flies can't get in). I had never had a driver's license.

The next day he took me to Canutillo and got me a commercial license to drive trucks. No questions were asked and no volunteering was done. He said, "I have a truck down at Watkins Chevrolet Agency getting a new motor. Let's go down and see if it is ready." It was. He told me to follow him and drive it to his house.

I had already driven in El Paso once. Sadie Taylor, Bud's sister, let me drive to town one day, and I turned left on a red light. I had no idea what those colors stood for. She told me. She said, "You sure don't believe in waiting for the green light, do you?"

Now there I was in the truck to take home through all those streetlights. I knew that if I should get messed up with those streets in El Paso, it would be like the time in Safford. Maybe I could find a one--armed man to help me. When I was taken to his house the first time by Aunt Hazel, the streets looked the same, but I had noticed some landmarks on the mountain, and figured I could find the place again if I had to. That was when I tested those landmarks and my sense of direction. I made it with very little trouble, and drove right into his yard just like he expected me to. To do those onions was just my board and room, but when I was a truck driver I got board and room and one dollar per day. Not a misprint. That took place about noon. We went into his house and into his office and he started counting out real money. He laid it on his desk with a road map. He marked off a trip with a man's name and address, and handed me the money. He gave me a bedroll, and told me to not go hungry, but don't eat steaks. When I got tired of driving to pull off the road and get into the bedroll. That is also when I saw my first road map. I sure didn't tell him I couldn't read it.

My destination was Dilly, Texas for a load of watermelons. In the afternoon I rolled that old truck out of his parking lot. It was a '36 model Chevy, 1 1/2 ton. I knew the direction I wanted, but I sure didn't know how to get there. I knew I must work my way down towards the river and find what looked to be the most traveled street, and turn downstream. I found it. I was finally out of town and on my way, and the truck was sure purring along fine. About sixty miles and the road made a left turn. That was the last I saw of the Rio Grande for a while. I rolled through Sierra Blanca with daylight to spare. About halfway between Sierra Blanca and Van Horn, that old truck came to a sudden death. I got it stopped on the shoulder so other cars could go by. My mechanic experience was less than my trucking experience. Now you get an idea of what I was up against. I found a few tools in the truck, and I decided somehow that it wasn't getting fuel. It had to be the carburetor. I took it untogether and couldn't find any dirt or grasshoppers, so I put it back together and back on the truck. By that time the sun had gone over the hill, headed for China.

I couldn't just sit there, I had to get going for those watermelons. Along came a larger truck with a large tank on it. Not a semi, as they were still not on the road, except specials. The old boy stopped and listened to me, then told me he had a rope he would tie onto my truck and pull me into Van Horn. The rope was about one inch in diameter and about a hundred feet long. He tied it onto my truck and left me back about fifty feet, and away we went. In those days, about forty--five or fifty MPH was high speed. It wasn't long before I had used up all my braking power to keep from running a wheel over the rope so I put the transmission in high gear and held the clutch in until I needed to slow down. That way when my brakes faded I could still slow my truck. Then it started raining, and I was just far enough behind to catch all the stuff his truck was throwing at me. I couldn't see the road, and my battery was going dead. I was trying to get him to stop and turn me loose. I used up my horn, my lights, my brakes, and couldn't even slow him down. I found that with it in gear and the wipers on I could let the clutch out and the wipers would work. They were vacuum type.

Then the worst part of all. I got sleepy, and just could not keep my eyes open. When my windshield was so dirty I couldn't see his tail lights I would let the clutch out for a couple of wiper swipes, and line up behind him again. I kept running off the shoulder of the highway into the ditch, but each time he would jerk me back up on the road. I would wake up for a bit and try to follow those taillights some more. I was at the end of my rope and couldn't turn it loose. He was towing me so fast that the only gear I could get was the high gear. When we arrived in

Van Horn, he came back to my truck and took his rope off. I told him thanks. I have no idea who he was or where he was going. He had pulled me to a little garage. I slept in my cab.

The next morning a fellow showed up at the garage and sure enough, my trouble was fuel, but the fuel pump rather than the carburetor. He took the fuel pump apart and I watched him close. Two little check valves in there. One of them had slipped the spring out from under the seat. He put it back in place, and I was on the road again.

Crossing the Pecos in those days was exciting. The road went all the way to the bottom of the gorge and the bridge was just over the water in the river. From there I could see where it met the Rio Grande. I went through Del Rio, Eagle Pass, and then across to Dilly. Dilly is halfway from Laredo to San Antonio. I arrived in Dilly the next morning. I found the farm and man I was looking for. We drove to the field. He put a man in my truck to catch the melons and stack them. I had about a foot of straw in the bed that was used to cushion the melons. As they were stacked, straw was put between them. I drove along the rows slowly and men tossed melons from both sides. Sure kept the stacker busy. When my truck was loaded we went back to the farmhouse. The women had dinner ready and just the men sat at the table and those gals served us. That was one great feast and I was hungry. I don't know how many chickens I must have eaten. All loaded and I was sure not hungry so was ready to head back to El Paso. I pulled into a gas station there in Dilly to top my fuel tanks before leaving. As I pulled away from the station, I was all of a sudden aware of the peddle to the metal and my truck was not moving. I hopped out and checked for fuel in the carburetor. None. Out came my few tools and off came the fuel pump. I wasn't surprised to see that spring had squirmed out again. I was able to get a new pump there and that solved my fuel experience.

I got my load to El Paso and J V was so pleased with me, he took me in the house and his wife fed me some of her very good cooking. He told me to get a shower and go to bed while he took my load to the market. My truck was unloaded and serviced for the next trip. That evening I was on the road to Dilly again, but a different farm. That time I was in tune with the country and knew what to expect in the way of service stations and restaurants. I got my load and was on my way back to El Paso.

When I crossed the Pecos I used my lowest gear going down and also for the climb up the other side. Where I crossed the Pecos River it was a very deep gorge. The road was carved from the rock walls down to the bottom, then a bridge across the channel. Today there is a high bridge across the top of the gorge. The old road is used for a boat ramp to get into the Amistad Lake. The old bridge is a bunch of feet under water.

I was almost to the top of the Pecos Gorge with my load on my return trip when I had an overheating problem. The fan belt was slipping. I tightened it, but it was cooked and ruined. I topped out about the time the belt left me for good. I had some ropes that I used to tie the canvas cover over the load with. I rigged a rope belt and used the last of my water and slowly I went. I carried a jug of water for that sort of thing. I remembered a windmill not too far ahead. When I was even with it I took my jug for water, about a fourth of a mile from the road. Three trips and my radiator was full and cool and my jug was full. I didn't go far, however, my rope belt wasn't doing too good. A truck driver came along with a spare belt. I bought it from him. I was soon on the road again.

When I arrived in El Paso that time, one of the other drivers was there. He was driving a new 1938 Chevy truck. He had been in some mud in the field where he loaded melons and most of it was in the floor of his truck. J V looked my truck over, then looked over the '38 truck, and turned to the two of us and said, "You boys trade trucks." The other driver was pouty, but I was sure glad to have the new truck. For sure I kept the floor clean.

With the dollar per day I was sure saving money. I had my eyes tested and got glasses, and that helped me a lot. I knew Mart was coming to El Paso soon, so I bought the glasses on credit. They cost me ten dollars. I bought her a watch with my money. She had it for many years. I think maybe she still has it. I paid the glasses off per agreement, and I used Mr. Seagle for reference for many years when I was trying to get a credit record built up enough to do me some good. After we moved to El Paso, in 1950 I went to him for glasses. He still had my record and remembered me.

Mart came to El Paso per plan. She stayed with her brother, Roy. I guess you know I was sure enough in tall cotton when I drove up to see her in my big truck. I told J V that I wanted to go see my girl and he understood. We went to a movie, that's all we could afford, then I had to hit the road again.

I hauled melons from the Dilly and Bradey Texas area until the season was over in that area. I sent to Dublan for LaSelle to come and work with me. He made the last trip to Texas with me then we started hauling from California. We drove day and night and sure hauled a lot of melons. We picked up some at Yuma and some at El Centro. We drove the dessert at night because the truck would overheat in the daytime. No sleepers on trucks in those days. LaSelle and I took turns driving. We rolled our bed out on top of the cab. The one sleeping there tied himself to the truck bed with a rope to be sure and not fall of in case of sleep walking. The truck bed was higher than the cab.

I had to get to the California field in time for the workers to load me out before 10:00 AM. It was so hot they quit at 10:00 AM then went back about two hours before sundown. One trip we tried to make the morning shift but missed it. LaSelle and I spent the hottest day of our lives in the field under a large tree. There was a canal of water close. We spent most of the day in the water. That was in El Centro.

It was night when we went through Yuma with the load of melons. Somewhere between Yuma and the mountain pass, I met a car on a curve on my side of the road. He didn't give an inch. I put my right wheels on the shoulder. The shoulder was soft sand. The sand stalled the right front wheel and I did a ninety--degree turn. Almost turned over. The truck seemed like it stayed up on the left wheels for minutes trying to make up its mind to go on over or settle on all fours again. When LaSelle and I got out and did a walk around, we found some of our watermelons had poured out on the ground. The only damage was a bent tie rod. We went back to Yuma and slept in the park that night and we sure didn't need our bedroll to keep us warm.

The last trip I made was to El Centro, CA. J V told me to stop in Mesilla Park, NM, on the return trip and sell melons from the back of the truck rather than going on into El Paso. In those days there were large cottonwood trees just south of the train station. We parked under one of them for about three days. We slept in the cab. One night it rained. The next morning we were sitting in a lake. I called J V and told him. He told me to send LaSelle to El Paso. For me to take the load to Capitan, NM, and sell them to the veteran's hospital.

A freight train was sitting there about to leave south and I told LaSelle to hop on it. He did. I was about ready to leave for Capitan when he came back all skinned up. He told me a fellow with a stick came along and knocked him off the train. The train was already moving pretty fast.

He got in with me and we took off for Capitan. He was driving. In 1938, the road was oiled over the Organ pass and down the east side to the bottom of the mountain, then just a bladed road along the edge of the white sands and on to Alamogordo. Not even graded. The road over the pass was so narrow it didn't have a center stripe. We topped the pass and started down the east side. It was quickly plain that we were in too high a gear and the brakes were going fast. Instead of using the last of the brakes to get slow enough to get a lower gear, he tried to downshift and lost it. I mean our speed was quickly breaking the law, and not a cop around to stop us and give us a ticket. I told him not to panic, stay in there and drive that thing to the bottom. Our speed was increasing fast when we went around an outside curve and down there on the next inside curve was a dump truck across the road filling a washout from the rain the night before. The dump bed was up in the air and he was starting to let it down. We had a choice of hitting him broadside or going down the side of the mountain. Either way we lose. I told LaSelle to stay in the road and he did. The truck driver got his load dumped and pulled forward as we arrived, and there was just room for us to zip by behind him. I don't know if the dump truck driver ever saw us. By that time we were in one hell of a hurry. LaSelle did a perfect job of handling our truck. We were going so fast that we were out in the flat country and almost to the white sands by the time we could get stopped. When we rounded the last canyon, the road was fairly straight, so all we had to do was stay calm and hold on. When we finally came to a stop, we both fell out and met each other at the front of the truck and we did some handshaking and abrasando. That was close enough to keep us jittery for a long time. I thanked him for staying put and not trying to jump. One runaway truck is enough for a lifetime.

We delivered our load in Capitan then went back to El Paso. I was walking on one of the streets downtown when who drove by but uncle Bill. He saw me and stopped to talk. First time I had talked to him since he bought the Benton Ranch at Cerro En Medio. He asked what I was doing and would I like to go to the ranch and work for him? I put my summer at Barranca with him on the back burner and told him yes. He told me what day he would pick me up at our ranch at Pajarito and for me to be ready. I quit my trucking job and went back home to the ranch to be ready when he came by. Sure enough, I saw the dust of his car on the day he had told me. I had my few things packed and ready to go make him a good hand. He drove up, and Dad and I met him at the gate so he wouldn't have to wait. Dad was telling me to work hard and make him a good hand, when I heard Bill telling me that he had changed his mind and wouldn't need me right then.

I sure felt well--stomped, once more. I was very upset because he had cost me my trucking job in El Paso. I was on the Jeffery fall roundup a few months later and he came by. He came over to me and told me that he had a job for me then and sure needed me. I told him thanks, but no I wouldn't go. He went to Dad and asked him to make me go work for him. Dad told me but said, "I'm not going to do that." I told Dad that I already knew he wasn't going to do that. I had already decided to go back to the mines in Bisbee.

In 1938, I worked on our ranch at the Pajarito. I had to stay home until the school year was out because I wanted to get my diploma with the class. I wished later that I had gone to school the full year even though I had enough credits to graduate in three and a half years. Then to El Paso and the truck driving job. Back to our ranch with the idea of going to work for Bill. By that time it was fall roundup time. Dad and I worked through the roundup with the Jefferys. When that was over, I packed my go--forth satchel and went to Bisbee.

8

Duncan

Duncan, Arizona is where Mom's family came to when they left Texas to start a new life. That was about 1916. Over the years they all married and left for other parts, except Mattie. She was younger than Mom. She married Warner Foote. He worked for the state highway department, and later he worked in Morenci, Az, when the copper mines opened up again after the big depression layoffs in the 1920's. Warner was one of the best men I ever knew. He was honest, a hard worker, and good to me. When we lived at Klondyke, we visited them once in a while, when we lived at Columbus we visited them once in a while, so when I was a freshman in high school, I went to live with them and attended school in Duncan. That was school year 1934--35. They treated me good and I learned to love them dearly. I was fourteen. Mom and Dad hadn't ever been out of sight before, so it was a new test for me. Those were times of no money. Dad paid Mattie ten dollars a month for my board and room. He would send me the ten dollars to give to her, and once in a while, when he could, he would put an extra dollar in there for me.

I had one pair of shoes, made in Mexico and so not the best. The soles soon wore through to my feet. I made a cardboard insole each day. Got along pretty good as long as I could stay out of the bullheads. I never told Mom and Dad. I felt lucky to be in school. When I went home for

Christmas, and they saw my shoes, Dad told me to go to the store and get the best shoes they had. I did, and they sure felt good.

Mattie lived between Duncan and Clifton. We rode a school bus to Duncan. The driver was Carl Duncan, we all liked him. Mattie's kids at that time were Jessie, Bobby, Louise, Sonny, and Harold. Jessie being the oldest, but younger than me. One grade behind me in school. They are dear cousins to me. They all treated me like one of the family. I felt like I pretty well earned my way, because I did the milking, wood cutting and wood hauling. They lived on the Gila River with about thirty acres of land. The land was full of mesquite trees and that was where I cut the wood for cooking and heating. I would take the wheelbarrow to haul the wood and put a rope around me and pull Sonny and Harold in their little wagon. Maybe we would take a lunch and to the woods we would go. Harold died the next year, he was my little buddy. Sonny always talks about when I lived with them, and what we did. When you take a country kid and put him all of a sudden in a place like Duncan, he sure had to pay attention and learn fast, or what he doesn't know will be found out, and that is bad. My first lesson was in the rest room. I just sort of stood around until I could see how all those things worked. All I had ever seen was a little house sitting over a hole in the ground. I think the worst thing you can do is take or send a cowboy kid to town.

That hurdle accomplished, I was a big kid and sure looked like good football potential, at least something for the team to practice on. Now I had heard of football but had never seen it. I played basketball, and if it was a ball it had to be fun. To the change room I went. I watched how those guys put on all that stuff, and managed to get mine on and most of it turned the right direction. I fell in with the players and down the hill we all went to the field. The school is on the side of a hill so as to be above flood stage of the Gila River. The first thing we got was a pep talk. That made my suit fit a little better, because now I was sure I was in the right place. Now get lined up there, two lines looking at each other, bend over and look at the fellow in front of you. I did, and about that time someone said something. I never did know what it was. Well sir, that son--of--a--bitch I was looking at hit me on the head and dominoed my bones all the way to the other end. Down I went and he was standing over me I guess to knock me down again if I was stupid enough to get up. I hit a rooster on the head with a stick one time and he acted like I felt. They started putting the line up again but my spot was empty. I was on my way to the change room. Coach Bricky sent one of his top players to the change room to bring me back. I told him I had done my last playing by football rules. If he took me back it would be by my rules.

With that behind me I could settle down to books. They had a good library and I sure used it. That was new to me also. I got my subjects lined up and one of them was Spanish. The first day of class Miss Eddins talked to us about what it was all about, then ran off a few words in Spanish. She knew we didn't understand what she said but by the end of the year we would. That was what it was all about. I looked around the room. I thought now is my chance to get in with those kids. I raised my hand, and told her what she had said. So she just tried me on for size. For the beginner's class, I did real good. She told me to report to Spanish II. She said she would give me two credits if I could handle Spanish II. I had two years of Spanish in grade school but we didn't get into conjugating of verbs, and that was eating me up in Spanish II.

Some time during the school year each class gave a program on the stage to the entire assembly. The turn was coming up for the Spanish class to entertain. Miss Eddins came to me and said, "Bill, if you will do me a bull fight that goes over good, I'll give you straight A's." Now the only bull fight I had ever seen, was when two old bulls wanted to make love to the same cow, and that was not what she had in mind. I asked if Bill Bass could help me. Yes, and he would have A's also. Bill lived about a mile down the river from me. We rode the same school bus and were good friends. It was assumed that because I came from Mexico that I knew about bull fights and could sing Rancho Grande.

We started looking for information on bull fighting and found muy poquito so we put our imagination to work. There was an unused woodworking shop in the basement of the school. We were given the keys. We made a bull. The head faced forward with big horns, and a two by four was fastened to the head to extend back over the back of the fellow who was to be the bull. With a blanket over him he looked pretty good. We made a place on top of the two by four to stick the sword into when it was time to kill the bull. The sword would stand up and we thought would look pretty good. We put a mark on the blanket where the sword spot was. We also made a horse for the picador to ride. The picador actually ran along side the horse but he was up wind from the audience so they couldn't tell but what he was riding. We talked two fellows into helping us, one to be the horse and one to be the bull. Bill Bass to be the picador and I the matador. After all, I was in charge. For the picador we had some ribbons on pins. Bill would run by the bull and hang a flag on him. I ran the cape around quite a bit. I was a little concerned that the bull kid might not play by the rules and decide to run over me. The show was supposed to last a whole period. After we had choused the bull for some time, he charged me and said he was sure getting tired of this, and for me to kill him and get it over with. The next charge I told him to make his stance and come at me, which he did. The mark on the blanket where I was supposed to stick the sword had shifted. I wasn't ready for what happened next, but I saw real quick that I was no longer in charge. The bull boy came out from under the blanket, threw the bull parts on the stage and said, "Damn you, you missed the hole." And at the same time I said, "... and damn you, you ruined my show." That student body just went loco. They thought it was all planned, and they tried all they could for us to do it again. We quit while we were ahead. I got my A's, and two credits. I learned more about bull fights than I did about Spanish.

When spring came along and the weather was nice, there were several of us who would use the last period to go down the hill and sit or lay in the grass at the edge of the football field. One was a good friend, Ellsworth Hill. His parents owned a ranch between Clifton and Alpine, which they called The Blues. For those days he wasn't a poor boy, and some times he would drive his mother's car to school. A Buick Roadmaster. He lived at Gutherie about five miles down the river from me. There were four of us together a lot; Jim Forehand, Bill Bass, and Ellsworth Hill. Jim lived across the Gila River from me. That day Ellsworth, we called him Toughy, said, "Let's see how fast that old Buick will go around the track and not jump it." The track went around the football field. He didn't get any passengers so he went by himself. They were practicing football out in the center. He made one round before anyone could believe what they were seeing, then he made the second round before they could put their thoughts together, but as he was about halfway into the third round he saw the coach waving for him to stop. Instead of stopping, he turned off the field and ran his car up to the sheds where the school busses were parked. He came walking back to where we were and grinning, sure funny. Coach Bricky took him by the arm and up the hill to the school building they went. About twenty minutes later he joined us on the lawn again. He was holding his back side with both hands. He said, "I won't ever do that again. I just learned that damn Townsend keeps a two foot rubber hose for when he gets mad." Townsend was the principal.

I have told that Trav Davis bought the Rafter G Ranch when we left there and moved to Klondyke. It is across the canyon from Mattie's, and I learned to like Trav real well. He was married to Warner's sister.

That year at Duncan was the first time in my life I was away from my horse and saddle. It was a whole new ball game for me. I had never been to dances where people got drunk in the name of having fun. Most of the entertainment sure looked stupid to me. Ellsworth and Bill were both heavy drinkers. Jim was like me, we could have fun without getting drunk. I look back now and I know they were both alcoholics. At that time I thought they did it because they thought it made them look tall. When I went to Duncan I didn't know that most of those people were from Mexico, and related to everyone I knew. I didn't know that the Foote family was Mormons. I did know I had some relatives in Virden. The Merrill families.

At Christmas time, Joe Memmott from Dublan went to Duncan to visit a Lunt family and Dad asked him if I could ride home with him. Mom and Dad wrote to me real often, and when I received the letter telling me of my ride home I thought the days would never pass. They finally did and I was sure glad to be home. The first thing I asked Dad for was the car so I could go to town and see Mart. She was glad to see me. Those holidays went by so fast, I wasn't near ready to go back to Duncan. During the Christmas holidays there were lots of dances and parties. Mart and I had lots of fun those few days. I sure wished I was going to the JSA instead of back to Duncan.

We had known the Karr family in Columbus. They did like we did, lived in Columbus for school and on the ranch in the summer. Only our school was in Dublan rather than Columbus. Their ranch was in the mountains southeast of Carretas. It was getting time for me to return to Duncan and I still didn't have a way to go, when John Karr and his wife stopped at our ranch to see us. They had been to Casas Grandes and were on their way back to their ranch. In the chatting, they told us they were going to Deming in three days and would be glad to take me with them. I went to their ranch. It was more like an Hacienda. Since I had a couple of days to kill there I took a hike up in the mountains, which were close. I only went one day, however, because it looked like it was too crowded for me and the bears. I saw lots of bear sign, and fresh. I didn't know anything about bears and I thought that was not the best time to learn.

They dropped me at the Greyhound in Deming and I ran in and bought a ticket to Duncan. I didn't ask any questions and so I didn't get any answers. I jumped on the first hound that came along going west. At Lordsburg I found out it was not going to Duncan, so I got off in Lordsburg. Now there is a town I didn't like then and still don't. A Duncan bus didn't come along until the next day. I spent the night at the Hollen Hotel. When I arrived in Duncan the next day it had been flooded from the Gila River. I had to take my shoes off and wade to the bridge. I walked across the river and hoped for a ride on down to Mattie's. People were good to help kids so I wasn't there long. Mattie said she thought maybe I wouldn't come back. I started and I was going to finish.

Warner bought a new 1935 Ford and it sure was nice. When school was out, Mattie and kids and Grandma took me home to Dublan. Dad met us in Columbus. I drove Dad's car, a model A pickup and Dad drove Mattie's car. Jessie rode with me. I have told about the drought of 1934--35. On our trip from Columbus to Dublan was when it started raining, and looked like it would never quit. There was lots of water and mud and we enjoyed it all. My brother, Sam, was born while they were there. They were there about two weeks, then Dad and I took them back to Columbus. That closed my Duncan schooling. I learned a lot by being in such a different environment, but I was ready to go to the JSA and be with the kids I was raised with and knew so well. And of course my girlfriend, Martha Taylor, was the magnet for sure that made the JSA so special.

9

Mangum

This is the Mangum story. I lived with them off and on for several years. I learned a lot from them. Rather than trying to make cowboys out of them, they made a town boy out of me. This is one fine family. Dez, their father, Tonie, their mother, Helen, Betty, and Jane, their sisters. And now this, about Owen and Ralph. Dez worked in the mines in Mexico, and sent the family to Dublan for school. The first getting acquainted with them was in the eighth grade. They had been in the Dublan school for a while but I hadn't paid any attention to them. They were nice kids and got along well with the crowd, but were still new kids and still hadn't been tested out real good. One of Dad's cousins, Gladis Gonzalez, moved to Dublan. She had two little kids. The Whipple house was divided into two apartments. The cousin in one and the Mangums in the other. The cousin sent word to me at school to come and see her after school. I did. She was having trouble with those Mangum boys because they were teasing her little kids. She wanted me to go out in the yard and whip them and teach them to behave. Now there is no way one guy can whip two, only in the western movies, and I hadn't seen any of those yet. I went out in the yard at her place and hunted up these two ornery kids, and I told them what I was suppose to do. They knew and I knew it would never happen. After we talked some, they said all they wanted was to be friends with the little kids. We got together with the little kids and the mama cousin, and we all agreed to be friends. My friendship with the Mangum boys started then, and has continued all our lives.

Our next get together was in high school. We were sophomores. Their dad was still working in the mines in Mexico. That school year their mother stayed with their dad and sent them to board in Colonia Juarez. They lived at the Harper Hotel. I had lunch there every day so we were together a lot. I rode the school bus from Dublan to Colonia Juarez every day. I would go to their hotel to get ready for the dance on Friday nights. The JSA always had a school dance on Friday night.

The next year their mother and dad moved to Colonia Juarez and I lived with them to go to school. I learned to love that family dearly. They didn't treat me like a boarder. They made me one of them. When their mother kissed them, she kissed me also, and she did that the rest of her life. Their dad treated me the same way. They took me fishing and hunting or whatever they were doing. If they took a trip, they took me along. Their dad had quit the mines and was making his income in other ways.

The Mangums had a stake--body truck they used for hauling anything for anyone who had something to haul. Owen used it to haul the school kids on hikes or picnics or whatever we were up to. A fellow named Tom Berkley bought the Casa Piedra Ranch. A beautiful place. It was up a big canyon and at the foot of the large mountain range about thirty miles north of Colonia Juarez, by crow. Mr. Berkley's niece, and her daughter from Oklahoma soon joined him there. The daughter, Marylee, boarded in Dublan, and rode the bus to the JSA. She was in my age group. Marylee also lived at the Mangum's part of the year.

The niece, Mrs. Daniels, decided Mr. Berkley's ranch was ideal to make into a dude ranch, so she went to work on it. The kitchen and dining room were about fifty yards down the hill from the rest. There were several bedrooms and a large living room for dudes. The bunk house was separate from those. I kept hearing about their dude ranch because she came to town on weekends and took Marylee to the ranch. When it came time for the grand opening, or the big fiesta, she asked me to go to the ranch and help to entertain the guests. She set the fiesta on a Sunday so most of the kids of my crowd were canceled out. Woodrow

Longhurst was Marylee's boy friend. He and I went home with them to the ranch after the Friday--night dance. That gave us Saturday to sort of get in mind what we would do to entertain the crowd. When we were planning for the grand opening I had told Mrs. Daniels to have Tom round up a bunch of wild horses and we would do some bronco riding. Saturday morning I went down to the corral to see what old Tom had rounded up. Sure enough, he had a bunch of mean looking broomtails ready for the show.

Tom loaned Woodrow and me each a .30--30 rifle and a couple of nice horses Saturday morning. Up the mountain we went to get a deer. The brush and timber was thick on the mountain, but shortly we spotted a couple of whitetail bucks. Off the horses real easy, rifles up, we could just see their heads, and pow. Those two deer just dropped out of sight. I looked at him and he looked at me. I said, "Well, we didn't have much chance in so much brush anyhow."

We went over to the spot and there the deer was, shot in the neck. "You got him!" he said in his excitement.

"Why do you say I got him when we both shot at him?" I asked. "I didn't shoot," he replied.

He threw out a loaded shell and I threw out an empty. Now to get the deer home. The horses we were riding would have no part of a dead deer. Back down the mountain to the ranch house we went. Tom told us to put a saddle on a blue horse that was there in the corral. He said he was sure gentle to carry a deer on. With Old Blue in tow we went back up the mountain to get our deer. We had tied a handkerchief on a tree so we could find the spot.

Sure enough, Old Blue stood real still for us to put the deer on him. Now I was good at tying things so I took over securing the deer to the saddle. The mountain was real steep with lots of brush and trees. When we put the deer on Old Blue he must have had his nose up wind, because when we turned him around and started to mount our horses, he jerked loose from me and was gone, downhill. He was bucking and having a fit like he was crazy. After a few jumps he was out of sight because the timber was so thick, but we could hear him going down the mountain. We were in shock, but thought, he would go to the ranch house so we would follow him. We were barely mounted up when there came Old Blue back up the hill still in a hurry, but the deer was gone. He ran up to us and stopped. He sure was puffing. We went down the hill to find the deer and I would sure tie it better next time. We hunted and hunted and we couldn't find the deer. We went to the starting point and followed Old Blue's tracks and made the complete circle that he made. We still didn't find the deer. Once more at the starting point and we followed the tracks closer and slower. We came to a tree and noticed that Old Blue hadn't gone around it, but had jumped it. There was our deer up in the tree. The mountain was very steep was the reason he could jump over the tree. I climbed up in the tree and pulled the deer down. It was a large cedar about ten feet high. I'm sure he didn't jump over the top. He jumped through it. I don't know why he didn't break his legs when he landed over the tree. I was sure glad the deer has been riding him instead of me. Old Blue was nervous and wouldn't let us put the deer on him again. So we put a blindfold on him and put the deer up there once more with him not seeing us do it. I tied it all the ways I knew and got on my horse. I snubbed Old Blue's nose tight to my saddlehorn and told Woodrow to pull the blind off. He went crazy again, but I was ready. Now that I knew what he would do, I could handle him. Each time he would go into a fit I would spin him. I had his chin snubbed to my saddlehorn, and that put me looking right into his eye balls. A horse can't do much with his chin up, and I sure wasn't going to let it down. He sure gave me a mean eye all the way down the mountain. Tom couldn't believe the old pony was so silly. We roasted and ate most of that whitetail deer over the fire in the fireplace that night.

   Sunday morning and we were up and ready for people to start arrivng. Woodrow and I each caught a horse for the day. Since it was early, we took a ride up one of the canyons to look around. The horse I caught was spooky and Tom told me to watch him. He enjoyed getting out from under riders. Sure enough he tried, but we stayed partners. Up that canyon we ran onto a wild burro. To me, wild means untamed for riding or petting. That burro came at us with his ears back and his mouth open and braying. I think our mounts were about as scared as we were. We ran out of his way, then teased him some to see how serious he was about biting and he would charge every time. That was not a good place to play, so we went back to the ranch house. We asked Tom about the burro and he told us to not mess with him because he would sure bite.

We tied our horses to the hitch rack out front and mingled with the crowd that was starting to gather. The barbecue was coming along fine. Sunday morning we had watched the fellow in charge of it checking it out. The barbecue was being done across the canyon and the aroma was sure in the air. A whole beef, and a big one. Something many people have never seen, is a real barbecue.

About ten o'clock, Owen and Ralph drove up in their truck with standing room only. Mostly they were our crowd from Dublan and Juarez and Sunday yet. Floyd Walser was one of them. He was a great hiker. He and some of the guests went for a foot hike up the canyon. I told him about the burro, and to sure stay away from him. When the hikers returned, they told me about the burro, and yes, he would bite. He bit Floyd on the chest. Walser went to El Paso for an operation on his burro bite.

Before I could get all the dangers pointed out to my friends, Ralph had untied my horse and climbed on him. I called to him to get off the horse real easy like, but he paid me no mind and rode him for a few minutes then back to the hitch post. He got off and tied him up. I said, "Ralph, that horse knows a green horn when he has one on his back, he has been bucking with me all morning."

At about 11:30 it was time to open the barbecue pit. That barbecue aroma filled the air and the guests all drifted to it. It was across the canyon from the buildings. Lots of food and lots of drinks. Soft drinks for us Mormonies, but lots of beer for those guests who wanted it, and some did. It sort of turned into two crowds. One of the Saenz fellows got to showing off with his pistol and shot one of his buddies in the leg. Just a meat shot in the calf, so the party went on. They were the beer drinkers. There were also Mariachis, and good music they made.

Dinner was over and everyone was having a good time. It was time for my part of the entertainment. A corral full of wild horses and plenty of vaqueros to put on a good show. Anyone in the crowd could ride if he wanted, and some did. There was a paint horse in there. Tom told me that he was a real bucker, so I told the vaqueros to leave him for me.

The vaqueros were the ranch hands. After a few rides, they caught old Paint. The crowd knew I had reserved him for myself. When they roped him, he didn't have a fit, he just behaved as a good bronco should. When they had him ready I climbed on with a leg boost from one of the vaqueros. When they turned old Paint loose he went berserk. He folded himself up with his four feet together and his head down there among them. He jumped high and used all four corners, north, south, east, and west. He was the only horse I ever rode that squalled when he bucked. He sounded like a mad bull. The riding was all done in the corral, no pickup man. Just ride until he quits bucking and step off. I did and the crowd went wild. I stole the show that day. That horse put on the best show of any horse I had ever ridden and was the easiest to ride. He bucked limber--legged like a mule. He was so easy to ride I even fanned him with my hat after a few jumps. He jumped high, but he didn't sunfish. Mrs. Daniels told me I had sure helped make the day a success and she thanked me a bunch. I think that was her first and last dudes.

That evening I rode home with the Mangums. I had enough fiesta to last me for some time. That grand opening was the only Dudes she ever had at the ranch. Her uncle Tom sold the ranch and left Mexico. She married Herbert Jeffery, who was our ranch neighbor. Mangums were living in Colonia Juarez because Dez had saved some money and decided to leave the mines and try his hand in the cow business. The cow business can get expensive quick when you are working on a falling market. There is more to the story than the market, but I am not qualified to tell that part of it. Some wrong partners. In the spring of 1937, Dez had all he could stand and something drastic had to be done. He and Owen went to Bisbee to work in the mines and Tonie kept things together in Juarez until school was out.

Joe Ireland was a neighbor of the Mangum's. One morning he told me he was going to the mountains to Pacheco and asked if I would like to go along. I had never been to any of the mountain colonies, so yes, I would enjoy the trip. He was driving a Model A. All Model A Fords had wire spoke wheels. From Colonia Juarez we started climbing to the mountains because Juarez is right at the foot of the high mountain range called the Sierra Madre. Very interesting. Up to the top then down into canyons. Follow the canyons for some miles then top out again, then down in the next canyon, but always going up. Pacheco is not at the highest part of the mountains, maybe about halfway. Colonia Garcia is at the top and on a large mesa. Pacheco is in a bowl. We were driving up a large canyon and went by a ranch house. A few horses and cattle lazying around the place and a bunch of mixed breed type dogs. Now those were real watch dogs. They watched us as we approached the ranchito then they chased us for half a mile up the road. They were barking like crazy and the hair was standing up on their shoulders. Sure enough bravo. Joe said, "On the way back this evening, I'll show you how to teach those dogs not to chase cars and I'll decrease their population at the same time."

We spent a nice day in Pacheco. On our way back down the mountain as we were getting near the ranchito where all those dogs were he stopped and laced a gunny sack into the wire spokes of each front wheel. On the way up, I had noticed that the dogs wanted to bite the front wheels. As we drove by the ranchito there came the dogs. I would hear a yelp and a dog would go spinning and not get up. They would bite those sacks and it would ring their necks. Sure did cut down on that ranchito's dog production. About thirty years later I was up that way. Some kids ran out to the road when they saw us coming and of course some adults also. My first thought was, "I hope they don't recognize me." We stopped to chat with them. They had an olla (Indian pottery) they had dug from an Indian village there in the canyon. I bought it and gave it to Gladys Nichols. There were four vehicles in the group. Sid Adams, Don Nichols, L C Ballard, and me, and our wives. They had wanted to take a rough camping trip and I told them to follow me. It was a week they all remembered.

After Dez and Owen went to Bisbee, and things seemed to be going fine Mrs. Mangum said she was not feeling well. By the weekend she was sure enough sick. She said to Ralph and me, "Boys, you have just got to get me to Casas Grandes to a doctor." Dez and Owen had taken the car so we were a foot. There was a family a few blocks away that had a Model T pickup. Ralph knew them and maybe they were friends of Mr. Mangum. Ralph and I went to see those people. May we borrow the T Model? We had no idea how to drive it, but we soon learned. I had watched Dad drive one when we lived at Klondyke. I would have been maybe four at the time. That kind of knowledge put me in the driver's seat and Ralph turned the crank. Before the day was over I wished that little T car would have never started. We drove it back to the Mangum house and helped Tonie with her things and helped her into the little car. No top, and summer was not just around the corner but was already there in full sunshine. It was just a few days before school was out.

In those days, one entered and left Colonia Juarez by way of the dugway. Colonia Juarez is in a narrow valley on the Verde River and in the mountains. The early Mormon settlers dug a road off the mountain, and down to the valley, thus the name dugway. We were leaving Juarez, and the last house before starting up the dugway was the Hatch place. Out in the front yard, as we were motoring by, was Bud Taylor from El Paso. He lived with the Hatches to do his senior year at the JSA. We stopped for a small chat. He told us he knew about Model T cars. Before he could tell us all he knew about Model T cars we had him in the driver seat and up the dugway we putt putt. Ralph and I were in the little truck box on the back. About halfway up the dugway we lost all forward motion. Out hopped the reserve horsepower and we pushed. It was still early morning so not too hot yet. With Bud's knowledge about T Fords and mine and Ralph's shoulders we topped out. I mean we got to the top of the first hill of our trip. Ralph and I reclaimed our seats on the run. There was one more hill to help it up, but not so steep. Then all hell broke loose. We started having flat tires. I have never seen so many flats on one little car in my life. However, I did remember that Dad had lots of flats on his T model at Klondyke. It was late in the evening when we arrived at Casas. About eighteen miles. Mrs. Mangum did not go to the doctor. She felt fine. We never knew which was the cure, the ride or the hot sun with no shade. Anyhow, she had a full day of both.

We drove that little car to Dublan to Demar Cardon's home. Maybe he could help us with those tires so we could get it back to Juarez and to its owner. Demar had an idea which we welcomed because Ralph and I had run out of ideas. He went in his house and out he came with a quilt. His mama was not home. We cut it in strips and stuffed it in the tire and forced it on the wheel. Sounds stupid? It looked pretty good, but I had no intention of heading to Juarez with it. We took a test run down the street. The tire came off and threw rags in every direction. We parked it at Demar's house and Ralph hired someone to haul it back to Juarez. Mrs. Mangum caught a ride home with someone that same evening since she felt so good and Ralph and I found a way back to Juarez the next day.

Ray Taylor had just bought a large new truck. He lived in Safford. Dez hired him to go to Juarez and move the family to Bisbee when school was out. They invited me to go with them. I talked it over with Dad and it seemed a good thing. I hoped I could get a job for the summer in the mines. One thing Dad knew was that I was in good company. We left Juarez early one morning and crossed into the US at the Berrendo Port--of--Entry. From there, we went by way of Cloverdale. That was an experience going down the mountain into Bisbee. Tonie rode in the cab with Ray and she had Betty with her. Betty was just a little tyke. The rest of us rode on top of the load. We sang and talked and got sun burned. We arrived in Bisbee after dark. Dez and Owen were glad to see us and especially to show off their surprise. They had a brand new 1937 Chevy four door. It was loaded with extras like radio, knee action front end, two sun visors, two wipers, and the antenna was hidden under the running boards. I have said they treated me like family and I enjoyed their new car right along with them.

The next morning Dez took me with him to the mine where he worked to maybe get me on at the same mine. The Briggs. I was seventeen and on the way to the mine Dez told me to tell the owner, Miles Merrill, that I was eighteen. I thought he was kidding. When Merrill interviewed me sure enough he asked how old I was. I told him seventeen. He looked at Dez and I knew right then I had messed up. Merrill said, "I'm glad you are eighteen because I couldn't hire you if you were seventeen." He told me to report to work the following day, and he would pay me $3.50 per day. Now that changes into muchos pesos at $5.60 for one. Sure sounded good to me. Owen took me to the Phelps--Dodge company store and helped me get outfitted. Owen worked for the P--D so he had a charge account at the store. Shoes, hat, carbide light, pants, shirt, and long handle underwear. I had no money, but

Owen put it on his account. The reason for the underwear was because the Briggs mine was on fire and very hot in some places and cold in others. That was so as not to change body temps too fast. I thought I had worked in hot weather on the ranch, but it was nothing to compare with what I found in that mine.

Now for my first trip down the mine shaft on the cage. Fifteen hundred feet. That cage dropped so fast I just sort of hung in the air all the way down. I learned later why. I held my breath and that caused me to float. Owen had showed me how to light my carbide lamp. I looked at that little fire and thought I would never find anything in the dark with it. What I didn't know was that it would be so dark that the little fire would make lots of light.

Miners are great to let a new man learn for himself as long as he doesn't get hurt. That first day I followed the men to the lunch room, and there they left the lunches. I noticed each one had a place and a way to suspend his lunch. I sat mine on a bench. At lunch time all the miners went to the station. It was a large room carved out of solid rock. That was the only level we were working and it was where the ore cars were put on the cages to hoist to the top. All my stuff was brand new. Lunch box, thermos and all. With all the new stuff there was no way I could fake my mining knowledge. Even though I had cleaned corrals with a shovel and a wheelbarrow it didn't count for much there. That first day Darwin Merrill, the bosses son, took me in tow to show me what to do and how to earn my $3.50 per day. Finally noon time arrived and we all headed for the lunch room. I noticed I had a lot of eyes on me but no one had yet said a word. I was sure enough hungry and when I opened my lunch box it was full of the biggest cockroaches I had ever seen. My lunch was gone. They had even tried to get the lid off my thermos. Those men could have told me but I guess I learned better that way. There was also a trick to hang the box. The roach couldn't go down the wire but he could jump from a beam if it was very close. In fact we had to be careful while eating a sandwich. Those roaches would jump off a beam onto the sandwich with you eating it. I have had them jump onto my sandwich, look me in the eye and wave their whiskers at me. They were about two and a half inches long. When we mashed a roach his buddies ate him right away.

Ralph was still too young to work in the mines. His job was making the lunches, and he sure made them good. A cousin, Gene Mangum, also lived with us and worked at the Briggs. We all knew but Gene that he was drinking coffee instead of postum. Ralph filled our thermos bottles from the same pot. The Mormon church teaches not to drink coffee because of its health hazard. Postum has no drugs at all. Gene lived his religion. He would even have the other miners taste it to see how good it was, and why they should drink it instead of coffee. The miners all knew. Gene was a hard worker and well liked. He was a college law student so was only there for the summer. He is now a retired judge from Phoenix, Az.

My job was trammer. That was the fellow who pushed those little cars from the mine--shaft station, through the tunnel back to the chute where the ore was being dumped by the miners from the stopes above. I filled the car, then back to the station at the shaft where it was put on the hoist and sent topside. I was in charge of four chutes and all I had to do was keep them empty. I had to take it out as fast as the fellows up in the stopes could put it in. I learned to handle four cars at a time. That gave me more rest time between trips. The chutes were about a half mile from the station. When I was asked what my job was, I told them I was a Tramming Engineer. The fellows who run the train engines were called engineers, so I felt I earned the title. I was engine and engineer all in one. In the early days the Briggs was one of the main mines in Bisbee and in those days a mule did what I was doing then. The track was upgrade going in and of course downgrade coming out. That was why I could push four cars at a time. I loaded the last car first and the first car last. That way when I started out with my train, as I bumped the loaded cars they would start to roll and so with a steady push they went on out to the station. If there wasn't much ore, or if I was caught up, I would only take one car in.

Some things I learned by thinking, and some I learned by not thinking. I have said the grade was downhill going to the station with my loaded cars. When I had one car I hung my light on the front of it. It was like a headlight. If I had more than one car I sat my light on top of the muck of the back car. One day I forgot I had left a loaded car down the line and hung my light on the front of the car I was pushing. That was the day I bought a new lamp. Another lesson.

As I was working I was thinking of how to get those loaded cars to the station and save energy or not have to work so hard. When I only had one car to take out to the station I would have to run to keep up with it on some of the downgrade. I pulled the chute and sat my light on top of the muck. I was tired and not in the mood to trot behind that damn car until it slowed down to be pushed on to the station. I turned it loose and just stood there and watched it go around the corner and out of sight. Now I do mean, out of sight. Have you ever been in the dark? I thought I had until now. It was so dark I couldn't even feel, much less see. Those cars would go almost to the station. Near the station was an upgrade to stop them unless they were being pushed. I had to crawl with my hands on the rails until I found that runaway car.

There was a main line, and tunnels leading off from it to the working stopes. The tunnels are called drifts. At each drift was a switch on the track that was kicked in the direction of the drift I wanted to go into on my next trip. I would kick it on my way out so it would be right for my trip in. It was easy to push the loaded cars out, but they were very heavy going in. Some of the miners thought it was funny to change my switch, so as I was going in with a good head of steam, my cars would turn into the wrong drift.

When muck was slow I didn't like to sit and wait. I would climb up to the stope and help with something there. The first time I did that, the miner, Bow Hunk, had just finished drilling the face and was loading the holes. They always blasted at noon or at the end of the shift. When he got the holes loaded, he looked at his watch. There was about ten fuses hanging down the face. He showed me which ones to light and he would do the rest. We did that with those little fires on our lamps. The fuses were cut to the length that gave time to light them and then get out and down in the drift before they reached the dynamite. I knew that, but when I set the first fuse on fire and it started hissing I thought that thing was going to blow before I could put fire on the others. I think he gave me three to touch off. I touched off one and when it started hissing I got nervous. I put my little fire on the second one and when it started hissing my feet started to run. It was maybe thirty feet to the manway that went down to the drift. I figured old Bow Hunk was right behind me so when I hit the manway I didn't take time to put my feet down first. I hit that thing head on and went all the way down head first. Old Bow Hunk came down a little later cool as could be. We sat there and waited several minutes before the holes started to blow. The fuses were cut at various lengths, and that way we could count and tell if we had a missed hole. A missed hole is one that for some reason does not go off. Those missed holes were a miner's nightmare. It meant there was a live cap sticking in a stick of dynamite some place in the muck pile. A shovel or a pick could set it off. I saw one miner that happened to and he carried the bag of rocks with him that were picked out of his body. He lived to tell about it. Most of them didn't.

I was getting to be a hard--rock miner, maybe two months already. I was up in a stope with a fellow who came there from Superior, Az. He was a little man but all muscle. He was doing some timbering in a place that was trying to get nasty. He was up inside a hole, about six by six and eight feet up trying to shore up the back (top). I was pushing timber up to him and I was nervous. Sure wished I had stayed down in the drift. The place was alive and kept sifting loose rocks and dust on him. He was sure working trying to hold it when all of sudden it caved in. I was out from under it and under good timber but there he was, almost buried alive. The timber he had been putting up in the hole was on him, along with the ore that he was trying to block off from caving in. The thing that saved his life was that when it caved, it blew him out under the timber where I was. There again, my feet started to run. In fact, by the time the cave quit coming down I was just ready to go down the manway to the drift below where I belonged anyhow. I heard him calling, "Bill, damn you, come back in here and get me out." I turned to go back after him but my feet kept trying to get to the manway. I moved some timbers off him and some ore, and about the time I drug him clear of that glory hole, it turned loose and filled the whole place up. It was good ore and they mucked on it for weeks. In it was a native copper boulder about three feet in diameter. It was left there because we had no way of getting it out.

The Briggs mine was interesting. It was one of the oldest mines in Bisbee. In the early days, when it was going strong, my job was done by mules. The fifteen hundred foot level was in limestone. For some reason it was the only cool place in the whole mine. This level had large rooms that were made to keep the mules in. Each mule had his own stall. A mule was taken underground when he was just large enough to work, and he lived there the rest of his life, or until he was too old to work. Since they had been in artificial light for so long they would go blind when returned topside in the sunlight. The mule station had electric lights, but when the mule went to work he carried a little carbide fire hanging from his forehead. Like the rest of the miners he had to see where he was going also. The place was a ghost town but only mules had lived there instead of people. It was all intact, even feed in the mangers. The only thing gone was the mules.

The Briggs mine was one of Bisbee's oldest and biggest in its day. It was a sulfide orebody which carried copper and some gold and silver. The mules were taken out of the mines when electric trollys went in. The Briggs was a very large orebody of sulfides. An orebody is mined by taking out the better grade and leaving pillars of the low grade to be mined last. Those pillars start to move and the friction starts the sulphur to burning. That was the reason the Briggs was so hot. It was on fire. The P--D (Phelps--Dodge) leased it to Merrill. Not only was it hot but it was very dangerous. It was abandond later and that was why I worked in the Whitetail Deer the second time I went to Bisbee. The Whitetail Deer was also a worked--out mine. We were just taking out the pillars that had been left. That is the most dangerous kind of mining.

In the mine we worked shifts, two weeks of nights and two weeks of days. After I had worked long enough to have a few dollars in my pocket I started looking for a car I could buy and pay cash for. While I was on night shift I had days to look around, and sure enough I found a car I could afford. At least the purchase price of $60.00. A 1928 white Chevy Roadster. It had a big bird emblem on the hood. It was soon christened The White Swan. I drove it home to the Mangum's to show it off. That was what life was all about. It made a hissing sound which I thought was sort of neat. The reason I learned later was lack of the air cleaner. The first thing to do was get Owen and Ralph in with me and we would take it for a test run, maybe down to Naco. I pulled into a gas station run by a friend. I told him to fill her up. He did and most of it ran out on the ground.

We drove back home and checked it out. Bad hose on the filler pipe. I was sure proud of my car. I drove it with the top down, and I sat so tall by now that I was looking over the windshield rather than through it. I was in the tall cotton. I was driving up Main Street in Lowell and I sure wanted to be noticed. There was lots of traffic. The traffic came to one of those sudden stops. I hit my brakes and you may think they didn't hold. Wrong, they did, but my steering wheel came off and there I sat. Horns were blowing with so many tones it sounded like an orchestra. I was holding the thing up in the air to let them know I had a little problem. I managed to put it back on the stub and steer my car over to the curb where I could take time to think what to do in a situation like that. The threads were stripped on the stub and there was no nut there to hold the steering wheel on. I had lots of experience with baling wire, but I couldn't figure just how to tie it on. My next thought was to get a hammer and brad the stub. The nut was lying in the cup under the horn button. One thing I was sure of, my horseshoeing experience wouldn't help me now. I went into a nearby store to look around for ideas. I spotted a triangle file. I rebuilt those threads and put the nut on. That was my first experience at making threads. I was sure there had to be a better way. I carried that little file for many years just in case.

Fuel tank now repaired, steering wheel now fastened on tight, and we were ready for the drive to Naco, some days later. Owen, Ralph, and I on the road for the shakedown. It was downhill all the way to Naco, about five miles, but on the return trip it was up hill all the way and The White Swan got hot. We went on home and the three of us had a pow-wow. We looked in the radiator and saw rust and junk. I went to a store and bought some Saniflush. It said right on the can that it will unclog anything, even toilets. We put in the whole can, ran the engine for a while, then drained and flushed it real good. Filled the radiator with nice clean water and parked the Swan outside the yard fence for a quick getaway the next morning. We had a trip planned the next day to go up in the Huachuca Mountains. The next morning as we approached it with hats on our heads and smiles on our faces, there it sat in the biggest pool of oil I had ever seen. A sure enough Texas gusher. I pulled the oil dipstick and it registered full... of water. Dez came out to look at it. I told him I was sure I had put the water in the right place. Like I said, the $60.00 was the first cost. We towed it back to the garage where I had bought it which belonged to Roy Hack. He put another block in the engine, cost me fifteen dollars. It ran good and I enjoyed it the rest of the summer.

When Summer was over and time to go back to the JSA, I drove the Swan to Duncan and left it at Mattie's. I went back to the JSA for my senior year. I finished at midterm but I stayed in Dublan until graduation so I could get my diploma with the class. There was lots of work to do. I helped Dad on the ranch, went on the Jeffery spring roundup for branding, and spent all my spare time at the Taylor home. The Taylor home was a magnet to me. Mart made me lots of candy, and she still makes good candy.

When school was out and I got my diploma I was ready to go. I went to Bisbee again hoping I could get in the mines. I was in touch with Owen and he told me there were lots of men in line for the jobs, but to come on out. I did. In Bisbee again and the first day there I went to a movie. Cost a dime but I knew the usher and he never charged me and the Mangums. As I came out of the movie, who should I meet but Mr. Miles Merrill, the fellow I had worked for the summer before. He was glad to see me and asked if I was looking for a job. "Yes, sir." He told me he didn't have a job in the mine right then. He told me that he was running the Whitetail Deer Mine and that he would put me on as soon as he had an opening. He told me his son, Demar, was building a home in Saint David. He asked me if I would like to go there and work for my board and room until he could place me in the mine. I raised my right hand and said I do. His son Demar was the hoist engineer. He lived in Saint David and drove to work every day. I went to the Mangums where my things were and Owen took me to the mine. I went home to Saint David with Demar when he got off work. Do not confuse Demar Merrell with a very close friend in Colonia Dublan, Demar Cardon.

Demar lined me up on what there was to do. They were Mormon folks so I fit right in with them. Pigs to feed, cows to milk, and a big flat--bed truck to haul sand. I had to have enough sand hauled and screened for the crew to plaster on the weekend. They were only working the mine four days a week. To keep his men working so they could live, Merrill had a contract of tearing down condemned buildings in Bisbee. Those materials were what they were using to build Demar's house in St. David. I spent about a week for my board and room. Mr. Merrill sent word with Demar that I could go to work in the mine. I could stay working for my board and room and ride to work with Demar to the mines if I wanted to, and I did. When there was enough lumber from the buildings for a load, I would drive the flatbed truck to work. While I was in the mine it would be loaded and ready to go. I would take it back to Saint David and unload it. Merrill was a good man. That time he paid me five dollars and fifty cents per day. With that and working for my board and room, I could save some money.

One night I came out of the mine and there was my truck loaded and ready to go. It was loaded heavy and lots of overhang in the rear. Mr. Merrill let me stay with the Mangums that night and go to Saint David the next morning. About forty--five miles. I put my gears in the bottom hole and climbed out of Bisbee to the top of the mountain pass. It was down hill from there to Saint David. I still stayed in low gears until I was off the steep part of the mountain on the St. David side. In those days there were dips in the road instead of bridges. The truck felt like it had power steering, which I had never heard of at that time, so I was being extra easy on the speed. I knew my load was tail--heavy. When I was off the steep part of the mountain, I shifted into higher gears and let the truck speed right on down the highway, like maybe forty MPH. With that load under control I adjusted myself comfortable in the seat with both hands on the steering wheel and my right foot on the gas peddle. I didn't need to give this old truck so much attention now so my mind drifted back to the ranch in Mexico. I was singing "Little Joe The Wrangler" with mucho gusto when I came to one of those dips. When the front wheels started up the other side of the dip, the front end just kept going up in the air and all I could see was blue sky. I got real busy with the steering wheel, and then I didn't know where was straight ahead for the front wheels. My feet hit the clutch and brake pedals at the same time. I knew the thing had got to come down but where was what had me worried. Sure enough, I had the wheels turned left and when it came down it zipped into the ditch along side the road. At that point it was a nice ditch and I came back up onto the road and started looking for the next dip.

There was a fellow at Demar's when I went there. He had done the same thing as I was doing. He started out working for his board and room. When he got on in the mines he stayed there also. Demar's wife would give me things to do if I should get caught up. The place had thick mesquite trees. They had about five acres cleared for garden. The garden was about a half mile from the house in a clearing out among those big thick mesquites. When I went to get garden stuff for the pigs I took the truck. A fourteen foot flat bed. One day she said, "Bill, when you go after some pig feed again bring me about four big eggplants, if you can find any."

I thought for a minute, and I better fess up, "What does an eggplant look like?" I asked.

"It's about so big, and sort of purple," she told me.

"Oh boy," I thought, "That's what I have been feeding the pigs." Off to the field I went in the truck to get some turnips for the pigs. Turnips was what I thought I had been feeing them but now I decided I was feeding them eggplants. I dug up a load for the pigs then picked out four nice ones and gave the rest to the pigs. I took them to the house and set them on the porch, then went on about my work. I heard her coming and knew something was up. She was laughing so hard she couldn't tell me what was so funny. She said, "Kid, you don't know your turnip from an eggplant." She told me more about where to look and that I wouldn't need the shovel. I went back to the field, a little smarter that time, and there I found them. She cooked them for supper and I have liked eggplant ever since.

I fed those two pigs good and before long they were ready to butchr. The Merrills had never butchered a pig and had planned to get someone to do it for them. I told them I had helped with a pig when I was at Duncan, and I was sure I could do it with their help. I had helped butcher beef all my life. We did a good job, and I was glad to see those pigs in the locker instead of the pen. Here is a good place to tell how much I don't like pigs. To me, a pig and a buzzard are about the same on the social scale. They both eat garbage of any kind, but when a pig gets through with it it's worse than when he started. Some laws have tried to clean up his menue but he is still a mess.

The first time I helped butcher pigs was at our neighbors' place in Dublan. He would take a pig out of the pen, cut its throat with a long knife then turn him loose in the corral to run around squealing and bleeding until he was dead. We butchered about six pigs that day and I still shudder when I think of the sight of all those squealing pigs. He put them in a smokehouse to cure the meat. Now that cured me from ever wanting to butcher a pig again. However, when I went to El Paso the first time looking for a job I went to the Peyton Packing House to check on an add they had in the paper. While I was waiting to be interviewed I decided to go into the plant and look around. That day was pig day and it didn't take me long to get out of there. I detoured the hiring office. A wide detour. When I helped Mr. Foote at Duncan I learned a pig can be done humane, the way we butchered beef. I have done several since. I still don't like pigs.

Time rocked along fine. I was sure working hard. We had Demar's house mostly finished and I was working full time in the mine. It was time to go live with the Mangums again. Mart was at the BYU, and I expected a letter every day. I'm sure she expected the same, so I made sure she got it. She spent the Christmas holidays there at the Mangums with me, and I missed her when she went back to school.

Now that I was back with the Mangums, Owen, Ralph, and I made plans to go to Duncan and get my car, The White Swan. They had a Model A coupe. We left Saturday evening after work, sometime in January, 1939. To Rodeo, Lordsburg, then on to Duncan. It started to snow on us about Rodeo, and was getting night time also. Sure was cold. That little A Ford had electric wipers and they burned out. It was snowing so much that the wipers couldn't clean the windshield and so the wiper stroke got smaller and smaller causing the electric motor to cook. That is when I knew that I never wanted a car with electric wipers. Most traffic was stopped along side the road, even the Greyhounds. We couldn't stop because we were too cold. We were snow blind and couldn't see the road. We got the idea of turning the lights out then all we could see was the road. We were sure glad to cuddle up to a stove in a Lordsburg service station.

We arrived at Mattie's at daybreak. She made us a good breakfast. I knew my car would need a battery and a couple of tires. We took them along. It had been sitting for about a year but we soon had the motor running and we headed back to Bisbee. It was around noon by the time we had the tires on and hand pumped them full of air and installed the battery. We decided to return through Safford, Wilcox, Pierce, and on to Bisbee. When we fueled up at Wilcox we had already used up all the daylight for that day. There was a problem with the headlights on my car, but we soon had them burning, and off we went. We had more headlight trouble before we got to Pierce. That time, in the dark we couldn't find the trouble, and we were about to freeze besides. I told Owen to take the lead and I would follow his taillights. That was our situation when we pulled into Pierce.

Pierce, Arizona, was a mining ghost town and still is. There was a combination bar, cafe, and gas pump, which was still open. Owen's A Ford had windows but mine was open, with just the top. We filled our fuel tanks for the final run, had a sandwich, got a couple of gunny sacks from those folks, and fastened them on the sides of my car for a wind break. I will say again, it sure was cold. Ralph was riding with me to try to help me stay warm. When we left Pierce, Ralph took his turn at the wheel and I would try to keep him warm. It was a very dark night so Owen's taillights were easy to see. As we left Pierce, Owen pulled in front of us and headed down the road assuming we were close behind. Well we didn't get close behind him and rather than wait for him to come back for us we tried to catch him. We didn't.

There was a cement bridge across the road, with the sides about a foot high. More of a culvert type. Ralph was maybe doing thirty--five MPH to catch Owen. He was running on the left shoulder with the left wheels and didn't know it. We hit the bridge in the middle of the front axle. When I quit seeing stars, and I don't mean those in the sky, I couldn't see anything. When the noise quit, I started to feel around on me to see what all had been rearranged. My nose was gone and bleeding in gushes. I was on the ground, and soon realized the car was on top of me. I was able to crawl out from under it. Then I remembered that Ralph was under it someplace. I crawled back under the car, I found him, and drug him out. I thought he was dead. I could hear the gasoline running out. I thought it might catch fire at any moment, so I drug Ralph a little more. Now I checked me over some more, because I sure had a headache. The old battery, which I had put in the rumble seat, had hit me in the back of the head and left a big gash there. I was over Ralph trying to get him not to be dead. Owen had missed us by now and I saw his headlights coming back to find us. When he saw my car upside down, he drove his car off the road and down where I was working on Ralph. The steering wheel had knocked the breath out of him, and he didn't have any breaks, but he still complains at me for getting blood all over him.

We were on the spillway side of the bridge. Over the years the rain water had washed a hole just our size. When the front axle of my car hit the cement it stopped. I mean the axle stopped the forward motion right there. The car leaped into the air and rolled to the left 180 degrees, and landed with the wheels up. It flipped while airborn, and came straight down. The front and rear bumpers of my car were on either side of the hole, and the old battery was in the hole with us after it bounced off my head. We went back to the cafe. The lady gave me some smelling salts and some cloth to hold over my face. We took off for Bisbee. Two things saved us that night. One was the hole we fell into and the other was the forward motion had been stopped.

We went straight to the hospital. A doctor went to work on me. He moved my nose around and started poking a string up each side. One side then the other then he looked it over for alignment. I was hurting and I thought he was playing with me. I went to work like that. I was on nightshift. The third night, I had a little string hanging out of each side of my nose. I tried to put them back in but they kept coming out again. I decided to just pull them out some and cut them off, but the more string I pulled out the better my nose felt. It was relieving the pressure, so I kept pulling. I pulled yards of string out. No wonder my head felt so big. When I got off work I went to the hospital. The Doc looked me over and said it looked good. He gave me some ointment and told me to rub it in and I probably would not have a scar. He was almost right.

The next weekend we went back to Pierce to check on my car. I sold it to those people at the cafe, range delivery for $10.00. That was the death of The White Swan.

Almost fifty years later, Mart and I drove by the place. I wanted to show it to her. The corner is still gone from the bridge, and the hole that saved our lives has been filled up with gravel washing under the bridge. Mesquites have grown up around it. Just not a good place for a car wreck anymore.

I went to see Roy Hack and tell him what happened to my car. He had a 1932 Model B Ford coupe sitting there. He offered it to me for $150.00. That time I took it out for drive and lookspection. I and those Mangum guys gave it a check out. It looked good so I bought it. Fifty down and fifty each month for the next two months. It was real clean and nice. I enjoyed it a lot. I caught a long shift weekend and went home to Dublan to see my folks. I took a fellow with me, Earl Peterson, who later became my partner in the cattle business. The Model B was the first Ford V8. Before I had it paid for, the mines were working fewer days and laying off men. I was one of them. I was ready anyhow. I was tired of underground work. I went to a store in uptown Bisbee and found a job unloading bulk oranges. That took most of the night. I finished paying for my car then I packed my things and told the Mangums thanks and adios, and left for Morenci. That was the last time I lived with the Mangums, but we have kept in touch all through the years. That was in the spring of 1939.

In the summer of 1943 I had been back in Dublan a few months from San Luis, Potosi when the Mangums came to visit the Wagners and other friends. Mart and I being some of the friends. Owen and Ralph talked me into going hunting and fishing up in the mountains near Colonia Garcia, another Mormon colony. I had never been there. I took my bed and my little Ford stake--body that Mart and I had brought back from San Luis. They said they would put in all the camping gear including something to eat. They assured me that we would mainly eat fish and deer and maybe a turkey. I had known those two guys for so long that I completely trusted them. The truck was loaded and up the mountain to Garcia we went and then over the hump (Continental Divide) and down to and on the Gavilan River on the Pacific side. What a place. Sheer beauty in every direction. Civilization had never found that place. Those guys were still not married, so they still hadn't learned to be responsible in some respects. By that I mean that when we unloaded all the good stuff for the camp, they had not put in the main box. Utensils and food. I took no responsibility, because it was their show and they told me to just bring my bed, and I did. Now we started to look around for some sign of previous inhabitants. We found a few old rusty cans, and boiled some potatoes that were in the pack. They caught lots of trout, but we needed a deer or turkey to go with them.

We went up a big canyon from our camp. There was lots of timber and undergrowth. I went up the left side near the top of the ridge, Ralph up the right side, and Owen went quietly up the bottom. We would meet at the saddle, unless someone saw something and started shooting. I had Dad's sawed off 30--30. They had more sophisticated rifles. Before we separated, a hawk flew over. Owen pulled his pistol and shot him out of the air. What a shot. The hawk wings stayed in the spread position and he came down in a whirl or flat spin. If Ralph and I should spot something just drive it over to Owen and he would shoot it for us.

I arrived at the saddle first. I was sitting on a log waiting for them. I had been there so long I hoped I hadn't gotten in the wrong saddle. I heard a little noise, and into the small clearing where I was sitting bounced a big buck. If I move he is gone and if I don't move he is gone, so I made a quick move to point my gun in his direction. He was about twenty--five feet from me. In fact, he almost ran over me, then he stopped to look me over. I started shooting from the hip. I forgot to use the sights. Instead of running, that old buck started jumping. He jumped around in that little clearing until I hip shot all my ammo. When I quit shooting he quit playing and I sat back down on the log. Owen and Ralph heard the shooting and were sure I would have something for camp. We were there about a week and hunted every day. We found deer and turkeys but never got any. It was great there however, three old friends together again.

Now in 1989, we are all retired and we are able to spend more time together. I have told how they took me fishing when we were kids. We all have boats and enjoy getting together. Owen's wife Margaret is from Colonia Pacheco. Ralph's wife Kay was raised in Bisbee. Our wives enjoy each other as much as the men so it really makes for lots of good get togethers.

10

Martha Taylor

When I moved to Dublan I was nine years old and I don't remember girls being very important. What I mean is they were just some more kids, but by the time I was in the eighth grade I had noticed that Martha Taylor was real important. She just stood out from the rest in special ways. She had the looks, and personality to go with it. We called her Mart and that is the name I will call her by all through my life story. We were in the same grade then, but I stayed out a year when we would have been freshmen and she went on to high school. Then I went to Duncan, AZ for a year. We were good friends by then, and when I went to the JSA the next year we went together most of the time. I will be writing a lot about the JSA. Those letters stand for Juarez Stake Academy. Her senior and my junior year was our best in school. We had lots of fun. I lived in Juarez with the Mangums that year so we only had school days together. No night dates or riding the school bus together as we had the year before. There was a school dance every Friday night and we enjoyed dancing.

Some Friday evenings I would take her with me to the Mangums, until it was time for her to get ready for the dance. Then she would go to the Skousen home and I would pick her up there. One evening we took a walk up the lane between the apple orchards from the Mangum's. They lived at the north edge of town. I took a .22 rifle along. Maybe a rabbit would jump out of the grass or maybe I would just show her what a good shot I was at some target. I did some shooting but she didn't seem very impressed. I decided to push the girl a bit and told her maybe she can just show me how it is done. She took the gun but just couldn't find anything to shoot at, so I came up smart again. It cost a peso to get into the dance, and I just happened to have my silver peso dance ticket in my pocket. I stepped to the fence across the lane, which was about fifty feet wide and set my silver peso in a wire splice that was there handy on the fence, and told her now show me. I didn't believe it then and I don't believe it now, but my ticket flipped off the fence. When I picked it up there was a hole in the middle. I had to borrow money to take her to the dance that night. I still have the peso. It makes a nice bolo tie.

Fausto Gerrard graduated from the JSA before we started there. He was very athletic and a good student, a very good basketball player, and well liked by everyone. His Dad had a store there in Colonia Juarez. Fausto didn't work. He just lived off his Dad. He got to drinking, and finally became a dangerous alcoholic. We all tried to stay out of his way. One day at noon, Mart and some of the girls were walking to the Rubio store near the JSA. That was her senior year. Who should be coming up the sidewalk but Fausto, and he was loco drunk. He stopped the girls and was trying to get hold of one of them. I was in the schoolyard and saw the girls had a problem with him, and I went to help them out. By the time I got to them, he had hold of Mart. I talked him into turning her loose and the girls went on their way. I chatted with him and walked him along the sidewalk until they were out of reach. I told him to go on his way, and not bother the girls. He smiled and left.

Later that same day word was sent to me that Fausto was in the school hall looking for me and sure enough mad. I thought I would go see him and get him settled down, but no way. He said I had interfered with his fun with those girls and he was going to whip me. The only person there in school that could handle him was Dave Spillsbury, my cousin. I knocked Fausto down and was holding him down when Dave arrived. As Dave was taking him away, he told me that he would catch me again, and next time he would have a knife. The word was out, and everyone was helping me watch for him. I was worried that he would catch me alone. I knew if he wasn't drunk he could whip me.

Time went by and I thought maybe he had forgotten about me. Not so. There was a special dance in the JSA gym and all the people of Dublan and Juarez were there. It was full of folks. Mart and I were dancing and as we whirled I saw Fausto come onto the dance floor and head our way. The gym was on the second story of that building. Now there was where and when dads came in handy. Mart's dad and my dad were on the side chatting and they saw him going our way. He was mucho loco. Mart and I stopped dancing and I was trying to make some quick plans, when her dad got him by one arm and my dad got him by the other arm. He had a little trouble understanding what they were saying to him until he felt Dad's .38 in his ribs, and not real gentle like. They led him off the floor and down the stairs, off the school ground, into the street and put the "splane" on him. They explained some things to him. When they came back upstairs Mart and I went over to them, and we thanked them for being there. They told me I wouldn't be bothered with him anymore. I sure hoped they were right and they were. When Dad poked him with his .38, he told Fausto he would kill him right there if he made a move towards me. I heard that part of the conversation but they never told me what they did or what they told him when they turned him loose, but he must have heard good. He never bothered me again. Mr. Mangum had to give Fausto a whipping not long before my trouble with him. He was trouble looking for a place to do it. Some years later I saw him and didn't know who he was. He had ridden a bull and got his face mixed in with the horns. It sure was rearranged. That was after Mart and I were married. Sometimes I would get in trouble with Mart and not half try. There was a play on at the JSA. I was to pick her up at the Ernestine Hatch home. Next door to my place at the Mangums was a family of Taylors. Her cousins. Two of the boys were home for some reason. They had been to college or working in the US. They had me over at their house and showed me so many things, time got by and I forgot to go get my date. When I remembered, they thought they had made me mad I left out of there so fast. It was so dark I couldn't see a thing. No matter I was in a hurry. My only transportation was my two feet and they were running so fast I could hardly keep up. Realize we walked everyplace we went. I had about a mile to go south on the north and south street. The JSA was about halfway and about a half mile at right angles to the street I was on. About halfway I met her, and I sure lucked out that time. She had decided to teach me a lesson and not wait for me. She had struck out alone for the JSA. Also about a mile from where she was staying. She was so scared she was glad to see me. In fact when she heard me coming she hid behind a tree, not knowing who it was, but as I got closer she felt sure it was me so she called my name. I hadn't seen or heard her and besides she hid behind a big cottonwood tree. There was no moon that night and it was sure dark. If she hadn't been so scared she would have let me go on by. Then I would have been angry and I wouldn't have had to take all the blame. At the point where I met her was where the swinging bridge crosses the river. Usually when we crossed the bridge I would swing her a little. She sure didn't ever like that. That night I took her across the bridge like the gentleman that I was. I wanted to hold onto all the luck I had so far.

Mart's junior and my sophomore year, 1935--36, was a special year for us also. We rode the school bus from Dublan to Juarez. In the morning I got on the bus first so saved her a seat, and in the evening she got on it first and saved me a seat. I was usually late because my basketball was the last period. I loved basketball. Most of the kids took lunches to school. I didn't. I had lunch at the Harper Hotel. On Friday nights we always had something at the school, usually a dance, so of course the bus went back to Dublan after the dance. The only passengers were the school kids. I couldn't afford to eat at the hotel both noon and evening. It was common practice for the boys to hit the school bus early in the evening and check out the girl's lunch boxes. On Fridays the girls would take an extra sandwich for the evening. I always raided Mart's lunch box. She sure made good lunches, and I always found a real good morsel of some kind. Maybe a sandwich, maybe some cake, but always there was something there. I thought I was sure being clever, and anyhow, she didn't know if it was me or some other guy raiding her lunch box. Years later a group of us were together and talking about our JSA days. I let my long--held secret out and told how I had robbed Mart's lunch box. She said, "Honey, I put those things there for you especially, I always ate at the Skousen's."

The school year of 1934--35 was the last year for the buggy days from the Pajarito Ranch to school in Dublan. I did the buggy one year in the eighth grade which was 1932--33. The other kids did it two more years, then we moved to town. By that time Bill had sold his cattle he had on the Corralitos and bought the Benton Ranch, the Cerro En Medio. Dad was now on his own, doing some buying and selling of cattle and making some money. We had a Model A pickup with the rear fenders cut off about halfway up the side of the bed. Dad bought it from Jack Helms. Jack had cut the fenders off so he could put a belt on it to pump water at the Buena Vista Windmill. We called it the Mud Hen. It would throw mud over the top and would cover the windshield. It really just threw mud in all directions. We had a man on the ranch, and part of his job was to keep plenty of wood cut. I would take that little A truck to the ranch and fill it up with chopped wood. Dad had made a frame on it to haul calves in as he bought them from the ejido people. That made it real good to haul wood from the ranch to Dublan.

On one trip at night to the ranch for wood, I asked Mart to go with me. We got Demar and his girl and off we went. It was a very dark night. I have told how the trip to the Pajarito Ranch was half in the lanes between farms. The other half was open ranch country. There were two large canals to cross in the lanes that ran water from the river to the farms. Sometimes the bridges were torn up, so we would go down in the canal, unless it had water. The first canal was full of water and the bridge was torn up. There were some pieces of lumber there that had once been part of the bridge. In the dark, we placed them for runners to fit the wheels and were able to get across. I say we did it in the dark because the only way you could tell if the lights were burning on a Model A was to scratch a match. We almost dumped that little A truck into the water. The two girls squealed, Demar adjusted the boards, and I drove. The next bridge was in the together stage so on to the ranch with no more problems.

We had an Indian at the ranch called Battling Sicky. He helped load the wood. As we were about ready to start back to town I had the idea to catch a couple of chickens for Mom to make some dumplings. That Indian went into the hen house and came out with two chickens. He rung their necks and put them on top of the wood. We headed back to town but we all knew, especially me, that we didn't want to cross that no-bridge canal again. The other choice was to go all the way around by Old Town Casas Grandes. There are two Casas Grandes towns with a bridge across the river between them. One, Old Town, is on the west side of the river, and the other, Nuevo Casas Grandes, is on the east side of the river, and near Dublan. That one we called the Station because it grew up around the water tank on the railroad. It was born as a water stop and grew from there. It would be about twenty miles farther but what was twenty miles when we were having so much fun. A Model A pick up fits two people, and there we had four.

As we were going down the hill from Old Town, I felt the load shift, I thought. Now it wasn't in the cab because there was no room to shift around so I stopped to give things a 360 walk--around. I found a flat tire on the left rear. Where was the spare and the tools? Under the wood. We were all young and frisky so we unloaded the wood, changed the tire and we were soon on the road again. I took the kids all home then went to my home to unload the wood. All of a sudden, my thoughts went back to the flat tire. When we had the flat the first thing I did was put my chickens on top of the cab so they wouldn't get bruised. I went in the house. Mom was waiting up for me. I told her about the flat tire and that I was bringing a couple of hens but I lost them when we changed the tire. She said, "Honey, why didn't you kill them and then they wouldn't have gotten away." I told her the rest of the story. That is the forerunner of what I have told my men for years. Don't lay tools under the hood of the car, throw them on the ground or out in the driveway, you can always go get them later. If you lay things on top of your car you should always kiss it first. You may never see it again.

I have told about the summer of 1936 that I worked for Bill at Barranca. Also about the black mules and repairing the cattle guard on the Pershing Road. That same summer Mart worked in El Paso. There came a car, and since we were repairing the cattle guard, the man working with me opened the gate for them, and they waved and drove on through. I didn't know who all was in the car but Mart was one of them. I didn't get a chance to speak to her. In fact, I just learned after she read this that she didn't even see me that day. I was busy driving nails, and anyhow I was afraid to quit working for fear of losing my job. I lost my job anyhow. The irony of it was that the fellow helping me was the man who got my job. That was my last day. His name was Julian Chaveria. A real good man. Bill hired a man to chop wood and milk the cows, so

Julian wouldn't have to do that. That summer is logged in my hind sight.

The lawns at the JSA were surrounded by cement walks, which were raised about six inches. When the caretaker watered, he just filled the areas. Mart and I were on the walk. I had her by the waist, and there was all that water. Temptation. I thought I would make her think I was going to put her in the water. I leaned her out over it. I thought she would put a foot in it, but she kept both feet on the walk. I got over balanced and dropped her flat in the water. By the time I could pick her up, quite a crowd had gathered. She went to the Skousen's and got some dry clothes. I had heard about wet hens. That was where and when I learned about wet girls. I did that no more, ever.

Another time I picked her up from a fall to the ground. I had let her ride my bicycle. With a dress and high heels, she had to be real careful. I was waiting for her by the front gate at her house. She rode down the street to the railroad track and as she came back to where I was waiting, she made a left turn to go into her yard. As the bike went over the ditch, the left peddle was on the down stroke and it clipped the heel right off her shoe. It caught on the bridge. She was going pretty fast and she sure had a wreck. She was sure scattered there on the ground for a few minutes until I could gather her up. It skinned her in places she wouldn't show me.

We looked forward each year to the springtime and the JSA school hike. We would spend two nights at the camp. Some of us liked to go horseback. I put Mart on my gentle horse, Boogers. She got along with him real good. She didn't wear spurs so I made her a quirt to pep him up with once in a while. She still has the quirt. Those hikes were in the mountains on a running stream. The last hike we were on was the spring of my junior and her senior year. There was transportation for all the kids who didn't have their own. The Mangums had a two--ton stake--bed truck. They drove it full of kids and camping equipment. They lived in Colonia Juarez and I lived with them that year. I sent my bedroll on a truck from Dublan. Mart sent her bed and groceries the same way. She fed me good. If she hadn't, I sure would have been hungry, because I didn't take any food. We arrived at the campsite in time to have lunch. Most everyone had arrived by then. The Mangum boys, Owen and Ralph, and I were very close friends.

We got together at camp and they told me that as they drove through General Guerrero's ranch, they went by the hacienda. Out there in the corrals was a bunch of horses. They stopped and talked to the mayordomo, Bill Ingram. He was married to the general's daughter. Bill told them to come back after lunch and watch them ride those wild horses he had gathered. The Mangums invited a lot of the kids to ride with them back down to the ranch. Mart and I were there. As we arrived at the corral I could see they were sure having a time. Ingram was sitting up on the fence, a pole corral, and telling his cowboys which one to catch and ride next. They were riding with a loose rope surcingle, and putting on a real show. They were riding in the corral so when the rider got off or was thrown off, the horse was still inside. It was a big pole corral made with the poles laying horizontal. It was easy to climb on and nice to sit on while watching the show.

We were all sitting on the fence enjoying the show when someone said, "Bill, why don't you ride one of those broom tails?" I hadn't seen anything yet that didn't look easy to ride. I went to Bill Ingram and asked if maybe I could ride one. Instead of saying yes, he called to his vaqueros to catch the grey horse that was in the herd. They did. "He is all your's," he said. That was one time I sure wanted to change my mind. There wasn't enough cowboys to hold old grey still enough to put the loose rope around his waist. When they finally got the rope around him they gave me a signal that he was ready. There were so many vaqueros holding onto that old pony that I could hardly find room to get on him. I was still getting seated when they turned that critter loose. He exploded. He bucked stiff--legged, and that just jerked me untogether every time he hit the ground. He went up in the north and came down in the south, for sure he was one sunfisher. On that sort of riding, there is no whistle to tell you, "That's enough, now you can hop off and go up to the pay window for your winnings." We rode real bucking horses, not kicking up horses like you see in our great rodeos with the flank straps. The only riding rules we had was stay on that old pony just however you can. You get off when you get ready or when the brono gets you ready. When he quits bucking you hop off, if you are still topside. There is a real trick to getting off. You must get off at the exact moment he quits bucking and starts to run. If he gets to running, you are in real danger. That day the change over from bucking to running happened as he made a dash near the pole fence. When he left the fence in a run, I was on the fence instead of old grey. I was so tired and completely exhausted that I couldn't stay on the fence. The vaqueros yelled, the kids yelled and clapped, and Bill Ingram emptied his .45 automatic into the air. It sure made my day but I was too tired to enjoy it for a little while. The ranch was later sold to Martin Jeffery. The same Jeffery who was our neighbor on the Corralitos in earlyer years.

Bill Ingram moved to El Paso. He worked for Cashway Lumber until he retired. In 1964, I bought a service station on 1805 West Picacho in Las Cruces, NM, from Jim Shelton. He was the owner of Cashway in El Paso. When I went to his office to take care of some papers, who did I run into but Bill Ingram. We had a good conversation about times before.

I have a very fond memory of Mary Taylor. She was Mart's mother. She always made me feel so welcome when I went after Mart for dates. If Mart wasn't ready, and that was most of the time, her Mother would entertain me. Sometimes she would tell me Mart wasn't ready but she would go with me. She didn't just sit me in the front room and leave me. She was my Trailbuilder teacher and all the kids loved her dearly. She had a special way with young boys and we listened to her. I have told that there were very few cars in Dublan in those years so we all walked wherever we went. Mart's mother had the nicest baby buggy in town. I thought any little kid would be happy to be a baby and get to travel in that buggy. At that time, Ethel was the one in charge and I would have gladly tended her just to get to drive the buggy. The buggy was on the order of a shopping cart only it had big wheels, like about fifteen inches. It also had brakes to keep the kid from having a runaway while parked unattended. It had a canopy for shade that could swing forward or back or overhead. It was made of braided straw and also had springs. Mart had her turn in that buggy and that is one reason she was such a happy little kid and then grew up that way. She got a good start in life.

If I would meet her in town, Mary, (she was Mrs. Taylor to me) would ask me to walk her home. Now that was a privilege to me. On the way, she would tell me how to walk with a girl, how to hold her hand, and to never put her on the outside of the sidewalk. When we would get to her house, how to thank the girl for the nice date. The girl goes into the house and the boy goes on his way. As I got a little older, however, I decided that she had left out the best part. The girl should give him a little kiss and then go into the house.

In April of 1937, she was buried in Mesa, Az. I went to see Mart, and when she came to the door, I grabbed her around the waist and swung her around. That was my common greeting. Then I noticed she was crying. I knew her mother was in Mesa for an operation. She told me her mother was very sick from the operation and she was getting ready to go to Mesa to see her. I was so embarrassed. I talked to her for a little while, then I left so she could get ready. She had five little brothers and sisters to get ready also. She didn't get to Mesa in time to talk to her mother. Only Mart can know what she went through at that time.

That was her senior year. I knew it would be hard for her to meet all the kids when she got back home from the funeral and had to finish school. The first morning when she was coming to get on the bus I got off and went to meet her and escort her to her seat. I'm sure that this was an instinct thing I had learned from her mother. Mart has told me since how much she appreciated me doing that. The way she took over and took care of the little kids and still went to school was just super. I was planning then for her to be the grandma to my grandkids. The next school year was my senior year and I rode the bus from Dublan to Juarez that year. I would get off the bus every evening and go to her home to see if she was taking good care of her little brothers and sisters, then go to my home, four blocks. She stayed home that year and took care of the kids. I thought how lucky her dad was to have her to do that instead of going to the BYU. Someday I fully intended to get her away from him.

The summer of 1937 I spent in the mines in Bisbee. I was glad to return to the JSA for my senior year and especially the girl I was lonesome to see. That was a great school year. I was student body president, and since Mart wasn't there for me to spend time with, I took enough credits to graduate at midterm. The teachers were good to help me get set up to do it. I rode the bus that year. I would get off in the evening at Mart's before going home. I thought she couldn't take care of those little kids without me. Sometimes they seemed as glad to see me as she did.

At Easter of 1938, the Mutual class chartered a bus to go to Mesa, AZ on a M--Men and Gleaner excursion. Mart invited me to go. I went to Mutual when I was in town and enjoyed it. Her dad was along also, but he didn't pay much attention to us because he was paying attention to Lorna Call. We arrived in Mesa after dark and there were lots of Mesa people there to invite us to their homes. No one had money for motels. Some of the group had relatives there. Mart and her dad went to stay with her sister, Beth Young. I had no relatives there but I had assumed that I would have a place to stay, that someone would invite me. I sure didn't have money to go to a motel. The group was all paired off but still standing around greeting and talking. I was the only one left without a place to stay. Beth and Ray had already taken Mart and her dad to their home. Mart didn't know I had been left. Someone from Mesa was supposed to see that everyone had a place to stay. No one in our group checked to be sure. I felt like a coyote I caught one time. What in the world have I got myself into now? I have never been good at asking. I'm sure now that whoever was in charge in Mesa didn't know that I was one of the Mexico group. The Mormon people just don't do that. Anyhow, just when I was at my lowest in feeling out of place, I heard a lot of yelling and about the same time I was attacked from the rear. When my surprise got back together, it was Owen and Ralph Mangum. Their grandmother Mangum lived in Mesa. They were visiting her, and they knew about the Dublan Mutual was to arrive that night. They hadn't expected to see me. They took me with them, and that turned out to be one of my most memorable trips.

The Mangums left to return to Bisbee a day before our bus left to return to Dublan. Our bus went through Bisbee en route both ways. We crossed the border at Antelope Wells. The Mangums took me with them, and I was to catch the bus the next day as it went through Bisbee on the return trip. We waited all day and into the night, and no bus came along. Finally the driver, Fernando Rubio, arrived with a tire to be repaired. It was ruined so he had to buy a new one. He didn't have the money. I loaned him money to buy a new tire. He had caught a ride to

Bisbee with his tire, and now Owen's dad took him back to the bus with his new tire. I asked, "Would you please bring Mart back with you?" Owen and Ralph each put in an order for a girl also. He brought the girls back and we all went to the Mangum home. Their mother sure fed us good. She made beds on the floor in one room for the girls and in another for the boys. While on that trip, Mart and I decided we would get married someday and we made promises to each other. About three years later we decided to keep those promises and she let me put a ring on her finger. I have said before what a nice person Mrs. Mangum was, and that was some more of her nice ways. She was raised in Dublan, and had lived with some of the Adams families. Some of my uncles and aunts.

I also loaned some money to Melvin Turley to buy a diamond for his girl while we were there in Bisbee. A few days before I could barely buy a hamburger, and now I was loaning money. I had a partner in the cow business who lived in Bisbee. I met him when I worked there the year before. He gave me some more money to buy cattle with. Mart and I made promises to each other while on this trip, April 18 1938. We didn't set a date. I went back to Bisbee and to the mines again for the same Miles Merrill I had worked for the year before. That was in 1937, and now it was 1938.

She went to the BYU. I lived with the Mangums in Bisbee. Mart and I kept the mailman busy. I sent her a very special valentine and in a few days there came one from her. I opened it and saw it was the same one I had sent to her. I thought she had sent my valentine back. I threw it in the garbage. Tonie, Mrs. Mangum, saw me do it. She knew it was from Mart. She asked me why I threw it away and I told her. Now she was smarter than I, or more curious. She picked it out of the garbage and read it to me. Mart had sent me the exact same valentine as I had sent her. I hadn't opened it to see what was inside. I was worried anyhow for fear she would find a sharp college boy and forget me. I thought she had already replaced me.

I have told how I teamed up with Earl Peterson while in Bisbee and we were partners in cow trading. Me doing the trading. Earl had a girlfriend at the BYU. He had not met her but they were corresponding, because of a mutual friend. Earl and I had some pictures taken together and he sent one to his girl at the BYU. We were standing together and he drew an arrow at the top of the picture between us. His girl was real pleased and showing her boyfriend around school. One day she showed the picture to Mart, and pointed out her boyfriend. Mart said, "Gal, you got the wrong one, the one you claim is mine." Then Mart told her the story.

At Christmas time 1938, the Arizona kids at the BYU chartered a bus, and Mart rode it to Mesa, to see Beth. Mrs. Mangum told me to invite Mart to spend the holidays with them, so Mart and I had our plans all set. I bought myself a round trip Greyhound ticket to Mesa and back to Bisbee, and Mart a round trip ticket from Mesa to Bisbee and back. I arrived at Beth's place in Mesa the same day Mart did and we went right back to Bisbee. I had to work the next day. There were lots of our friends in Bisbee, so we enjoyed visiting them. Some we visited were her folks and some were mine and some just friends. All our friends were betting that she wouldn't go back to school, and they almost won the bet, but we decided she better go back. She spent about a week in Bisbee and what a nice Christmas it was.

Those years, in the 1930's, were tough and my job wasn't that secure. And sure enough, in about two months the mines started to layoff men. I was one of them. That was when I went to Morenci, Az. By the time the BYU school was out, I was working in Morenci. I planned to meet her in Safford, and we would spend a day there before she went on home to Dublan. We stayed at Vangie Taylor's. I arrived in Safford before her Greyhound, and found out it was coming in late. I went on west to Geronimo, about twelve miles and met the bus there. I got her off the bus, and I have never seen a prettier girl in my life. Very early in my book I told about Sam Hinton. He is the man who gave me Bounce, my dog. The Hintons lived on a farm near the Geronimo bus stop. I wanted them to meet my girl. I hadn't seen them for years, anyhow, so we went to their place. They were glad to see me, and of course were enchanted with Mart. Mrs. Hinton went to work on dinner, and I believe that was the best chicken I ever ate. We went on to Safford. I had to go back to Morenci, and Mart went on home.

Mart's sister, Rinda, took care of things at home when Mart went to the BYU. Harve soon married Aunt Rhoda and then the girls were free to get married or whatever they decided to do. I got a letter from Mart telling me she would be in Safford and when. I met her there and we set a date to get married and I gave her a diamond. It was Sept. 16, 1939. Was I one proud guy to put it on her finger. However, she asked me again for a promise. We decided that if we couldn't be married in Dublan with blessings of those so important to us, then she would come to the US and we would get married on our own. Now the promise she asked for. She said, "Dad is very strong and determined, so promise you won't let him talk you out of it." I promised and we sealed it with a kiss.

Sure enough, in a short while after she returned home with her diamond, I heard from her dad. Would I meet him in Safford? "Yes", and I did. That was the first time I had ever talked to him man--to--man. His proposition: If I would join the Mormon church, he would send us both to the BYU for a year, and then we could get married. I listened to him good, I had always liked and respected him. After he had talked to me for some time, he said, "Now what is your decision?" We were sitting on the bed in his room at the motel.

I said, "Harve, there is only one thing that will change my mind, and that is for her to say no to me." One of the great moments of my life happened right there in that motel room. He jumped up off the bed and faced me and said, "Bill, that is what I hoped you would say, I just had to be sure of how strong your love is for her. She is so special to me. I would like you to be married at my home and I will pay all the expenses." We shook hands and no one ever had a better father--in--law than mine. The more I knew him, the better I liked him. Now fifty years later and I'm writing my life story, remembering those words that I have always held so close to my heart.

Mart and I set the date. It had to be on a Sunday because my boss was a crotchety old bachelor, Mr. Reed. He gave me Monday off only, and let me know that if I took more I would be out of a job. I lived at a room and boarding house, up the hill above the company store. Vinton Baxter lived there also and we were good friends. He had a Teraplane coupe. A one seater. He took me to Dublan. We picked up Vangie Taylor (Mart's cousin) as we went through Duncan. She lived in Safford. Owen and Ralph Mangum met us at the Mexican border at Antelope Wells. They were from Douglas. Baxter and I left Morenci after work Saturday. We worked six days a week with Sundays off. It was night when we crossed the border. We arrived in Dublan just about daybreak, and we went straight to Mart's house and got her out of bed. She came down the stairs in her robe. I grabbed her and put her in the car and we ran around town until we had the whole town awake. Owen had a Model A coupe, and a pair of loud air--horns on it and I don't think he ever turned them off. The next day people were telling us that they knew when we arrived in town.

We were married that night, October 29, 1939, and Monday morning we headed for Morenci. Dad was going to El Paso, so we rode with him to Antelope Wells. That is where the four of us, Vangie, Baxter, Mart, and I, tried the little coupe on for size. In those days a two door car had only one seat. I held Mart on my lap to Morenci. She only weighed about 110, but it still about ruined my legs.

I had rented a one--room apartment. It took us a few days to get things together to cook in our little room. In the meantime, we ate at the Longfellow Inn, which was close by. I would go to work with a lunch and she was supposed to go to the Inn for breakfast and lunch. I found out she wasn't going because there were too many men, and they all wanted to be friendly. We soon had a three--room apartment. Housing was so scarce that some of the people were living in tents. Since Mart and I have been friends since the fourth grade and sweethearts most of our lives, it is obvious that I could tell a lot about us. I have tried to hit the funny things that we have done, but there is no way I can tell the real inside feeling I have for her. She has shaped my life and I totally give her credit for our successes, and such a fine family we have. She comes from a very good family and she is a credit to all of them. We have come a long way together and are still going. I think we have a love for each other that would be hard to put in words, so I won't try... MART, I LOVE YOU THE MOST.

11

Morenci

I left Bisbee in the spring of 1939 with a smile, because I hoped to get a job topside in Morenci, rather than working underground. I sure did. It was summer and it was hot. I felt it was a start in the right direction. I liked my job in Morenci. My first tools were furnished by the Phelps--Dodge. A pick and shovel. I was on the B bull gang and we dug ditches for pipelines. Some of the ditches were about a foot deep and some, I could hardly throw the dirt out. There were lots of people there looking for work, and I was one of them. So when the boss said, "Dig." I said, "Which way and how deep?" I was going to be the best ditch digger in the gang. I didn't plan to stay a ditch digger very long.

In about two weeks I was promoted from the B gang to the A gang. The A gang moved things about. We moved the bricks from the Clifton Smelter to Morenci for buildings in the pit. I was in the Morenci pit on the unloading end. It was all done by hand, brick by brick, no pallets, and no forklifts. There were two of us on the unloading end. We had been hauling bricks for a few days when the top bull gang boss drove up. Stepped out of his car, and was coming over to me. The day before he drove up the same way and fired a truck driver for running over a water line and breaking it. I was unloading the bricks while the poor driver was getting a ride to the pay window. The boss said, "Adams, get in with me." I didn't ask any questions, but I sure didn't know what I had done. We were driving along, and my heart had already stopped, when he said, "Adams, how would you like a better job?" That got my heart back into some sort of rhythm, but then my ears had gone bad. He took me to the machine shop and turned me over to a new boss.

I got a raise from $3.00 to $3.25 per day. We worked six days a week. No forty--hour weeks in those days, and for sure no minimum wage. If you wanted more you worked for it. If you worked, you got paid. If you didn't work, you didn't get paid. Just plain simple arithmetic. There was a crew that worked for the machine shop but worked in the mill, which was just up the hill. I was turned over to a machinist in the mill as a B helper. That was the day I started doing the things that were natural for me. Machinery was my dream. The machinist was uneducated, like about maybe fourth grade, and he was very touchy about it. He was a good machinist, which he learned as an apprentice with the railroad. He had very little tolerance for my dumbness, and he rode me hard. I worked hard for him and when he said to jump a foot I jumped two feet just to be sure and have enough. His name was Herb Payne.

There was another machinist also worked with us. One day Herb was on me and riding hard, he was a little man. The other machinist saw and heard him. We were all on the same job. He said, "Herb, I don't know what you have in mind but one of these days you are going to find out what this Adams kid's limit is, and when you do I want to see it." His name was Henry. The next day the boss told me that Henry had talked to him and would like me to work with him. The two machinists just traded helpers.

Henry took me under his wing and started to teach me things. He had me running the cranes, and the hoist that was on top of the hill, plus anything else that needed to be done. He showed me how to weld and let me practice, and we got along fine. In the meantime, Herb saw what he had let get away. Herb then became a very good friend and helped me a lot.

Herb got on me the first time because I didn't know how to use a crescent wrench. I was using it upside down. Any cowboy kid should know better. He would send me down to the machine shop for various tools, most of what I had no idea of what I was going after. I had been on the job for a while and I kept hearing tales about some dumb kid that was sent for a skyhook. I always listened good because I was learning from the conversations that those skyhooks were sometimes hard to find and the poor guy would run all over the place looking for it. Each time he would get to the place he was told he could find it, he would be told that someone else had it. Seemed there was only one and it might be anyplace and sure hard to find. They told a story about a kid that was sent for a skyhook and when he caught on that they were playing a joke on him he decided to turn the joke backwards. About a month later he returned and reported that he was unable to find the skyhook. He had traveled all over the US looking for it. He collected his wages and expenses.

Well my boss Herb told me to go down to the toolroom at the machine shop and get an outside caliper. I knew by then that I had better find out more about it, because I thought maybe I was going on a skyhook trip with another name. I told him I didn't know what it was but please, don't fool me. He drew me a picture of an inside and an outside caliper and I have never forgotten. I never use my calipers that I don't think of that day.

We had both rod mills and ball mills on the same floor of the mill. There had been a delivery of rods. Henry was to move them up and over all the machinery and to the other side of the building. The rods were three inch diameter, and ten feet long, in bunches of about twelve. We had overhead cranes on all the mill floors. Henry tied them on and gave the signal for the crane man to hoist and take them over to me. I was to take them loose from the crane hook. The last bundle was way up in the air and coming over to me to take off the chain when the chain slipped on one end of the bundle. That stood them vertical just long enough for the other chain to give way. Down they came, or down they went. They went through two floors and lodged in the third. All the floors were cement, about six inches thick. They missed all the machinery and all the people. Henry was taken to the pay window.

A new machinist was brought in right away, but Herb took no chances of him getting me. He asked our boss, Whitey, for me and I was glad. Herb and I worked together the rest of the time I was in Morenci and he taught me a lot. I cut one of his fingers off and he still liked me. Herb smoked a pipe, and wore those funny little round glasses. He was constantly lighting his pipe and pushing up his glasses. The pipe was so ripe I could find him by smell anyplace in the mill. Sort of like having a bell on him.

One day we were working on the classifiers. He dropped his pipe into the tailings chute and away it went. The tailings was moved by running water. The tailings went through more agitation and flotation and finally wound up at the bottom of the mill in a large tank where there was a large agitator. The final tailings flow was down the mountain to the tailings dump. He got a new pipe but kept it in his pocket more. It just didn't smell good. About two months later there was a problem with the agitator in the bottom tank. Herb and I went down to repair it. We had to drain it in order to work on the equipment. We were in that tank looking over what had to be done and all of a sudden Herb let out a yell. He found his lost pipe. He wiped it off and stoked it. Things were back to normal, smell and all.

That was an old C&A mill that Phelps--Dodge acquired when they bought up all of Morenci. It was being used as a test mill to find out the best way to mill the ore from the pit. Low grade with lots of pyrite. The manufacturers brought in their machinery for testing. Our job was installing it then taking it out and installing for someone else. Very interesting, and lots of experience moving heavy stuff. The new mill and smelter were being built and the railroad was being put in the pit to haul out the ore. The test mill was supplied by dump trucks, big ones. Those companies were all competing for the contract to supply the new mill.

I worked hard and wanted to learn because there was the schooling for the machinists that would run the new mill. After a few months I was made an A helper and they gave me a B helper. I was still under Herb, but he was given another B helper and the two of us could handle lots of jobs. I sure liked the idea of a helper to send for tools. I was given my own tool box and it was kept on the main floor of the mill. Many of the tools we would use during a day had to be checked out at the machine shop at the bottom of the hill. Like I say, I was glad to have my own helper. I was up to $3.75 a day then and getting lots of overtime. I sure liked the overtime because my wedding day was getting close. I started a savings account at the bank, and I had a passbook at the company store. With learning to run cranes, and handle heavy equipment, and weld, I was on my way to better things.

We wore safety belts with chains on them to tie wherever we were working, much of the time high up in the rafters. One day I was walking on the crane track, my chain hanging down, and it hit the 440 volt line that supplied the crane. I had to get a new belt. One of the fellows called from below, "Adams, you are going to get killed before your wedding day."

One of our jobs was replacing liners in the various mills, cone crusher, ball and rod mills. We had one ball mill that was about ten feet long and about twelve feet in diameter. Sure was hot in there. The liners were about four inches thick and weighed about a hundred lbs. each, and it took a bunch of them to cover the whole inside surface. That ball mill was shipped in from Cuba. We had to rebuild it all the way. We put it on the second floor up from the main floor. The main floor was about in the middle of the mill from top to bottom. The road came in there for bringing in supplies and equipment. From there, we moved it up or down the mill. We moved the big stuff on a track that ran up the mountain on the outside of the mill building. At the top of the hill was a large hoist and that was the way we towed things up the hill to the floor we wanted to install it on. Herb and I had overhauled the hoist on the hill and he had showed me how to run it. One of the jobs we did was to reline the brake. When the mill came in from Cuba, I was an A man by then and I was put on the hoist on the hill and then on the crane inside the mill on the floor where we installed the big ball mill from Cuba. I sure liked sitting in the crane cage up high and watching the fellows below. I took signals only from Herb, because I was in a position to hurt a lot of people if I didn't give them exactly what they called for.

I was working on the main floor when I heard a scream, and down fell one of the electricians. He had a small job to do above the crane track, and should have red--flagged the switch. He didn't take the time to climb up to the cage. He had one foot resting on the track when someone started using the crane. The cage and controls hang underneath the crane so no way did the crane man know some one was standing on the track. It cut about half his foot off.

I mentioned earlier that I cut one of Herb's fingers off. We were relining one of the cone crushers at the very top of the mill. That job was a first for us but that was no problem. It just took different tools. The nuts we had to remove were about six inches across. We used open end wrenches with about a twelve--inch handle. The wrenches were about one inch thick so were pretty heavy. One man held the wrench on the nut and the other man hit it with a double--jack. The man with the double--jack stood with his feet on the level with the wrench. He was turned with his back to the man that was holding the wrench in place. The wrench was held with two hands spread apart so there was a place for the double--jack to hit. The double jack was swung backwards between the feet of the double--jack man. And all of it in a stooped position to start with. We were working under the walkway of the crusher.

I was on the double--jack and I told Herb I was sure getting tired. We had better change off or let me rest a bit. That was the last nut and it had started to move. He said, "Hit it," and I did. I bumped the double--jack handle on something and it threw my aim off. Herb held his finger up for the high sign, but it was gone. He said, "Adams, you just cut off my finger." I felt so bad I just couldn't say anything, but one of the men there did.

He said, "Herb, he told you he was tired, and you told him to hit it, and he did."

Shortly, the two safety men were there and they called a meeting. All I could think of was; the pay window, here I come.

Things were not going good for me when a fellow welder stood up and said, "There is no way we can blame Adams, here is the fault of the whole thing. We all know that a double--jack with a long handle is dangerous and it should have been cut off down in the shop where it was installed." I always felt that he saved my job and probably Herb's also. The handle was cut off right then and it did make a difference. Herb would flash his stub at me some times after it had healed just to make me feel bad.

The union moved into Morenci and started trying to get members, but none of us in the mill wanted to join. The union folks didn't give up, and they finally had enough to join that they told the rest to join or lose our jobs. We all joined. One of the benefits was free hospital and pay while off work. I had tonsil trouble for years, and they were bothering me at that time. I told Mart it was a good time to get them out. We had been married only a few months. Her tonsils were taken out when we were in high school.

The doctor gave me a local, so it was quite an experience for me. I sat in what was sort of like a dentist chair. He took them out in the morning and I went home in the evening. He had a little piece of baling wire with a loop on the end. He went down my throat and lassoed one tonsil at a time and squeezed it loose. As he pulled each one out he showed it to me and I could hardly believe all of that was in my throat. No wonder it hurt all the time. I still have to rinse my food out of the holes with water. Two nights later, I hemorrhaged. Mart and I tried to stop the bleeding all night but couldn't. The next morning when Herb came to work he loaned me his car to go to the hospital. The doctor reached in my mouth with a pair of pliers and pinched the hell out of my throat. I thought he was going to wipe me out. I spent a night in the hospital and never had any more trouble.

Bob and Jane Carson were married about the same time we were and we rented adjoining apartments. Their's up and our's down. We communicated with a broom handle. We tapped our ceiling or they tapped their floor. So many taps for we are coming up, or you come down. Bob worked in the pit on night or day shift, changing each week, and I worked in the mill on straight days. Our place was up on the side of the mountain. In the evenings, our pastime was a walk down to the company store and post office. Bob and I would each buy a milk nickel then we would split with our wives. They were made on two sticks, I think for that very purpose. Kids with only one nickel.

The Phelps--Dodge Co. had leveled a hill nearby, and were building a residential town, called Stargo. Bob and Jane were getting a house in Stargo the same time we were. One Sunday the four of us decided to walk over there and see how our houses were coming. About two miles, one way. We started in the morning so needed jackets. I was wearing a real nice sweater I had bought in Bisbee. Along the way, my sweater was too hot so I asked Mart to carry if for me. She refused, so I insisted. Pretty soon I noticed she had my sweater by one sleeve and was dragging it on the ground. Now that was just going too far to show me how ornery she could be. I took my sweater and carried it myself, and we continued on our trip. Bob and Jane thought it was funny that she had gotten the best of me. The incident passed but I never forgot. Forty--five years later, in the home where we now live, she asked me to bring her sweater. It was a nice one and she loved it. The stage was set for what I quickly had in mind. We had friends visiting and we were going out for dinner. I came dragging her sweater by one arm into the front room. I really thought she wouldn't catch on to what I was doing. She did, and she called out, "Oh no, not after all of these years."

I said, "So you remember how ornery you were that day?" Just another little thing to remind us how great our lives have been together.

We never lived in our house in Stargo because we went to San Luis Potosi, Mexico, but on vacation we visited Bob and Jane in their nice house. And of course to show off our little kid. They had a little girl the same age as Floyde. Before I leave the Morenci part of my story, I must say that my time there was one of the best learning times of my life. I enjoyed every bit of it. When I look back, I feel that it was a mistake to have gone to the mines in San Luis because I hated underground work so much. I didn't learn a thing that I wanted to spend my life at. Not only that, but I was on the get--ahead list for the new mill and had already been told so. After I had been in San Luis a year, I took my vacation and we went to Morenci to see old friends. While we were there I met one of the big--shots I had known when I worked there. He offered me a job if I would like to come back to Morenci. I have wished many times I would have taken it. He was the father--in--law of my mine--superintendent at the San Pedro Mine in San Luis Potosi. His name was Tex Neil. I say he was a big--shot. He was the man left in charge of Morenci while it was shut down during the depression years. Tex was a good man to know.

12

San Luis Potosi

We were married October 29, 1939. Mart liked Morenci. We made some nice friends, so the time passed quickly. The Phelps--Dodge Mining Company was building a new housing town called Stargo. We put in for a house and were accepted. We were waiting for it to be finished. I had also been told that I was in line for a machinist job in the new mill. We had been married about eight months when I received a letter from Bill Holmes offering me a job with the American Smelting and Refining Company, known as ASARCO. He was the assistant general superintendent at the San Pedro Mines in San Luis Potosi, Mexico. Remember back at Barranca, Bill Holmes was partner with my uncle Bill in the cattle ranching. We were thrilled. Mart's brother, Mennell Taylor, and wife, Florine, were there. He worked in the smelter. The smelter was near the city of San Luis but the mines were about fifteen miles from town and in the edge of the hills. We enjoyed that job, and especially because we made good money. Floyde and Sid were born there so they are Potosinos. Up to this point in my story, when I have talked about Floyd, I referred to my brother. After this, my brother will be referred to as Tio, and Floyde is my son. Also, notice the names are spelled different. When I registered Floyde at San Pedro I added the E by mistake. He likes it, so the correction was never made.

I accepted the job in San Luis. We took two week's vacation at Dublan with our folks. Then we went to Ciudad Juarez to catch the

Pullman to San Luis. We rode the train three days and two nights, and arrived in Aguas Calientes. We spent the night there in a hotel, then took a different train to San Luis. We arrived in the evening and there was Mennell and Florine to meet us. I called Bill Holmes at the mine. He told me to go up to the mine the next evening and meet Mr. M.F. Tynan. Tynan was the overall mining superintendent. Bill Holmes was next in pecking order to Mr. Tynan.

Mennell and Florine took us to San Pedro to meet the people. Bill Holmes was at the Tynan's home and they were waiting to meet us. I was not used to being around those kinds of folks and I sure wanted to do things just right. Just step right up and shake hands with everyone. No way was I ready for what happened next. Large front room, tile floor, polished to a mirror finish, and throw rugs here and there. I held my hand out to shake with Tynan, and at the same time I stepped on one of those little rugs. I had done some roller skating, but nothing to compare with that little rug. It took off down the room with me on it. I missed all the hands that were reaching for mine. I managed to jump off just as it ran under a couch. We said our howdies and I was told when to report for work.

I have told that Mennell and Florine met us at the train when we arrived in San Luis. They took us to their home where we spent the first few days. We were there at the San Pedro Mines for three years and spent many very exceptional times together. They are not only kinfolks, but our very special friends. The special friendship is still very much intact.

After a short while, we were pretty well established there at the mines. Floyde was with us by then and sure had our attention most of the time. Mart had become used to being married and taking charge of the house, the maid, and Floyde, and sure enough she just added me to her list. One day I decided to have a little game with her. I said, "You want to wear the pants, so I'll just try them on you for size." It was a long wrestle and she was sure hard to hold to put them on her, but I finally did. I said, "Now see, they don't fit very good do they?" She admitted they didn't. We have laughed about that many times.

The mine area was fenced in and had a twenty--four hour watchman on the entrance gate. Our house was furnished. The confidential employees, which included the shift foremen, lived inside the fenced in area. I was a shift foreman. We never locked our doors. Our house was the closest to the mine office with the mine shaft between the two, about a hundred yards to the office, so you see, I lived very close to my work.

The first year I was there we only had two shift foremen. We each had charge of the entire mine on our shift. I was guided through the mine one time then turned loose. I had a pocket full of maps which I couldn't read, and three hundred men scattered all through the tunnels and stopes. To run all that, I had two shift bosses, level bosses, a stope boss in each stope, and an underground secretary. In the mine office were the mine superintendent, the mine foreman, and two shift foremen (me one of them) a moso and a secretary. In the main office were General Superintendent, M. F. Tynan; Assistant General Superintendent, Bill Holmes; the Mining Engineer and staff, and the accounting department.

Our house had maid's quarters unattached. We had a full--time maid until Floyde came along, then we had two maids. One to cook and tend him and one to do the laundry. I had taken on all that at the old age of twenty.

Soon after Mart and I moved to San Luis, Dad sold the cattle I had bought with the Peterson money. I sent half the profit plus the investment to Earl Peterson. He was pleased and so was I. Dad used my part to buy the L7 brand and cattle from Wilber Stevens. I think about fifteen head. They were already on our ranch. I was then a cowman on my own.

I spent three years underground mining in San Luis. I didn't like underground work in Bisbee and I didn't like it there. After two years I handed in my resignation, but Tynan called me into his office and offered me a raise if I would stay. I stayed one more year, but I just couldn't take it any longer. I knew there had to be a better way to live than like a gopher.

Now, about the mining. I worked shifts. One week, days, and one week, nights. The night foreman was also in charge of the third shift, but he could run it from his house. There were phones in the mine and in our houses, and of course in the offices. I would line the third shift boss up, and if he had a problem he could call me at my house from underground. The third shift lowered timber, explosives, cut chutes, hauled out the used and broken timber which there was lots of, and of course took care of the honey wagon.

Mining is very dangerous. Safety is something we preached to the men constantly. The only man that was killed in the mine in those three years I was there was cutting chute on third shift. As ore was dumped in the chute, the fine stuff builds up and must be cut out with a pick. The chutes were on a forty--five--degree angle up and about a hundred feet long or high from the drift. The chute must reach from the drift up to the stope being worked. The stope was where the body of ore was. We used the top--slice system. The first cut at the top of the body and then eight foot cuts to the bottom of the ore body. The ore bodies were surrounded by limestone or porphyry. It took lots of timber. The San Pedro Mine was very heavy and we had to timber everything. We had men who did nothing but replace timber to keep drifts and other permanent working areas open and safe. The posts were about eight inch diameter and six feet long. They were installed on five foot centers with eight by eight inch caps on top. The caps were about two feet long. As a cut was worked and timbered, a floor was laid with two by twelve lumber. The next cut was taken from underneath that floor. The timber was pine. However, while I was there we tried using some posts of palms. There was a palm jungle near there. They were very rough and heavy to handle and wouldn't hold heavy weight for very long periods. The real trouble, however, was that they wouldn't explode when we blasted a stope for caving. Many times we would have to crawl into a stope that didn't cave good and drill those palms again and blast them. I just never got used to being that brave.

With that little explanation it will help you see the potential danger. The man got into the chute at the top. A rope was tied around his waist and over a beam so he could let himself down as he picked the ore loose. He laid some boards over the top of the chute so that if a rock should fall it wouldn't get into the chute with him. The fellow did just that, but he didn't get the boards close together and a rock about the size of a goose egg fell down the chute, hit him on the back of his hard hat, caved it in and broke his neck. It was one of those freak accidents.

I will give some background about the San Pedro Mine. It was discovered and mined by the Spaniards. In those days it was very rich in gold and silver in the oxide ore. The oxide ore was above the three hundred meter level and that was the richest. When I was there the oxides had been pretty well exhausted. There was still some very rich ore in small veins and we had to patrol that area because of stealing. We called the thieves gambosinos. They would gouge the ore out of the veins and carry it out of the mine on their backs in sacks. We kept heavy iron grate type doors over the old entrances to that part of the mine but they would get in anyhow.

To check the part of the mine where those gambosinos worked was considered dangerous duty so we would send one of the shift bosses with a backup man to check it out about once a month. Mainly they went to see how many doors had been busted open. They would send some one to repair them. One day I decided to go with my shift boss so I would know more about what I was sending a man into. I have never liked to send someone where I wouldn't go. It was an experience and once was enough. We found two doors busted open. We knew there was someone in there or there had been so we were very cautious. There were drifts or tunnels in all directions, so lots of places for a gambosino to hide. There was no way we could find those guys because they had the drop on us, and really we didn't want to catch them. We found some sacks of ore in the drift where they had dropped them to go hide from us. We did not hunt for them but we sent men to lock the doors again. The Spaniards had mined that part of the mine the very same way the gambosinos were doing. That part of the mine was in solid ground and didn't need any timber. I have wondered since; how come the company didn't let those guys mine the ore then buy it from them instead of chousing them?

The Spaniards had put down an inclined shaft to haul the rich ore out. We used that shaft to ventilate the mine. There was a very large suction fan at the entrance of the inclined shaft. It pulled the air down the vertical shaft and out the incline shaft. That was the reason for the doors in the drifts. To control the air flow. When ASARCO leased the mine, they drove a three compartment vertical shaft and went on down into the sulphide ore body which was very large. The ore we mined was rich enough that it was not milled. It went straight to the smelter.

The first year I was there I had the whole mine to run on my shift so I would go through part of it in the first half of the shift then the other part in the last half. It was pretty well divided with the upper part oxide and the lower part sulfide. I never went through the mine in the same sequence so my men never knew when I would be checking them. I had a few that would take a siesta if they thought they had me figured out. I was making my run one day and as I arrived at a new stope we were driving, I saw all the men down in the drift looking at one of their buddies they had laid out on the rail track. They told me he was dead from gas up in the stope. They were suppose to turn the air hose up there and blow it out before going in. That fellow had been in a hurry to get to work. I made a quick decision. I didn't want a dead man on my shift. I rolled him onto his belly and went to work on him. After a few minutes he took hold of some air on his own. Before long, I had him sitting up. I made some good points that day and a very good friend.

Another day I was making my run through the mine and a runner or messenger had been sent to find me, and he did. He told me one of the men had been cut on the arm and was bleeding to death, and that he was being taken to the four hundred meter station. A station in the mine was where we had access to the cages. In the San Pedro Mine there was a station at each one hundred meter level. When I was there we used the three, four and five hundred meter levels. By the time he arrived at the station I was there, and what a sight. They had tied string around his arm from his shoulder to the tips of his fingers. His arm was already swelled out over the string. His hand had already turned black. We had a hospital in the town of San Pedro, about a mile from the mine. I called the office and told them to have a car ready, that I was sending a man out that needed quick attention. Then I cut that string they had wrapped him up with and took it out of all that swelling. His blood started to squirt. Then I showed a man how to find and control the artery near and just above the elbow. If it flows a little, OK, but don't let it squirt. I put them on the cage and sent them topside. He got to the hospital and his arm was saved. I have always thought maybe the whole man was saved. Some more good points I got that day.

Before long I was to find out those good points were sure needed. I think any time someone is in charge of so many men, there will surely be some of them who don't like the boss. I got along well with the men. They worked hard for me and my tonnage was always good. However, I had one fellow who insisted on giving me a hard time, and pretty regular. I was not tolerant of no--goods and I had a few. I was to learn later that those no--goods were heavy union, and mostly stoolies. The union had me fired, but the company labor man, Fritz Delius, went to bat for me. I was rehired the same day. When I came out of the mine that day I was told the story. Fritz was a good man, very well liked. While we are at this point, let me tell about Fritz. He was a very young boy on a German submarine in World War I. When the US got into World War II, Fritz was fired. He had many years of good loyal service with ASARCO. Everyone at the mine disagreed, but after all he was an ex--German soldier. The story I heard was that he was on a submarine and the crew jumped ship when they went into Vera Cruz when they saw they were losing the war.

About the fellow who was giving me some lip one night: We were down in the mine. He got real smart before some of the other men. I told him what I wanted him to do and went on my way. Most of those men traveled by foot or in buses to work from the ranchitos around in the hills. They were mostly sandal--footed Indians. Good people and good workers. Very few could read and write. I always went out of the mine in time to be showered and changed by the time the men started coming out. We ran two double--decker cages that ran counter balance. I would go to the mine shaft and watch them as they came topside, and check with my bosses to see that everyone was accounted for. That night, one of the fellows who heard me having trouble with the old boy, took me off to the side and told me he thought the guy was sure out of line. He said, "Senor Alamos, (they never learned to say Adams) just tell me and I will kill him on the way home tonight."

I said, "No, let's don't kill him tonight, let's give him a little more time to shape up." The guy did shape up and made me a good hand. The men called me, "El Viejo". I was twenty--one at that time.

The ore came out of the mine in little cars that were pushed or pulled on rails by hand. All the drifts were equipped with the rails. The same type job I had in Bisbee. We also hoisted lots of waste. We used all the waste we could to fill in places where we took out ore, but in some cases it was easier and cheaper to hoist it to the surface. There was a train that ran from the mine to the smelter in San Luis. It ran in the canyon behind and underneath the mine office. The ore was trammed over to the edge of the canyon and dumped in a chute and into the train cars below. The waste was pulled by a horse over a bridge that crossed the canyon, then some distance around on the other side of the canyon and dumped. When it rained, there seemed to be a lot of lightning. I was on day shift and when I came out of the mine in the evening there was still excitement. The little man that drove the horse to pull four or five cars of waste to the dump was still in shock. Lightning had killed his horse when he was about halfway with a load to the dump. That little man was very nervous about continuing that job. We got him a mule to pull the cars with and told him not to worry. Lightning will never hit a mule. He was still desconfiado so he drove the mule in front of him at full length of the lines.

I came out of the mine for dinner or supper, depending on the shift I was on. The mine was very hot in some places and cool in others, so we wore long--handles to keep from freezing when we came out of the hot places. The stopes were hot and the drifts were cool. The mine was ventilated with a very large suction blower. The air was pulled down the working shaft and blown out an old incline shaft. The wind was so strong that, on the main drifts we had iron doors to control it, or send it to the places we wanted to cool. In each drift there were two doors about thirty feet apart, because the wind was so strong we couldn't have opened just one. We went through one and closed it then through the next one.

I came up for supper one night. I showered and changed clothes per usual and left my work clothes with Shorty. He was the office moso for my shift. He kept a hot fire and hot water to shower. When I left for my house he would put my clothes on the backs of chairs near the stove to dry for when I returned from mid-shift meal. The mine was so hot in some places that we always came out wet with sweat. We wore rubber boots and we would pour sweat out of them like water. The miners came out dry because when they arrived at their working place they took their clothes off and worked naked. Huaraches, hard hat, and a cloth between their legs tied to a string around the waist. The office moso on my shift was called Shorty and he took good care of me. He also kept my gloves washed. My gloves would get caked with sulfides and sweat. Washing gloves was a thing I started there at the mine.

I have told that my house was about a hundred yards from the office. I was eating supper when a big boom rattled my doors and windows. I was trying to put my thoughts together when there was a knock on my door. As I opened my door there stood my moso, Shorty. He was so scared he couldn't talk. His clothes were all torn off and just hanging in strings. His eyes were as big as pesos. He finally got said that the office had blown up and about killed him. He said he was putting my clothes to dry when it happened. I rushed over there and he was right, the roof was gone, and so were my clothes. The only thing left was my long-handles. They were straddled of a rafter. They must have been spinning as they were going up because they were wrapped around the rafter.

The office was on the bank of the canyon where the ore train ran below. I never found the rest of my clothes. The roof was pretty much all together down there in the canyon. Many times when I was showering at night, Shorty would have the water heater so hot it would be dancing, but I never had an idea it was about to blow up. The pop-off valve was bad or gone and that was why it blew. That night he just finally built up too much steam. It blew the top off the hot water tank so the pressure or explosion was up. It blew all the roof off, mostly in one piece. The water rained back down in the offices. Sure was a mess. The roof was most of the damage. Hardly cracked the walls. The office was four rooms and a rest room. Art Hall's room, Carl Beecroft's room, shift foremen room, and the change room.

I have told that we used lots of timber in the mine because it was so heavy. The mine that is. Another job of third shift was to hoist out all the old timber that had been replaced with new. We had men that did nothing but cut up the old timber in stove wood lengths and deliver it to our houses. I guess they would have put it in the stove for us if we asked them, but we had a maid to do that.

By the time Floyde joined us, we had a 1940 Chevy. Our first car and we were sure proud of it. Mart had older brothers and so she had never learned to drive. In Dublan there was one car per family and most families didn't even have one. I taught her and I must say she is the kind of a driver that I feel at ease with. We take turns driving now with our motor home. I go to the bed in back and take a nap. I must tell a story on her anyhow. When we thought Floyde could make the trip, about a month, we put a few things in the car, mainly those special little pants he was wearing, and headed for Monterrey. Our very close friend, Ernie Hatch, was there on a church mission, and we were sure she wanted to see our little kid.

We left San Pedro when I got off work in the evening, and drove all night to get there. When I told Bill Holmes we were going to Monterrey he told me that there was a large river to cross, and that we had to cross on a chalan (ferry). It was very fortunate because I'm sure I would have driven into the water had he not told me. It was night and very dark by the time we got to the river. The car tracks went right to the edge of the water. It was a gravel road and I would have driven in just like the river I was raised on. The chalan was on the other shore and a fellow came over for us. It was tied to a cable across the river and was moved by hand. Those tracks at the water edge was where the cars were driven onto the chalan.

I will try to tell you a picture of the beauty of the river and chalan part of the trip. The river is named Tamesi. It flows into the Panuco River a few miles before finding the ocean at Tampico. From San Pedro we climbed the mountain range which is in the tropics. Then we dropped down into the valley where the chalan crossed the river. The valley is called El Valle De El Salto (the valley of the water fall). The valley was thickly timbered with palms about fifty to sixty feet tall. At this point, I say "was" because the last time I was there all those beautiful palms had been taken away and the valley turned into farms. I'm sure the palm timber we used in the mine for a while came from that valley. From the chalan we drove up the river about five miles to a most beautiful sight. The entire river falls off the mountain into the valley. A little over three hundred feet straight down. If you get closer than about a hundred yards you get rained on. So you take an umbrella, a rain coat, stay back, or get rained on. Mart and I got rained on. I will give you an idea of the amount of water. At the chalan the river is about two hundred feet across and about ten feet deep, and just as clear as glass when not in flood stage.

The road was very mountainous. It was graveled from San Luis to the Mexico City highway which was paved. When we arrived at the paved highway we were on our way. We thought clear sailing on north to Monterrey. I was tired so we decided Mart would drive and let me rest. At that time she had only been driving about three months, and that was all in the daytime, and flat country. When I gave her the wheel I thought we were out of the mountains. I soon learned that on that road one does not get out of the mountains. She had only been driving a few minutes when we became aware that we were not out of the mountains. When we became aware that we were still in the mountains and big ones we started watching for a place for her to pull over and let me drive. Before we found a place where she could pull off the road to change drivers, we met a car on a curve with his bright lights on and we were blinded. I knew if Mart dimmed her lights she would be able to see a little better. I told her to dim the lights. Since she hadn't driven at night she didn't know where the dimmer switch was except somewhere down there on the floor. She looked down there trying to find it and things were going to adios fast. She was still on the throttle. I grabbed the wheel and was able to hold it around the curve, and until the road was straight again. We got stopped and we were scared. She was so scared that I thought if I take over now she may never drive again, and I sure didn't want that. We talked for a few minutes. I talked her into driving until she got over being scared, then I drove the rest of the trip. We took some bedding with us and when I was too sleepy to drive anymore we found a place to get off the highway a few feet and tried to sleep until daylight. Between Floyde and the tropical bugs, we didn't sleep much. We left Floyde in the car. We sure didn't want the bugs to get him. We got to Ernie's house in Monterrey at about breakfast time. We drove that road several times. Each time we went around that curve we thought how near we came to losing it all right there. We couldn't see the bottom of the canyon. We were on the inside of the curve.

I will tell a little bit about teaching Mart to drive. The shift lever of our car was on the steering column. That in itself was confusing because we had always driven with floor shifts. It was a vacuum booster shift so only needed a finger to start it in the right direction and it would shift itself. To shift into reverse the lever must be lifted then moved by finger only, forward, but never when traveling forward. Mart didn't understand the finger only part. When going from low to second she would get a handful of shift lever and into reverse she would go. I sure thought she was going to take out the transmission a few times. Automatic transmissions were still way in the future. After a few lessons she felt confident to drive around camp to visit the other ladies. I came out of the mine one day and as I walked up to our little Chevy I noticed the right front fender was gone. There was a fire hydrant near our house under the same pepper tree where we parked our car. When she backed out she hung the fender on the handle that turned the fire hose on and guess what. That hose proceeded to beat hell out of that poor little car. Bill Holmes heard the commotion and came out of his office and called for help to get the water turned off. He told Mart to tell me that he did it. She did and I believed her.

When I went to San Pedro there were only two shift foremen, but after a year they hired two more foremen and divided the mine. I was given my choice on my shift of taking the upper or lower run. I took the lower. I was given my choice of my two shift bosses and I took Enrique Urista. He couldn't read or write. He was good with the men and knew the mine. When I had all that settled I got busy. It would be about a month before the new men arrived. I started teaching Enrique to read and write enough to make out reports to me. I told him to start transferring men. Put the good ones on the lower run. By the time the new man arrived I had the men switched around and no one had ever caught on. My mining problems went from a few to none. The new man, Tennis, sure had his work cut out for him. He was a new mining engineer from El Paso. After about a year of me with no problems, the mine super said, "Adams, I'm just now figuring out why Tennis has so much hell with his men." I told him that I had told Enrique to adjust the men the way he and Tacho, the other boss, wanted them. Enrique forgot to tell Tacho what he was doing.

Sometimes on Saturday night, if the day shift had gotten out good tonnage, I would make a deal with my men. It was always important to beat the other shift, and mostly I did. When I saw I had to really get after things to beat the day shift, I would tell my shift boss to tell the men as he went through his run, that when they had one more car of ore on top than the day crew we would go home. They had never heard of such a thing, but they went for it anyhow to see if I would really let them go early. They worked through lunchtime and it wasn't long before we had the tonnage out. I also told them to be sure and drill and blast so we would have muck for Monday morning, because if our Monday tonnage was down we would never do it again. We had done the same thing in Bisbee once in a while and we liked it.

My men made so much noise when they got topside that night and went home early that the whole mining camp knew about it before I could tell my bosses what I had done. I was called to the head office for a little chat. I had set a precedent that all the miners liked, but the superintendent was afraid of. He was afraid we would get in too big a hurry and make some of the working places dangerous. Maybe I should say more dangerous because it was by nature a dangerous mine. He didn't tell us not to do it anymore but he did say to not do it very often and then only after talking to him. He told me that the test would be if I had left muck for Monday, and if I had a bad tonnage run we would discus the issue some more. I told Enrique to be sure the men understood that we were all in trouble if we didn't get a high tonnage Monday. We did because I had developed the best crew in the mine.

I got two weeks vacation time per year, but the mine foreman, Carl Beecroft, got four weeks. Carl and I were the only men that didn't have a degree in mining engineering. He was mine foreman and I was shift foreman. I was given his job while he was on vacation, and I sure had my hands full. By that time, Art Hall, the Mine Superintendent, had been transferred to Charcus, and Ralph Bateman was put in his place. I knew I didn't like Bateman, but I didn't know why until I had to deal direct with him. He absolutely did not know mining. To this day I don't know how he held his job, unless he was related to someone high up in the company who wanted him out of the way. When I saw what I was up against in trying to run the mine with him, I decided to go over his head. I went to the Chief Engineer office and told Campbell what I was up against in trying to run the mine with Bateman. He wasn't surprised but in no way would he talk. He told me to come to his office each evening and he would go over the details with me so I could keep things going in the right direction, and not blast into something I shouldn't. I had to know what and when and where to cave stopes, and that had to come from the engineer. I should have been able to get it from Bateman. Another thing I didn't understand was that Bateman knew I was going over his head and he never said anything about it. After I was in El Paso and had my own service station, who should come into my drive one day but Ralph Bateman. He had retired and was living there. He was glad to see me and we talked about the San Pedro mining days. He had the nerve to tell me how he had held my job for me. I was thankful he couldn't read my mind. He wouldn't have liked it.

I have told that the mine shaft was three compartments. The third being a man way with a ladder from top to bottom. The ladder zig zagged in the shaft, so there was a platform about every thirty feet. About two hundred feet down was a crystal cave. When the canyon ran water from rain the water found a passageway from the canyon to the cave then right on down into the mine. If it rained and ran the canyon for more than a day, we would shut the mine down and just bail water. We had large buckets that we exchanged for the cages and that way we hauled the water out.

They had spent lots of time trying to find where the water went into the passageway from the canyon but never found it. Not only was it a very hot mine but also a very wet mine. We carried slickers to go through the rain part of the mine. I climbed down to the cave and carried out some beautiful crystals. I gave them to my mother when she visited us. My little brother, Sam, destroyed them with a hammer. I never went back for more.

On my days off, which were Sundays, we drove to the country and saw lots of interesting things. We found a little town that had hot springs with bathhouses built there and we enjoyed that. On one of our trips to one of the ranchito towns, we saw a fight going on and quite a crowd gathered. I knew the men, they were on my shift at the mine. One of them had a knife and the other one had a pitchfork. They were dancing around like a couple of roosters. One of them never came back to work. One day, on a Sunday, we saw some fellows on the waste dump across the canyon from our house. One of them cut the other open just above the belt. I won't even try to describe it except the poor guy sure had his arms full. Quite often on Monday I would miss a man and ask about him. "Oh, he got into a fight and was killed."

The cages had safety dogs to catch the guides in case of a cable break or anything that would cause the cage to fall. The dogs were checked once each month. The safety was removed from the pin holding the cable to the cage and then the pin jerked out quickly. The dogs must stop the cage in about four feet or less. The guides had to be replaced sometimes because the dogs ate them up on those tests. I was there three years and my shift had to climb out of the mine once. I was on day shift. We had a new man on the hoist. When the cage was about halfway down he hit the hoist brake and gave it a good bounce. When it free floated it turned the dogs loose and that was where the cage stopped, but the hoist man didn't know the cage had stopped. He dropped the rest of the cable on top of the cage. The cage was going to the four hundred meter station but he bounced it at about the two hundred meters and so dropped two hundred meters of cable on top of it. The cable folded over into the compartment of the other cage so it was also out of service.

We had to walk out of the mine that day. The mine was fifteen hundred feet deep, and that is quite a walk straight up. As my men started single file up the ladder, they started to sing, and it echoed from top to bottom as they climbed. I always encouraged my men to smile and be happy, and there they were after a hard day's work, having to climb fifteen hundred feet to the surface and singing. Enrique and I climbed out last.

I have told about the chalan (ferry) on the big river we crossed on our trip to Monterrey. It is the Tamesi river. After a year we had a two week vacation and of course we went home to Dublan. We drove east to the Mexico City highway then north to Monterrey, then east again to Laredo, and then to El Paso. We spent a day in El Paso doing some very needed shopping and then we crossed the border at Antelope Wells, NM, and home to Dublan. We reversed the sequence for the return trip. As we drove through Linares, on our way back to San Luis, a fellow ran a stop sign and I hit him broadside. Linares is south of Monterrey. Floyde was sitting in the back seat eating a banana. It threw him to the floor and poked the banana into his mouth. He sure was upset about the whole thing. The fellow I hit was an officer of some kind. I was sure I was in some big trouble. He took me to the courthouse, before a judge and told how I had hit him broadside and ruined his car. Then the judge asked me for my story, and if I hit the man's car in the side. I told him yes, but that the light was green and I thought I was OK to go through. He asked a few more questions, then told me to get an estimate for my repairs. I did, three hundred and fifty pesos. The judge made the fellow pay me in cash right there in his office. I left there knowing that I was one lucky gringo. The judge thought I was a tourist. Con la boca cerrada no entra la mosca, which was a favorite saying of my father--in--law. It means, with the mouth shut the flies can not get in.

    The car wreck in Linares was behind us and we were on the last leg of our trip back to San Luis. When we arrived at the big river with the chalan, it was gone. I mean the chalan was gone. The river runneth over. There had been so much rain that the river had overflowed the banks and washed the chalan away. A new one was being built and was almost finished, but the river was still too high to cross. We sat there on the bank three days waiting for it to go down. It kept raining and we were running out of food and pants for our little kid. A 1940 Chevy was not much room to live in for three days.

    While we were waiting, bus loads of people arrived on each side of the river, and since the buses couldn't cross, it was decided to cross just the passengers and luggage. The chalan operator had a small boat tied to the cable with a rope and a pulley arrangement to pull light load trips across and it worked fine. Then they got in a hurry and put too many folks and luggage on board and started across. In the middle of the river the current was swift and was about to swamp the boat. The passengers panicked and moved forward instead of back, and sure enough the little boat went under. It dumped the people in the water but most of them held onto the boat. A man was washed loose from the boat and he couldn't swim. He was splashing and crying for help. We were all on the bank watching when someone in the crowd said, "HAY VA UNO." We were still watching him fighting the water for his life and going down the river when again some one said, "HAY VA OTRO." There were several washed loose from the boat and each time, "HAY VA OTRO." The operator couldn't do anything because the passengers had all piled on the bow with him and so they just sat there midstream until enough washed loose so he could get the others to move to the back. He lost most of that load. Searchers ran up and down the banks but never found any of the missing. Only one could swim and he had no trouble getting to the shore. Swift water is more fun to swim in than a pool, but takes more care. About two hundred yards below were rapids. Not even a good swimmer could survive that.

I put sticks at the edge of the water to see if it was rising or lowering. It was doing both, so on the third day we went back to the Mexico City highway then south to Ciudad Valles. We had spent two nights in our car at the river so we were glad to get a motel. We left our car at the motel and caught the train to San Luis. The same river was flooding there at Ciudad Valles. We had a little trouble getting to the train station because of high water.

That was a beautiful train ride. Over and through the mountains. I have never seen so many tunnels. When we arrived in San Luis, Mennell and Florine met us. San Luis was flooded. Water was all around the train depot. The road was barely passable to the smelter as there was no bridge. It was a month before the weather cleared so I could go for our car. When I parked it I put the emergency brake on hard. When I went for it, I couldn't get the brake shoes to release. They had rusted and grown in place. I have not been an emergency brake fan since.

We spent lots of time with Mennell and Florine. They were really good to us. We went on lots of picnics. One place we especially liked was a grove of large trees. Maybe about a quarter mile square. The trunks were about three to four feet diameter and maybe about two hundred feet tall. They were very pretty and I have no idea what kind they were. That small grove was the only trees we ever saw of that kind. It was a nice place for an outing so we went there several times. One day we had the tablecloth spread out on the ground with all kinds of good things to eat right under one of those big trees. I was laying on my back looking at the trees and admiring them when I spotted an owl in the very top of the tree we were under.

We had a Taylor family reunion in June 1990. Mennell and I were talking about our San Luis days, and I asked if he knew what those large trees were where we went for picnics. He said, "Oh yes, they were eucalyptus trees." And he remembered the owl also. I have added this rather than change my story.

Mennell and I liked to hunt so we took our .22 automatic rifles with us on those outings. I took a fine bead on the owl and pulled the trigger. He just sat there on his limb and I leaned my gun against the tree and laid back to watch him some more. I didn't expect to hit him anyhow. The tops of tall trees have a lot of movement. After a few moments he fell off his perch and dropped a few feet and caught his feet onto another limb, but he was upside down. I was the only one that knew he was coming down. I watched him as he dropped a few feet at a time then the last drop was about twenty feet and almost onto our lunch. He was such a pretty bird I wished I hadn't shot him.

On a Semana Santa we went fishing at Tampico. We closed the mines for the week. No miners would report to work anyhow. Carl and Helen May Beecroft, Lester and Eva Skousen, and Mart and I were the ones who made that trip. At Tampico we chartered a boat with a driver. A large river, called Panuco, runs through Tampico. He took us first down the river and out in the ocean. Before long Carl was hanging over the side and begging to go back. We didn't catch anything out there, but the porpoises sure liked to play with us. Then we went up the Panuco River and caught some large fish. We caught Yellow Tails and some Tarpons. The Yellow Tails we got into the boat but the Tarpons would get loose before we could get them to the boat. They would stand on their tails and shake the hook out of their mouth. They are a real game fish.

Our main recreation at the mine was tennis. In the City, at the smelter, it was bowling. We had one court so we played mostly doubles. Carl and Eva, and me and Helen May. Three years of that and we got pretty good. One evening we were playing, and of course there was always a crowd watching, and waiting to play. I had gotten pretty good at reverse spinning the ball. It would hit the court across the net and spin backwards. Eva was playing net and was determined I would not get to spin one out on her. Instead of spinning it, I hit it hard and straight, but she anticipated my move and was there. Instead of catching it on her racket, she caught it on her throat. I was embarrassed, and she has never let me forget. When I see her, she reminds me that I hit her with a tennis ball.

Someone bought an old mansion in San Luis Potosi City and made it into a tourist museum type hotel. They had a grand opening and invited all the ASARCO people and important town people, including the governor. When I met the governor, the handshake was one to never forget. His last two fingers were gone. Keep this in mind because he and I meet again about five years later. His name was Delgado. The Roberts invited Mart and I to ride to town with them for the party and we were glad. He was in charge of the warehouse there at the mine. I had heard he was bad to get drunk at parties, but I had never seen him get out of line. I had never been around drunks so really didn't think anything about it. At that party he sure enough took advantage of the free drinks. When the party was over, I had to almost carry him to the car. Mart and his wife were in the back seat, and I was driving. About halfway home, he should have asked me to stop and let him out, but he didn't. No one but a drunk could make such a mess in so many ways. That was one time I was sure glad. Glad we were in his car instead of mine.

When I made up my mind to quit the mines, I traded our car for a '41 Ford half--ton stake. We went there with a suitcase and needed a truck to leave with. It included two little kids. Our little kids seemed to enjoy the same things we did, so they were no trouble to take along. In April of 1943 we drove down the hills and away from the San Pedro Mine for the last time. We both shed some tears, but were glad we had broken loose.

We didn't want the US border hassle so planned to travel up the center of Mexico to Dublan. Lester had done that and told me how to go. To Monterrey, Torreon, Jimenez, Delicias, Chihuahua, and then to Dublan. Sounded easy, but after Torreon there was no road. Jump ditches and follow trails, and ask every man you see on a burro if this is the trail to the town you hope you are headed for. It took us more than a week. We arrived in Torreon at night, tired and hungry. I pulled up to a hotel on the main drag. When we had our truck loaded for the trip, the last things on top was our luggage, and four brand new tires I had bought through the company. The war was on and there were no tires to be had. I went in to get a room and was only gone a few minutes, but when I came out there was a guy on top of the load cutting the rope that held the luggage and tires. Mart was telling him to get off but he paid her no attention. When I came out he jumped down and ran. We stayed the night there. Those places have a corral for the vehicles and a watchman. That was two day's travel.

The reason it took us two days to Torreon was because Bill Holmes wanted me to look at a ranch that was for sale on top of the mountains before we got to Monterrey. He thought we might want to buy it if it looked good. It was a large Spanish--grant hacienda on a high plateau. For some reason the area was a large high flat country with very little rainfall. What grass there was had been ruined by the prairie dogs. They were everyplace. I spent a whole day with the mayordomo looking it over. I just couldn't see any chance of ever making it work. I turned it down.

There is a large river between Torreon and Gomez Palacio. There was a bridge at the crossing, however. We will see that river again some day later in my story. A short distance after we went through Gomez Palacio we came to a fork in the road. The left looked pretty good and the other not so good so I stopped to look them over on foot. As I got out of the cab, two guys jumped off the top of my truck and ran into the brush. I had my .22 Colt Woodsman on the floor. I grabbed it quick and fired a few shots in their direction, but into the bushes. They had hopped aboard as we passed through the last town going slow. The ropes were cut and they were just ready to start unloading my tires and luggage. I tied them on once more, and after that Mart would stand on the running board as we went through a town.

I checked the roads and decided to take the best one. It seemed to be going in almost the right direction. We traveled until in the afternoon and came upon a large earthen dam being built. That was the end of our pretty good road. I should have taken the right fork. I talked to some people about if I could cut across to Jimenez, so I didn't have to go clear back to Gomez Palacio. We had no map, so we just sort of kept the radiator facing to the north.

The road, or tracks they showed me, looked about like our ranch road so I decided for the shortcut. By then I had been stopped by a police, but I never knew why. He asked if I had a gun. Thoughts went through my head. If I lie and he finds it I'm in trouble, but if I say yes, he will take it and let me go on my way. I said, "Yes" and took it from the floor of my truck so he could see it. To my surprise he said, "Muy bien, sige." That was how close Floyde came to not having that pistol today. We traveled on that road until evening and made camp out in the wide open country. We got an early start the next morning, and by night we had made about fourteen miles. I still wonder why I didn't turn back. I kept thinking it would get better and Jimenez was out there someplace.

We were passing lots of riders and wagons all going our way. The next town was having some sort of Santo celebration. I noticed some riders loping alongside of us and I thought I better stop and see what they are up to. Would you believe they were cutting the ropes loose again on my tires and luggage, from horseback yet? So after that, when we passed riders, out went Mart on the running board. She got real good at it. That part of the trip was mostly flat country, but we came to a place where the road or trail went up a hill. It was so steep that we almost didn't make it. In fact, I was able to make it by slipping the clutch, and that I knew was my last stand. We topped out and what a sight. It was flat country on in to Jimenez and the road was recognizable. We could see the tracks without guessing.

We made Jimenez that evening. Out of gas, almost. I knew gas would be a problem on the trip so I had a twenty--five gallon drum extra. It was in the fuel tank already. I ran onto a rancher I had known and he had a fifty gallon drum in his truck. I asked him for a few gallons and he turned me down quick. I could not find any gas in Jimenez. We thought maybe we could make the next town, and if no gas, then we were at the end until we could find some. It was very night when we drove into the next town. There were people walking in the park. I started trying to find out where I could find some gas, and there just was none to be had. A man came to me out of the crowd and said he knew where I could get some gas. He would go with me and show me. He hopped on the running board and started giving me directions. Mart and I were sure nervous. He was taking us to some of the back streets. He held up a hand for me to stop and he went inside. When he came out he had another man in tow. The fellow said he could let me have ten gallons. It was expensive but we had to have it. I tipped the fellow who took me there. We put the gas in the tank and hoped it would take us to Delicias. I mentioned way back in the Rafter G Ranch chapter about Dad and Nichols buying alcohol in five gallon square cans. That was the way the gasoline was sold that I bought that night.

We drove a little farther that night and made camp. It was so dark we couldn't tell where we were, so we rolled our bed out on the ground and got in. We made a little bed near ours for Floyde and Sid, but they kept crawling out so we put them between us to keep them from getting away. The next morning we couldn't believe what we saw. We had camped on the bank of a large canal and it was full of water. Sure no place for little kids to be running around in their sleep. That was a few miles south of Delicias, our next MUST fuel stop.

At Delicias we pulled in to a gas station with our fingers crossed. We got all the gas we needed. My barrel was full again. We made Chihuahua City that afternoon and got a room at the Victoria Hotel. We bathed and ate and slept the rest of the day. The next morning we got an early start for the last lap on to Dublan, a long day's drive. When we arrived in Dublan, our folks had been worried about us, and so had we.

When Bill Holmes saw that I was going to quit the mines and go back to the ranch, he helped Bryan Brown and his brother, Art Holmes, and me form a partnership in cattle. We each put up one thousand dollars US. Then they would pay me $100.00 US per month to run the operation. That was the reason he wanted me to look at the ranch near Monterrey. He thought it might be a good buy for us three partners.

I had registered for the service with the El Paso Draft Board, but would not be called as long as I was in the mines. When I went home I sent in my change of address and job, and was called in July, 1944. By the time I went to the service I had about a hundred head of cattle in the partnership.

13

Dublan Second Time

In April 1943, we were back on the ranch again at the Pajarito. I was glad to be out of the mines. It sure seemed good to have a horse under me again, I thought. I had been out of the saddle for so long that I had lost my balance. There had been some changes while I was away. One, Dad had sold all the cattle, including mine, and sent them south to the Sudderth Ranch. The Sudderth Ranch was on top of the mountain north of Chihuahua City. Sudderth hired Tio to drive the herd to his ranch, and then hired him to run the place. Tio never went back home again only to visit. Raymon was there for a while at the Pajarito but he was gone when I returned from the San Pedro Mines. Dad had gotten into buying and selling cattle and was making some money. I fell right in with him and was sure getting set when I was called to the service. World War II. I had about a year and half before being called so I was able to get a lot done. My folks lived in Dublan, and Mart and I lived on the ranch.

Dad had traded for three bronco horses. He told me to break all of them and take my pick of one for myself. Tio had started riding them and had them doing pretty good when he left, then Raymon took them over, then I got them. I learned later that they had been bucking Raymon off. Tio could ride them. The first thing I did when I returned was have a special saddle made. A saddle with a good seat to sit in while a horse was trying to get me out of it. I had one before with a good seat so

I knew what I wanted. A saddle maker in Casas Grandes made it for me. Dick Fitzpatrick. When he had the tree ready, I sat in it, then as he put the covering on, I sat in it. He put leather on and shaved it off and reshaped the seat until he made me a perfect fit. Most saddles are very uncomfortable.

I rode the three colts. They were three years old, and two of them were sure messed up. One of them bucked all the time and kicked my feet at the same time. I finally told Dad, "This bronco wants to get on so I'm getting off." The other one was not dependable, and I told Dad he wasn't worth my time, so Dad gave me the third one. I called him Sueno. He made a good horse and gentle.

There was a fourth horse in the deal that I haven't mentioned yet. Bill gave him to Dad, a three year old from his Benton Ranch. Lorin, their brother, had broken him. Lorin Adams was a master with a young horse. That horse was so gentle and so good that Dad got careless with him and leaned too far over his neck. That colt popped Dad on the ground so quick he hardly knew what happened. Tio took him over and was able to ride him, but after he threw Dad he looked for any excuse to buck, and he was a spinner. When Tio left to drive the cattle to the Sudderth Ranch, Raymon took him over, but couldn't ride him. His name was Streak. When I got him he was a mess looking for where to do it. He was just too good a quality to throw away. Dad told me the whole story on him so I was ready.

I had my new saddle and had it pretty well broke in, most of the squeaks out. I was on him and penning some cattle. One cow turned back rather than going into the corral. Streak turned with it, but then forgot about the cow and put all his thoughts into getting rid of me. I have told about my Chinate horse, and how he would spin. That Streak horse was then and there teaching me about a real spin. I stayed for about two 360's then I flew upside down and landed that way. He was spinning so fast that instead of being popped onto the ground, I sailed out then skidded on my back. As I left my new saddle, my spur raked across the seat, and those marks were permanent. Mart came running out to help me get up, but my arms and legs and head seemed to point in the right direction. I told her to stay back so I could catch my horse. He stood there for me to get on and we would try that again. I rode him some after that but I never trusted him. I knew that if I was ever unbalanced just a little, he would do it again.

While at the mines, Mart had two maids to help with Floyde and Sid. A very nice house and things to go with it. At the ranch we had nothing. She did all her work and did a real good job and no complaining to me about it. No wonder I love her so much. Sid was still little, but Floyde was big enough to get into things he shouldn't, so needed more watching. He had been used to the maid being close. With his new type of life he was enjoying his freedom. Mart heard him playing and laughing outside the yard. It seemed he was having so much fun she better see what he had found that was so funny. He had found a little rattlesnake and he was teasing it with a little stick. When the snake would strike at him he thought it was funny to see it jump. Each time it jumped he would jump, so it hadn't bit him yet. It was just a matter of time before the little snake would catch him.

We had a large water trough in the corral and he loved to get in it. It was real dangerous because it was about two and a half feet deep, and that would sure drown a little fellow. I knew someway I had to outsmart him. I couldn't keep him out. I thought maybe I would let him get in, and not let him out. See how long before he has had enough water. He played for a long time, and I began to think I had lost that round, when, "Daddy, I want out." That's what I had been waiting for. I said, "You better swim some more." Pretty soon he was begging to get out, but I kept him in until he was real sure he had enough, and believe me he never went near the water trough again. That took care of my biggest worry, because I was gone so much. Floyde was old enough to learn nursery rhymes and we had taught him several. He had trouble with the Ba Ba sheep however. He called them brown sheep. One day I decided to take some time with him and get him to call them black. He said, "Daddy, I can't say black sheeps, I just can say brown ones."

Dad was buying and feeding cattle in town. A feedlot near the house. Then shipping them when he had a few train--car loads. That year the farmers had raised lots of beans and they were full of weevils. Dad bought those beans by the ton and wheat straw by the ton. That was what he was feeding them. He had a man there that cooked the beans in fifty--gallon drums and took them to the feed troughs in a wheelbarrow.

Those beans gave the cattle Montezuma's revenge, so one must be very cautious about getting in the corral with them. Especially the south end if the cow was headed north. He would feed them a few days and then ship them to El Paso and get some more cattle to feed. He was the only bean buyer in town.

I hadn't been back in Dublan very long when I ran into Mr. Bob Cook. He was in Nuevo Casas Grandes, or as we called it, the Station. The same one I have told about that raised paint horses. I asked him if he had a good paint colt he would sell me and he said he did. He would take a hundred pesos for him. I gave him the money, and he would deliver the colt on his next trip for supplies. He was still in the mountains and came down to the Station about every two months. I was passing the stockyards about two months later and I recognized Cook's pack mules and camp there in the corrals at Casas Grandes. Sure enough, there was a paint colt. A two year old and I thought he must be mine. I went into town and found Cook in one of the stores buying supplies. Raymon was with me. Cook said he would be back to the corrals in about two hours, and yes that was my paint horse. Raymon and I drove back to Dublan to the feedlot and saddled our horses. Then back to the stockpens to pick up my colt.

My paint colt was not taught to lead so he was completely raw, and that was the way I wanted him. He knew nothing, but also no bad habits. I rode into the corral and pitched my rope on him. He came along pretty good until I was leaving the corrals with him on the end of my rope and then he changed his mind about being a good horse. I hate a horse that won't lead. I thought that by the time I got him home he will have learned, and good. I cinched my saddle tight and tied the rope to the horn and started home. He choked and fell down, got up and ran, hit the end and was jerked down. That went on for several times and Raymon said, "Bill, you are going to kill him before you get him home."

I said, "I'm going to lead him home, not drag him, and now is the time for him to learn that." After a few more choke downs and fall downs, he decided there were two ends to the rope and he better quit pulling on his end. He came up to me all sweaty and puffing. I petted him and talked to him, and told him how smart he was. He stayed by my side and never tightened a rope again. He made a good horse, but was never gentle.

He was bald faced with a round red spot on his fore head. I called him Penney. He had a white ring around his eyes, on the eyeball itself. Dad told me he had mean eyes, so don't ever trust him, and he was right. He always looked for a chance to kick me, and he never got over it.

I have told that Tio stayed on at the ranch he delivered the cattle to when Dad sold out. The ranch was in the flat country on top of the mountains north of Chihuahua City. When Mart and I got settled back at Dublan again, we decided to go see him. Mart made a lunch and away we went in our stake--body Ford. In those days, the Ford V8 had the fan on the crankshaft. After we passed El Valle, it was new country to me so I had to watch my roads very close. Realize, when I say road, I'm talking about ruts, or car tracks that seem to lead in the direction I want to go. We came to a canal full of water and no bridge. I waited for a wagon to cross to give me an idea of how deep it was. It was about two feet deep but only about ten feet across. I turned around and went across backwards, and fast. Even then, it drowned my engine. When it dried off we continued on to Namequipa. We had been in valleys until the Namequipa town with mountains on either side. At Namequipa was where we went into the mountains and climbed out on top of a high plateau. That was where the ranch was we were looking for. The Sudderth Ranch.

As we left Namequipa I heard a noise I didn't like. When I investigated, I found the front spring leaves all out of place on my buggy spring Ford. That was when Ford still only had one spring in front and one in rear. We called them buggy springs. The center bolt had broken and let the leaves slide around. Those springs are not hard to change with a spreader tool, but I only had a jack and very few other tools. I had my twenty--five gallon drum full of gas. It was just after noon and a good lunch and there we sat. I also carried a spare center bolt. Spring trouble was one of Ford's headaches. At that time Mr. Ford had his money and I for sure had the headache.

I did not turn the main spring leaf loose on the ends. I knew I would never get it back in place with what tools I had. I jacked the car up and sat the drum under the front bumper then let the car down so the spring could fall out of the saddle. There were no broken leaves. I was in luck. I had a tough time getting the head of the center bolt to go into its seat and that was a must. Darkness arrived just as I finished the job. We arrived at the Sudderth Ranch after midnight, and when we awakened Tio, the first thing he said was, "How in the world did you find the place at night? Most people can't find it in the daytime." We spent a few days there with him.

He showed us the ranch. It was large. One of the problems they had was lots of wolves. He carried a rifle and pistol when he was riding the range. He rode the range in a pickup. I have told that the ranch was on top of the mountain range. Very flat and easy to drive anyplace with no road. Lots of grass but no rocks or chuckholes. When we would jump a wolf we would take after him and I would shoot him out the window when Tio got alongside of him. We hunted coyotes on our Buena Fe Ranch from the vehicle and they were smarter than the wolf. When we would get in pistol range of a coyote, he would turn and go the other way and by the time we turned the car around to go after him again, sometimes he had found a hole to go into or a fence to go under. The wolf ran crooked but didn't turn back unless we really crowded him. Our biggest problem with those wolves was getting enough speed to catch them.

While we were there, Tio had to go to Chihuahua City. He drove the company Lincoln Zephyr. I followed him off the mountain to the Chihuahua Highway and left my truck at the junction until we returned from Chihuahua. There was a service station and restaurant there. He showed us a great time. We returned home around the mountains rather than over and through them.

About my Ford, I was on my way to the Pajarito Ranch from Dublan. I had a canal of water to cross and no bridge. It was early in the morning and I was in a hurry. I drove into the water easy like. The fan caught the water and drowned my Ford dead. Remember, those Fords had the fan on the crankshaft. I gave it mouth--to--mouth language but it still stayed dead. It was sitting there in the water and I was still talking Ford language, which I was learning fast, when along came Lalo Gavilando. His ranch joins the Carretas Ranch which at that time belonged to Gordy Boyd. I thought he would pull me out of the water. He told his chauffeur to get out and look things over. He did and hopped back into the car. He drove around me in real bad water, out the other side, and I haven't seen him since. I decided right then I didn't like him. He was driving a Chevy. Many years later I landed my plane at his ranch with a message for him. I didn't tell him that I was the fellow he left sitting in the canal of water.

I spent all my spare time repairing the front spring on that little Ford. One day I had enough. I went to the Station and started looking for a buyer. Ernesto Jaramillo, who had a store on Main Street, gave me five thousand pesos for it. That was the same man and the same store where I tossed the egg to Demar Cardon when we were going to the JSA.

I went to Ciudad Juarez and bought 1934 Chevy. A nice little car. That was in the days of knee action shocks. Dad, Raymon, Albert Wagner Sr., and I were driving over the ranch we were buying from Wagner, when we jumped a couple of coyotes. Dad said, "Run up alongside of them and I'll shoot them." I did, and he got one right away but the other one gave us quite a chase. By the time he shot the other one my car seemed to be handling rather funny. We got out to take a look. The arms on the knee action had bent and I had about three inches negative camber. There was no front--end place closer than Deming. I jacked it up and heated those arms and bent them until it looked about right. Those nature trails kept the speed limit to about thirty MPH so it worked real good.

I was driving down the street in Dublan in my 1934 Chevy and came upon Manrique Gonzalez trying to start his International pickup. It would have been made in the early 1930's. He lived a block from our house. I stopped to help. He had lots of trouble with his truck. He said, "Bill, I'll trade you straight across right now where they sit." I would rather have the truck so we traded. He drove my car off and I walked back to our house. Two blocks because he had his truck out in the street where he had been trying to get it started. I told Dad what I had done. He went with me in his car and a chain and we towed my truck home. When I traded for the International pickup it was in the winter. That was the reason Manrique couldn't start it. I mean it was frosty and cold that morning.

My newly--traded--for truck had twenty--one--inch wheels, and of course the fan was up where it should be. I could go anyplace. 1941 was the last new cars built because of the war. A few of them were called

1942, but only a few were built. The next new cars were built in 1946 but were the same as the last ones that were built. There was such a demand, that used cars sold well and new cars had lines of buyers waiting a turn. No discounts, and lots of extra goodies. I felt lucky to have an old car or truck that I could get around in.

The twenty--one--inch tires made it especially good for my ranch work. It was made in Mexico for Mexico's roads or trails. I could go anyplace and never hit high center on those ruts we called roads. I soon wore out the tires that were on it, but no problem. I had four brand new tires I brought from San Luis, only they were fifteen inch. I found some Plymouth wheels with the same hole pattern and put my new fifteen--inch tires on my truck. It sure looked better, more like a car than a buggy. I got the new tires and wheels on it and headed for the Pajarito Ranch, ten miles, at night, and no moon.

My little truck didn't have very good lights, but no worry because I was raised on that road and knew it by the foot. Floyde was sitting in the middle and Mart had Sid on her lap. I was one happy cowboy heading for the rancho. It had been raining, so there were plenty of mud holes in the road, but I knew them all. I just drove into them and out the other side. About halfway to the ranch and just before we left the farm area, I came to a large mud hole. I could have gone around, but why, when I like to splash mud anyhow. In the middle of that mud hole was where I learned the difference between twenty--one--inch tires and fifteen--inch tires. That little truck hit high center and all four wheels were not on the ground. It was cold and we only had our jackets. I got out and scouted around to see what I could find. Near there I found a stack of wheat straw. I guess where the farmer had run the thrasher. In those days the thrasher was stationary. I got Mart, Floyde, and Sid, and took them to the straw stack. We dug a hole and put the kids in there and covered them up. Then dug one close to them and got in there ourselves. That straw kept us warm and we crawled out the next morning in good shape. I was able to get out of the mud before long. I never quit wishing for the twenty--one--inch tires. I still had the wheels but couldn't get tires for them.

Our lease was about up with the ejido on our Pajarito Ranch. We had been there about fourteen years. They would not renew the lease so

Dad started looking for a place to go. He bought the Wagner Ranch, which was about ten thousand acres. It was south of Casas Grandes. The fence on the Wagner ranch had been destroyed during the Villa revolution and was never put back. Wagner had not been using it since Villa's time. It had been used all those years by the ejido people, and they had no intention of giving it up without a fight. An ejido is a large amount of land owned by the government but run by the people of the town it is designated to. The ejido law caused many problems for the adjoining ranchers. The ejido was created after the Villa era to try and give the campesino a place to work and live. The ejido at Pajarito was called Guadalupe Hidalgo. The ejido south of Casas Grandes is Colonia Madero. That would be our new neighbors and not friendly already.

We took the fence from the Pajarito Ranch and put it on the Wagner place. We called that ranch Buena Fe. We moved in the early part of 1944. There was a group of men determined that the fence would come down. They would tear it down at night and I would put it back in the daytime. Then Dad and I would patrol at night with the .30--30 loaded, and the car lights out. but we never caught anyone. We didn't really want to catch anyone. We just wanted them to know we intended to stay. When we were out there, they stayed away. By the time I went to the Navy things had quieted down and we didn't have much trouble.

When we moved the cattle from the Pajarito, we took them to Jay Robinson's ranch northeast of the Dublan Lakes. We leased from him until we could get our place fenced. Dad drove the cattle the first ten miles to the river and I took over and drove them the next seven miles to Jay's ranch. We had some cowboys to help. The river was running full, bank to bank. I went around by Old Town with my pickup loaded with wire and posts then met Dad at the river on the Dublan side. It was interesting to see the herd cross. I have seen that sort of thing in the movies since, but that was my first experience in swimming a herd of cattle across a river. I had seen a cow swim but never a herd. It was difficult to get the first cow to take to the water, but when one did the rest followed and there was a long string of cattle swimming. The water was swift, so they got out about a hundred yards downstream from where they entered. Once they were in the water, they were left alone to find their best swimming angle with the current. The little calves swam in there just like the cows. We didn't lose a one.

Dad took my truck and I took over the cattle drive at the river. The country was flat and easy to travel. After Dad sold the herefords he decided to go into black angus, so the herd we were moving was black. Black cattle will fight for any reason or no reason at all. The cattle herd was moving along nicely when one of the bulls stepped on a devil horn and it caught on his hind foot just above the hoof. A devil horn is a dried and matured seed pod of a very beautiful desert flower. He was almost carrying that foot and I sure didn't want to turn him on the ranch with it on him. I told one of the cowboys to get ready and I would rope the bull by the foot that had the devil horn on. I wanted him to be ready and jump from his horse, run up to the bull and get the thing off the bull's foot and run to the side. I explained to him twice because that old bull would quit pulling and turn and fight in a matter of seconds. I told him to be sure and run to the side and I would hold the bull until he could get on his horse.

I roped the bull, and as he pulled, his leg stretched out. The man jumped off his horse and got the devil horn off. The bull looked back and said, "I'm gonna get me one vaquero." No problem, the cowboy would run to the side, and I had the bull stopped in his tracks. Nothing could go wrong. Well, not much anyhow.

It just didn't work out that way. The cowboy panicked and forgot what I told him. He ran towards me, he ran by me and kept going. His chaps were sure flopping and he was outrunning that bull. The bull came by me after him. That gave the bull the fun to chase him twice the length of my rope. That vaquero did exactly what I told him not to do. However, he was winning the race until the bull hit the end of my rope, and broke it. That old bull had all the time he needed to catch, and I thought, kill my cowboy. All I could do was sit on my horse and watch. The bull was fast getting in a position to pick his hind pockets. Or maybe just clean his nose on the seat of the vaquero's pants. The guy stepped in a hole and fell down and I quit breathing. No way could I get to him in time to save him. The black cattle don't have horns, so all the bull could do was mash him up. Killed by a bull comes out about the same no matter how he does it. The bull stopped and stood over him, pawed some dirt, blew his nose on him for good measure and then went back to the herd. I had to turn the guy over and stand him up. He thought he was dead. He told me he was sorry he made the mistake and ran the wrong way.

While we were fencing the Buena Fe Ranch, a neighbor, Alberto Varela, fenced off a piece of our land that joined his ranch, and moved his sheep onto it. Dad had gone to El Paso so I was by myself and in charge. Mas o menos. I had the ranch all fenced except the piece he had taken. I had my fencing crew ready to go and told them to set the posts on the line and I would asked the herder to move the sheep. The herder refused so I went to town looking for Alberto. I found him in Casas Grandes at a service station. I needed gas also. I went up to him and told him that my men were putting the fence on the line now and would he, por favor, move his sheep, and he could move his fence later. Well sir, he became unassembled. There was quite a crowd gathered. He sure cussed me, and tried to get me to fight him or just hit him. All that time he had his hand on his .45 pistol. I knew that if I didn't stay cool, that old boy would kill me, and he would have all the witnesses he needed. I told him I was right and he was wrong, so I would go to the law, and I left.

I found an official of some kind at the courthouse and back to the sheep I went. When I arrived with my help, Alberto was already there, and the sheep were leaving. I drove up near his car. He came up to me and wanted to shake hands. He was sorry for getting so mad. He said I had embarrassed him before all those people. He would move his sheep and would have his fence moved before I could get my fence closed up, and he did. We were friends after that, never anymore trouble. About seven years later we sold all our cattle to him and his partner, Francisco Anchondo. Soon after that Mart and I moved to El Paso with a one--way ticket. Never to try to live in Dublan again.

We got the fence all finished and moved our cattle from Jay's ranch to ours, about four miles. The Dublan Lake was between the two ranches. We had lots of trouble with the ejido people who had used the ranch for free for so many years. They would cut the fence wires between each post for about a mile at night and I would repair it in the daytime. By the time I went in the Navy we had things pretty well calmed down. I would splice the little pieces of wires together when repairing the fence, and it was a mess. Three or four splices between every post. New wire was hard to come by and sure cost when we could find it. Another war shortage. I knew I would be called to the service anytime so I tried to have things in order when I would have to leave. I traded my pickup to Joe Memmott for a Dodge Coupe he had picked up in Chihuahua. Dad wanted the Dodge Coupe, so I sold it to him.

It was wheat--threshing time and Mennell, Mart's brother, asked me to help him for half of the ten percent we would get for cutting. We worked hard. Mennell drove the tractor and I ran the thresher. It was not the self--propelled type like today's machines. It had to be pulled but had its own motor for threshing. It had a large hopper or bin that caught the wheat. When it was full we would dump it into a truck, then when the truck was full we would run it to the mill. Every tenth truckload was ours. I kept enough wheat for Mart's flour while I would be gone to war, and sold the rest. Mennell sure treated me right.

Sid was too little, but I would take Floyde to the field with me sometimes. He would play on the ditch banks in the shade while we were cutting. Round and round the field we were threshing. We had just made a turn to go back to the end of the field where Floyde was playing when I saw a dog going in his direction. As we got closer, I could tell it was a mad rabid dog. Its tongue was swelled out of its mouth was how I could tell. It trotted right on by Floyde and over to a farmhouse nearby, and started fighting with some dogs there. A fellow came out of the house and killed it. I was afraid to leave Floyde there, so I took him on the thresher with me. I put him in the bin because I was afraid he would fall off the thresher. My controls were lower than the bin so I would leave them to check him every few minutes. As the wheat came in he was having a good time playing in it. It was a good field and the wheat was sure pouring into the bin. It was about time to look in on him because the bin was getting full and I sure didn't want him to fall out. I looked in there and he was gone. Only one place he could be and that was covered over with wheat. I dug him out and he was almost gone. I ran my finger in his mouth and got the wheat out so he could breathe again. He had gone to sleep and he didn't know that he was covered up, and would never wake up. He sure was drowsy for a while. That was his last trip with me to the field. It was just too dangerous.

While I was cutting wheat, Sid got into trouble also. In those days a Mexican nickel was about the size of a US quarter and made of copper. Dad was always giving the kids money. That day he gave Sid a nickel. Later in the day Sid went to Mart and pointed to his throat and tried to tell her that was where his money was. He was just learning to talk. She didn't think he could swallow it. He couldn't eat or drink so we knew something was in there but surely not the nickel. We decided she better get on the train and take him to El Paso. When she got to the border, the American officials wouldn't let her go across to El Paso until the next day. By then, he was sure getting sick and weak. When she got him to the doctor the next day and they took the x--ray, there was the nickel. The doctor very carefully removed it. He told Mart that if it had broken the skin in his throat it would have poisoned him and killed him right there. He was so hungry she could hardly get him filled up. I have never forgiven the immigration man for not letting her go to El Paso the first day. I don't know what was the problem because we crossed there all the time.

I made sides on my International pickup to haul my paint horse. I made a long tailgate for him to walk up to get in. In those days you didn't see many horses that would ride in a pickup so it drew some attention. Tio came to see us for a few days from the Sudderth Ranch where he worked. They needed a good milk cow and we had one. She was a jersey from the J & M dairy in El Paso. Joe Memmott gave her to Dad when she was a little calf. He owned part of the dairy. Tio bought her for Sudderth and hired me to take her to his ranch in my pickup.

Mart and I left with the milk cow early one morning because it would be a long day. We went the usual route to go to Chihuahua City until we got to the road that went up the mountain to the Sudderth Ranch. It was about ten miles to the top of the mountain and then it was flat country the rest of the way. The climb was pretty steep from the Chihuahua highway to the top. As we were going up a steep part of the road my truck just would not pull the load. The road was narrow so I had to back down to a place where I could park and try to find my trouble. I couldn't find what was wrong because the engine revved up good so I tried the hill again. The same thing, loss of power. The next time I backed farther down the hill and got a good run at it. I made it to the top of the ridge but the next canyon was steeper and farther up and I couldn't get enough run to make it.

I noticed that the engine ran good on level ground or when I backed up to get a run it ran good. I had used the procedure of backing through water that was too deep to go through front first. I turned the truck around and sure enough it ran good going backwards. The reason was because the fuel pump was weak but with the back end uphill the engine got enough gasoline to run. Yes sir, and I don't mean maybe, I backed that little truck with the milk cow in it all the way to the top of the mountain. It didn't have rear--view mirrors. I owl--headed all the way. Like I said, it was about ten miles to the top. The road was barely as wide as my truck.

I knew that my time was near to be called to the war service and there was still lots to do getting the ranch fixed up. My folks lived on the ranch, but Mart and I lived in Dublan. Dad had bought a windmill but couldn't find pipe for the well. Mart and I went to Chihuahua City to see what we could find. I still had my International pickup. We spent a few days there in Chihuahua City and I was able to find some pipe that had been used to transfer oil from someplace to someplace. The inside was a mess but the pipe was good. It was three inch ID. The pipe, for some reason had been cut in ten--foot joints, but that was still quite an overhang for my truck.

We left Chihuahua for Dublan real early with some lunch for the road. That pipe slowed us up more than I thought it would. Between El Carmen and Galeana was one deep and narrow canyon. Maybe six feet deep and twenty feet wide with steep sides and only one place to cross by car. I slowed down and shifted to low gear. I was at the bottom of the arroyo and ready to climb out, but I didn't. That International went to death city right there in the bottom of the canyon. In checking, I found that it also ran out of gas right there. So what, I had a twenty--five--gallon drum of gas and a siphon hose. I soon took care of that. Still wouldn't go. Starter dead. I found one of the cables had jumped off the battery. Still no go, but the motor would spin, however. I had coil trouble before so I looked at that and sure enough it had been hot and squirted tar out. I carried an extra coil and I put it on. With all of my trying to start it, I had by then run out of energy in the energizer. The sun had just gone behind the mountain. There was very little traffic on that road, especially at night. Mart and I got ready to spend the night. One thing for sure, if someone did come along he would have to help us out of the arroyo in order to get by. At that place there was no wood, period. It was grass only country, but guess what there was lots of instead of firewood. Not buffalo's but cow's. Not much difference in buffalo chips and cow pies. They are made about the same way and make the same kind of a fire, mostly smoke. We gathered a large pile to last through the night and had just lighted the fire and settled in our blanket when we saw car lights coming from Chihuahua City way. I told Mart to get in our pickup because they would have to push us out of the canyon. When we hit the top I would hit the gear while he was still pushing and if it started we would be gone. It started very easily. We got home to the ranch just in time for breakfast. That truck sure was hard on coils, and I could never find out why, so I always carried a spare. I had to leave to the Navy before the well work was finished.

The mail finally brought the greetings from Uncle Sam for me to report for duty in July 1944. Floyde and Sid stayed with my folks and Mart went with me to El Paso. I told that Dad bought the Dodge Coupe that I traded my pickup for. He had taken the rumble seat out and put a pickup bed in there. I think it was a Model T box. We had been to Mart's folks place to tell them adios. Mart was driving and Dad and I were riding in the truck bed. In those days a coupe was a one seater. Dad was sitting up on the edge of the pickup bed as we were going to the train station. Mart drove over a bump in the road and it threw Dad into the air. We were in forward motion and when he came down his seat was gone and he hit the ground tumbling. He wasn't very happy with the driver but he didn't say much. He really did say a bunch, but it was while he was still tumbling and she didn't hear him. The train was there and ready to leave and that was the way I left him when I left for the war. Mart and I got on it and went to El Paso. Only those who have been there know the feeling I had that day. I felt like I had been given a one-- way ticket away from all I knew and loved.

14

U. S. Navy

July 1944: I was in the El Paso courthouse being sworn into the Navy. There were thirteen of us that day. Hundreds took the physical the day I did. Everyone I talked to said they had asked for the Navy. I felt lucky to be one of the little seagoing crowd. We all held up our right hands and swore to go kill Japs and Germans. That is not nice language today but it sure was then, and we meant to do just that. When we were in, I mean committed, like too late to change the mind, the judge came to me and handed me a sealed brown envelope. He said, "Adams, you will deliver these orders and these men to Los Angeles." I asked who I should give them to. And he said, "When you get off the train, there will be a Navy man there to greet you, and he will ask you for your orders."

We were all delivered to the El Paso train depot to wait for our train. We all had folks there to see us off. Mart and I knew it was adios for a while. We rode pullman, and had good meals. Our train left El Paso in the evening. We rode it all night, all the next day, and arrived in Los Angeles after dark. No matter, the Navy man found us, took the orders, then gave us some. Orders that is. Line up, get in step, and then some other words I didn't understand. We didn't line up, and we sure didn't get in step, but he still managed to get us on the train for San Diego. We were thrown into the main herd at the training station to wait till morning. That was Boot Camp, and it didn't take me long to know why. Every time I turned around someone gave me a boot.

Breakfast was on time, then to the barber shop, and I mean lots of barbers. By the time it was my turn I could see what to expect, and sure enough, a close clip. I didn't realize there was no humor in the Navy, so I said, "You guys must have come from a sheep ranch." I never picked up and swept up so much hair before or since.

Then back in line and hipity--hop to the next stop. My next orders were, "Take all your clothes off and put them in one of those little bags. Tag the bag to be mailed home or throw it in the bin for Goodwill. Keep nothing, not even a toothbrush." It was a large building, and what a sight. That roundup was a new experience for me (puros machos). We moved along passing the various booths. First the underwear, "What size scivies you use?" New words were coming at me; dungarees, whites, blues, kerchief, seabag, ties. The ties were little ropes about a foot long for tying the clothes. The clothes were rolled up tight and put in the seabag in a special order, then socks, and then last were shoes. One pair for marching, and one for dress. My dress shoes were still new when the war was over. The shoes were too big. They told me that when I got out of boots they would just fit. They were right. I wore 8 1/2 when I went in and 10 1/2 when I came out.

I learned real soon that there were three ways to get in trouble, the right way, the wrong way, and the Navy way. In a very short time a little herd of boys was cut out of the main herd and given a number and was called a company. As soon as the little herd was given a number and called a company, there was sure no chance to break out of it. Seemed all they did was stand me at attention and count me to see if I had escaped yet.

We were lined up in front of our barracks, when the CO saw a cigarette butt on the deck. He told a Mexican boy to pick it up. That boy was tall and marched behind and next to me. He said he didn't throw it there. Then the CO gave an order very loud and rank pulling. The fellow still refused. They gave him three days, bread and water. The fellow's name was Perez. When he came back to the company the CO threw a butt on the deck and ordered him to pick it up. He did. He told me he sure had enough bread and water treatment.

    We marched everyplace we went. The Perez guy was out of step most of the time, and if we were in close, he stepped on my heels a lot. I told him and told him to not do that, but he just didn't know his feet apart. One day we were into some hot maneuvers and he was all over my heels. I turned around and told him that the next time he stepped on me I was going to whip him. A little more marching and he got me again. I spun around on him but he caught me by the shoulders and turned me around. He said, "Adams, I'm not doing that on purpose, but don't fight me because you'll sure get us both in trouble, and I don't want bread and water again." We went on and he did improve some. I had showed him how tough I was.

    One of the things the companies competed in was boxing. Two companies would meet at the boxing bleacher and volunteers would get in the ring. All fun and no one got hurt, until one day a professional from the other company got in the ring with our volunteer boy and sure messed him up. Just a few licks and our boy was on the deck for good. Our CO asked for a volunteer to get in there with that guy, and we all started looking around to see if we had someone so foolish. My good enemy--friend, Perez, stood up and volunteered. Perez climbed in the ring and was charged for a quick kill. The other guy was a toe dancer, and would go around his man looking for an opening and then put a glove in his face. He went at Perez with his dance, and Perez was watching the guy's feet. As he would get ready to hit Perez there would be a foot signal that Perez recognized, and bang, Perez gave him a face full of glove. He gave up and quit before Perez killed him. He never hit Perez one time. Perez came back to his seat not even breathing hard. I jumped up and greeted him and said, "Mr. Perez, old mate, you can step on my heels all you want to." It turned out he was a champion boxer from L.A. He never stepped on me again. I know he wasn't afraid.

    Everyone had to go to the church of his choice, and that was where and when I got in the habit. We were marched to church just like everywhere else. At church I ran into Clarence Wagner, Chester Brown, and Dale Farnsworth, all of us in different companies, and all of us from Mexico. Dale and Clarence were very friendly, and we got together every chance we could. Chester was never friendly to me in school at the JSA, so when he said hello the first time, that was enough for him. He was a good person, we just never ran in the same crowd.

My company was a bunch of ornery kids, mostly eighteen and nineteen year olds. The companies compete for a pennant and it was hung over the door of the barracks of the winner. The winner got it for a week, and each time, the winning company got an all night liberty to San Diego. My company was the worst and we got no pennant for that. We went through three COs and one day we were marched to the grinder and put at attention. The grinder was a large paved area for putting boots through the paces of learning the Navy steps, and I don't mean dance steps. Our new CO climbed up on a platform and gave a short speech, but to the point. He said, "You are the worst company in boot training. You have done in three COs. I am only used to winning the pennant. I won't ask you to do anything I can't do, but I will make you do anything I can do, and if any one of you think I can't, come forward now." No one did. Boots was twelve weeks and we had six to go. He soon learned who were the trouble kids, and he would take them out one--on--one and put some instructions on them that they would remember. The first week we could march and follow orders pretty good, and by the second week we were darn good. He would march us by the review stand to show us off. We were so good that one day we were marching and he got mixed up on his calls and we marched over a flower bed. That was the end of those flowers. He first called, "Get the hell out of those flowers," but we kept on going (bad command). He gave us, "To the rear march," and got us back into the street, stood us at attention, and used some Navy words that were new to me. Then, "Forward march," then, "Right face march." When he said, "Halt" we were up to our waists in the bay. The water sure cooled us off. Then he had us double--time until we dried out. We held the pennant for the last three weeks of boots.

We got our liberty, and I called Mart. She was in Phoenix. I told her which hotel to meet me at. We were both in the lobby and she was checking all the sailors but couldn't pick me out. I was so burned and peeled from all that sun, I hardly knew myself. We spent a real fun day at La Jolla Beach. We took our first ride on the roller coaster. That was her first and her last.

I finished boots and had two weeks leave. I took a shortcut home to Dublan. I mean I got on the fastest train I could find to El Paso. The one that dips down into Mexico before crossing the Colorado River. I sure hated to go back when my two short weeks were up but I was afraid Uncle Sam would do like he did with Pancho Villa. Send someone after me. I figured my time close. I could take the train from Dublan to Ciudad Juarez and be just in time to catch the train to San Diego. The Dublan train goes through the large Salazar Cattle Ranch. They have very good hereford cattle. The train stopped, which wasn't unusual, but then word came back to the passengers of why it stopped. The engine was derailed. I went forward along with the rest of the passengers to see what had happened. Two of Salazar's big bulls were fighting on the track. The one facing the train jumped off the track. The other one stood there shaking his head, and bragging about being the best bull when his victory was his last. Well maybe not really, because the last thing he did was knock the train engine off the track.

A crew came to the rescue with some special irons they put in front of each wheel that was off and drove the engine back onto the track. It took hours, and all I could think of was missing my train in El Paso. While the train was being repaired, the soldiers and a lot of the passengers made a fire and had eaten most of the bull by the time we were ready to go again. They were cutting steaks from him while he was still under the train. I made my train to San Diego but it was close.

From boots the company was scattered. I was sent to Port Hueneme, near Oxnard, CA. It was a cargo--handling school. We learned to use the steam winches for loading and unloading a ship. We used two winches, a control for each hand. The cargo was handled from a gin pole that was swung out over the side of the ship. Two cables were fastened to the hook that picked up the cargo. One cable went through a pulley on the top end of the pole and the other cable was on a pulley at the top of the second pole. One pole was swung out over the edge of the ship and the other pole was swung over the hole in the ship where the cargo would be let down into. One cable lifted the cargo and the other placed it over the hole to let it down to the deck it would be assigned to.

There was a cargo hole on each deck and if they were all uncovered the cargo could be let down to the very bottom. A very tricky manoeuver. I thought I was doing well and getting along with the instructor. The cargo we practiced with was very large wooden blocks to start with then as we got pretty good we loaded a dump truck they had there for the test. It had less than a hundred miles on it but it was literally beat all to pieces from banging on the side of the ship. Realize the mock ship was made of concrete so we couldn't tear it up also.

I had been used to working with gloves on, so I asked for a pair. The instructor laughed at me and used some un--nice words on me. Twelve weeks of boots and they still didn't have me well--broke. I was on the night shift school. The next day I went to the first Lieutenant and told him my story. He listened to me, then asked how many were on my shift. He gave me an order for a pair of gloves for each man, and I sure thought I would get some brownie stripes. The stuff we were handling was rough and dirty. None of the fellows had ever used gloves. They were pleased that I thought of them, but the instructor had one fit. I had gone over his head and he got mean. I couldn't do anything right. We were told at the start of the school, that one man was always held back when the class was shipped to somewhere else.

When it was time to leave we all put our seabags in a pile and as our name was called we picked up our bag and got on the bus. When the bus drove off, me and my bag were the ones that were left. When I was able to get my tears stopped I looked around and tried to think, "What now?" I went into the office and was told I would be there for four weeks on mess cook. Then it came to me, go to the phone and call Mart. She was still working in Mesa and staying with her sister Beth.

I will never know what that old boy put on my records but I do know that I was kept off the winches on my ship until one day in New York the winch boy messed up badly. I took over his winches and finished the loading. I had learned on steam winches and they were sure enough wild. The ship winches were electric and controlled like the ones I had run in Morenci. By that time the war was over and I wasn't trying to make brownies anymore.

I had to work the noon meal and the rest of the time was mine, and I had weekends off. Now about mess cooking, I was still of the opinion that life should be fun, and that one should enjoy what he does. I was put on the butter tray, little squares, and give one square to each man. The butter was cold and on waxed paper. I bent the outside tongs of a fork at right angles to the others, then snap the bent tongs into the patty of butter, then by snapping it on the handle of a knife, it would pop onto the man's tray and stick there. Those guys got in a hurry for their butter. They would hold up their tray and I would shoot them a butter. At first two or three men back then more. I got so good I was shooting butter for thirty feet. Those long shots were really easier than say one ten feet, because the guy had time to move his tray and still catch it if my aim was a little off. Once in a while there would be a complete miss if I should shoot a curve, but someone in the rear always caught it.

It was bean harvest time. I got a job in a large warehouse where the beans were brought in from the fields and shipped. I worked there weekends and some evenings. They paid good and I worked hard. Those sacks of beans sure got heavy by the time the day was over. On the base we had ship's stores and I could buy things that were gone from the public. Those bean boys all wanted watches. I had learned my three times tables in school and I put them to work there. 3 x cost = profit.

I was to meet Mart at the bus depot. I waited for a long time and finally went to a hotel nearby, but couldn't get a room so I slept on a couch in the lobby all night. The next morning she came down the stairs all nice and fresh. She had arrived earlier and gave up waiting for me, so went to the hotel and couldn't get a room, but the clerk thought she looked like a nice person so he let her have a room of someone who was out of town at the time. We found an apartment, a room, with kitchen privileges. An old dairy that had the stalls made into rooms. Most of the stall was still intact. The place hadn't even been swept out good. Cow signs here and there. Mart got real sick with asthma so could only stay a few days. I had to almost carry her to the Greyhound. The driver saw how bad she was. He took her out of the line and put her in a special seat. We sure did appreciate it. As I'm writing this I'm remembering all the lines I stood in, and how I promised myself that if I live through the war I will sure be hard to line up again. Well, it hasn't been 100%, but damn close.

My next move was to T.I. (Treasure Island). The buildings were from the World Fair. They were so big we had several companies in one. That was where the ship's crew was put together. I was assigned to the USS General MB Stewart AP140. A troop transport. It was still being built in Oakland. I was on T.I. for three months. One of the buildings was the chow hall. Four galleys, and each one fed about three thousand men per day. I spent most of the time in some sort of school. Each galley had its own scullery (dish washing). By that time I had learned a lot of things about survival. One of them was why start at the back of the chow line. Start up near the front, just far enough back to not cause too much commotion, and always pull in front of a little mate. I had just politely forced myself into the chow line one day at noon, and there came the master--at--arms of my galley. I knew I shouldn't mess with that guy. He carried a big stick hanging on his duty belt and it was always ready for a fast draw. He took me to the very front of the line, told me to get my food and where he wanted me to sit. I did, but I wasn't ready for what happened. He said, "I have been watching you. You seem to get along well with the men. You break into the line anytime and anywhere you want. How would you like to come in early and eat, then take charge of the scullery?" I did but again I wasn't ready for what went with it. I could go on liberty every night and have every other weekend on liberty. I called Mart, "Come to San Francisco, the weather is fine."

On the scullery job I had about six men and they had to hop to keep up with the trays as they came in. The trays went through a steam and hot water bath so it was plenty warm in our shack. I had one Black boy and he was a good worker and no trouble at all. We all liked him. One day he came to me and told me that one of the boys was harassing him and calling him a "nigger." I called the two of them to one side and into a corner to ourselves and asked the other boy if he liked his job. He did. I said, "Let this be the last of harassing or you will be turned over to the master--at--arms and when he gets through with you, me and this Black boy will take you to the recreation building and he will give you some lessons in boxing." I was sure that Black boy would sure mess him up and he thought so to. Boxing was a very good way we had of settling with two boys who just had to fight. That way, no one got into trouble. I was called on by friends to be observer while they tried to kill each other with gloves. All I had to do was keep it fair no matter which one would win. I would let them fight until one of them had enough. It seemed to always make them into good friends. He didn't give me any more trouble. I was in charge of the scullery until I went aboard my ship.

After that problem was solved, I had a very smooth and pleasant bunch of boys. One day the master--at--arms came into my work place. The scullery was a building for doing dishes and was built inside of the large world fair building. It was maybe 25x25 feet. He took one of my boys and sat him in the corner and started talking to him. I had no idea what was going on and I sure didn't ask. I couldn't hear what the master--at--arms was saying but what ever it was the boy was sure paying close attention. That went on for several minutes then the master stood up and started telling the boy what to do. The boy did everything he was told. He was supposedly hypnotized. I had heard of such but had never seen it and of course I didn't really think it could happen. After he had put the boy through several things the master told him it was getting cold. It kept getting colder and the kid was about to freeze and he finally found a jacket to put on and he sure seemed to be getting cold. His eyes looked like he didn't see anything. I was still doubtful, however. The master kept telling the kid how cold it was getting and it appeared he was really about to freeze. By that time my scullery was surrounded by onlookers. Then the master started to warm the boy by telling him it was getting hot. He took the jacket off. The master kept telling him how hot it was and he started taking off his clothes and broke out into a sweat. Just before the kid boiled the master clapped his hands and brought him out of it. The kid was sort of dazed for a few minutes. It was not a fake. The kid was too tired to work so we sat him on a chair for the rest of the shift.

We found a place to live, and Mart got a job in a steak house. My sister, Domer, was there also. We three lived together. Dick, Domer's husband, was already overseas. Domer and Mart worked at the same place. When Mart went home she left me her electric iron. I made spending money ironing uniforms. I charged $1.00 to iron a neckerchief, and had all I could do. I had my Navy pay sent to my bank in El Paso so I had to make my spending money when I wasn't standing in line for something.

I went to gunnery school at Point Mugu. When we studied the Mark 14 sight, I knew that I wanted to be on the trigger end. I knew that was the most important place, if we were going to shoot those Japs before they shot us. I did well and when I went aboard ship I was assigned to the quad 40 remote control. That was my general quarters battle station. I was high above and away from the guns I was firing, with good visibility. We practiced a lot and when one of those little target planes went up, I looked at it as if it was a Zero, and I put some holes in it.

I will tell here a little about the gunnery school. I liked it and I sure wanted to be good enough to get on the trigger part of the gun and I had fallen in love with the forty millimeter. I didn't like the twenties because the barrels would get hot and bend and if they were not changed in time I thought maybe they could bend into a U shape and just shoot hell out of me. We had shot and learned about those two guns while in boots.

We learned about the Mark 14 gun sight, which at that time was the latest and best thing on the market. It went with the gun I liked so I took very special interest to learn about it and hoped I could be assigned to it when I went aboard ship and was assigned my battle station. I was feeling pretty sure of myself because at the shooting range I was put on the forty millimeter with the Mark 14 sight. I fired two guns from the one sight. The target was a long sock pulled by a very brave pilot. He would circle out over the ocean then fly over us and we would shoot the sock. Maybe I should say we would shoot at the sock. I was still thinking like when at home on the ranch. If I couldn't see the target I didn't shoot. One day the instructor came to me and asked why I quit shooting so soon. I said, "Sir, I couldn't see the target anymore." He said, "Adams, if you can't get the ammunition out there I will put someone on that gun who can." After that, for sure, I shot my share of the ammo. I would start shooting at the sock before I could see it and shoot at it after it was gone over the hill. Just squeeze the trigger and stay ahold of it. One day I was doing that very thing and all of a sudden I realized I had the plane in my sight instead of the sock. I made a quick correction without releasing the trigger. Word came to us the next day that when the target plane landed the pilot found some holes in it. We were told in Navy language to shoot the sock and not the plane because it makes the pilot nervous when he finds holes in his plane. After a few days we got pretty good with those guns. It was real easy to shoot the cable just in front of the sock and let it fall into the ocean. That was a no--no because it took the pilot several minutes to get another target for us.

Mart stayed in Frisco until my ship was about ready then she went home. We had two little boys that needed her also. My ship was commissioned and when it looked like it was going to float, we went aboard. We had trouble the first thing. The prop caught the demagnetizing cable and wound it up like a fishing line. Then the shake down. First trip out in the big water.

The following dates and places are actual records that one of the yeomen made for everyone in the ship's company. It was mailed to me after I arrived home. I kept it, but at the time I had no idea that I would ever have any use for it. Now that I am writing my life story it is priceless for making my Navy era more interesting.

USS General MB Stewart (AP140) c/o Fleet Post Office, San Francisco, California

RECORD OF VOYAGES

3 March 1945: Went aboard the USS General MB Stewart and put ship in commission. Went to Oakland Naval Supply Base to load supplies and equipment for ship. That was the hardest work I did in the Navy.

8 March 1945: Left Oakland NSD (Naval Supply Depot) and went to San Francisco. That was where we tangled the prop in the cable.

14 March 1945: Left San Francisco for Long Beach, California, for shakedown. We had a guy in ship's company from deep in the Tennessee woods. Joe Knoe. He never bathed and wouldn't work, but he went to the training schools with the rest of us. One of the schools was how to see at night, and spot something out there in the dark. They stressed to us that if you think you see it, report it, because there is probably something out there. That was the only time I remember of using the crow's nest, and they put Joe up there. I think to get him out of the way. It was a very dark night. The watch stations were, bow, port, and starboard on the bridge, port and starboard amidships, fantail, and the crow's nest. Joe in the nest and I was on the fantail. We all had head phones, so we all heard what anyone said. We had complete silence until around midnight, Joe broke it but good.

"Bridge, bridge, I think I see two submarines."

Bridge, "What is your position?"

Joe, "I'm standing up."

Bridge, "Where are you?"

Joe, "I'm on watch."

Bridge, "Where are you at on watch?"

Joe, "I forgot the name of it."

They rode Joe hard to try and teach him but he refused to learn. He was the most worthless person I have ever known. He liked me for some reason. I never abused him. They couldn't make him mad. In New York a piano had been brought aboard and was still on the deck, topside on the fantail. I was walking down the deck on the opposite side when I heard piano music like I have never heard before or since. When I came around the corner and saw who was playing, I was in shock. It was Joe Knoe, and his face was just bright with pleasure.

15 March 1945: Arrived in Long Beach, and started a twelve day shakedown of the ship. The rope storage locker, or room was on the fantail, one deck down. I was put in charge of it. Then later they added the paint locker to my care which was near my ropes. Then before long I was also put in charge of ship's stores when taking on supplies. I liked my job.

28 March 1945: Shakedown completed, went to San Pedro to load more supplies. 31 March 1945: Left San Pedro for San Diego.

31 March 1945: Arrived in San Diego, and started loading troops for the first trip with passengers aboard.

2 April 1945: Underway at sea with a load of Marines, fresh from boot camp.

8 April 1945: Arrived at Pearl Harbor. At that time it was the advanced base. The advanced base was where supply ships went to from the US, then other ships ran from there to the front bases. My ship ran to those advanced bases. The AP ships carried troops from the US to the advanced bases. The APA ships carried the troops from the advanced bases to the front or where the fighting was. The advanced bases were at first, Pearl Harbor, then Manus Island, then the Leyte Island in the Philippines. We unloaded our troops onto three APA's that were waiting for them. We had a day liberty in Honolulu. 12

April 1945: Underway at sea again with a load of patients and sailors. Some of those boys were sure in bad shape. Casualties going home.

18 April 1945: Arrived in San Francisco. Unloaded passengers and started loading supplies immediately.

26 April 1945: Underway at sea again with a load of two hundred and fifty Waves and the rest of sailors.

2 May 1945: Arrived in Pearl Harbor. Unloaded Waves. A very exciting voyage. The Waves sure made WAVES. We took on supplies there. Mainly pineapple juice and milk. Both in square metal five gallon cans, and sealed. I have told how I was in charge of the rope and paint locker rooms. I had the rope locker fixed up pretty nice and I had it open to those who liked to come and relax. I made sort of a club, and of course the ones who wanted it that way were the ones who put me there. I was put in charge of a detail to unload trucks and bring the juice aboard. The milk went into the cold storage and the juice to the supply store, about three decks down. Now when I had one of those details, I always had one of the club boys in the lineup. They carry one can at a time on the shoulder and it was like a continuous march. The club buddy would brake out of the line at the right time, and detour to my rope room, drop his cargo and get back in line. I did that for anything we were loading. The big thing was cigarettes.

Anything I had in the locker was for the club's use. I never allowed anything from there for trading or to be sold. There was about a dozen members and mostly rated men. They were the ones who talked me into getting into trouble when we crossed the Equator. One of the members was the chief cook, and we ate good all the time. Some of the club guys liked to play poker. When we had soldiers aboard, they would hunt out some with money, and some of them had a bunch. They would go down to my rope locker and play all night. I served them coffee and sandwiches. The cook had given orders at the galley for them to give me what I asked for. In poker, every hand is won by someone, and every winner put $1.00 in the kitty for me. I never gambled, but I sure had a winning hand. They shifted what looked like lots of money to me. The cook and Dudley were the heaviest players. The first Lieutenant would come down once in a while for coffee with us during the day.

3 May 1945: Underway again with a load of sailors headed for Manus Island in the Admiralties and Leyte Island in the Philippines. While enroute we went by Guadalcanal and New Guinea. The only escort we ever had was from Manus Island to Leyte. A Destroyer. It was much faster than our ship and it ran zig zag course in front of us. We ran a straight course following the Destroyer. We ran a zig zag course from Pearl Harbor to Manus, and that took longer to cover the same distance. Those waters were all sub dangerous. Our escort picked up what they thought was a sub, when we were off the coast of New Guinea. It ran circles and dropped some depth charges, and we continued on course. It later caught up with us but I never heard any details. Some things they didn't tell us.

10 May 1945: Crossed the equator and the International Date Line and received initiation for Polliwogs to become a Shellback. War was over in Europe. That Shellback game was the worst experience of my time in the Navy. I almost got into some real trouble. A few days before we were to cross the equator the Shellbacks started getting ready to work over the Polliwogs. They were making us do all sorts of silly errands, run around in our shorts, take one of our shoes and tie it around our neck. We were doing everything they wanted, and no complaint. The day before we crossed the equator, some Shellbacks and some Polliwogs had gathered in my locker room. Club boys and all friends. The Shellbacks just kept harassing us. I said mates, let's take them, and we did. We took all their clothes off, and the shillelaghs they had made to whip us with, and threw them overboard. We had the Shellbacks outnumbered but it was one hell of a fight. The shillelagh was made from sewing a tube of canvas, filling it with beans and soaking it in salt water. Three Shellbacks and about six Polliwogs. It was hot and we got so sweaty we couldn't even hold on to each other. We sent them topside like that. They sure looked silly. They had given us a bad time about not being very tough Polliwogs.

By then we were hot and LOCO to get things going. I knew the Shellbacks were having a big meeting on the bow of the ship, and getting ready for us the next day. Now most of the Shellbacks were officers. They had been in the Navy longer. I told the mates, "Let's just finish the job and whip all the Shellbacks." I climbed to the top deck, they right behind me. We ran forward yelling, "Calling all Polliwogs, let's get--em." By the time we got to the bow we had a bunch of followers just waiting for orders. I took about ten with me up the ladder of the forward gun tub. The gun there was a five inch 38. I told the rest of the Polliwogs to take care of things on the main deck below me. I was up in the gun tub, and we were looking down on the Shellback meeting. They didn't know we were there. I broke out the fire hose, and when I pulled the trigger there was so much pressure I couldn't hold the hose by myself. Some mates grabbed the hose with me and we were then in control of it. I mean I had pulled the trigger on that water pistol and it was loaded with live ammo. Saltwater.

The first thing I did was wash all the meeting people away. They went for the ladder up to the gun tub but my troops would kick them off. If they held on I would turn the hose on them and off they would fall to the deck. Now, the bridge was where the controls were, like steering, captain's quarters, and other important things. It was about thirty feet from my position across to the bridge, and about the same elevation. By then I was wound up and my reasoning was all gone. I saw some folks on the bridge and I turned the hose on them. I sure didn't want to miss anyone. I noticed one of them was yelling something at us from a mouthpiece. I turned the hose into the mouth horn. It was sort of like a funnel. I guess I about drowned him. I felt one of my helpers tugging at my shoulder. He had to tug pretty hard because I had my mind on those folks on the bridge. He finally got right up to my ear and I heard him say, "Adams, that is the captain, and he says, "MAN YOUR BATTLE

STATIONS." I pulled the water trigger to the off position and down the ladder we went. As I hit the main deck I saw a couple of guys leaning over the side. They had a Shellback and was ready to drop him. That old kid was sure begging. I talked them into not dropping him, and to get to their battle stations. They hadn't even heard the orders, they were so intent with the fellow they had begging.

We were kept at our battle stations long enough for the officers to get the ship back under control. It turned out that everyone had left their duty stations and entered in on the fight. I went back to my fantail locker room where the whole thing started in fun. The guys we started with, in the first place, had showed up also. They started telling me how much trouble I was in. That I had caused a mutiny on the ship. Of course I said, "It was all in fun," when there arrived a messenger from the captain looking for Bill Adams. He handed me a letter from the captain, and signed by the captain. It mentioned some of the things he could do to me, and one of them was have me shot. I got scared and started to shake, and I have never gotten over it. Like I have said before, it was hard for me to learn that the Navy does not enjoy jokes of any kind. That letter was too hot to handle. I was afraid the word would get around and I destroyed it. I have wished many times that I had kept that letter.

Now for the next day and initiation. A guillotine, which I tore down the day before with the water pistol. A tank of water with a chair sitting up on the edge and turned with its back to the water. A thirty foot canvas tube about twenty--four inches in diameter, and full of mess--hall garbage, mostly chicken guts, and sure enough ripe. A word here about those chicken guts. I have already been questioned of how come we had those guts on the ship, and did we really have them. I don't know how they got them. I had assumed that they came out of the chickens we had been eating. I had seen chicken guts all my life so they were not new to me. What was new to me was crawling in them in the tunnel on my belly. Now believe this. I had already gone through so much hell by the time I got to them that I don't even remember the smell. The Polliwogs were in shorts only. Lined up for a turn at getting whipped while fastened in the guillotine. Another reason I hated to stand in lines. Some of those Shellbacks sure took advantage of the pleasure.

First the guillotine, a wooden blade with a notch cut in it to just fit the neck. When the head was in place and the blade let down, the tail was the only thing that could move and it couldn't move far. About like the football line. Head down and tail up. When everyone that wanted to, took a swat then the poor guy was turned loose, most of them crying, then to the chair and dumped backwards into the water. Two big guys in there to be sure you almost drowned, then to the tunnel. There we had to go between two lines of guys with paddles and they hit until we got into the tunnel. When you came out the other end, you were a Shellback and could get in line and have fun whipping those still to go through.

I put my head in that guillotine and they dropped the blade. They whipped me until I couldn't stand up. They would stop and start to turn me loose, and the captain would call, "Give him hell" and there came some more paddles. I finally just sagged to the deck, and they turned me loose. I got in the chair and they dumped me in the water. Those two big fellows held me under until I took in water. They raised me up and let me blow, but down I went for the intake. While I was up I heard the captain say, "Kill him". He was on the bridge with his mouth horn. They kept me in the water until I knew I couldn't make it, I had given up. I guess those guys felt me go limp. They picked me up and threw me out of the tank. I thought I had gone to heaven it felt so good when I hit the deck.

The guys at the gut chute helped me get up because they wanted me to go through their line. I took a run to get in the gut chute but they whipped me so hard and fast I didn't make it. By then I had the water blown out and I was mad. I told them that I was going to walk up to the chute and get in and if there was one paddle laid on me I would come back on the fight, and the hell with the consequences. They believed me, and let me get in, but about halfway through someone stepped on the tube in front of me so I couldn't go forward, and they began to whip me. They knew they had the captain's blessing. I yelled to make them feel good, and they finally let me go on out. What they forgot in their fun was that a fellow had gone into the tunnel with me. When I couldn't go any farther I laid down flat and the little guy crawled on top of me. They almost killed him. They were sure mad when I came out and asked them to help me get the other fellow out. We drug him out and I carried him below to the hospital. I sure felt sorry for him, but I sure had all I could take.

What I didn't know was that one of the officers was taking movies of the Shellback meeting, and when the water started he got movies of the whole show. On our next trip he showed it on the movie screen. We had movies for night life. He got a good shot of me squirting the captain. The way the sailors yelled and clapped when they saw it, I wasn't sure if they were for me or against me. I got some bruises that day that I will never get over.

We were carrying about 4500 troops. They were confined to their quarters during the Shellback games. The passengers were not allowed to roam the ship anyhow but less that day. The ship was built for troops and so they pretty well had to stay in their part of it and that was not topside. One time some of the boys we were bringing back to the US got a little unruly and would not return to their quarters below decks. We broke out the fire hoses and cooled them off. Actually we told them we were washing down the deck fore and aft.

16 May 1945: Arrived at Manus Island of the Admiralties. Unloaded part of the passengers.

17 May 1945: Underway for Leyte, Philippines. Manus was bombed the next day. 21 may 1945: Arrived at Leyte in the Philippines. We were anchored in the bay. Philippinos came out in canoe type boats to do trading with us. I traded for a grass skirt for Mart but didn't get home with it. Someone stole it. The standard procedure for trading was to lower a bucket on a line to haul things up and down. We traded from the fantail which was about twenty feet above the water. Someone tied a bucket on with a bad knot and was lowering it. A little kid was looking up to catch it and get his prize, when the knot slipped and the bucket fell. It hit the kid on top of the forehead and peeled the skin down over his eyes. With our language barrier we had a time convincing him to come aboard. We had a hospital and a doctor to sew him up. We let a rope ladder down to him but he wouldn't get on it. I guess he thought if we got hold of him we would finish killing him. We sent for a Philippino, that was one of ship's company, to come and talk to him. There are so many different languages in the Philippines that he had a time making the kid understand. Finally he came slowly up the ladder, and he was like a little animal that had been captured. The doctor sewed him up. We brought him back to the fantail and turned him loose. That little fellow jumped over the side and went down the ladder so fast we hardly believed it.

In all our trading, one of the Marines got a very large grass hat. Everyone was trying it on. When it came my turn, I rolled the brim like a western rancho type. The Marine boy went loco and decked me. He put a choke hold on me with my mouth and nose covered with his arm. I was running out of air and ideas, but I had one option. Bite him. I tried to bite a piece out of his arm but he turned me loose too soon. There were a lot of witnesses and they all thought the bite looked OK but him. He was not friendly but never bothered me again.

Someone brought a monkey aboard when we took on passengers at Leyte. I think one of the soldiers had him in a bag. I heard about the monkey and that he would have to be put to sleep. I started looking for him and sure enough he was down with the soldiers, but no one would claim him. They all told me to take him so I did. I took him to my rope locker, where he would be safe, then went to the ship's doctor to see what he needed to be a legal sailor instead of a stowaway. The doc went to my rope locker where I had him and looked him over. He said he would give him some shots and I could keep him.

That little monkey was the most entertainment we ever had on ship. He had friends and enemies, and he never forgot or forgave. He liked to go for a walk on the top deck. He would follow along but if someone made a move at him he would land on my shoulder, straddle my neck and hold onto my ears. I put a cot in my rope locker and slept there most of the time. I had to tie the monkey to keep him out of my bed. He liked to sleep with his head next to mine, and that was just too close. He liked to play. He was swinging by his tail or getting into my ropes and messing them up, he absolutely would not behave. Some of the guys taught him to smoke. I mean he got the habit quick. Everyone that came in, he would go for their cigarettes. I was worried when he started trying to light them himself. I sure had to be careful with matches. I had permission to take him off the ship, and the day we arrived in San Francisco, someone stole him and got away with it. It had to be someone with more pull than I had, and I had a bunch. I have always thought it was an officer that liked to take him for a walk. Floyde and Sid will never know how lucky they were that they didn't get the little monkey. I had planned to send him to them.

22 May 1945: Left Leyte and went to Guignan on Samar to unload rest of passengers. Men on Samar were loading into LSTs with full packs.

24 May 1945: Left Samar and returned to Leyte. Saw ships and airplanes that were disabled during the battle of Leyte.

30 May 1945: Left Leyte with load of soldiers, sailors, airmen, Coast Guard men, and USO women. There were many casualties among them. Routed via Aniwetol, of the Marshals. The only war scare, was caused by a single Jap plane on patrol. We manned our battle stations and I sure tried to get him in my Mark 14 sight. They had him on radar, but he never got close enough to shoot at. We were in sub waters for about two weeks. Lee Dudley, a close friend from Burley, Idaho had a ship shot out from under him a few months before out there in those Jap waters. We slept on cots topside with all our clothes and shoes on and our life belts on. We sure didn't want to be below decks at night if we should take a torpedo. Besides that, I was captain of one of the life rafts, and I sure didn't want to miss it. We had life boats and life rafts. The boats would be loaded by those assigned to them then lowered to the water, but the rafts were dropped by pulling a wooden stake from the rope it was tied to. We had to jump overboard then get into the raft.

12 June 1945: Arrived at Honolulu. Unloaded part of troops.

13 June 1945: Underway for San francisco.

19 June 1945: Arrived San Francisco and unloaded rest of troops. It was so foggy we couldn't see the Golden Gate as we went under it.

26 June 1945: Left San Francisco for Norfolk, Va.

5 July 1945: Arrived at the Panama Canal on the Pacific side. The worst storm I was in was off the coast of Mexico someplace, at night. It was so rough that the ship changed course in order to hit the waves at right angles. I was not on watch that night. My quarters were on the fantail, one deck down. I tied myself to my bunk in order to stay in it. I always tied myself in. Another thing Dudley taught me. I was on the top bunk, four high. That storm was so rough that the screw would come out of the water when we went over some of the waves. It shook some of the boys out of their bunks onto the deck. The ship would rattle like it was about to lose some parts.

It was very interesting going through the locks of the Panama Canal. We were pulled through the locks by little engines on the bank, called donkeys. They had a cog rail in the middle for traction. Three locks on the west side and three on the east side. Once through the locks on the west side we used our own power to go through the canal and into the lake. At Colon we were let down into the Atlantic. The canal is on the Pacific side, a few miles and then a lake on to the Atlantic side. The locks raise the ship to the lake level. In the lake ships can pass but not in the canal. The ships have to wait their turn to go through. We were there a day and night on the Pacific side. The canal is in mountains, and very shaley, which means they are sloughing all the time. Sometimes the canal will be closed until a slide can be cleaned up. It has to be shoveled into a barge and hauled out of the canal. We went through in the daytime. It was beautiful. Everything tropical. There were barges in there cleaning up a couple of slides when we went through.

6 July 1945: We went through the canal, and started on to Norfolk. Enroute we went by Jamaica, Cuba, and Haiti.

11 July 1945: Arrived in Portsmouth, Va. We were there ten days. The ship was completely painted inside, and I'm sure a lot of other things were done. We had lots of liberty and the mates from the east coast went home.

22 July 1945: Left Portsmouth Navy Yards and went to Norfolk NSD and loaded supplies for our next trip.

24 July 1945: Left Norfolk, enroute to Naples, Italy. We passed close to the Rock of Gibraltar and the Isle of Capri.

4 August 1945: Arrived in Naples. Unloaded mail and picked up orders and left for Leghorn, Italy, also called Levorno. By then I had learned that everyplace we went people came out to the ship and wanted to buy cigarettes. I would buy a few cartons as we were going along in order to have a nice supply in my locker because when we were anchored, the ship's store was closed, so we couldn't buy and sell. We would drop a bucket over the fantail on a line. The buyer would put in his money, and once we had his money we would let down his merchandise. We would make about 500% profit. I never drew any of my Navy pay. I had it sent directly to my bank in El Paso.

5 August 1945: Arrived in Leghorn, Italy. There we saw a lot of war destruction that the US had done. We had a day of liberty there. Went to see the Leaning Tower of Pisa. There was not a natural harbor there so it was manmade jetties, with only one opening for the ships to go in and out. When the Americans flew in there it was full of German ships. Like Pearl Harbor, they were sitting ducks, and like Pearl Harbor, they tried to get out to sea where they would have a fighting chance. The fly boys let the first one get to the entrance and sank it right there. That was enough to plug the hole, and then they sunk the rest of them. The ships that were tied to the docks were still there, only rolled over on the side. We tied up to a sunken ship, and crossed over it to get to the docks. The ship that was sunk in the gate had been cut into pieces and stacked to one side so we could get in.

The town had a beautiful park, and in it was a fenced off place, maybe 50x50x6 feet and full of small arms, pistols and rifles. I need to mention here that one of the things we had to watch for was stealing. We had guards everyplace on the ship and those Italians would get aboard and put on clothes and wear them off. They were the stealingest people I have ever seen. Another thing new to us US sailors were the rest stops built into the walls along the sidewalks. No covers for privacy, just walk up and do what ever you can't hold any longer. There are high walls along the sidewalks very similar to Mexico City.

7 August 1945: Left Leghorn with a load of soldiers, enroute for Panama Canal and then to Manila.

10 August 1945: Stopped for water and fuel at Gibraltar. Mart's birthday.

14 August 1945: Japanese surrender. "END OF WORLD WAR II". We were in the area of Cuba again headed for Panama. Floyde's birthday.

15 August 1945: Received orders to change course and go to New York.

19 August 1945: Arrived in New York with a very happy bunch of soldiers. We were the first ship to hit New York after the war ended, and what a reception we got. Boat loads of people with lots of girls singing with bands met us and really made us feel welcome. They met us out on the ocean side of the Statue of Liberty. The troops we were bringing home would not stay in their quarters. They went topside and of course all on the side of the ship where the action was and the ship listed so much that they had to be moved. I'm talking about our passengers. Some of them had already quit taking orders very well.

When we docked I was on the detail to tie one of the moor lines on the dock. I just stayed down there and partook of the milk and donuts and kisses those girls were handing out. I finally got enough and decided it was safer on the ship. The soldiers could hardly get off the gangway before they were hugged and kissed and handed milk and donuts. Milk was the big thing that was missed, and that included me and I had never drank milk before, and I haven't since.

I made some spending money after we turned towards New York. Those soldiers wanted to look sharp when they went down the gang way, so they all wanted their pants and shirts pressed. I was good friends with the tailor. He had his locker or room like I had for ropes only he did a little different type of work. He had a steam press besides his sewing machines. He told me that he had made all the money he wanted. He was tired of pressing clothes and would I like to help him. I did. We worked around the clock until we arrived at New York. We charged $2.00 for each pair of pants and each shirt, and it took me maybe ten minutes to do both. I don't remember ever counting the money I made, but I sure wasn't broke when we hit New York.

There was a long troop line on the ship all the time when we were under way. We carried as many as 4500 troops. They were given cards to be punched. They could eat twice in 24 hrs and they could fill their canteen with water once every 24 hrs, and then they were in line again to get me to press their pants and shirt. I had to run my rope locker in the daytime so I pressed only at night.

23 August 1945: Left New York for Marseille, France. We were running empty going over, and we sure did live good. No troops to worry with and short shifts. Sunny--side eggs and things like that. The cooks seemed to be trying to get on the good side of the rest of us. We ate steaks cooked the way you like it. And the weather was good. None of that Atlantic ice hanging on the cables and wherever else it could get.

3 September 1945: Arrived in Marseille, France. I have told about selling cigarettes. We had the word that France paid top dollar, so we loaded ourselves down and headed for town. We put cigarettes in our clothing every place we could and still get off the ship without limping. We were off the ship and there was a stake--body truck waiting to take us to town, standing room only. We still had to go out the gate of the pier on the truck and there were guards there checking for the very thing we were doing. Now those guards were not new at the cigarette game we were playing. They took the merchandise and worked it themselves. When the truck stopped at the gate for inspection, a guard jumped up on the front of the truck and started to shake the boys down. Cigarettes literally came out of everyplace. There was so much excitement I thought maybe I would just move around and wind up behind the guard and he would miss me. He was making such a haul that it worked and I got into town with a full load.

Now, how do I find a buyer, and for what price? While I was still thinking, a Frenchman popped out of a door and asked if I had cigarettes. I asked him what he would pay, and he offered $20.00 per carton. I was hardly in town yet so I thought I would test the market. I told him I had to have $30.00. He jumped on them and I sold him the four cartons I had. The invasion money was a different color so I had to exchange it for good money on the ship. The French people were more friendly than the Italian.

I think the most interesting thing I saw in France was the horses. They delivered to the ships at the docks with horses and wagons. They were percheron type horses and the smartest or best trained I had ever seen. The drivers could mostly talk to those horses and place the wagons to the exact spot they wanted for loading or unloading. The harbor at Marseille was large and there were lots of ships in there.

4 September 1945: Left Marseille for New York.

15 September 1945: Arrived back in New york.

17 September 1945: Went to the Todd Shipyards in Hoboken, NJ for ship service. That time the ship was put in drydock and the hull was sandblasted and painted. Sure was a sight to see that big thing sitting high and dry. We enjoyed lots of liberty and the people in New York were very friendly. I had dinner at Jack Dempsey's restaurant and bar. There is where I drank my first and only beer with a raw egg in it. Just don't bite it. I didn't.

25 September 1945: Out of drydock and back to New York to load supplies and fuel.

27 September 1945: Left New York for Calcutta, India. Ice flows were far enough south that we had to detour around some large chunks. I didn't see them but they showed up on the radar. I liked to go to the radar shack and see the course they had plotted and how things showed up out on the water that we couldn't see.

11 October 1945: Arrived at Port Said, Egypt. We took on fuel oil there and started through the Suez Canal that night. I have told how we had to watch when docked because of thieves. When we tied up to a dock we put rat guards on the lines so the rats couldn't come aboard. The rat guards are about four feet in diameter with a hole in the center for tying to the line. They are shaped like a funnel with the funnel facing down. The rat climbs up into the funnel, and can't go on. We put one at the ship and one at the dock. In Port Said we had a guard at each line on the ship in case a rat or person should try to go up the line to the ship. And they did. The rats were big and the kids were little that came up the lines. The rats didn't get onto the ship but some of the kids did. Those rats looked like cats when they were climbing the line.

We were at Port Said all one day and there were kids swimming alongside all the time. We would throw money down to them. I have never seen anyone swim like those kids. They were like fish. They would get hold of the line, pass the first rat guard and come overhand up to the guard next to the ship, and while they were trying to get by it we would knock them off and back down in the water. With all our watching, one of them got aboard and went below and got some clothes. He put them on. We thought it was so funny that he got by us, we just picked him up and threw him over the side with the clothes on he had stolen. Those kids knew we wouldn't hurt them even if we caught them.

The day we spent there was a memorable one even though I didn't get to go on liberty. I was put on guard duty. By that I mean I was on shore patrol duty that day, but on the ship. When on shore patrol we wore a white belt and carried a big stick. When we were in a foreign country there were always some of the fellows drew shore patrol duty. Port Said was my first time to draw that kind of guard duty since I left T.I. We were not the regular shore patrol with sticks and pistols. We were fill ins and only got sticks.

As the daylight was getting ready to go somewhere else I was told to send for a large box and sit it there near the gangway for when the liberty fellows started to return to the ship. I was also told to search every man as he came aboard, especially the officers. They will try to bring liquor back with them. I was not told how to perform the search. I didn't want to be feeling of those guys so I was tapping the bulges with my stick. I tapped one bulge a little too hard and he was an officer. Instead of getting myself into trouble I was commended for the way I handled the situation. As they came up the gangway they were taking the bottles from their hiding places and sure putting them in the box. I had to send for a second box.

On that trip there was an opening for a Boatswain third class, and I was one of the seaman chosen to take the test. I didn't get it. I came out with the same rate I went in with. I went to the yeoman's office to see what I could find out about where I had messed up. The chief yeoman was a good friend of mine. He told me some things that he shouldn't have, and swore me to secrecy. First that I had the highest score on the test. I kept his secret, but I also changed my ways. On my record was that I had been in charge of three hundred men in the mines. That was OK, but they were Mexicans, and that was not OK. They thought I would want to handle White boys like I did Mexicans. I don't know what they thought was the difference. Then the equator thing was there also. I didn't have a chance. I had filled in various duties for the rated men all the time I had been on ship and we got along fine, but no one would stand up for me because of that equator thing.

The boy that got the rate was Sam Bassille from Minnesota. He was on my gun crew. When we had the plane scare at New Guinea, he didn't make it to his station, which was loading my guns. After General Quarters I went to look for him and he was under his bunk crying his eyes out. I never reported him. All of a sudden he was my boss and he was for sure going to make sure I knew it. He had about four of us painting some spots on the top deck. I had my gloves on. He told me to take them off. I didn't. He didn't like the way I brushed the paint, and told me so. I finally got enough of him. I went after another bucket of paint. We filled a gallon pot from a five--gallon bucket there close. There were some brooms near that we had used to sweep before starting to paint. I came back with my paint. The other guys could see I was up to something. I poured the whole thing on the deck and swept it around with one of those brooms. Now let me tell you, that little sailor got mad. He would like to have jumped on me right there, but he wasn't that mad.

He told me that he was going to teach me a lesson. For me to meet him in the bottom of the ship in one of the troop compartments. We were running empty. He told me what time, and I promised to be there. I didn't think to invite any of my close friends. He did invite his. When I got down there, he was ready with about six of his close buddies. I had no one on my side. One of them was the Marine I had bitten at Leyte. They all stood on the ladder (stairs) so I couldn't change my mind and try to escape. Sam and I looked at each other, and I said, "Sam, do you want to spar around and see who is the best man, or do you want to fight to kill?"

He said, "Fight to kill, you son--of--a--bitch." Enough conversation already. I went to work on him so quick he didn't have time to get ready.

What he didn't know was that he had suggested the very thing I had spent twelve weeks in boots training to do. I grabbed his shirt and pulled him to me, up went my knee, and it found the mark. As he came forward I caught him on the throat with a hand slice. Then we were down and rolling and I was after his eyes. He started yelling, "enough," but I made sure he meant it before I turned him loose. When he stood up, he said, "Adams, you tried to kill me." I told him that was what he had asked for, but he thought it would go the other way. His old head was sure scratched and bruised and his clothes were gone. I thought his buddies would hold me for him, but they let me go up the ladder. They did tell me that I was the dirtiest fighter they had ever seen.

Shortly a runner came to me with a message to report to the chief boatswain and first lieutenant. I walked in and Sam was there. His friends had reported the fight. They thought they were doing Sam a favor. When I walked in, the Chief looked at me then he looked at Sam. I didn't have a scratch or lose a button. He said, "I just can't believe this. Sam you are torn all to hell, and Adams isn't even scratched, what were you doing?"

Sam said, "I was trying to get loose. He had me down and was trying to kill me." Chief Sandler asked me if that was true. I told him yes, and I told him why. Sandler said, "You boys shake hands, and if I ever have a report on either of you again, you will both go to Court Martial." Sam and I had no more trouble, and when I left the ship, he came to me and big tears ran down his face when he told me goodbye.

12 October 1945: We were still in the Suez Canal at daybreak. Saw piles of cut--up ships that had been taken out of the canal. The Germans had sunk ships in it and blocked it from traffic for some time. The patrols were riding camels along the bank. They were also cleaning the canal there but not with large shovels. There were lines of people with baskets on their heads. They went down and filled their basket and climbed back up the bank to dump it. We got out of the canal and into the Red Sea. Religion tells us that this is the part of the earth that God chose to do all His great things in the beginning. I guess He figured that if man could survive this, he could populate the rest later on. It was so hot, the top deck buckled in waves. We ran around in shorts only, and for some reason I did not sunburn, I just turned brown.

16 October 1945: Out of the Red Sea and into the Indian Ocean. Much cooler, but still hot.

24 October 1945: Arrived in Calcutta, India. We went up the Hooghly River. We had to ride the high tide up the river then wait for the high tide in order to get back out to the ocean. I went on liberty there and what an experience. We were told to be sure and stay in groups of at least four or five. We did. There were lots of soldiers stationed there. We took out 4500 of them. We noticed the soldiers each carried a long stick, and we asked why. They told us to knock those Indians down if they got too close. While we were talking and getting information, a gal came up to us and wanted to sell or trade her baby for just anything. We kept backing away from her but she would follow right up to us and stick the baby onto us. The soldiers kept telling us to knock her down, or she won't leave. There was no way we could do that. After it got out of hand one of the soldiers hit her with his stick and knocked her out in the street. I thought sure we would have those Indians all over us any minute now. No one paid any attention. Those people were literally starving to death.

As we were going up the river we saw bodies floating by. Something to do with their religion, they throw the bodies into the river and they go out to sea. They also cremate them. There were people dying everyplace. On the sidewalks and in the streets, and fires burning them as fast as they could. I had seen animals dying and kicking their last, but never humans. We walked around them, no one paid them any mind. I sold my wrist watch for a hefty sum to an Indian that just had to have it. We went into the market place, and before we got out of there we wished we had stayed away. Mainly when we got in we couldn't find our way out. Those people just smothered us. They got so very close and there were so many of them. I still think about how close they got to us and never touched us. When we finally got out of that mess, we went into a carpet house and took a nap on a pile of them. Then back to the ship. We had had enough.

I was called to the yeoman's office while we were there in Calcutta. He told me that orders had come through for my discharge when we returned to the US When I was in New York the last time, I received a telegram from home telling me of my brother Sam's death. Also a letter from Dad telling me of the ranch fence being torn down by the mile. Mart having a very bad case of the flu and effecting her hearing. I thought, I have never gone to the Chaplain with any of my troubles. I'll just test him out on this. I showed him the letters and telegram. He took them, and sure enough I got an early discharge.

27 October 1945: Left Calcutta for New York with load of soldiers, civilians and Polish refugees. Combination load of Red Cross, Chinese, Indians, and Missionaries. When the tide came in, we went out. Our ship's prop drew so much water that the river was about five feet fuller behind us than in the front. The river was barely wide enough to steer the ship in. When we hit the mouth, or where it dumps into the ocean, we hit a sand bar, and came to a very sudden stop. We sat there while the top brass came up with some ideas. The last of which they sure didn't want to exercise. That was call for help. It isn't good for the captain to have his ship sitting on the ground. They decided to drive it off, and gave it full throttle forward. It churned that old sand and just made a thick looking mud, and went into a vibrating shudder. When it started to move I think we all yelled at the same time. The sun was just going down and I think that was one of the most beautiful sunsets I have ever seen, at least I remember it more. There I was on my way home and my ship was sitting on a sand bar halfway around the world.

30 October 1945: Arrived in Ceylon (now Sri Lanka), took on water and fuel. Some of the guys went on liberty to town. We were there all day. In the evening we saw a truck coming towards the ship and it looked like another truck was trying to catch it. Those guys, about ten of them, had gotten into some sort of trouble in one of the bars. The police were going to put those sailors in jail if they could catch them. The sailors ran out, stole a truck and there they came. They jumped out and ran up the gangway with the police on their tails. There were two of us on guard duty, and we stopped the police. We called for higher authority to come down and help us. From the captain came the word for the police to go back to town. Come back in the morning and get the boys and punish them. I thought to myself, I'd sure hate to be in those boys shoes to get turned over to the police and left there. By morning we were on our way well into the Red Sea again. We knew then that we had a good captain, but I was still thinking of my bout with him at the equator, so I had to salt him a little.

31 October 1945: Left Ceylon for Suez.

8 November 1945: Arrived city of Suez and started through the Suez Canal.

9 November 1945: Arrived at end of Suez Canal at Port Said. Took on fuel and continued on.

23 November 1945: Arrived at New York City.

25 November 1945: I was transferred to the Navy Hospital in New York for a checkup before discharge, then from there to the separation center. The ship's doctor thought I might have some kidney trouble, and it should be corrected before I went home. I was in the hospital about a month, and felt fine most of the time, I guess because I was so anxious to go home. The hospital was built like a horseshoe. One mile from point to point. A long hall from point to point with wings on each side all the way around. The personnel rode bicycles to make their rounds. We had brought lots of wounded back to the US, and that was where many of them were being treated. Some of them that the Japs had split their tongues so they couldn't talk. They also couldn't control the saliva. They carried a small towel. In the wing I was in, someone died about every night, and someone fighting in an oxygen tent all the time. Our wing had a sort of kitchen with a large ice box with goodies for in--between meals. I was designated to take the goodies around to the ones who couldn't get out of bed.

My turn came around for my checkup. They didn't feed me and got me all cleaned out for the tests the next morning. Into a wheelchair and down the long hall I was being pushed. I was sure getting nervous. As I was pushed past some of those doors I could see one guy opened up and another with tubes running in or out of him from all over, and by the time we got to the room where I was going, I could hardly stay in that wheelchair. I was wheeled inside, and there was a thing that made me think of being tied in that guillotine. They were going to give me a spinal, so they could put some dye in there and look at it.

I was told to just stand up to that thing and we will tie you, hands, feet, everything so you can't move. I stood up but instead of getting close enough for them to start tying me up, I panicked and ran. Those old boys couldn't catch me so they yelled down the hall to some of their buddies to stop me and hold me for them. They did, and there came the wheelchair again and we started over. That time when they told me to get next to that thing, I fell on my knees and begged them to not do that to me. They told me they had to check me out so I couldn't come back at the Navy later in life, with some sort of claim. We talked a little while and they told me that if I would sign a release they wouldn't put me through the test. I for sure signed right then and there. I was carrying food to fellows who had gone through that and it just didn't seem like the thing I wanted to do. I didn't feel like I had that much trouble. I would live with it. That has been forty--five years now and I have had one bad flare up. The doctor told me to drink lots of water. I carry a canteen in my car for when I am traveling.

They didn't even take me back to my wing in the wheelchair. They turned me loose and said, "GO." I went to my wing. I was sitting on my bed trying to figure out my next move. I had already found out that it was harder to get out of the place than it was to get in. I went to the office and asked them to send me to the separation center. I was told that they were so far behind with paperwork, that it would be at least two weeks before mine would come to the top. While the officer was telling me all the reasons he couldn't just go in the stack of papers and pick someone out, the gal helping him said, "Did you say your name is Adams? Is it Willie Roy?" My head was moving up and down. I was at attention or I would have done a little dance. She said, "I just picked it up from this stack I'm processing." The officer told her to hold it and to fix me up. That evening I was gone from the hospital.

20 December 1945: At the separation center I found a bunch of excited boys. There were hundreds of us in the barracks and about midnight all quiet as it should be, someone called out, "Anyone here from Texas?" That building came alive. Sounded like we were all from Texas. It never got quiet the rest of the night. The next morning we were marched, I should say we were escorted as we had already forgotten how to march, from building to building to be deregulated (discharged). The last thing we had to do was sign some papers and pick up $300.00 then go to the last briefing.

The last day in the separation center and the last act of getting free was to pass by a table with fellows handing us papers to sign. The first guy said, "Sign here that all boys eighteen years old should serve two years in the military." I wouldn't sign it. Then to the next table and sign up to stay in the reserve in case we need you quick. I wouldn't sign it. They threatened to send me to the bottom of the class and send me through the whole process again.

I told them, "One thing I have learned in this Navy, is I just don't give a damn. All out or all in." My bluff worked. When they started calling the reserves back in for Korea, I sure was thankful I stood pat that day.

We were told at the last meeting in the separation center that some of us would have some trouble adjusting back to civilian life. Not me, just open the gate and let me out. Well about that time they did and said adios and good luck. There was about a foot of snow on the ground. I was outside the gate and no bus to pick me up and no one cared where I went or how I got there. My adjusting trouble had already started. Somehow I got myself in to New York, and to this day I don't remember how. I went straight to Penn Station to get a one--way train ticket to El Paso. It was still morning in New York City. Not a chance. The lines of kids going home were going in circles to stay in the building. I finally got up to the window, a gazebo type place with ticket windows all around it. The man looked at me for a minute then told me to come back to him at four o'clock in the evening and maybe he would have something for me. At four o'clock I was in his line and as I got closer he looked up and saw me and smiled. I could hardly wait for my turn to his window, and sure enough he had me a ticket. I got on the train about dark and arrived in Chicago the next morning at daybreak. I had a full day layover in Chicago. Wasted time.

21 December 1945: I left Chicago in the evening with designated seat all the way to El Paso. I got in my seat and was sure happy when the train pulled out. I kept looking at the fellow seated with me, and he kept looking at me, and finally he said, "I got it, you are Adams aren't you?" I admitted that he was right. It turned out we were in boots together. He was a yeoman and had spent his time in the offices in New York. We had been in the same boot company in San Diego. He told me that he had kept track of our company, and that most of them had been killed in action. Our company was trained for hand--to--hand combat, to take over the Jap prisons with knives. No guns because of noise. We spent all our time in boots learning to kill with bare hands and knives. When boots was over a few of us were sent to Port Hueneme for cargo-- handling school. The rest went overseas. Then I was pulled from the cargo handling school bunch, and they went overseas. I sure felt lucky after talking to this guy. I think he got off the train some where in Kansas.

23 December 1945: Arrived in El Paso in the evening. I went straight to Roy and Della's home. Mart's brother. They were going to Dublan for Christmas on the NorOeste train the next morning.

24 December 1945: Arrived in Dublan. I went with Roy and Della. Mart, Floyde and Sid were at the train. Not to meet me, because she thought I was still in the hospital in New York. When things started to happen I didn't have time to let her know. We had planned for her to meet me in El Paso, so she was waiting for the word. Sid saw me first and said, "Mama, there is Daddy." I was getting off the train, maybe I should say I was falling off the train. I have never seen a more beautiful girl or cute little kids in my life, and they were mine. My folks were there also. The train went from El Paso to Dublan every other day and everyone turned out to see who got off and if any mail came in for them. That was one memorable Christmas for us, and what a great gift, for us to be together again.

15

Dublan Third Time

There I was, home again in Dublan. Home from the Navy. December 24, 1945. I shouldn't have any trouble taking up where I left off eighteen months before. A little money in the bank, a few cattle on the ranch, Mart and the little boys were fine, her folks and my folks were fine, the cattle were fat and my two horses, Penny and Sueno, were fat and needed riding. Bright sunshine everywhere I looked but I was restless. I sure wanted to make up for lost time. The first thing I needed was transportation. I bought a 1940 pickup. It was in good shape for being worn out from use in Mexico. It needed tires, a new engine, shocks, brakes, clutch, and it had many rattles for me to listen to. To this day I can't stand a rattle or a squeak. Mart and I wanted to go to El Paso anyhow. There were no tires in Mexico and you had to know some one in the US to get them. Dad knew Orie Pernell and told me to go see him. He had a service station on Mesa Drive. He didn't have the tires I needed, 700x16, but he was able to get them for me. He got me four tires and tubes. We also bought some furniture for our house. I threw those tires on top of the load and we headed for home. In those days we always crossed the border at Antelope Wells, NM. The officials on both sides treated us good, and of course we treated them good.

When we arrived at the US Customs, about closing time, and about night, I was told that the only way I could take the tires out of the US was because I needed them, and in that case they must be installed on the vehicle. It was very night and I was very tired when I got those four tires legalized. 700x16 tires sure hold lots of air strokes with a hand pump. In those days the US office was about a mile from the border, but being the friend that he was, he went with me and unlocked the gate. After the tire delay we were finally on the Mexican side but no problem there. We knew those people also. They were always very helpful even at odd hours. The Americans controlled the gate and if they would open it the Mexican officials let folks go. Of course we were good to help them also. It worked both ways. I have even arrived at the border on the Mexican side and walked the mile to the American office and they would let me through.

While I was gone to the Navy, Dad had caused the windmill to take its position over the well. The stock water storage tank was built and things sure looked fine. One thing bothered me, however, and always has. Before I left for the Navy we discussed how to build the water storage tank for the cattle. He wanted to use rocks and cement and make it about 20x20 feet square. Two feet thick at the bottom then up two feet then narrow down to one foot, then another two feet up. That left a one foot step. That was fine but he wanted to put the shelf on the outside, and I showed and told him how much more water he could store with the same size tank by putting the step on the inside. Someone told him I was wrong and so he put the step on the outside like he wanted to in the first place. He thought the tank would be stronger. He always wished he had listened to me because the water storage was very marginal. He was afraid the water would push the walls down, if he did it the way I wanted it. He made it so strong anyhow that he really only needed the one foot thick wall.

When I got home he was in the process of digging the well deeper. It was an open well and the water was drying up. A man was down in there digging and a man was hoisting out the muck and what water that came in so the digger could work. When we bought the ranch, the water table was about six feet. There was a gravel strata near the surface, but with so many farm wells being put in the water table was going down pretty fast, and the gravel strata was dry. Under the gravel was a clay conglomerate that was just wet but no water. After a few days of digging the man below said he couldn't dig anymore because of too much water. We hauled him out and I went down there to see what he had found. He had chopped into a little stream of water about the size of a pencil that actually squirted out of the conglomerate wall. About sixty feet down. I guess it was a good one because we had plenty of water and it is still doing OK.

I had been home a short while and was still trying to get adjusted to a normal life when I received a letter from a fellow in New York. Henry Caldwell, 340 Park Avenue. He was a major we picked up in Calcutta. I had no idea who he was. He said he had watched me working on the way back to the US and he was very impressed with me. He wished he would have let me know his interest in me, but since he wasn't sure of his financial situation until he could get home and sort things out, he just watched me and stayed on the sideline. When he got home he found his money would allow him to pursue his dreams. That was to buy several hundred acres in the east, on a river, in the country, containing both meadow and woods, and the river had to be navigable for small cabin cruisers with access to the ocean. And of course with a house, and barns and stables, and a couple of horses for him and his friends.

I wrote to him and told him to pay my way and I would return to New York to meet him and talk it over. He answered me right away saying that he would go to Mexico and meet me. Now picture me trying to entertain that rich gentleman from Park Avenue. He arrived on the NorOeste train per schedule. He wanted someone to help him choose the place and then be the manager. We talked a lot, and Mart and I took him to a dance in Colonia Juarez at the JSA. He was very impressed at what he saw in the people there. Mart and I talked it over and decided not to risk what we had and the way we were raised for something that would be so strange to us. I could see getting back there in the east and becoming a Moso to a rich man, and that wasn't what I had in mind for my life.

Some time passed and I got a letter from him telling me that he found the place he wanted and was going to put in a factory to make pots and pans, and would I reconsider. I wouldn't. Then a letter telling of his wedding coming up and would I come to New York and be his best man. I decided right then that the man just didn't know how to think like a poor boy. Again I turned him down as best I knew how. The last letter I had from him contained pictures of his wife and baby. I have no regrets for not going with him, but I have always wondered what I missed.

    Dad had been waiting for me to get home and help him brand the calves and other things that needed doing. I was sure glad to get on my horses. Dad had ridden Penny while I was gone but not Sueno (sleepy). The name because he never looked wide awake. We were working some cattle as they came in to water, and I was on Sueno. Now, he hadn't been saddled for eighteen months. A calf broke out to run away and I jumped Sueno to him and roped him. Sueno went to bucking and squalling, and threw me over his head. I landed on my feet running. I grabbed onto my rope, which was tied to my saddlehorn, got hold of the calf, and flanked him. I was sitting there on the calf when Dad rode up and said, "Just what all did you do in the Navy?" My horse stood there and held the rope tight just as I had taught him to do. He had never bucked with me and I was sure surprised then. If I had watched his ears I would have known that he wasn't uncocked. I got on him again and I thought we were friends.

    A few days latter we had a herd together and I was cutting on Sueno. He was pretty good for a young horse. I cut out a few head, and a cow was determined to get back into the herd. I pushed him to help me change her mind. I think he got mad, because he went to bucking, but that time I was more ready. I didn't have a rope in my hand with a calf on the other end. All I had to do was get a good hold on the horn, sink my spurs into his belly and let him know I was home now. While I was thinking all that, I became aware that my saddle was not under me anymore. Even so I was still grabbing for something, just anything to hold onto. He stood me on my head in a mesquite bush, and when I came out of that bush I had my bridle in my hand. He stood there looking at me and that was the first time I understood what is a horse laugh. I put the bridle back on him and climbed aboard. That time with the full intention of not making him mad again. I decided to let the fence rider ride him for a while. Get some miles on him, and maybe improve his manners. The fence rider man saw him buck me off so he knew what he was getting into. The first day about noon, there came Sueno back to the ranch house without the rider. Dad and I hopped in the car and went looking for our man. We found him walking in. I gave Sueno to

LaSelle Taylor. He had a big ranch and was a good rider. I don't know what he ever did with him.

Mexico had foot--and--mouth disease in their cattle in the southern states. The US closed the border for importing cattle from Mexico. The Casas Grande area cattlemen had formed a company and were building a packing house. It was under construction when I returned from the Navy. That way they could ship the canned meat to the US. The walls were pretty well up, and I got a job there installing the equipment in the rendering plant. The equipment consisted of two boilers, two tanks about 4x20 feet to be installed horizontally, a grinder that chopped the bones, and a very heavy duty press. The tanks were hoisted in the lazy position like laying on their sides. The rendering plant got the part of the cow after the meat had been removed. The packing house was only a cannery. No steaks only those that were stolen, and that did happen.

The bones went first into the grinder then into the tanks for cooking by steam and then the press. It was a many ton press. It squeezed out the tallow which had some market value. That left a pressed round cake about 1x3 feet, similar to a cheese mold. Those cakes were sold for fertilizer. The only part of the cow not salvaged was the beller. If we would have had video cameras at that time we could have saved that.

That was my first job after returning home from the Navy. My experience in Morenci came in very handy then, only I didn't have any cranes to do the lifting. They told me to pick any six men from the whole work force. Those men were running wheelbarrows full of cement. When I asked one to come with me he jumped at the chance. I chose six good men and went to town and bought the hydraulic jacks I needed. Then I cut all the 4x4 and 6x6 timbers I needed for bulkheads. They gave me the prints of where the machines went, and I went to work. It was a very dangerous job, and I sometimes thought they had saved it for me. It was dangerous because of the way I had to do it. The two cooker tanks had to be raised about five feet. The bulkheads had to be positioned so the cement pillars could be framed and poured in the proper place. I will say one thing, no one messed with me and no one ever came around and told me to hurry. I had my men stop and rest a lot because we were so nervous. Those machines weighed in the bunch of tons, and as we were going up with them they wiggled like they would wipe us out at any moment. We got the job done and no one got hurt. Safety was another of my Morenci teachings. There were two boilers. I had to build the bulkheads inside of them and raise them two feet. I have visited the place in later years. I look at those tanks and boilers and wonder how I did it. I sure needed the money. I was getting $20.00 (pesos) a day. Exchange was $5.80 to one in dollars. $3.45 a day doesn't sound like much for a guy who had very recently quit his job of traveling all over the world for the biggest company in the world.

The building was up, and much of the equipment was installed, or on the floor to be installed. My part was coming along fine. The roofers were putting on the tar paper with melted tar. They had the tar buggy on the roof where it would be handy. The roof was large and flat with just enough slope for runoff if it should rain. I heard someone call fire, and sure enough there was big smoke on the roof, and people running in all directions. The tar buggy was on fire. They soon had a garden type hose up the wall and onto the roof. A half inch hose, and carrying water about a hundred and fifty feet. The working end had very little pressure, and of course no volume at all. One of the things we trained very much at in the Navy was fire fighting. It takes three things to make a fire: oxygen, fuel, and heat. Remove any one and the fire is gone.

I climbed to the roof to see how they were doing, and I found them with the hose squirting the water in the air over the flame. I watched and tried to tell them they were going at the thing all wrong, but no one could or would hear me, and they would not give me the water hose. The fire soon got out of control and everyone was ordered off the roof. The roof itself was not on fire yet because enough water was on it but the cooker was ready to explode. When the fellow with the hose dropped it and ran for the ladder, I grabbed the hose and was able to get close enough to spray water on the bottom of the cooker. A couple of fellows stayed on the roof to watch me, but from a safe distance. They could hardly believe it when they saw the blaze go out. I thought when I went down the ladder off the roof I would get all kinds of handshakes and good words. I got a left handed thanks from one of the contractors. I somehow got the feeling that they wanted it to burn. I have always felt like I messed up something that I didn't understand.

There were three open wells on our Buena Fe Ranch. The rest of my story about our ranch in Mexico will be about Buena Fe. Only the one at the ranch house had water. One was in the horse pasture. We used it to put garbage in. The other one was about in the center of the south pasture, and about twelve feet deep. I was riding my horse in that area one day and for some reason I rode over and looked down in it. There were some hoot owls that lived in there, and I guess I wanted to check on them. When I looked in, what I saw was not owls but a yearling calf down there. He hadn't been down there very long. He was standing on his feet so no broken legs. He looked up at me with pleading eyes. I rode back to the ranch house, got Dad and three long poles for a tripod, a block and tackle, and we took my pickup to see if we could save that calf. I went down in the well with him and tied a gunny sack around his middle and a rope on each end of the sack. I tied the rope to the bumper and I gave Dad signals. When the calf arrived to the surface I swung him to solid ground. When his feet hit the ground he jumped out of the sack sling and he was gone.

The reason we had those long poles to make the tripod with was because we had bought a lot of poor cattle. We were buying and selling. We had overstocked the ranch, and some of the cattle were needing help. We had poor cows all over the ranch hanging on tripods. We would lift them up in the morning, take feed and water to them, then let them down at night. Sure kept us busy. We saved most of them. When I think back on some of those days I wonder why in the world does anyone want to be a cowboy.

Mart and I lived in Dublan with our two little kids, but we stayed at the ranch a lot. One night we were at the ranch, supper over and Mart was doing the dishes. A very dark night. Dad was aggravating her about something, and he said he would bet her he could outrun her to the cattle guard and back. About two hundred yards one way. She didn't pay him any attention, only to say there was no way he could beat her. She went on doing the dishes, and for some reason she went to the front door and let it slam shut, but she didn't even go out. Dad had settled in the front room. When he heard the door slam he knew she was getting a head start. He went out the back door in high gear, with his house shoes on. There was a barb--wire fence from the house to the cattle guard. The back door faced the cattle guard. Mart and I were in the kitchen, maybe I was helping her, when we heard Dad come back into the house. We didn't even know he had been gone. Well now, he had left out of there so fast, because he knew she was out there in the dark and running, that he veered a little too much to the left and hit that barb wire fence. The fence was parallel to his track. His clothes were torn all to pieces, and he was cut and scratched all over. Then he was upset because she hadn't even left the house. The next morning I repaired the fence. He had knocked down two posts. When I saw the damage to the fence I decided he was lucky not to have done himself in.

I liked to play jokes on Dad and once in a while I would get him pretty good. I pulled the engine out of my truck at the ranch, and took it to an auto shop in Dublan to have it rebuilt. I took the truck in there also to do some welding and frame repairs while the engine was out of the way. Dad towed it to town for me with his car, but when it was ready to take back to the ranch there had been a heavy rain and the road was sure too muddy to pull with his car. I borrowed a commando type truck from Edgar Wagner. After the war there were lots of those type vehicles sold in Mexico. I wanted Dad to tow me but he didn't want to try to drive the commando. We tied a chain to my truck, and to the commando, and Dad was in the driver seat of the towed pickup. About the last mile to the ranch was very slick and muddy. I noticed that when I goosed the commando, it would spin the rear tires and throw mud on the windshield of the truck I had Dad in. I flung a little mud and he wanted me to stop and clean the windshield. He started waving his hand out the window. I was watching in the rear view mirror. Before long I had the windshield covered up. He was waving his hand for me to stop, then he couldn't see through the windshield and he stuck his head out the window, and I soon covered his glasses. He took them off and stuck his head out again, and was trying to keep the mud off his face, no luck. When I got to the bridge on the canal, and the cattle guard I took it easy. I quit spinning the wheels so he could stick his head out the window and see them. Then I pulled him on up to the house. I fell out of my tow truck laughing so hard, he had to laugh with me. He was sure a mess. I was towing him in ruts and he couldn't have gotten out of them if he had tried, but he thought he had to see where he was going. He laughed last, however, while I was cleaning my truck. I told him it was worth it.

While I was in the Navy, Dad gave Floyde and Sid each a horse, and they went where they wanted to on the ranch. Ada was a little older and the three of them rode a lot together. Ada is my youngest sister. A good life for little kids. When we moved to El Paso I sold their horses to Tio and he took them to Alabama to some other little kids.

When the Corralitos lost part of their land to the ejido they decided it was time to sell the rest of it to the ranchers. The ranchers who were leasing got first chance and most of them bought their ranch. There was a ranch southeast of the railroad between the Corralitos Shipping Pens and the San Pedro Pass. That part had never been refenced since the revolution days of Pancho Villa. Joe Memmott, from Dublan, and Ed Lunt from Duncan, Az., bought it. They had part of it fenced. When my packing--house job was finished I made a deal with Memmott to run his ranch and run my cattle there. He paid the expenses of the operation. I had about a hundred head and moved them to the Memmott Ranch.

Joe had drilled a well about 350 feet deep. He had fenced the outside line of his land. There were no other improvements, so my work was cut out for me. He took me to the bank and told them to honor my signature the same as his and gave me a checkbook to run the ranch with and to buy and sell cattle. At that time the US had not quarantined the northern Mexico states. I went to Durango, Mexico, and bought three hundred head of two year old black angus heifers to stock the ranch with. Jim Reynolds was the commission seller of the cattle. I was to meet him in El Paso. We would fly to Torreon, and be picked up there by the rancher for the trip to his ranch. I had planned to fly from Casas Grandes to El Paso, but when I went for a ticket, I was told the plane was weathered in someplace south and would not make the flight. It came from Mexico City to El Paso, then to Casas Grandes and return to El Paso every day. I had to be in El Paso the next morning.

I asked Mart to go with me in our pickup and she could stay in El Paso until I returned from Durango. I would be gone three days. We left in the evening, and drove at night out through the sands. We had gone past San Pedro and I misjudged the depth of the road ruts and hit high center. I was going fast enough that I skidded on the axles and all four wheels were off the ground. I was working to get off, when I heard a plane, and there went the plane to Casas Grandes. A little late but there it was. By about sundown I was ready to roll again, and there went the plane back to Ciudad Juarez. I was caught with a full night of driving when I should have been on that plane and in El Paso in a few minutes. Those were DC3 planes.

After passing San Pedro, the road had about ten miles of dry lake bed, no vegetation and smooth, then about ten miles of sand dunes. After the sand dunes was the Chihuahua highway and it was paved. When the wind blew, and that was often, the indication of anyone foolish enough to have ever traveled that route was wiped out. The next traveler could find his own path through there. I had heard stories of folks going in circles on the lake bed at night when they couldn't see landmarks, so I was sure not going to let that happen to me. It was a no--moon night. I knew about how long it took to cross the dry lake bed and I was still on it when I noticed I had some car tracks to follow and they seemed to be getting easier to see. You guessed it. Each time I made full circle, the road was easier to follow. I stopped and got out to check for the north star to be sure I didn't go back to San Pedro. I kept the north star in sight while I drove slowly trying to find where to get into the sand dunes. After a while I found the opening in the sand where we should leave the lake and go into the sand dunes. On the lake I had been driving pretty fast, like maybe thirty or forty, then I found the sand entrance and had to slow down.

I hit the first sand and came to a sudden stop. The right front fender dropped as if I had fallen in a hole. I carried a flashlight and emergency tools. When I inspected my problem, it didn't take long to realize the right front wheel was gone. It was there close. I hadn't gone far without it. I carried a bumper jack, so I didn't have to dig in the sand. The nut had come off that holds the wheel onto the front axle.

I found the nut, the washer, and the bearings, and cleaned the sand off as best I could. I put them all back together and a cotter pin to keep the nut from turning off. A short distance and off came the wheel again. I found all the parts again. It's hard to believe I found them the first time, but to find them in the dark a second time was sure using up my luck fast. With closer checking I found that the threads were gone from the axle. I tightened the nut as best I could, and I could see it would shear the cotter pins right away. Among my tools was a small screwdriver. I drove it into the cotter pin hole and bent it so it wouldn't fall out, and we were gone again. We made it to El Paso and I was in time for my flight to Torreon. I didn't get much sleep that night. When I got back from Durango, I went to a parts store and bought a tool for chasing threads on front and rear axles. There were special undersize nuts for those chased threads. The bearings still had all the balls in so I cleaned the sand out and didn't replace them. When I say I cleaned the sand out I mean I wiped them of as best I could. A little grease and they went back where they came from. The cars in those days had tapered rear axles and hubs. I think that tool is still around the shop. That little screwdriver was also in my tool box for a long time.

Jim Reynolds and I flew to Torreon, Coahuila where the seller met us that night at the airport. He took us to a hotel and sure fed us a good supper. Then we left for his ranch, about fifty miles somewhere in the foot hills of the big Durango mountains. He was driving a pickup, and his wife was along. Jim and I rode in the back of the truck with a canvas over our heads to keep some of the cold out. We were sure cold and aired out when we arrived at his ranch. It was in November.

The next morning we had a good breakfast and I walked down to the corrals to look around. I jumped across a little ditch, and didn't have my pants pulled up tight and those damn things came apart from the crotch to the belt. I did some quick thinking, and looked around the corrals for some barbed wire I could tie them back together with. That fix seemed better than what I knew I had to do. I reached back there and sort of held the pieces together and went to the house to ask the lady I had just met for a needle and some thread. She could see I was in trouble, and she guessed what kind. She told me to take them off and hand them through the door to her and she would have them together in a minute. I asked her to please double stitch them and she did. There I was a big time cow buyer about to write the man a check for many thousands of pesos. I was sure feeling pretty tall but hadn't expected to get too big for my britches so soon.

The cowboys were sent out early to bring in the herd and they soon started coming in. The herd was black angus cattle that originally came from the Benton Ranch near the US border which was then the Adams

Ranch. It belonged to Uncle Bill, and was called Cerro En Medio. I liked the heifers and bought all of them. Well I didn't buy one of them. The wolves had been after it and had it torn to pieces. Mainly the hind legs. A wolf goes for the leader just above the hock. One wolf teases the head while another runs by and bites above the hock. When they finally get the leader torn where the animal can't stand and sits down, then they go for the jugular. Nature can be very cruel. The cowboys must have scared the wolves. They rounded up those cattle early in the morning and that probably saved that little cow. She was ruined, just not dead.

The cattle were to be delivered to Jimenez in December. I wrote him a check for the earnest money and the balance to be paid on delivery. I would receive them at the Jimenez Stock Pens on a day we set in December 1946. I went back to El Paso. Picked up Mart and we headed for home back across the sands again. That time my wheel was on a little better and the other one checked out also. In about thirty days I was to receive the cattle in Jimenez. For some reason the seller didn't bring all the cattle I had bought. He planned to bring the rest at a later date. It was his big mistake because Chihuahua border was closed for any cattle coming into the state from any state south. The cattle market came to a complete standstill. That was due to the foot--and--mouth disease (AFTOSA). I flew to Chihuahua and took the train on down to Jimenez. The seller was at the hotel and the cattle were being herded about three miles out of town. The next morning we got in his truck and went out to the herd to see them and have breakfast at the chuck wagon.

It was cold and those Mexican cowboys used a serape instead of jackets. A hole cut in the center to stick their head through, and it hangs down around them. They were just changing the guard as we drove up. One of the men going to the herd was still flipping his serape for adjustment as he was riding out to the herd. The cattle were still bedded down, but as he rode towards them, they jumped up all at the same time and stampeded. I mean they left there, and I was sure glad they still belonged to him. Those cattle were so scared and loco that it was noon before they settled down enough to pen them at the railroad stock pens. That was the first and only stampede I had ever witnessed. I had seen corrals and fences after the stampede but not the actual run. You don't try to stop a stampede. You haze the leaders and try to circle them until they will get to milling and hope one doesn't break out and start the whole thing over.

I had ordered five train cars to ship them in. I would ship to Ciudad Juarez then change trains and then ship to the pens just outside our ranch on the NorOeste Railroad. The sellers' ranch was near the border of Durango and Chihuahua. As cattle came into Chihuahua they had to be dipped for ticks, and then again at Jimenez before I could ship them north. He had paid a little mordida and not dipped them when he crossed into Chihuahua. Now I had to have them inspected, then dipped. If the inspector were to find a tick he would quarantine the herd for a week after dipping. Then they would have to be dipped again. I found out that my cars were not coming for a week, maybe two weeks, no promise.

I asked a fellow cattle buyer at the hotel about ticks, and how to tell if there were any and where to look. I had seen rabbit ticks and knew where to look for them. On rabbits. But I had never seen a cow tick and had no idea where to look. I heard what you thought, "On the cow." I was concerned because I knew Durango was a tick state, and my cattle were not dipped. He told me to go among them and lift their tails and look up there where they are fastened on. I did, and the first tail I looked under was full of ticks. I checked several and found all the ticks I wanted to see in my little herd. I knew then that I had big trouble. Cattle not dipped, no cars, and I couldn't get any, and lots of ticks. The seller had my money and had gone in high gear just ahead of his dust. In fact I could still see his dust when I realized I had a mess on my hands. It looked like I was about to get a very expensive lesson in cow buying.

I went to a farmer and bought all his hay. Enough to keep my little cows alive for maybe about a month. I had no idea how long it would take me to get out of the mess. Then I went to the inspector and asked about inspecting my herd. I was covering the top of his desk with pesos while we were talking. I sure would like to not have to dip them in such cold weather. He went into the corrals and walked among the little cows and didn't see any ticks. He didn't lift any tails. I kept them milling and spooked, which was easy to do. He agreed that they were sure nice cattle to put through that dipping again. He assumed they had been dipped at the Chihuahua border. The papers I had, said so.

The fellow I met at the hotel was a big cattle buyer and a big shipper. He had his own train. I found out that he had some cattle on quarantine at times. I made another trip to the office of my friend the inspector. As I was talking to him I was putting pesos on his desk again. I told him that I needed five cars. In about a week the big buyer's trainload of cars arrived. When he got his cattle all loaded that the inspector let go, he had five cars left. I went to him and asked if there was any way he could let me ship in those cars. He did and put my cars right on his train and pulled them to Juarez. I gave him the feed I had left for his quarantines. SUCH A DEAL.

I have tried to tell my story like it was. When we unloaded the cattle in Ciudad Juarez, and the man that my friend was buying the cattle for, saw five of his cars had carried someone else's cattle and his cattle were left in Jimenez, he became unhappy. I didn't stay close for all the conversation, but the last I heard as I was trying to get out of hearing distance was, "You damn, dumb, stupid son--of--a--bitch." I was going to thank him but I changed my mind. I had already thanked my friend in Jimenez. My friend might have lost his job, I don't know.

I need to sort of explain why I did the no--dipping thing. First for personal gain. I was in a bind and had no intention of acting like an Opossum. In all my life I had never seen a cow tick. "How come we never had them?" I knew those would not be the first ticks to be shipped towards the Corralitos. That left me only one conclusion. Those kind of ticks can't live there or they would already be there. It was not the right climate for them. Actually by the time we branded those little cows we didn't find one tick bug on them. Tio helped me with the branding and he had tick experience. I unloaded them in Ciudad Juarez in the morning and loaded them on the NorOeste in the evening for their last ride to the Memmott Ranch. They drew lots of attention so I stayed with them all day and kept them spooked so no one could get a chance to look under their tails.

When we left Jimenez, my five cars of cattle were all on the front of the train next to the engine. That was back in the steam--engine days.

The rest of the train was behind them, then the caboose where I rode. My five cars were next to the engine because we loaded them last. The cattle were loaded with the train backing up. I don't know why. We left Jimenez in the evening. The first time the train stopped for water I went to see if my cattle were all standing. If one gets down, he will be killed by the others stepping on him. They were all OK and I started back to the caboose. The train was already rolling, and I almost missed getting on. At the next stop it was night. I checked them out and decided to stay in the cattle car with them until the next stop. That was a mistake. Black cattle kick like mules. I had to sit up in the little window of the cattle car until the next stop. I knew that if I went to sleep and fell inside, the cattle would get me and if I fell to the outside, well, I just would not go to sleep. I about froze sitting in the window of that cattle car. The next stop, I checked them and went back to the caboose. It sure felt good to be by the fire in the little stove.

The next and last stop was at a water stop north of Chihuahua City. It was just daybreak. I went up front to check my cattle one more time. By then I had thought the thing out. I would walk to my cars and check them and then climb on top of the train cars and walk them back to the caboose. I had seen railroad fellows do that so I knew how it was done. I checked my first car first and the back car last and up the ladder I went. By the time I was topside, the train was moving. I was running to the back of the train and jumping the space between the cars. The people on the ground were all yelling and waving, and I was thinking how friendly, or maybe they thought I was pretty clever to be running along the top of the train. I looked back over my shoulder just in time to see the water pipe, and it was coming towards me fast. It was still hanging over the train. I flopped down on the top of the car and it went over me. That was one close call.

We unloaded in Ciudad Juarez before noon and I had no trouble getting cars to go south on the NorOeste Railroad. I had them in the Juarez pens about five hours before they were loaded on the other train. Everyone was looking at my nice little cows and I was in the corral with them to keep them stirred up so no one would be tempted to look for a tick. I was sure glad to get them on the homebound train. It was MUY NOCHE when we arrived at the Corralitos Stock Pens to unload them.

I would leave them there until morning then drive them to the ranch. About three miles.

When we got to the Corralitos pens, the engineers told me to get them unloaded PRONTO because the engine had a water leak and it was putting out the fire. When we had them all in the corrals, the engine was unhooked from the train. They told me to get on the engine with them and they would try to get to Casas Grandes before the steam was gone. I did, and I have never had such a bucking ride before or since. I had no idea those engines jumped around so much. There were two seats on that old engine and I didn't get one. I stood up and sure had to hold on to keep from getting bucked off the thing. They went pretty fast and I really thought it might jump the track any minute.

I lived a block from the track, and as we pulled into Dublan, I told them my street. It was a very dark night. They slowed the engine down some and told me to jump. I planned to land on the road where it crossed the track, and I did. I rolled and tumbled and banged into something, and thought I was being killed. I had my satchel in my hand and never turned it loose. I finally got stopped from rolling and was able to walk on to my house a block away. My second Christmas home since the war and it was Christmas Eve. I got home from the war in good shape but that second time from buying cattle, I was damn near killed. When Mart saw me all dirty, skinned, and clothes torn she thought someone had worked me over. I was worked over alright. When I told her what happened she told me that the railroad was mad at her dad. They dug a big ditch the day before at the crossing so he couldn't use it. That was what I jumped into. Her dad's house was a block east of the track and ours a block west of the track.

Chihuahua closed its border to Durango the first of the year so the rest of the cattle could not be delivered. I went to El Paso and quarrelled with the seller one whole night to get him to refund the money I had paid down on them. When he saw I was determined, he gave me a check. It was a lot of money to me.

When Memmott bought the ranch he only fenced about half of it because of the ejido people who wanted to keep it as they had it for so many years. The ranch was part of the Corralitos but had not been refenced since the Pancho Villa era. It had been used all those years like public land. In other words like it was ejido land. The land went to the top of a big mountain and Joe wanted me to go ahead and fence the rest of it. He told me there was a sheep herder up one of the large canyons and that there was permanent water up there. I put my pickup in grandma gear and drove up the ridge looking for the sheep ranch and also for a place to send my men to cut some ceder fence posts. There was no road or even ruts, just pick and choose my way. At the foot of the big mountain I spotted the sheep camp down in the canyon. I left my pistol in my truck. I heard the sheep man was sort of mean, and I didn't want him to think I was looking for trouble. I walked over to the edge of the bank, about forty feet high, to take a look around.

That old boy was sitting in the shade of his hut with a .30--30 looking eyeball to me. I thought he was old, but I wasn't sure because he was covered with long hair and beard. I called to him, "Soy Amigo." He looked at me for some time, and I looked at that rifle for the same amount of time. He finally told me to come on down and tell him what I wanted. He turned the rifle across his legs and I sat there on a rock to talk to him. I had almost forgotten what I was there for anyhow. I told him that was my land and I wanted to cut posts and fence it. Then I was looking down the sights of that gun again. Backwards. I could see I must change my thinking quick. I told him he could stay there because I would need someone to look after that part of the ranch. Quevedo was my neighbor to the north. He had put the old man there for the same reason I told him he could stay. To watch the place and not let anyone in there. After we talked for a while I told him I would go on up the canyon and look around some. I thought we had become friends by then. I was wrong. I was looking down that damn gun barrel again, and he told me I had gone as far as I was going, and not to come back. The old man had long hair and a long beard, so all I could see was his eyes, and they looked mean. After I left the ranch, Memmott had him moved off and put the fence where it belonged. It was all in the court process when I went up there, but the old man hadn't got the word yet from Quevedo.

When I took over the ranch, I hired a cook and two men to help me build. There was nothing but the 350--foot well and it was bad. A six inch well with a four inch cylinder and two inch column pipe. The bottom check was not holding, so I had to pull the whole thing to get to it. A very poor setup for any well, much less a 350--foot well. Memmott had told me how many joints of pipe were in there. They were twenty--foot joints and no windmill tower. The water was pumped by hand. The well was set up for a windmill but in the meantime it had a handle attached to the sucker rod for those thirsty enough to push it up and down. Same idea as a pitcher pump, just a longer handle. All I had to pull those pipes with was a tripod made from three twenty foot joints of two--inch pipe. We would pull a joint up then unscrew it, then hold it up enough to unscrew the sucker rod. The two had to come out together and stay together until we had them on the ground. The only good thing was that they were not full of water, because of the bottom check leak. When we had all but the last two joints laying on the ground, I decided to pull the last two without taking them apart. One joint came up and all was fine. We kept pulling and out came the next joint, but it was not the last one. There was one more joint down in the well than what I was told. Now I had forty feet of two--inch pipe up in the air and it was leaning south, or north, or someplace besides straight up as it should. I couldn't go any higher with it and I couldn't put it back in the well. I had large pipe wrenches and we were finally able to unscrew the two pipes that were up in the air enough that they toppled over and broke themselves loose. They were ruined but no matter because I had a new cylinder and three inch pipe to go back into the well.

The next project was to build the windmill tower in order to install the heavy pipe. I should have built the tower first anyhow. I had a flatbed truck 4x4 army surplus. I went to a sawmill up the Tinaja River, which is in the mountains northwest of Colonia Juarez, for a load of lumber. I got four 8x8x20 foot timbers for the legs and 2x6 lumber for the braces to build the tower. The rest of the load was 1x6 lumber for gates and log edgings for the corrals. When I started off the mountain with my load, I went to four--wheel--drive and the lowest gear I could find. Floyde and Sid went with me. Sure was a long slow drive but I had no intention of changing gears while coming off that mountain. I still remembered the runaway at the Organ Pass near Las Cruces, NM with that load of watermelons.

Mr. Albert Wagner Sr. had drawn plans for the tower and the stub to fit an eighteen--foot windmill. A windmill is measured by the diameter of the wheel. I went to work on the tower. I laid two 8x8 timbers at the proper angle and nailed on the braces. We did that to two sides, then we had to stand them on edge to nail braces on the top side then turn the whole thing over to bring the bottom to the top and brace that side. I had no way to do that only pure man strength, four of us.

When we had the two sides made and ready to stand on edge, I cut a three foot board. We were ready to lift the first side onto its edge. The four of us were able to lift it the three feet and I told my cook, who was one--legged, to stand the three--foot board under it so we could get a better hold and stand it on up. My one--legged cook was Peggy, the boy we raised at the Pajarito Ranch. When he turned loose to get the board, we couldn't hold it. My other two men jumped out of the way and the thing fell on me.

I was doing the splits with it on my left leg near my hip. I just knew I was busted all to pieces. It took four of us to lift it the first time, and three were trying to lift it off me. They would lift it some then drop it back on me. I was trying to get them to listen to me. They were excited and grunting so loud they couldn't hear me. I finally got their attention and told them to get a long pry board. I finally got them to quit bouncing it on me and use the pry board. When I crawled from under it I couldn't get up. The men took hold of me, however, and stood me up, and after checking all my parts, I found them unbroken, but twisted a little. My left leg was stiff at the knee, but I was able to hop around and we finished the tower and stood it up. My left knee has never fully recovered.

My tools were the flatbed truck to pull with, a set of four--pulley rope blocks and lots of rope. We moved the tower to its almost location, planted a post at each of the bottom legs then with a long rope tied to the truck, and in four--wheel--drive, we were able to stand it up. I tied a rope to it also and dallied a post to keep it from going on over when it stood up, just in case. It tried to do just that but I had too many ropes on it in too many places. We walked the tower around until it was centered over the well, then poured footings and fastened it forever to stay put.

It was a couple of weeks before I could bend my leg enough to ride in the cab of my pickup truck. Mart would drive for me and I would stand up in the back.

I put a 6x6 timber across the top of the tower to tie the rope blocks to and then we were ready to put the well back in the hole. Memmott came out to help me with that part. We were in the well with all but the last two joints of three--inch pipe. Memmott took the clamp off and we were about to let the next twenty feet into the well when the 6x6 timber broke. The rope blocks barely missed Joe, and the whole thing went down the well.

We all took turns looking down the well to try and see what we just couldn't believe. So near finished and we lost it. No one got hit with the falling timbers and rope blocks so we could put our thoughts on how to get hold of the pipes and pull them out again. We came up with zero ideas.

I went to Dad's ranch and told him what had happened. He told me how to drive a wooden pin into the bottom of a pipe and sharpen the end going down in the well. That served as a guide to find the threads on the pipe in the well about fifty feet down. I spent the whole night finding a joint of pipe to use for fishing. I found it at the Corralitos Hacienda. I arrived at my camp at daybreak and my men were already up and breakfast was ready. While we were pulling the pipe out Joe was in Casas Grandes finding a new cylinder. He was there with it by the time we had the pipe out of the well. I was able to get hold of the pipe on the first try. We had to pull the whole thing and start over because the fall bent the cylinder on the bottom. It had to be replaced.

I had already moved my cattle there from Dad's ranch and they had been without water for two days. I stopped the well work on the third day and we drove the cattle to the river and let them fill up. It was about three miles one way. I drove them back to the ranch real slow so they wouldn't spill all that water they were carrying. That would have to last them for two more days if I was lucky to get the well going again. I did and they were sure ready for more water. I used a pump jack while I was getting the windmill installed. The water storage I had was a five hundred gallon trough in the corral so I had to pump water everyday.

We were finally ready to install the windmill on the tower. The wheel was eighteen feet in diameter. It sure looked big laying there on the ground, and I had to put it about thirty feet up in the air. Mr. Wagner came and helped me build and install the stub on top of the tower for the mill engine to sit on. When his son, Edger, knew that he was going to help me he said, "Bill, Dad is an old man so be sure you don't let him climb up the windmill tower." I saw no problem with his request until we were at the ranch and started to work. Edger forgot to tell me how to keep him off the tower. He went right to the top and worked with me. I used a two--inch pipe for a gin pole to pull the pieces up to the top. I ran three guy--lines from it because I knew it would not take the weight of the engine without some help. I nailed 2x12 boards on the tower as runners to slide the engine on as we were pulling it up. I was using four--pulley rope blocks. I got Dad to help me. I tied the pull rope to the front bumper of my pickup and put Dad in there to drive. That way he was facing me and could see my signals. I gave Dad the up signal and he moved backwards watching very closely for my stop signal. I built the slide alongside the ladder, so as the engine was pulled up I could climb the ladder alongside it and keep it on the track. We took it up slowly and finally had it onto the platform. I have said that the wheel was eighteen feet in diameter. Put a little arithmetic to that and it means the engine had to sit on top of the stub another ten feet above the platform. That was not so bad, but I had to raise it another four feet to clear the stinger, and then let it down onto its seat on top of the stub if and when I got the stinger in the hole. I think the engine weighed about three hundred pounds duty weight.

OK, so you want to know what duty weight is. That is the weight the US uses to collect import duty on cattle shipped from Mexico as they come off the scales on the US side. It is also the weight that cattle buyers use to pay for the cattle. The buyer contracts a price per pound duty weight. What that means is that the cowman in Mexico rounds up his fat calves very carefully, then ships them to El Paso. They spend a day being dipped and inspected in the Ciudad Juarez Stockyards. In my days they were then driven by horseback across the bridge to the El Paso Stockyards and then onto the scales for duty weight. By that time those little cattle would have shrunk as much as 30%. What I'm trying to get across is that the engine had been laying in the sun for a few weeks so surely it shrunk some. Maybe not quite 30%.

Up to the platform, I could work alongside the monster but from the platform on up I had to be under it. Things were sure getting touchy. I gave Dad some more up--signal and he gave me an inch at a time, just what I needed. My guy--lines were so tight I could hear them playing tunes in the wind and the weather was very calm. I had a safety belt on and I was high enough on the stub so I could guide the stinger into the hole once we had it high enough. Dad was moving it up for me as he read my signal, and we were within a quarter inch of being high enough when one strand of a guy--line broke. I was under that thing looking up at it and had to make a decision. I couldn't go back down, it was in a bind. I looked up into the blue sky and said my own kind of a prayer and motioned to Dad to give me some up. He did, I got the quarter inch and guided the stinger into the hole. I gave Dad a down signal, and as he gave me some down another strand broke, but before the third and last strand broke we had that engine in its home resting place. I didn't turn my safety belt loose for a few minutes for fear I would fall. I had to put myself together again. I noticed Dad was bent over the steering wheel, and when I climbed down and went over to him, he was crying. We had sure played it close.

I put a new line on my gin pole and we were ready to put the hardware onto the engine, that being the wheel and the tail. They weren't heavy like the engine but were still tricky to install. They kept trying to knock me off the tower. I put the wheel up first, because it would be easier to control without the tail if gusts of wind should happen along, and they did, pretty regular. The wheel wasn't much trouble until we had it half on. It came in eight sections. We had to install each section from the bottom of the wheel, working on the platform. You have heard of throwing a monkey wrench in the gears? That was exactly the way I put the wheel up. I would climb on top of the engine and my men would turn the wheel far enough for the next section and I would put a monkey wrench in the gears to keep it from turning backwards. Then came the tail and it had a mind of its own. It tried to knock me off the tower a couple of times when I was trying to get it pinned in place. I had been pumping water with a pump jack so when the windmill was finished all I had to do was hook up the sucker rods and it was soon pumping water.

With the mill up and working I could take time to fix a place to live so I could take Mart and the kids to the ranch to be with me. Up until then I was just camped under the stars. I had built a small cook shack to keep groceries in.

Mart and I went to El Paso and went to Silver's. I think he sold something of everything. I bought a large tent, about 12x12. The tent had a center pole and was only one floor. Dirt. We didn't have to climb any stairs. You might say we lived on the ground floor. We had our beds and a stove in there, and we were sure happy because we were building on our future. Floyde and Sid dug little holes in the floor to play marbles.

They had a little dog they called Shorty. One night it snowed about four inches, and the coyotes were sure playing and yelping. They started running around our tent and we thought they were going to come inside, and so did Shorty. He wanted to run outside and fight them. Floyde and Sid could hardly hold him. I ran outside with my pistol to try and get them to go play somewhere else or I would decrease their numbers. They yapped at me and ran away with me shooting at them. It was moonlight. They didn't come back. The next morning there were coyote tracks everyplace. When they almost came into the tent, I think they smelled Shorty and wanted him to go play with them. They would have torn him to pieces.

I had built corrals and a horse pasture, and the men had hauled enough rocks to start building the house and other buildings. I had a rock mason there and was ready to go, but then Memmott decided to sell the place, I didn't buy it, so he told me I would have to go. I rounded up my cattle and took them back to Dad's ranch at Buena Fe.

We had a very rainy summer while at the Memmott Ranch. There were two large canyons that came off the mountain through the ranch. One on the west side and one on the east side. The west canyon ran close to the headquarters. It rained so much one day that it ran it over and it washed out the railroad bridge. The railroad brought in new timbers for the new bridge. The old timbers had washed down the canyon a few hundred yards, and most of them had been carried away but one. A 14x14 by about fifteen feet long. I took my 4x4 truck down there and tied a chain to it and drug it to our tent. Mart and I would sit on it in the evenings and talk about how lucky we were. We had a real nice tent and all the work we could handle. She made candy often, and it was a treat to scrape the pan. We have a picture of Floyde and Sid scraping on one side and Shorty licking on the other, all sitting on that log. Not long ago some ladies at our church were talking about some of the hard times they had gone through and one of them said, "Martha, you wouldn't know about that sort of thing."

Mart replied, "Have you ever lived in a tent?"

When the US border closed to importing Mexican cattle, Memmott and Lunt decided to sell the ranch. They offered it to me for $30,000.00 dollars. Nothing down, and pay as I sold cattle. Sure sounded like a chance of a lifetime to me. I sent telegrams to my partners, one in San Luis Potosi, Bryan Brown, and one in California, Art Holmes. Art gave Bill Holmes, his brother, his vote or proxy. Bill lived in San Luis. I flew to San Luis to meet with them and explain what a good deal I thought it was, but they both voted to turn it down. We were partners for several years after that, but I knew then that I would someday make some changes. I would sell out and pay them off, or someday buy them out. Otis Jeffers bought the ranch a few months later for $80,000.00. I moved my cattle back to Dad's ranch, and left for El Paso to find a job. At that time Mart had a contract teaching school there in Dublan and couldn't go with me.

16

El Paso

In the early part of 1947, Mart and I went to El Paso to find a job and try to make ends meet. Floyde and Sid stayed at the ranch with my folks until I could find a job and a place to live. We first rented one room with kitchen privileges on Montana St., no kids allowed. I went to Fort Bliss where General Electric was doing rocket research and filled out an application. I was told to come back the next day for an interview. I did and the interview was very short. The answer was no. They just didn't need any cowboys. I was upset, and I turned loose on that poor old boy in the big chair behind the big desk. I had a lot to say about fighting a war, then not being able to find a job. He just sat there and let me have my say, and when I started to leave, he told me to sit down, and let him talk. He told me he would give me a job on the bull gang and I could go from there. My problem was that I didn't know how to tell him what I did know. I reported to work the next day and it sure felt good. I had to work two weeks before getting any pay but that was OK. The bull gang was just doing the odd jobs around the place such as moving things in and out of the warehouses. Lots of stuff was being shipped in. The program was new and there was lots to do. In our moving of machinery I told my boss of my experience in Morenci, and he soon saw I had some experience.

I had been on the job about a week when some very large and delicate heavy equipment came in on a truck. The bull gang was to unload it.

My boss told me he didn't have the experience for that job, so he would turn it over to me. If I messed up we would both be out of a job, but if I unloaded the truck with no problems he would sure see that I would get to move on when some department came to him for a man. There were two large machines on the truck, in crates. I was given a crane and told to choose my help. I picked one man and told my boss to keep the rest out of the way. That was my test and I had to make it work. The main thing I knew was how to put the cables on the package so it would not slip and dump it when we went up in the air and over the side of the truck. For some reason they couldn't take the truck side rails off. All I had to do was sit it on the ground. The shipment came in late in the evening. I told them I couldn't unload it by quitting time. I was told to unload it and take the time I needed. There was a large crowd of important folks watching, and it all went very smoothly. I got a few hand shakes, and especially from my boss.

The next day I was picked up from the bull gang and sent to the machine shop as a boiler maker. We had boiler makers in Morenci, so I had an idea what it was about. They worked with sheet metal. I had no experience at all in that line. I had practiced welding when I was in Morenci and I told them about that. I had been in the shop a few days when there was an accident with one of the welders. His bottles were standing up but not tied. The oxygen bottle fell over and broke the gauge off and it went to spinning like a top. For some reason it went out the side of the metal building. The hole it made was the only damage, but the welder lost his job. I filled in his job for about a month until they hired a new welder. We boiler makers made the containers for the instruments that went into the test rockets. Those little boxes had to be made to a very close tolerance. One man did nothing but check tolerances, and if it didn't pass it went to the scrap heap and we started over. I got myself some gauges like the Inspector used. I soon learned to make my jobs right the first time.

I will give some background on what we were doing. When we ended World War II in Germany, we captured as many Scientists as we could before the Russians got them. Those men were shipped to the US and put in Fort Bliss. They were inside a chain link fence with the gates open. They were given housing and schooling for kids and living quarters. The men were allowed to report for work. They supervised and taught us. All the captured V2 rockets and components were there also, and that was what we were doing. We would build up a rocket, and then send it to White Sands to be fired and tested. Those Germans were smart, and they learned English so we could talk to them and understand what they wanted. Dr. Werner Von Braun was the leader of the pack, about six of them.

We had a rocket ready to send to the firing--range and the Germans were doing some final tests. They were talking German and going in circles because they couldn't get continuity in the exhaust system. The rocket's parts were put together in three sections then the sections were put together on a track there in the shop for the last test before leaving for White Sands. Finally the Germans got some tools and started taking off inspection plates. They found some old pants stuffed in one of the pipes. No one admitted doing it, but the Germans told us that would be reason to be shot in their land. That same rocket was the one that went out of control and landed in the graveyard of Ciudad Juarez. It sure shook up both towns. It was the rocket fuel that exploded because they didn't carry any bombs.

I was working hard and learning a lot. The boss came to me one day and asked if I would like to work with a German on the sandbag. Sure, why not. The leather sandbag was about two feet high and about two feet across. That was the way we made odd shapes of sheet metal for wings and such. I worked with Von Braun, and for sure he was an artist with a rawhide mallet and a sandbag. I soon got so I could hit where he wanted and how hard he wanted. He liked me because I tried to do as he wanted. I was the third man he had tried to teach the sandbag maneuver to.

In the planning was a two--stage rocket. GE had tried to contract the mock up with a California company, but they wanted $5000.00 to build it. GE decided to give the job to Von Braun and I was on the ground floor with him. He gave me the blueprints and told me to go to work. I had a helper, and with Von Braun I built the world's first two--stage rocket. It was a mock--up to study before building the real thing. Most of it was done on the sandbag because of the odd shapes. I got pretty good at shaping sheet metal. My two stage project was different from anything else going on in the shop so we created lots of curiosity.

Mart and I soon found a place to live where we could bring Floyde and Sid out from the ranch in Mexico. They had some kids over and were playing in the backyard one day, and were talking about what race they each were. Mart heard Sid tell them we were half--breeds. Floyde and Dad are Americans, and he and Mother are Mexicans. He was right. He and Mart didn't have their citizenship papers yet.

I started taking flying lessons on the GI bill but before I could solo we left El Paso for higher ground. Mexico City.

By then the aftosa program was getting well underway. Curtis Morris, a rancher in Mexico I had known all my life, asked Dad where I was. Dad told him, and he said, "We need him with the aftosa. We need someone there that will let us know what is really going on." He told Dad to tell me that if I was interested, to go to the courthouse there in El Paso and see Dr. Redman. I was to tell him that Curtis had sent me. Curtis had already talked to Dr. Redman. It took me longer to quit my job than it did to get hired for the aftosa program in Mexico.

We had a little airfield at the ranch. Curtis flew in there to tell Dad that I had the job. He was flying a Cub. He made a bad touchdown. About half of the runway was left behind him and there wasn't enough runway left to get stopped. He punched the throttle for a go--around. He was too fast to stop and too slow to fly. The road was at right angles in front of him with a fence on our side for the ranch, and a fence on the other side for the Wagner farms. It was a lane about two hundred feet wide. He saw he couldn't get his plane back in the air so he decided to jump the two fences. He jumped the first one, then bounced in the middle of the road, but he didn't quite clear the next one. It tore some holes in the wings and bent the struts on the landing gear, but he did a good job of keeping it right side up. He got it stopped in Wagner's alfalfa field. Dad went over there and they put the tail--wheel in the back of Dad's truck and towed it over to our place. At Casas Grandes there was a saddle maker who was also a flyer, and a fixer. He had built and flown a plane using a Model A Ford motor. It had three wings. He crashed it on its first and only flight. On take--off he hit a rat mound and went airborne but not for very far. His name was Fitzpatrick.

I quit my job with GE and took a week off before going to Mexico City. We went home to the ranch, so I was there when the plane was being repaired. Curtis was there each day watching the work. He just wanted it patched to fly to Deming for proper repairs. When it was ready to go he told Fitzpatrick to fly it straight to Deming and that he would meet him there and bring him home by car. What Curtis didn't know was that Fitz liked to play around in the air. He had done a lot of barnstorming in his younger days. He took off and climbed out beautifully, gave it a little check--out then started diving and rolling and sure put on a show. Then he would buzz us. He buzzed us twice and Curtis was sure using some cowboy language on him. He pulled out his .45 automatic and said, "If he comes by one more time I'm going to shoot him." I don't know if Fitz heard him or saw him with the pistol in his hand, but the show was over. He went out of sight towards Deming. I thanked Curtis for getting me the job, and told him that some day I hoped to have an airplane. I had already landed once there at the ranch with my instructor. That was how come Curtis to fly in there.

We spent a few enjoyable days with our folks then went back to El Paso to get our shots and fly to Mexico City.

17

Aftosa

August 15, 1947. We spent a short few days with our folks in Dublan. Then back to El Paso to catch our plane to Mexico City. A DC 6. We were used to the DC 3, so the DC 6 sure was big. We had a short stop in Monterrey and then on to Mexico City. We arrived at night and when I saw the lights of such a large town I knew I was in for some surprises. Later I was surprised at how many surprises. When I was given my papers in El Paso, I had the information of the hotel to go to and the address of the aftosa offices. We were told to hold onto our luggage because that is the stealing capitol of the world. I was to find out later how true. They even have a school to teach thievery. Pick pockets especially. Mart and I held onto our luggage and our two little kids. We got a taxi and told him the hotel and the address. Our first ride in Mexico City was one to remember.

The taxi man delivered us to the hotel, nervous but unscratched. At the hotel we freshened up a bit and went to the restaurant for supper. When we were seated I knew right away that we were out classed in that place. We were not used to waiters, and they were pushy. I finally got them tipped enough so they left me alone. We didn't go back there. I had been told how much money I was going to make, but I hadn't seen any of it yet. I had to be careful with what little money we had.

The next morning I went to the aftosa office. A taxi ride again but that time I could see better what we were almost hitting, or what was almost hitting us. I tried to tell the driver that I wasn't in a big hurry, but he listened badly. At the office I met several fellows like myself, just arrived. I was hired as a sanitary technician, whatever that was. Sounded pretty good when I was told in El Paso. We would be allowed so much money for living quarters in Mexico City, then a perdiem when in the field, then the salary I was told about in the first place. I was rated as a GS6. When on that job I drew my living allowance, and perdiem. I had them deposit all my salary in my bank in El Paso. We found an apartment on the Paseo De La Reforma. That is the main street entering the city from the west, and we were near the Chapultepec Park. Floyde and Sid enjoyed the park. I was sent the next day to my job, in Morelia. Sure a nice place. I would go out on a couple of jobs for training then be given a crew of my own. I found a place to rent and called Mart to bring the boys and come to Morelia. She did and still talks about that bus ride. Rest room especially. First come first serve, and no door. I went in a government car with a chauffeur. Morelia is a days drive north of Mexico City, and all mountains. I was given a vehicle with a bilingual chauffeur. I was soon to learn that those chauffeurs were just about running the show. I had trouble with mine the first thing. He didn't drive to suit me and sure didn't interpret to suit me.

Aftosa means foot--and--mouth disease. It is highly contagious in split footed animals. It came to Mexico from France. France has a large white beef animal called Charlais. The story we got was a Texas rancher wanted to get some of those cattle. They were shipped to Mexico at Veracruz and finally smuggled across the Rio Grande, and were being trucked to their destination when they were caught. The Veracruz area is where the aftosa broke out in the first place, and it spread rapidly over the southern part of Mexico. The idea was to eradicate it before it got to the US, and the only known method was to kill all the split--footed animals in the infected area. The US furnished all the money and personnel to buy the cattle at market price, put them in a trench, shoot them and cover them up. The Mexican Government furnished personnel only, which was a counter part to the US. The counter part Mexicans were paymaster and appraiser.

I went out on two jobs and I was then ready for my own crew. I got orders to bring my family to the hotel where the aftosa people had set up a field office. We were told to not go out on the street because there had been some aftosa fellows killed in a little town near there. A mob had turned the Jeep over and killed the guys with rocks. Some of the fellows there were ready to quit and go back to the US, where it was safe. We worked closely with the Mexican Army, and it was some soldiers who were killed. While we were waiting in the hotel, about a week, for orders to go back to work, I got orders to go back to Mexico City. That was where the main office was. I went in a government car with a chauffeur again and Mart and the kids got another bus ride going the other direction. Back to our apartment in Mexico City. We kept the apartment because we knew we would be going back and forth.

I reported to the Mexico City office the next morning. The meeting room had a long table with all the important folks on one side and four of us who were being looked over on the other side. One of the men spoke to us and said, "We are forming a new job designation, and you fellows have been highly recommended. We need to know more about what is going on and how the program is being carried out. You fellows will be inspectors, and will report to the man in charge of the district you are sent to. Then you will come to Mexico City once a month and report to us here at this office." We had to be bilingual, and be recommended by one of the veterinary doctors who knew us. Dr. Wardlow was from El Paso and he recommended me because he knew Dad and Uncle Bill. He told those at the table interviewing us that, "This boy has to be OK."

They sent two of us to Guadalajara. The fellow they sent with me was from Cananea, Sonora. They raised me to a GS8. They took us to the Transito office and got us each a driver's license so we could be free to go and come as we wanted. They gave us each a new Chevy and we were gone. We had never driven in such traffic, but when we were out of the city, we were still together and no bent fenders. We arrived in Guadalajara at night and went to the designated hotel. Again I called Mart and she got another bus ride. By then she knew what to expect. We found a real nice place to live. We liked living there. Floyde and Sid liked Guadalajara also. They had a nice backyard to play in, some nice lemon trees to climb, and a pan--dulce man that came around everyday with the best goodies.

I traveled the country a lot so I was out of town most of the time. Part of my job was to travel north beyond the quarantine line and look for sick cattle. The new Chevy I took to Guadalajara was for one of the head doctors. I was given a Jeep, a water jug, a bedroll, and an army cot, so I could stay where night overtook me. When I was in a town on the road traveling I would ask for someone to take me in. I would pay them for my meals and a room to put my bed in. I got along very well with those people.

The first morning at the office in Guadalajara, I was standing around getting acquainted, on the outside of the building, with all the fellows. I had been inside and reported to the chief. The chief doc came to the door and called out that he needed a volunteer to go with someone someplace, and before he could say where or who, I told him I was ready. I was given a Jeep and introduced to the general of the state of Jalisco. He needed to go to some towns near the Sayula Lake. I shook hands with him. All day we traveled and talked and I was bothered because something was trying to come to my mind. I just couldn't clear it up. The general had a thumb and the two fingers next to it. The other two were gone. You never shake a hand like that without noticing it. I was sure I had shaken that hand sometime in my life, but I couldn't place it. I told him how I was raised in Chihuahua, and I had worked for the AS&R in San Luis Potosi. He told me that he was governor of San Luis at that time. Then it came to me. I have told in my San Luis story about a party I went to. A mansion was turned into a tourist attraction, and I had met the San Luis governor at that party. The man I was driving for was that man. He remembered the party, but of course not me. I had the pleasure of working with him a lot, and we became good friends. He always asked for me when he traveled. His name was Delgado. I don't think I ever knew his first name because he was General Delgado to us.

Many Mexican people didn't understand the program, and the killing of their cattle, so he put out much effort to help them. Being a general they trusted him. When I arrived in a town with the general the people would gather around. He would get out of the Jeep and talk to them, and I was at his side. The first thing they would do was bow and some of them would get on their knees, take off their hats and say, "Mi general."

Now the inspector job was a little touchy because I traveled alone and went into some rather hostile spots. When I returned to those same towns I had been to with the general, the people gave me the same respect they had given the general because I was, "El Senor que anda con nuestro general." All I had to do was be good to them and they would do what I asked. I took the little kids for Jeep rides, all that could hang on. Sometimes I couldn't see out for the kids.

The cattle were mainly milk cows or oxen to pull the carts and plows. I went up on the Altos de Jalisco to inspect herds and get permission for the vets to go there if I could find any sign of the aftosa. I went as far as Aguas Calientes. Those people were bad to hide their cattle, and they were surprised where I could go in my Jeep and find them. They had never seen 4x4 cars and they were also surprised that I knew where to look. I had a state map that sort of helped me know where I was most of the time. I spent the night with a family in a town there on the Altos and I wanted to check out a town but I couldn't figure from the map how to get there. I gave a fellow a few pesos to go with me and show me the road, and I promised to bring him back. He told me it would take about four hours but that he would walk back. It turned out that when we started off the Alto, which is a very high large plateau, we went down into the mountains. When we arrived in the little town I could hardly believe what I was seeing. We had dropped off the Alto into the tropics. It was a large bowl, maybe five or six miles across. There were orange trees full of fruit, flowers, and smiley folks, and irrigation ditches full of water. I didn't find any aftosa down there but I found big trouble on the Alto. They ran the Quarantine line then on over to Aguas Calientes. My guide told me adios and that he would be home in about one hour. On foot there was a trail he could take. With a few trots and a gallop he would be home.

I took Mart and Floyde and Sid with me on one of my trips. It was at the town called El Salto. El Salto means waterfall. There is a large waterfall there where the entire river falls over a rock formation. The waterfall is called El Salto Juanacatlan. When the kids took us to see it they called it Niagara. A beautiful water fall about fifty feet high right in town. It was a large river spilling into Lake Chapala called Rio Santiago. I got two surprises there. The people were white, and a lady got after me with a machete. It was a Spanish town and they had stayed Spanish all those years. Sort of like the Mormon colonies in Mexico. They discouraged mixing colors. When I went into a new town I always went to the captain of the Army there, or I hunted out the padre. In that case I was in front of the church and looking for the padre. He showed up just as I was trying to tell the lady I was a friend. The padre got her to quit swinging her machete and listen. I had no more trouble there. The folks were really friendly and showed us the waterfall and the town in general. That was the northwest part of the state of Jalisco, but was not being worked yet because it was supposedly clean. I had found what the aftosa folks were afraid I would find. Then I could concentrate on the rest of the state where the aftosa program was already at work, and see what I could find there to report to help the chiefs make their decisions.

I was back in the area that I traveled with the general. When I say cattle it will include pigs, goats, and sheep. The fosa was where the animals were destroyed. Sacrificed was the word those people used. The fosa was an excavation, tres metros wide, tres metros deep, and cincuenta metros long. One end being sloped so the cattle could walk down into it and be driven to the other end. As they arrived at the other end they were shot and others driven on top of them until there were three layers deep.

On one of my inspections it was a big day. There were two fosas near each other and lots of people. Part of the job of the sanitary technician crew was to disinfect all the people and horses as they were leaving those fosas where there had been infected cattle all day long. A pond was prepared of lime water, about 8x8 feet square and about six inches deep. Everyone had to walk in it as they left and the vehicles all had to drive into it. The horses had to walk in it and the rider had to dismount and walk in it himself. There were soldiers there to see that those orders were obeyed. I had been there all day but after lunch I took a paymaster and a couple of soldiers in my Jeep to go down the river and inspect a little town. My Jeep had a canvas top and canvas doors. I had two soldiers in the back seat. They were my bodyguards. As we returned to the fosa, the work had had been finished and everyone was leaving. I drove up close enough to see how things were going. It all looked OK to me, then there came a guy on a horse. He walked his horse in the pit but would not get off and walk in it himself. The soldiers told him to get off then proceeded to make him. I saw trouble coming, and sure enough the fellow spurred his horse and took off. The soldiers started shooting at him and he was shooting back. The timber was very thick and he was soon out of sight, but the shots were still being fired by both parties. Now when the first shot was fired, I fell out of my Jeep and Vergeraunt fell out on his side and we met under the Jeep. We looked at each other and couldn't believe what we were seeing. Those two soldiers were already there. To this day I don't know how they beat us out of the Jeep. I guess those doing the shooting emptied their pistols because the shooting stopped. No one was hit and folks walked in the pit.

Vergeraunt was a paymaster and for some reason was at the fosa that day but not working. That was the reason he could go for the ride with me. I had just met him so I didn't know anything about him. However he comes in strong a little later on and I sure enough got to know him.

On my inspector job I tried to go where they were working a fosa unless I was given a special place to check out. There was a town southwest of Guadalajara that I went to once with the general and hadn't been back. A brigada was sent there to work. On my round that week I wanted to go there and see how the work was going. The chief had told me to give him a report on how that brigada was doing. None of them could speak Spanish and their interpreters sometimes messed them up. All roads were good but not paved. As I was getting near the town I could see quite a dust up the road and coming my way. Only one thing could make that much dust, and that was several vehicles like a brigada.

The brigada consisted of three vehicles. The three vehicles were for the appraiser, paymaster, and sanitary technician. When we met, they were all excited and on their way back to the office in Gudalajara. I thought maybe they had some equipment trouble. No sir, those Mexicans were mean and were about to pounce on them. We talked for a while and I was trying to get some details. That was the main part of my job, to see why some of the fellows were having trouble with the people. They said the town was full of people just standing around and ready for something. I think some smart guy said boo to them. I talked them into following me back into town and, "Let's see just what is going on." They agreed, but said they would sure leave at the first sign of trouble. I told them to follow me and to stay in their cars until I told them it was OK. All those towns have a nice park in the center and that was where people got together in bunches, to chat and walk. I drove into town and drove around the park. I couldn't see any indication of a problem, so I picked out a group of fellows, and stopped my Jeep. I hopped out and went over and shook hands with all of them and told them what we were there for and that I would like to see the town mayor, the padre, or the lieutenant, or whoever was in charge. While I was talking to those fellows some more men walked up to me, and they were important. I told them my story, and they said they were expecting someone to come and help them with their sick cattle. They said those other fellows drove into town but left right away. I told them that since that was the first work we would do in their area, would they call a meeting and let me explain what we were doing and why. I called the rest of the men to come over and meet those people. I told them that we would go to a meeting with them. They had a large building at the school and I mean the town turned out. There were a few speeches then it was turned over to me. Speaking in public is something I have done muy poquito. I looked over the crowd and I knew they expected me to be good at what I was there for. I had their full attention. I started to speak and my Spanish has never flowed better before or since. When they started to ask questions, I knew I had it made with them. They kept me up there on that platform much longer than I had planned. It was noon or a little after when they let me get out of there. When it was over I tried to shake hands with everyone there. I didn't but I tried. Then came the surprise of the day. While we (men only), were in that meeting, the ladies got together in one of the large houses and made dinner. It wasn't just something to eat, it was a several course banquet. They had arranged a long table on a long porch and I'm sure all the important folks of the town were there. We didn't do any work that day. We sat around and talked and got acquainted. One of the people took us into his home for the night and at supper time they served beans, and some other things, but nothing to eat with but tortillas. It was arranged puro Mexicano. I think they did it on purpose for the Gringos. I helped the guys with their tortillas and they got the hang of it quickly and sure didn't leave the table hungry. We were given a room to put our beds in. We all carried bedrolls and cots. Those fellows never quit talking about how they had panicked and misjudged that little town. I felt like I had earned my money that day.

I was looking things over at a fosa. Everything was in order. As I was walking around I met up with my friend, General Delgado. We chatted some and he asked if I liked to shoot, and I replied that I did. The cattle were suppose to be shot only by the soldiers. He called the two soldier shooters over and had them give me one of their guns and he took the other. They were .22 rifles. He told them that we would do the shooting and for them to load the guns for us. We were on opposite sides of the pit but shooting in the same direction. We had shot a lot of cattle. If the animal was facing us, we had to hit the curl on the forehead. If it was 180--degrees from facing us, then we would shoot just between and behind the horns, or whatever was up there. If no horns, then the ears would do. I was shooting away when a fellow came to me and told me that a boy had been shot. I knew I was not suppose to be shooting, for that very reason. That was why the soldiers were there. I went to check on the boy. He was maybe twelve years old and lying there under a bush. He was shot in the leg, flesh only just like the movies. I told the general. He walked over and looked at the boy, patted him on the head, and said, "I think one of my bullets must have hit a horn and bounced off and got your leg." That little kid got up on his feet, removed his hat and bowed and thanked the general. I wanted to take him to town in my Jeep but the general told me, "Let's finish shooting the cattle, then we will take him to town." He told one of the men to put him in the shade of a tree so he would be comfortable. When I took him to town in the evening, that little fellow sure did thank me for being so good to him.

Much of what I reported when I was Inspector was not acted upon. I think the American chiefs wanted to know that the Americans were behaving as they should, almost. Some of them were a little overbearing, but mostly they did very well. I was very free to go and come and see and report. As far as I know, my reports were never aired in the field.

Since those people could not read or write or count, they were very vulnerable when they received all that money in cash. No silver, only bills and nothing larger than $100.00 pesos. They were afraid of banks so they carried it home with them in a woman's stocking. I think their wife's, maybe. It took me a while to get used to seeing them with a stocking full of money thrown over the shoulder and headed home.

The American paymaster was inside his tiger cage vehicle, army surplus. In there also was the Mexican paymaster to see that he counted the money right, and then the man that all the world trusts, the padre. The cage was enclosed so that no one could see inside only at eye level except the inspector (me) who could get into positions to see things as they really were. I have told how the cattle purchase tickets were paid in $100.00 peso bills and smaller. Most of the money paid was $100.00 pesos. The American paymaster counted the money and handed it to the Mexican paymaster, who counted it to be sure, then the padre got it for the final count to be sure that it was right. He smiled and handed it out through a small window to the fellow with his hand ready if it was a small amount or a stocking if it was a lot of money. Some of those folks received many thousands of pesos. The American counted above the table, but the two others counted in their lap. If it was a small amount, it went by all three unshrunk, but if it was a large amount it was shrunk a few bills by each of the last two. As I have said most of the bills were $100.00 pesos. Mostly the people could not count all the money they were getting so they insisted on someone to keep the Gringo from cheating them. This really isn't a true statement, because they trusted the Gringo more than anyone, but the US didn't want to take any chances of ever being in a position to be accused of cheating. We were paid well and took no bribes. There is no telling how much money was siphoned off by those two types during and over the entire operation.

A fellow who had sold a lot of cattle and had lots of pesos, asked me to take his money and put it in my bank until the aftosa was over, then we would buy cattle to restock the area. I told him I was in no position to do that and for him not to give his money to someone like that. He said he trusted me because I was a friend of General Delgado.

The thing I wanted most with the aftosa program was to be an appraiser. The appraisers were in charge of the brigada, and made a lot more money. The brigada was the entire crew that worked a fosa. I walked into the Guadalajara office one morning and I got orders to report to Mexico City. That time, they made me an appraiser and sent me right back to Guadalajara. I was glad for that because I sure didn't want to have to move Mart and the kids again and I knew the area and lots of the people by then. We liked it there.

Most of the appraisers were older men who had bought and sold lots of cattle. They sent two other fellows with me. I don't remember why they were called. When someone was called from the field it usually meant a raise. We went to Mexico City in a Jeep station wagon and a chauffeur. Those mountains are very high with very curvy roads. We were going through the worst part at night. The driver turned out the headlights every time he met a car, until they pass. That is a custom there that I didn't like. The other fellows thought they had to take what ever those bilingual driver boys handed to them, but not me. I was in the front seat and I told him to not turn the lights out anymore. We met a car and out went the lights. I told him once more in a little better Spanish. The third time he turned them out I decided he still didn't have his ears on. I reached over and took the keys. No locking steering so I was safe. I told him he could get out and walk or get behind the back seat. He decided to ride. I was the only one of us with a Mexico City driver's license. I got the wheel. All was OK until we went over the top and started down into Mexico City. Mexico City is in a tremendous caldera rimmed in on all sides. The valley is 7440 feet above sea level. So one is high in the sky before climbing to get out of there. I thought maybe I should get him back in the wheel seat, but then I decided to stay with what I had. About that time it started to rain. It rained all the way down the mountain and into the city. It rained so hard I couldn't see the road but there was so much traffic I sure couldn't stop. I was following some taillights and things were going fine when all of a sudden the taillights disappeared. There was a large ditch of water alongside the road and he went into it. The taillights went out of sight in the water and I have no idea what happened after that. I found some more taillights and they stayed on the road on into the city. My apartment was on the same side of the city where we went in so it was easy to get to. It was the same road into the city that goes from the city to Acapulco.

The next morning I went to the aftosa office and they gave me the good word, and raised me to a GS--12. I was then an appraiser, and I sure felt good. That afternoon we started back to Guadalajara. The same two men with me and one extra to leave in Hidalgo as we went through. My driver asked them to put him somewhere else because I wouldn't let him drive so he was not with us. It was night when we arrived at the Hidalgo Hotel to drop off our passenger. He got out with his luggage and was knocking on the door of the hotel. I waited to see that he got in OK. Many of those Gringos were scared anyhow. A Chinaman that ran the hotel came to the door but wouldn't let him in. He said there had been a killing there and they told him that if he let any aftosa people stay there they would kill him. I told the fellow we would find him another place to stay, but no way. He put his things back in the Jeep station wagon, and hopped in, and went with us to Guadalajara. I think he was more scared than the Chinaman.

On one of my trips to the Mexico City I decided I would drive my car and take Mart and the kids and see the Chapultepec Park. We lived close to it. We especially wanted to see the Chapultepec Castle, where Maximilian lived when he was emperor of Mexico for about three years. It is up on a large rock formation out in the middle of the park. The El Paso office gave a letter to all personnel as they were sent to Mexico, from the Mexican Consul in Washington, D.C. We were told that if we should get into any sort of trouble to present the letter. It explained who we were, why we were in Mexico and to treat us with courtesy and help us out. Many streets in the city were one way, and traffic was like ants.

I was in the park and sure enjoying the sights when I made a wrong turn. I was in the flow of traffic, but they were all going the wrong way but me. I heard whistles and saw cops coming on foot from every direction. The one that got to me first wanted my driver's license. I gave him my Mexico City license. He put it in his pocket. They had me out of my car and were sure telling me about all the trouble I was in. I was trying to find my letter. I fumbled it out of my billfold and handed it to the fellow who took my license. He read it then turned to the other cops and told them that I was some kind of an official. He gave me back the letter and then handed me my license. I thanked him very mucho, and asked him which way I should go to get out of the mess. He took his cap off and bowed and said, "NO LE HASE". (it doesn't matter). The cops stopped traffic and waved to me to go on. I was able to turn around right there and get everyone going in the same direction again. I still have the letter.

About our apartment in the city. It was three floors up spiral stairs, no elevator. I have mentioned how they steal there. Our door had three locks on it and a peep window to look out of if someone should knock on the door. We bought bottled water for drinking. In the morning Mart got us all bathed then filled the bathtub with water to use during the day, because it was turned off at noon and then back on the next morning, maybe. We kept the tub full all the time. The first earthquake, and things started to swing and the water was trying to jump out of the tub, Mart thought she was sick and went to bed. She told some friends about it and they told her she had just gone through an earthquake. Each apartment had a clothes drying pen on the roof. Each person had his own lock. The pens were made from chicken wire and were supposed to keep the clothes from being stolen. Mart had her own maid, but she lost clothes from the wash to the pen on the roof and back. Some of the thieves would run a wire into the pen and twist socks or underwear around it and pull them out through the chicken wire. The place had a high steel fence around it, and a door to get into the building. It took three keys for the gate, three keys for the main door, then three keys for home base after you climbed three flights of stairs. We were young in those days or we couldn't have carried all those keys. Much less run up and down three flights of stairs in a circle yet. The thing they didn't steal was kids. Floyde and Sid went to the park by themselves and played there by the hour. The big danger was crossing the street. Paseo De La Reforma. Six lanes on each side of the median, which was itself a park about a hundred feet wide.

I went back to Guadalajara and was ready for my first appraiser lesson. I was sent with an old timer to get my first and only lesson in appraising. I watched him and tried to learn. I had been watching the appraisers all along anyhow and thought I could find a better way to get the job done. They would spend hours arguing over the guessed weight of some animal. There were no scales. The guy couldn't even speak Spanish. The Mexican appraiser was never satisfied and he would hold out for the last peso. An animal could not be killed until both appraisers agreed on the weight. The price per kilo was set by the market in the city and we got a new list every week. We guessed the weight to come up with the price. Different prices for different types. Pigs, goats, sheep, cows, and calves. The most expensive were the oxen, and some of them were big. Each week we got a sheet from the city telling how each appraiser was doing and what he was paying, and of course they liked the appraiser who could buy for less and still be fair. We were not told to try to cheat the people.

A Monday morning at the Guadalajara office I got my first appraiser assignment. I was to go to Atoyac on the dry Sayula Lake. I knew the area well because it had been and it was a real hot spot. I had worked it as Inspector alone and with General Delgado. I was not given a Jeep but was told to ride with the paymaster. The first time I had met him was when we jumped out of my Jeep and found my bodyguard soldiers already under it. His name was Vergeraunt, and he was from California. The paymaster vehicle was an army van enclosed with wire mesh. A tiger looking cage. He had a chauffeur. As I have told, the paymaster had a Mexican equal who went along, the appraiser had a Mexican equal who went along, and the sanitary technician had his own vehicle and a crew that he took along. That should have been three vehicles heading out that morning, but we were one short, MINE. Vergeraunt got in the front seat with his driver, and I and the other two got in the cage. The first stop was at the bank to pick up $250,000.00 pesos. At that time the exchange was $5.60 for one dollar. Then we were on the road and I was getting unhappy by the numbers. No one knew it but the inside of me. I had something by the tail there and I had to be real careful or it would get me by the tail.

The Mexican appraiser they sent with me I knew by sight and reputation. He was little and hard to get along with. The other appraisers refused to work with him, which was the reason I got him. He carried a .45 on his hip. He was tough and it showed. I was mainly mad because I didn't get a Jeep and then that no--good paymaster should be driving and me sitting in front with him. There was also an extra passenger in the cage with us with a .45 on his hip. One--eyed and sure tough looking. I didn't know just where he fit in but I thought he might be a backup for my Mexican appraiser. I'm thinking I have a tough man here with a tough backup. With all the rest that was making me so mad, what I was thinking of those pistoleros didn't help. Just before I blew the side out of that tiger cage I was in, we came to a little town and Verge had his driver stop. He walked to the back and opened the door to the cage and said, "Come on Adams, let's take over." He told his driver to get in the cage. The driver got mad and refused to get in. He was supposed to drive and to interpret. Verge told him in perfect Spanish that he needed neither one. He could get in and come along or find himself a ride back to the office in Guadalajara. He didn't get in. I blew out a lot of air to get me down to my normal size again and Verge and I started to talk and get acquainted. He was definitely my kind of man and we worked together a lot and became very good friends.

That part behind me, I could start to think about how I was going to handle the situation I was in. The town I was going to ran the appraiser out the week before. I was going into a town with the fosa ready and the cattle there ready and the people all mad as red ants. They were mad because they thought the Gringo was not paying them enough for their cattle. The Mexican appraiser had convinced them of it. I was going in there with the meanest Mexican appraiser of the lot.

We arrived into town and drove around some, looking for a place to stay. We went to the Quartel and talked to the captain and asked him to recommend a place. We stayed in people's homes. No motels in those towns. He told us where to check. The people were nice and glad to have us. We were given a room inside the patio. Verge took the money box and kicked it under the bed. He said, "Let's walk around and see the town." Now this Verge, in his rounds in the south of the state had picked up a one--eyed pistolero, and used him for a bodyguard. He told me, "Don't worry about the money." Verge paid him out of his own pocket. I was glad to know the pistolero was with Verg and not the appraiser. I soon decided the bodyguard pistolero was a good idea. That weekend when we went to Guadalajara I went to the chief and got permission to put him on the payroll. That way, he was part mine. I never worried about my back when he was around. I used him for a bodyguard and also he was my informer. He sure was good at both. He could see more with his one eye than most folks with two. I was the only appraiser with that sort of setup. One of the things he watched for was to see that all the animals I bought went into the fosa. When I was

Inspector, I noticed some didn't. Those people get smart. They would let the animal get away and sell him again later on. I found that was happening to the old appraiser they sent me with to learn. A fellow came to him to sell his cow and the appraiser told him that was the fourth time he had bought the spotted cow and would give him his ticket after she was shot. She was put into the fosa that time.

One of the crew of the sanitary man was what we called a gut--chopper. After the cattle were all killed and ready to cover the pit, he went in there and cut open all the bellies. They didn't do that at first. In one of my inspection trips I found a fosa uncovered. After a few days the thing explodes and throws all the dirt off. Then the predators, dogs and coyotes, went in there and away went the germs. All those people were hungry and it was hard for them to see so much good food shot and buried. Lime was also put on the animals so the people wouldn't go in there and dig them up to eat. My pistolero came up to me after we were through killing one day and told me to watch the gut--chopper. The chopper was down in there doing his job. He was also cutting the tongue out of some of the animals and tossing them to folks waiting on the bank. They all carried morales (shoulder bags). I had the soldiers inspect bags and make them throw the tongues into the pit. I had the sanitary man fire the gut--chopper and hire a new man. We hired our labor at the place where we worked.

I was in charge of the brigada and I was sure starting to like the paymaster but I had to take over the operation and make it click. All he had to do was pay any voucher that I signed. The appraisers were responsible for the success or failure of the program in the field. By then I had done some thinking and decided how I planned to go about taking charge. Everything was out of control. I had to make those people want to work with me rather than me trying to work with them. We made plenty of appearance around town to be sure everyone knew we were there. The next morning the people started gathering their cattle at the fosa, which was only a short distance from town. My men and I all met in the dining room and had breakfast. They were ready to get on with trying to deal with those people and watch me get the boot. Finally my paymaster couldn't stand it any longer and he asked why I didn't go out to the fosa. He knew also there had been trouble there, and he also knew the reputation of the man I had to work with.

I laid my plan out to him. "I don't intend to work today. The first thing I want them to know is that I'm in charge, and if I go out there today they will be in charge. When they spend enough time out there waiting for me to show up, and I don't, someone will come here to see why, and it will probably be the tough appraiser." Sure enough along about noon, we were still hanging around the dining room drinking hot chocolate, when there he came, and was very upset. I told him that before I was going out there to try to buy those cattle I wanted to be sure the people were ready to sell them. I knew that some cattle were dying every day, and we were not suppose to buy dead ones. I told him to tell the people that I would be around the dining room all day and if any of them would like to come and talk with me I would be glad to talk with them. Before long the patio was full of people. They were not mad. They were good people with sick cattle. I went out in the patio to meet them and shook a lot of hands, and they were all friendly to me. In the yard a tree had been cut down and the stump was still there, about a foot high. I climbed upon the stump and told them how I would be able to work with them, and expressed to them my authority. "You have not let the appraiser last week work with you, so I have been sent here especially to take care of this area one way or the other. I will work with you and buy your cattle at a fair price, or I will quarantine the area, pull all my men and equipment out and let your cattle die, and you will get no money at all. I will not send anyone else in here to help you." Now I did not have that kind of authority but no one knew it but me. I knew I had to get the attention of those folks or I would fail just like the appraisers before me. I wasn't used to failing when I was given a job to do. The thing that saved me there, was that I wasn't used to government ways. I looked at things in the field and made decisions accordingly.

The response was great. "Senor, come to the fosa manana and we will work with you." One of the fellows in the crowd told me that one of his cows had died during the night and was there some way I could help him. I asked him to take me to it so I could inspect it and then I would deal with him tomorrow at the fosa. It was freshly dead, so I told him to dig a hole and after he put the cow in it, to slice it so it would not explode, and cover it well. Tomorrow I would send someone to see if he had done a good job. He had and I bought his cow first at the fosa. I made a friend right there and he told all his buddies. The next morning I had my crew report to the fosa to see if we could really get this thing off left of dead center. Verge already told me that he had worked with several of the appraisers and he had seen some of them in trouble but none stupid enough to stick his neck out there for the machete. I told him to watch me, because I intended to get the smart little pistol packing tough appraiser into the trouble he thought he had me in. I will call him Jose.

Jose and I met at the fosa and shook hands then we walked among the cattle and shook hands with the owners. When in Mexico you shake lots of hands. I still do. Each owner had from two or three to maybe ten or twenty head of animals. Very few had more than twenty. The way it was set up to buy the cattle was that each appraiser had a preprinted pad with the different types of animals we purchased. A line for each of type, weight in kilos, and the price in pesos, and of course a total at the bottom. When we agreed on a herd of one owner we signed each other's copies and gave a copy to the owner which he had to accept and take to the paymaster for his money. All payments were made in cash only. Each of us kept a copy. A copy went to Mexico City, to be later hooked with the copy that went through the paymaster. After we made our rounds among the people and everyone was nervous for us to get started and get to arguing and shaking fingers and maybe even a fist once in a while, I called him to one side. I had a good hand shaking talk with him. I told him I knew of his reputation and I didn't come to quarrel with him. I came to do a job and I needed his help. I told him that I had also heard that he knew cattle real well and was able to estimate them very close and that I like that.

I told him I was from a ranch in Chihuahua, and I wanted those people to get a fair shake. "Now, I'll tell you what I'm going do. We will look over the cattle together and you will put down what you feel is fair and if I feel you are close I will sign it and we will go to the next bunch. Just don't mess with me." The first bunch, was about ten head. We walked among them and I wanted him to think I was sure guess weighing them. He finally came to me with his estimate, and he was sure giving me a test. I had him show me each animal and explain to me why he thought it weighed so much. He did, and I told him, I would sign his sheet like he had it, but I told him in his kind of Spanish, don't try to pull that on me anymore, or we will go home and I will do what I said yesterday. "I will shut her down."

He assumed that I was telling him that he over weighed them and that was what I wanted him to think. I didn't know how close to right he was. I had never seen a cow on a scale in my life. We did the next bunch and I had him show me again. That time I told him I liked that better but there was one of them I just couldn't go along with him on. I picked a large bull oxen out and told him he was for sure twenty kilos too much on him. Another herd bought and as we bought them they were driven down into the fosa and shot. As the day went along things got better, and I had that little man doing a fine job. Each time I would brag on him some more and then I would pick out another large animal and tell him that we should give the owner thirty more kilos on that big bull. He went over to the man and told him what I said. The day was perfect and that evening we went back to our dining room for some more of that good chocolate. Verge told me that was the smoothest he had ever seen a fosa handled. I told him, "Yes for starters it was OK, but now I hope I can keep it going as smoothly, because the people expect the appraisers to fight. If they don't then they think the Mexican is playing footsie with the Gringo." We were still talking about it when we heard a commotion in the patio.

There was a large crowd and they had my little compadre in front of them and looking for a place to hang him up to dry. They were serious. I jumped upon the stump once more. I got what I wanted but I hadn't planned on having to protect him. They were saying he was no good because we didn't fight at the fosa. I said, "If that is what you want we can do that right here. He has a .45 on his hip. If one of you will loan me a machete we will put on a fight for you, and I think I will lose." I got some good laughs from the crowd. While I had their attention, I explained to them how I wanted to run the operation. "I didn't come here to be unfair with you, so this man does not have to ride me. He knows cattle. He is an expert. I have told him to buy your cattle at a good judgement fair price and I would sign the ticket." I reminded them that I had even let him buy the dead ones, if they had just died. After that I had a town full of friends and especially my appraiser. He just got better and better and he was tough. When they brought him into the patio, it was him checking me out as much as the people. He had to be sure where he stood, just how much authority he really had. I gave him a bunch, he thought.

The area I was working was a large area and there had been so much trouble there that it was behind schedule. The disease was getting ahead of the killing. My operation went so smoothly that the office people couldn't get my fosas dug fast enough, so I asked permission to take that over also. They gladly gave it to me. We worked in the field on weekdays then back to Guadalajara for the weekends. After the first week I was given an army truck of some kind, then about the third week, a fellow drove to my field headquarters and told me he had come after my vehicle. Some quick awful thoughts went into my head that I will never let out. I thought they were going to leave me without a vehicle again. It was evening and we were having our chocolate break. I went out to the street with him to give him my truck and there was a brand new Dodge Power Wagon. He said, "I have orders to trade with you." Now for sure my cotton was really growing good. Some of it was getting pretty tall, and that was when I sure had to be careful. I was just a kid out there among those old timers. They had been buying and selling cattle for many years. There was a story happened some years back that was a good lesson to me, and which I used in this case and have used it through the years. Two little words. (SPETY SPETY) Comes from Esperar. It means don't get in too big of a hurry.

I got to know those folks pretty well and I knew which ones were the leaders. I asked one of them if he would like to have a contract to dig fosas and guide me in the mountains, because by then I was starting to get pretty well caught up in the flat dry lake area. He rode one of the prettiest horses I had seen around there. When I commented on the horse he told me the story. When they had horse shows in San Antonio, Texas, someone would go there and steal a stud and run him across the Rio Grande and into Mexico and into the mountains of Jalisco. His horse was from one of those studs. He put a crew together with picks and shovels and they looked like a bunch of gophers. I had him dig some of the fosas cien metros long and leave a petition in the middle. We could put cattle in from each end. The other appraisers knew I was paying too much for my cattle or I couldn't be doing such a fast job. When the first sheets came in from the Mexico City office, I was one of the lowest buyers. Like I said, I had to watch my cotton, or someone would start chopping on it.

I had also taught my man--Friday how to buy large herds like, say, one to two hundred head. We would walk around in the herd together and look at the whole herd and see which size group fitted the most of them. We would find and agree on maybe thirty head of larger types, then the rest would be pretty much the same size. We would come up with a weight for the herd then a weight for the thirty head, then count the whole herd as they went into the fosa, sign the ticket and go on to the next herd. Some of the appraisers were taking two days to buy a herd like that.

We had finished up early one Friday and were on our way to Guadalajara when we came across one of those very deals. We stopped to chat and found the two appraisers almost ready to have a fist fight. They had been going at it all day. I asked him if he would like for me and my man to try to buy them and he was sure glad for me to take over. There was about three hundred head. We started walking among them, and trying to come up with how many in the various sizes. I always worked from the big ones down, for the count, then from the small ones up, for the weight. In about forty--five minutes we agreed on the cuts and the weights for each cut, ran the cash total up, called the owner over, and gave him our appraisal total. He looked off into space for about two minutes and turned his head to us (he was horseback so was looking down on us) and said, "Muy bien, a la fosa." We went on to town and let them kill their cattle. One of the problems they were having with the owner was, they would give him the numbers for different grades, but they never did give him a total and he couldn't do numbers well enough to tell what they were doing. I bought that herd for a lot less than they had been offering all day and the owner wouldn't take it. They had never totaled their numbers for him. I had learned real quickly to give a man the total and not the little numbers in between. Most of those people signed for their money with a thumb print.

Aftosa

My first trip as appraiser, the paymaster took $250,000.00 pesos. After that he would go by the bank as we were leaving for the field on Monday morning and pick up $500,000.00 pesos. Some weeks I would have to send him back to town to get another $500,000.00. I had built up a good business. We were working a large bunch of cattle one day and things were going fine. My friend, the general, was there to watch me in operation. During the day a fellow came up with the biggest ox I had seen at any of the fosas. Big Red. He was fat and just a monster. We estimated his size and could have been low as he was so big and fat. He was clean, with no sign of sickness. After I had him all bought and paid for I asked the general if it was OK for me to give him to the people to butcher. He was very pleased as I knew he would be. I asked him if he would give him to the people and then shoot old Big Red for them. He told the people, but he made me the good guy instead of taking the credit for himself. He walked up to the old bull and with his trusty .45 he fired into the curl right between the eyes. Front and center. The ox just stood there. He was a work animal and was taught to behave himself. The general fired another shot and that time a little blood trickled out the hole and the ox blinked his eyes a time or two. Three shots in the curl and he was still standing at attention. The general walked around to the side of him and put the next shot in his ear. Now that made that old bull mad and he decided to leave there. There were two ropes on him and lots of holders but it wasn't enough. The bull was getting away. The general borrowed a rifle from one of the soldiers and that bullet in the curl put him down. Machetes were at the ready and he was still falling when they were cutting chunks off him and putting the meat in the morrals they all carried. I went on working and after a while I looked to see how the butchering was coming along. It was over and all that was left to show there was ever a bull there was a small stack of grass. His last meal. To do what I had just done was a no--no and I knew it. I also knew the word would get to the office before I did, and that was the reason I worked so close to General Delgado. After that little boy was shot that day I knew the general would stay by me, as long as I was doing a good job, and helping him to help the people. I had those people eating out of my hand that the office folks thought were hard to handle. They sure didn't want to mess up what I had going. I was reminded that I wasn't suppose to do that, but if the general wanted me to do it again, to be sure it was a clean and well animal.

That whole area had many old Indian Montezumas and many of them had never been dug in. When I contracted the fosas to be dug by hand, those fellows looked for the soft places to dig, and that was the old Indian ruins. They dug up complete skeletons and lots of pottery. Mostly they broke it up in their digging. They had no appreciation for what they were destroying.

We were working a fosa out in the middle of the old dry lake bottom. Verge and I had explored the whole area and knew the good and bad spots for driving a vehicle, and also that there was a wet area there in the lake. No water, just mud and no bottom to it. The road back to town went around the mud. The sanitary man was from New York. How he ever got a job in Mexico, I never figured out. Anyhow, there he was, not dumb, just no savvy about some of us country boys' ways. It was his first trip with verge and me. We got through early that day and Verge and I challenged each other and that old boy to a race back to town. We each had our own vehicles. We wanted him to get ahead of us so he could beat us. We figured he would take a shortcut straight through the dry lake, and if he did... well, we grinned in anticipation of what was going to happen to him. One more lesson for our New York buddy. We lined up side--by--side and revved our motors and Verge gave the go signal. Sure enough, Verge and I were left in the dust and sure enough he went straight towards town. We went around the road and on into town. We enjoyed some chocolate and he still didn't come in. We went out to find him, pretty sure where he would be. He was there alright. He was going so fast when he hit the mud that he just floated on top of it and I mean he was in trouble. My Power Wagon didn't have a winch but the other two did. We would have to pull him out backwards. We tied the two winch--cables together, his and Verge's, but when we ran the winch it pulled Verge's truck in, rather than pulling the other one out. We got some rope and tied my truck to the back of Verge's and we finally got the old boy out of the mud. He knew he had been had and was good natured about it. We hadn't planned on him going so far into the mud however, so the joke was on us too. It was one of those types of mud places that looked the same as the dry ground, almost.

Aftosa

We soon discovered that the dry lake was great rabbit hunting at night. The white--side jackrabbits would come out of the brush that was on the edge of the lake and at night they would run and play. There was no vegetation, just smooth white alkali for miles. Those rabbits would run in pairs and there were lots of them. Verge and I were each issued a .22 rifle and ammunition by the case. The rifles were semi--automatic. We would lay the windshield down and run those rabbits in the car lights. Great sport. I have read since then that those rabbits are an endangered species. We sure endangered a lot of them at that time.

I had the valley cattle all killed off and was ready to go up in the mountains and get the ones that were not brought down. The mountains are high, steep, and very thickly timbered. Travel was only by trail and horseback with a guide. The captain gave us horses and saddles. That was my first time to get sore from riding a soldier type saddle. No bueno. The horses were big and stout and fat. We got an early start and rode for about three hours to the fosa we would work that day. We sure had lots of cattle and it was almost dark when we got through. There was about twenty of us to come back off the mountain. The trail up there was wide and laned with a rock fence, but we took a short cut coming down and some of it was very steep. The horses which were shod would sit down and slide down on their hind feet. Some of the slides were forty or fifty feet down. I had the New Yorker with me. He told me that was his first horseback ride. He was getting sores in some unhandy places.

The return trail was strictly single file, and it was very dark because there was no moon. The timber, I think, would have blanked it out anyhow. I got behind my guide, put the New Yorker behind me, and Verge behind him. The other men had to keep up or they would be in those mountains all night. One man that didn't keep close to the man in front of him might take the wrong trail at a fork. He would lose himself and everyone behind him, and that sure happened that night. That was the reason I got next to my guide, then NY, then Verge. I had no intention of getting lost in those mountains, especially at night. We were riding under limbs and I was holding them for New York so he could catch them and hold them for Verge coming behind him. There came a fat limb and I held it as long as I could but I could see he was too far back to catch it properly. It hit him and almost knocked him off his horse. I told him he was too far back. He said, "Damn, if I get any closer you'll kill me." It was too dark for him to see the limbs. He stayed closer and got along fine. I would call back to him when I had a good one for him and he would get ready for it. Then we came to the first slide. I wasn't ready for such a steep thing. The guide had told me about the steep trail but I supposed the horses would take little steps going down. When I saw the sparks coming from the hooves of my guide's horse, I knew he was not taking steps. The horses had shoes on. I knew to turn my horse loose and let him have his head. I called back to my buddy to not pull on the bridle or you will dump him. Hold onto the saddlehorn and let him go. First I had run him into the mud, then I had hit him with a limb. There was no way he would trust me and turn the reins loose. Can you imagine trying to teach a New Yorker, in the mountains, on a dark night, in the middle of a forest, on a narrow trail, how to handle his mount on a slide? I sure thought I had lost him. The more his horse tried to get his balance the more he pulled on the reins. For some reason they hit the bottom with the horse still on his feet, and NY scared to death. I told him there will be some more slides and when he saw sparks from my horse and heard him sliding, to slack his reins and get hold of the saddlehorn and his horse would take care of him. He said he would sure be glad to get back to the subways. We came off in about one hour, compared to three to go up.

The next day we had another fosa in the mountains but a little different area. An army man came out from Mexico City for that one. We would be at his home town and he wanted to see that everything was done right. He had planned a big barbecue for when we got through in the evening. He had told me what he was going to do, so I had time to plan my getaway. He sent some soldiers to the mountains to kill a tigre. They were to take it to his ranchito and make barbecue for us. The tigre is a mountain lion. We would have a fiesta. The soldiers I used were a captain and two or three men. I dealt direct with the captain. The Mexico City man had a high military rank, I don't remember what it was. Everything went fine and we got through early in the afternoon. We all headed for the ranchito. The old boy was telling me about the tigre they had killed and how sabroso (delicious) it was going to be. As we approached the ranchito we had to cross a small river with running water.

I had told Verge and NY to stay close to me and I would be watching for a chance to leave out for down the mountain. I figured we could get off the mountain before dark. I knew all the others were wanting to eat that tigre. As we came to the water, everyone else rode on to the buildings and dismounted and tied their horses. I told Verge and NY to let their horses drink all they wanted while those folks were going inside. They did and I came up out of the river and headed down the mountain, not even thinking that I might get lost. One thing for sure, I wasn't hungry for tiger barbecue. We were almost out of site of the ranchito, when I looked back and there came a soldier after us. We were on top of the mountain where it was flat and there was lots of timber. It was about a mile from the ranchito to where we would start down off the mountain. We pulled up and waited for him to catch us. I told Verge and NY we just as well get ready to eat that tigre. I was sure he had orders to bring us back. He said, "I have orders" (and that was when I turned my horse around) "to go with you off the mountain so you don't get lost." I was glad he came along because there again we took a shortcut and went down some more slides, only that time it was light and we could see them. NY was sure, then, that he had seen and done it all.

The next evening the tiger man was having a few drinks at the sidewalk bar in town and as I passed he called me over, and told me to sit down. When I sat down, he pulled his .45 and laid it on the table, facing me. I mean I was looking at that big hole in the barrel. He was well drunk and I was well nervous. He wanted to know why I didn't stay and eat some of the tiger he had done in my honor. He gave me a long lecture about my manners, and every once in a while he would rearrange the .45 a little, and each time that hole looked bigger. He wanted my attention, and for sure he got it. There was lots of quiet all around that sidewalk bar, except for El Hombre Grande telling me off. He finally ordered mas Tequila and told me to go. My feet tried to jump up and run, but my head said, "spety spety." I thanked him and shook hands and sort of melted into the crowd. I don't know what his Army rank was but it was over my captain.

I received a letter from Bill Holmes, who was still in San Luis Potosi. He told me that Ray Bell was looking for a Master Mechanic for his ranch in Durango and that he had recommended me to him. The aftosa was temporary and we were already starting to wind it down. My area was almost cleaned up. He told me how to call Mundito Bell at the Bell Ranch and set up an appointment if I was interested. Mart had about all the Guadalajara climate she could stand and we needed to get back out into the desert type country. Bell paid my expenses and I flew to Torreon. He sent a car for me and I spent a couple of days at the ranch. I was impressed and I took the job. I needed thirty days to get loose from the aftosa, go back to Dublan for a little vacation, then go to Atotonilco, Durango.

Mart and the boys, Floyde and Sid, went by bus to San Luis Potosi. I went by car to Mexico City to get checked out. I would fly to San Luis from Mexico City and they would get on my plane there and we would fly home to Dublan together. We would be on the plane that went from Mexico City to Chihuahua, Casas Grandes, Cananea, then to Nogales, a DC 3. I got to San Luis and no family. I didn't know what had happened, that she didn't get on my plane. When I arrived in Chihuahua, we had a layover because of bad weather in Nogales. I was sent to a hotel in town and then I would continue the next morning to Casas Grandes. I was very concerned about Mart and the kids because I had no idea what had happened or where they were and I had no way to find out. When I got to the hotel and started to register I noticed that Mart was registered there already. She had bought a ticket in San Luis Potosi on the plane just ahead of mine and also had a layover. We had a paid--for night in Chihuahua. I had a little problem with the hotel folks. They weren't going to let us stay in the same room. I don't know how they thought they could keep us apart. The next morning we got on the same plane and had a nice ride on home. Again our folks were glad to see us and we sure enjoyed our vacation with them.

18

Bell Ranch

We were home again in Dublan from the aftosa program. We always called Dublan home and still do. I was busy getting things together for our move to the Bell Ranch at Yerbanis, Durango. The name of the ranch is Atotonilco. When we moved to El Paso I sold my pickup to Mennell, Mart's brother. Before we went to El Paso, I bought a four-wheel trailer from Mennell and put high sides on it to haul my horse in, or two horses if need be. It didn't have springs and my horse hated it. It would be fine, however, to haul our things to Durango but I didn't have a car. Mr. Hardy had a Plymouth four door that he had nothing but trouble with. He sold it to me for $300.00 pesos. I drove it around Dublan a few days while we were getting ready to go and I was having no problems with it. What it would do was stop for no reason at all and then it would be hard to start. After it rested for a while it would start. Sometimes a long rest and other times a short rest. No one had been able to find the trouble. It was running so well that Dad wanted to go with me to Durango, then buy it from me and take it back home with him. His car was worn out. His car was a Dodge he had bought from me when I went into the Navy, a 1936 one--seater coupe. The Plymouth was a 1937. My car would be furnished at the Bell Ranch. In fact I would have eight of them to look after. Four cars, three pickups and a 1 1/2 ton truck, all 1941 Fords. I repeat, the trailer had no springs. The sides were made of 1x4 lumber with about eight inch spaces and they were about five feet high. We loaded all our possessions into the trailer. We would have been money ahead if we had built a fire and put everything we had in it. That no--spring trailer destroyed it anyhow.

Mart's Singer sewing machine went in first in a choice spot, covered over with a blanket for protection then I turned my saddle upside down on top of it. Her prize machine and my prize saddle. My saddlehorn had a screw in the top, and being upside down that screw jumped up and down all the way to Durango. It wore a hole in the blankets covering the Singer, then proceeded to wear a hole in the top of the machine. The machine is still that way, we never tried to repair it. I have always complained that her machine sure messed up my saddlehorn.

We were loaded and ready to leave bright and early for Atotonilco, Durango, and that we did. It was slow travel but we would put some miles behind us. We had plans for a nice motel in Chihuahua City for that night. We actually made the second night in Jimenez, Chihuahua.

After leaving Dublan, the first test was the Chocolate Pass. There was a large canyon to cross and the Plymouth would not pull the trailer out of it. We were about halfway up the bank when it stopped. Not dead, just not enough power. I was new at trailer towing and I could not back that four wheel trailer down the bank to start over. I took along a bunch of rope just in case I should need it. We were not out of sight of Dad's ranch when I needed it the first time. I still have that rope habit. I always have some rope in my truck. I put a few rocks behind the trailer wheels, unhooked it with the rope tied to the tongue and Dad and I let it down to the bottom of the canyon. There was a road that went around the steep place, so we hooked up again and made it up that time.

As we traveled I was hearing noises already that I didn't like. I jacked up the rear wheels one at a time and decided I had a bad bearing in the left one. We unhooked again. We carried plenty of food and water. There was no shade there. Dad, Mart, Floyde, and Sid got under the trailer for shade. I went back to Dublan, about six miles. I went to the Fomentadora auto shop and replaced the bearing. I had a few tools so I did the work myself. Back on the road and the noise was gone. I found my passengers glad to see me. Of course they could see me coming when I left Dublan, almost. They could see dust moving on the road and headed their way. The roads were dirt and not even graded. Anything that moved made dust, especially cars.

There were many more washes to cross but I learned to get a run at them and was able to make it out the other side. The road from Dublan to the Chihuahua highway was just ruts to follow. The El Paso--Chihuahua highway was a gravel dump or road bed and worse than the ruts because it was full of holes. We traveled off the dump most of the time! Down in the ditch that was dug alongside the road bed. The ditch was where they got the material for the dump. From Dublan to Galeana, then to San Buenaventura and from there to El Carmen. I had never been that way but before but was told the road was better, and I needed all the better I could find. I had always gone from Galeana straight through the valleys to El Carmen. A shortcut, but bad.

I was not told about the mountain range I had to cross after leaving San Buenaventura. It was a gradual climb from San Buenaventura to the top. I was sure happy the way things were going when all of a sudden I topped out in the pass and all I could see was blue sky. The ground had dropped out from under me for at least two thousand feet. I hit the brakes and went for low gears, and got them all at about the same time. It wasn't enough. I knew that my brakes would go out if I used them very much so I used them as sparingly as I could to keep my speed down so that I could make the curves. That was when I wished for sure we had set fire to all our things including the trailer. It looked like that trailer was going to kill us all. I told Mart to be ready to throw the kids out and jump out herself if I saw it was getting away from me. I had plans to bank it and hope it didn't roll over the edge. It was a long drive to the bottom and we were all sure nervous. I was remembering the truck runaway on the east side of the Organ Pass at Las Cruces in 1938. I didn't like it then and I was not going to like this one if it got away from me. I think I was the only one who really knew the real danger we were in. At the bottom of the mountain was a long straight away of about five miles and it sure felt good. Then about ten miles to El Carmen. Remember, we were not on paved roads and that mountain road was almost wide enough for a car to fit on it. There we were with a trailer to try and make those sharp curves.

We arrived at El Carmen and bought a cold soda pop at a roadside stand. Sure was good. El Carmen is one of the old Terrazas Haciendas. Probably the largest. Someplace after El Carmen, and in some very thick mesquites, we crossed a very small wash, and that was where the Plymouth took charge. It died and intended to stay dead. It was just a little after sundown. That was where we spent the first night, not in the hotel in Chihuahua City, but Hotel Monte. I had tried to start the motor several times. Sometime towards morning I thought I heard the motor running. I asked Mart, Floyde, Sid, and Dad if they could hear it and they also thought they could. We had spent the night trying to keep a little fire warm that I had made. I told them all to get in the car and while we thought we could hear the motor running I would go through the gears to see what would happen. It moved, and we were gone again. How many times I had tried the starter and nothing, then for some reason it came to life. I hadn't done anything to it but talk to it and I went out in the mesquites to do that.

We arrived in Chihuahua City but it was too early to quit so we got a good meal and went on to Jimenez. We stayed at a motel with a patio to put our car and trailer in for security. When I drove through the gate, it was too low or my load was too high, and the two got together. Knocked the top beam off the gate and about tore up my trailer.

We had a good night's rest and cleaned up and hit the road the next morning. That day we hoped to make Gomez Palacio, near Torreon. We did, but on the way we hit some very fine dust. That area is old dry lake bottom. When we finally got out of the flour type dust, we stopped to look things over, if we could see our load at all. We couldn't see our load. It was gone. We had suitcases on top of the load, kids clothes, our clothes, cameras and film, movies we had taken of the aftosa and our folks and the ranch, things we could not replace. All our pictures and typewriter. It seemed like all the important things were gone. We unhooked the trailer. Dad and I went back as far as we thought wise and found nothing. The road just was a bunch of trails running in the same general direction, and we couldn't even tell which one we had been on. We gave up and turned back. I didn't want to leave Mart and the kids for long, anyhow. We made it to Gomez Palacio and stayed in a nice motel, again with a corral for our car and trailer.

The Nazas River runs between Gomez Palacio and Torreon. There is a bridge there, but to go that route through Torreon was some what further than if we went straight to Atotonilco. But on that road there was no bridge over the river. We still had to cross the river but at a different crossing. The bridge was under construction. In fact, the highway was under construction from Durango City to Chihuahua city or maybe the other way around I just don't remember. Up the river is the El Palmita dam. Water was turned down the river at certain times for irrigation. That was the day it was to be turned into the river. If we hurried, we could get across the river before the water got to the crossing. We hurried and there was the river and some water, but not the flood they would turn down. I could see the car tracks going into the water on our side and I could see them coming out on the other side. I looked up the river and saw no flood coming, so into the water I drove.

About halfway across the river, the old Plymouth just refused to pull the trailer any further. The motor didn't die, but the old Plymouth just sat there in the river and refused to pull the tailer out of the water. Not only did it act like a burro, but it was the same color and at that point I thought it looked like a burro. I jumped out in the water, got my kids, along with their dog, Shorty, and carried them on across to the bank. I told Mart to get under the wheel. I would unhook the trailer and Dad and I would push and maybe we could get the car onto the bank. The motor never did quit us, or we would have lost it. The gravel and sand would have had the wheels set tight in a very short time. With the car on the bank, out came my long rope. I went into the river and tied onto the trailer tongue, expecting the flood to arrive at anytime. We were told what time it would not be safe to cross, and we had used it up. We were already borrowing time. I tied the rope to the car, which was about two hundred feet from the trailer. Mart was driving, Dad pushing, and I was out in the water trying to keep the trailer tongue pointed in the right direction. It insisted on going downstream because of water pressure on the tongue. We finally got it onto dry ground. We were still hooking it back onto the car when the head of water went by.

We went on down the road a few miles and it was time for a rest and lunch. We thought about how lucky we were. The kids ran and played with their dog, Shorty. After a good lunch and a little rest we put things and kids in the car and down the road we went. We had gone a few miles when the kids realized they had left their little dog where we had lunch. I unhooked the trailer and left Mart and Dad with it. The kids and I went back to find Shorty. We looked around where we had lunch. They called for him, but no Shorty. We saw a car coming. He stopped and asked if we were looking for a little dog. He had seen him running down the road back towards the river. We caught him about a mile down the road. He was in high gear. I don't know who was the happiest, Shorty or the kids. The fellows that stopped to tell us about the dog were Joe Jarvis and his brother. They were from one of the Mormon colonies also. They told us they had a ranch in that same area near the Bell Ranch.

With Shorty found and on board, the trailer was hooked up once more, and we were on the last lap to Yerbanis. That was the small town on the railroad where we went through the gate and onto the Bell Ranch, Atotonilco. The ranch was 200,000 acres in size. I have told about what it took to get that far, and we were still in good spirits about the trip. We were looking at the gate we would go through in a few minutes. When we went through that gate we would be in or on the Raymundo Bell Ranch. It was about seven miles on to the Hacienda. The Hacienda was in the center of the ranch. The highway and railroad were parallel to the ranch fence line. I made a ninety--degree turn left off the highway and headed towards the gate. I had to cross the railroad. Remember back when the old Plymouth died after we came down off that mountain. You get one guess and that is all. Right. It died straddle the railroad. When we were coming off that mountain I asked for help in my own way and got it. When we were stuck in the river I asked for help again and got it, and now there I was needing help again, I mean the special kind that makes one think right in tough spots. I got it and have never forgotten. I was thinking like the old boy up the tree with the bear down there. Please help me start this car or stop the next train. The car started and as we were going through the gate into the ranch, a train went by.

About the gate. It was locked at all times. A man lived there with a telephone to headquarters. A few men had a key. After that day I had one. The gate was locked but a fellow lived there just inside the fence. I told him who I was and he called the headquarters to check me out, and since I had told him the truth he let me in. The Bell ranch was an old Spanish Hacienda and in very well kept condition. 200,000 acres of old Spanish--grant land. Dad spent a few days with us. Mundito, Raymond Bell Jr., took Dad on tours of the ranch. Dad enjoyed that.

Dad left early one morning to return home and someplace en route the Plymouth died while driving along and he couldn't get it started. He had used most of the daylight that day. Along came a big truck and offered to pull him to the next town. The sun had already gone over the mountain. Dad had all the rope with him, because I sure didn't need it anymore. He wanted to be sure that he wouldn't run into the rear of that tow truck so he left about fifty feet of space between them. Away they went. It was night by then and Dad's lights were getting dimmer by the minute. The trucker kept going. Dad was getting sleepy and tired and decided he had enough, but he couldn't stop the truck. Then the truck slowed for some reason and Dad was a little slow on the brakes. He ran a front wheel across the tow rope. The truck picked up speed again. Dad put on brakes, flashed lights, and wore the horn out, and finally the battery. That old boy did him the favor of towing him to the first town and stopped to turn him loose. Dad always carried his .38 special. He said he thought seriously of just shooting that truck driver. First, the tires wore out then the wheels wore out, sparks flying, and the driver just kept on trucking. It cost Dad more to get it repaired than the car cost in the first place.

Mr. Bell was a tough man and ran a tight ship. 200,000 acres and only one gate into it, and a security guard at the gate. If you were in, you could only get out with permission, and if you were out you could only get in with permission. Those with standing permission carried a key. There was no liquor allowed... period! At the ranch there was a school, dance hall, hotel, daily mail service, electricity, airfield, jail house, and cemetery. Name it and they had it. We had a very nice home near the hotel.

We were told that a few days before we arrived, the working folks had a dance, and someone had smuggled in some hard liquor. Some of the men got drunk and into a fight. A fellow was killed on the dance floor with a knife. They were still trying to get the blood stains off flour when we were there. Bell's policeman put the killer in the jail, and sent some men to dig him a grave. Then they stood him by it and, with everyone looking on Mr. Bell pulled his .45 and shot him. He fell into the hole and they covered him over that same night. The policy was that if someone wanted to get on a drunk, all he had to do was ask. He could have all the time he wanted to leave the ranch and get it out of his system then come back to work, but you couldn't make the mistake of doing it on the ranch. And you especially couldn't kill someone. If someone only got drunk he was just put off the ranch. Mr. Bell tolerated no people--trouble. He had over fifty people there.

Mr. Bell was well--liked and respected by his men. He actually had his own registered Mexican Army of about twenty--four men. The .30--30 rifles were lined up on the wall of my office. I say my office because that was where my desk was. I saw the army called to duty one time while I was there, and will tell about it later. I went along.

The job of master mechanic was a big test for me. The Bells had a very well organized system. My job was to supervise the departments and see that the system was carried out. I had a very good auto mechanic, a windmill man, a blacksmith, and a carpenter, and each of them had their respective crews. Then there was the cowboy "caporal," who was not under me. Rodolfo Corrales was the secretary and head man, and he was good. Before I would make any decisions I would talk it over with him to be sure I was on the right track. Mr. Bell was gone a lot.

The Bells kept the penthouse or top floor of the Blackstone Hotel in San Antonio and the Del Norte Hotel penthouse in El Paso. Mrs. Bell spent most of her time in El Paso and he spent most of his time in San Antonio. Mundito, the son, ran the ranch. He was a very smart and likeable.

They bought gasoline and salt for the cattle by the train car. Four wagons were busy every day distributing salt over the ranch. They used grain salt instead of blocks and put it in wooden troughs for the cattle.

When we were getting ready to leave Dublan, Mart went to the school and got the material she would need to teach Floyde. She saw that he learned well. She sure made him work. He and Sid loved to go with me when I made my rounds on the ranch which was every day. I had the ranch divided into three parts for making my rounds, and it took me a day to check each part, so I was on the road all the time. In the morning I would go to the various departments and get my men all lined up for the day and started to work. Then I would go back to my house and Mart would give me a good breakfast. She would also fix me a sandwich and I would be gone for the day. We had about twenty--four water places for the cattle and I had to be sure they were OK and that no cattle were thirsty. Mart tried to work Floyde's studies so he could go with me a lot. My car was a like new 1941 Ford coupe. The cars all had twenty--one--inch tires for getting over the ranch roads.

The Bells had two ranches. The other one was southwest of Durango City, about a hundred miles away. Mundito told me that as soon as I felt acquainted with Atotonilco he wanted me to go to the San Juan Ranch and get to know it. It was a little larger and in the high mountains. Atotonilco was also all mountainous, but lower hills. Mundito was installing two--way radios between the two ranches. They had the unit installed at Atotonilco. He sent me to take the radio technician to the San Juan ranch to install the unit there. I have told that all gates and doors were locked and only the men with the right keys could open them. Each department head had a key to open any door that pertained to his work. I carried the same key that Rodolfo carried, which was a master that opened almost everything. So, when we arrived at the San Juan gate I had a key. No watchman there.

There was a small light plant at the San Juan Ranch that they thought was big enough to run a few lights plus the radio. I was along with the radio man to get him to the San Juan Ranch and also to see that he got the mechanical means he needed to run the radio. In those days the antenna was a long wire stretched overhead. He got the radio installed and we could hear Mundito from Atotonilco but he could not hear us. The electric generator ran well and sounded good, so I thought the problem had to be in the radio. The technician kept telling me we needed more power. I didn't know how to get it. The little light plant was inside a room and the exhaust went out through the adobe wall then turned ninety--degrees straight up to the top of the roof to get the noise away. It was one and a half inch heavy pipe and was about twelve feet high.

We fought it for two days and I just had to think of something. That was what I was there for. When I had used up all my ideas I called the foreman over and told him to take the exhaust pipe loose, maybe it was plugged somehow. The little engine just didn't sound like it was winding up. I knew a car could be choked down by plugging the exhaust. The plant was running while he was taking the pipe loose, and the minute it came apart, that little engine went wild. The problem was back pressure from such a long pipe. The tech and Mundito got their signals going, and when everyone was happy the tech taught the cowboy foreman how to talk to Mundito. The radio was installed so the foreman could make a report to Mundito every day. The radio worked real well. If there was a problem at San Juan I could go up there and get it taken care of.

The next morning we were on our way back to Atotonilco. I was driving along pretty fast, like maybe forty--five or fifty MPH, when we blew the left front tire. It was not an oiled road but a good graded road with lots of nice rocks on it. In those days in Mexico, they didn't have nice crushed gravel for the roads they were building. They made the road bed with whatever was close and with whatever size it happened to be. The tech man was in the front seat with me, and Floyde and Sid were in the back. My car was a coupe. That little car wanted to do everything but stay in the road, but I was doing OK, until the tech got hold of the steering wheel with me. I lost control and out in the boonies we went. Sure looked like I was going to lose it but it came to a stop with all four wheels down. The first thing the tech said was, "Sure was a good thing I helped you." He was lucky that I was too busy to knock him loose. He said that in Spanish, and he will never know what I was thinking in the same language.

For some time, Bell had been fighting with the Durango state road people because they wanted to cut a road through his ranch. They wanted to go straight from Torreon to Durango. They had already gone in and cut a right of way through the mesquites on the ranch. Actually, they were not mesquites but pepper trees. He got that stopped. That was before I went there, but the work they had done was very visible. I don't know how many years the fight had been going on. The state was very determined to put the road through the ranch. It would have been a bunch of miles shorter.

Mr. Bell was in San Antonio. Mundito was in El Paso. As I have told, Rodolfo was in charge. We knew that there was a road crew working from Torreon, and coming our way. We heard they had orders to continue straight when they reached the Bell Ranch, so Rodolfo had a scout watching for them. The Bell Ranch was low hilly country, and much of the outside fence was made of rocks stacked without mortar. When the Spaniards fenced their ranches it was before barbed wire. They had lots of cheap labor and lots of rocks. There are many miles of rock fences in Mexico. The road at that time had to go around the outside of the ranch, and it had to make a ninety--degree turn where it met the ranch line.

The scout came in one evening and told Rodolfo that the road crew had torn down the rock fence and was camped inside the ranch. That night Rodolfo called in the cowboys and gave each one a .30--30 rifle and asked if I wanted to go along. I did. I have always wondered why he went at night instead of waiting until the next morning. He put all these armed men in the back of the stake--body truck and we went to the road camp. Those road men were all standing around a large campfire. Their equipment was close by. They were singing and joking as those people do. They didn't seem surprised to see us drive up. Our men had orders to stay in the truck and be quiet, unless they got orders from Rodolfo to do otherwise. Rodolfo and I did not carry guns. We walked up to the fire and shook hands with the men. Handshaking is a must--custom in Mexico. Rodolfo told the road crew, their boss really, that he would like for them to move outside the ranch line and to please repair the fence like they found it, and that he would be back the next day to look it over. They said, "Si, senor," and they did. We stayed and talked to them for a while then went back to the headquarters. They had no argument with twenty--four rifles. The ranch was later willed to the state of Durango for the orphans, so the state came out ahead in the long run. Rodolfo made no threats that night but the message was very clear.

The wind was undependable for the windmills, so we had a pump--jack at each windmill. Sometimes we would pump for a month at a time at one well. A week was common. The pump--jacks were all very old and worn out. In the warehouse were brand new jacks for every well, and Mundito told me that as soon as I could adjust my time he would like me start a program of getting them installed. It took me some time to get them all changed out because I had to do it when I could spare the windmill crew to work on them. The new ones were red one lunger International Harvesters with water hoppers for cooling. When I put those pumps to work they were determined to eat my tacos. I couldn't keep oil in them. They threw it out the seal on the crankshaft next to the flywheel. Not very bad but, there shouldn't be any. I was convinced that they all had bad seals, but it was a pretty big job to change them. I planned to get them all installed then go after the seals as they got too bad to ignore.

Then we installed one that threw the oil out as fast as we could pour it in. I decided to experiment with it. I sure couldn't do it any harm. I drilled a hole in the fill plug, which was nothing more than a pipe plug. At least it would not throw oil all over the engine as was then happening. I found out the engines were not vented and they were building up pressure. The vent holes solved my oil problem. I need to say here that I hadn't been there very long when Mundito left and didn't come back. I knew he was in El Paso. I was told that Mr. Bell had given Mundito and his sister each a large sum of money and told them to go it on their own. That was probably when he willed the ranch to the Orphans of the state of Durango. That was probably one of the ways he could hold such a large ranch until he died without a lot of trouble, and probably the reason he could stop the road from going through. I had no one to turn to with a problem like the oil. Since Mundito was gone, I had to lose sleep over it all by myself. There were two windmills that hadn't pumped water for some time, and a spring that was full of moss and going to waste in a location where it should water lots of cattle. I had the new engines installed and working fine. I discussed the windmills and spring with Rodolfo. He was for giving them a try. The water on the ranch was very deep, over three hundred feet, or it was springs and just ran out on the top of the ground. At the headquarters was a large spring. They had a small lake there for boating.

There was one spring up in the hills that was lower than the storage tank they wanted the water to run into. It didn't make much water but filled a hole we could pump from. The hole was about eight feet square and maybe ten feet deep with about six feet of water. There were some logs thrown across it to set the pump on and it was a mess. We needed to wall it up about four feet, and I wanted to do it with rocks. We had a mason that did very nice rock work. The problem was, and the reason that had never been done before was how to keep the pump in operation while the masonry work was being done. The pump worked on a windmill cylinder, so had to be over the water. There were many cattle watered there, so the pump had to stay in operation. I went back to my mining days for some ideas. I told the windmiller to haul some lumber up there and build a free standing scaffold out in the water to support the pump. He did and braced it well. We made one of the nicest looking water holes on the whole ranch, and it was all my idea. When the rock work was finished we put some timbers across the top to fasten things to and it all worked like a charm. The spring had no pressure. No water ran out of it but it would supply the pump all day.

When I had a pump going at a windmill I would put two men on it. There were times that I had three pumps going at the same time. It was not a windy country. We had three burros. I would send two men with a burro and tell them which pump to go to. They would take chuck along for a few days, and if they ran low one of them would go back to headquarters with the burro for more. The headquarters was in the center of the ranch.

They had lots of trouble with the old engines. I soon found that those pump boys had too many tools, and they could take too many things off the engines. The idea had been to give them the tools so they could make small repairs. I came up with the idea to give them no tools so they could make no repairs, not even change a spark plug. The windmill had to be disconnected and the pump jack connected. I put seals on all the engines so no one could get to a spark plug without cutting the seal. The seals were made from lead with two holes to run the wire through. The wire was twisted and the lead was crimped with a special tool I made. I kept the special tool with me. That way I could do a repair job and reseal the part. I told those guys that the sky would fall on them if they should mess with the seal. I put wing nuts on the sucker rods and made a special tool to remove them with, and that was all they could do with it. The same tool could remove the oil filler plug so they could add oil and that was it. So all those pumper boys could do was put in oil, gasoline and water for the hopper, and sleep. It cured my pump breakdowns. You wouldn't believe what those sandal--foots could take apart with a pair of pliers and a monkey wrench. I have called them sandal--foots because that is what they were. They are the mozo or servant class. Uneducated but very good people and dependable workers. They are very dedicated to their Patron. They are at the very bottom of the working class in Mexico. They make sandals mostly from worn out tires. They cut a patch to fit the foot and tie it on with strings around the ankle and between the toes. The miners in San Luis Potosi were mostly of those people.

I have told that gasoline was bought by the train tank car. They had an underground storage tank with a service station type pump but the tank developed a leak. When I went there they were using drums to store fuel in. The leaker tank had been uncovered but was still in the hole. They found the leak. The windmill man had used a welder some so they were going to have him get down in the hole and weld the leak. Gas weld. They didn't have an arc welder. Now that old boy was afraid to do that. One evening when he thought no one was looking, he slipped up on that tank, lit a match and dropped it down the fill neck. When I went there those boys would hardly get close enough to look into the hole much less think of repairing the tank. It had a big crack in one end where the small leak was before. Mundito asked if I could weld it. I told the men to take it out of the hole so we could fill it with water, then roll the hole to the top and I would weld it. I surprised them again when I showed them how to wrap a rope around the tank and roll it up on the bank. There were so many things like that on the ranch that needed doing. I got them pretty well caught up while I was there.

The windmill crew used the stake--bed truck. I talked to the crew boss and we decided on which non--producing wells to try first. There were two wells that had not pumped water for some time. I had the logs of those wells and I studied them and decided to give it a try. They kept very good records of everything. We pulled everything out of the first well and there seemed to be some water at the very bottom. We used a slush bucket and we bailed sediment for two days. It was loose stuff that had filled in over the years, and sure enough we got into water. Enough to keep the storage tank full and water many cattle. We were about a week on the first one and were ready to tackle the other one. It wasn't as easy and was a deeper well. However, it came in well. After that success my crew thought I was a pretty good patron, and they worked for me real good, and sure thought I knew about windmills. I had been around them all my life and helped work on also.

We had been working on one of the wells all day and were going home tired. Floyde and Sid liked to ride up in the truck with the men. I was in the cab with the driver. On that ranch there were no cattle guards, but many gates. It was fenced off into pastures to control the arrangement of the cattle. There were many rabbits. The guys in the truck would fill their pockets with rocks and try to hit a rabbit as we traveled along. Floyde and Sid included. We had stopped to go through the gate and there sat a cottontail in the shade. Floyde threw a rock and killed it dead. There was so much excitement in the truck I thought something had gone wrong. They all wanted to help Floyde get down there to get his rabbit. When we got home he ran to his mother and told her how he had killed it with a rock and would she peel it and cook it. She did. There were lots of deer and lots and lots of rabbits and lots of rattlesnakes. I had my .22 pistol with me. Many evenings I would take Mart and the kids for a drive and we would shoot rabbits out the car window. Mart got pretty good with the pistol, but I had never noticed how she was holding it to shoot. It was automatic and the carriage flies back to eject the empty and reload for the next shot. She shot a rabbit, but held the pistol too close to her glasses. It broke one lens and glass got in her eye. I have told how on the trip down there we lost so many of our clothes and things. Mart went to El Paso to do some shopping and get us back in shape. She had returned by way of Dublan to see the folks, her's and mine, and then flew to Torreon. I had just picked her up in Torreon the day before and we were sort of out enjoying each other's company when she was hit in the eye. I knew Mrs. Bell was catching the train that day at Yerbanis just outside the ranch. She was going to Torreon and then flying to El Paso. I rushed Mart to the train and she went along with Mrs. Bell to El Paso. Mrs. Bell took her to her penthouse at the Del Norte Hotel. Mart stayed at the McCoy Hotel. She got the glass out of her eye and flew back home the next day. That time I met her in Torreon, to bring her on home. I don't think she ever shot the pistol again.

Another thing we killed lots of was rattlesnakes and scorpions. I think the scorpion is Durango's state bug. The rattlers were so many that the Bells paid a bounty on them. The men were paid each Saturday and they would bring in their rattles that they had accumulated that week for their bounty at the same time. They would have hands full.

There was also a gardener and so we had lots of fresh vegetables. They also butchered a beef each week and sold it in the store at a very low price. We always got choice cuts and we got pretty well spoiled for good meat. We could buy staples at the store, and could order anything we wanted through the warehouse. I was getting $300.00 US per month, but since everything was furnished I had it sent to my bank in El Paso. After one year I was to get a raise to $350.00. When I had been there a year, I went to Mr. Bell's office to talk to him about it and he fired me right there and then. I knew there was trouble in the family but I didn't know I was part of it. He said, "You were hired by Mundito and he isn't here anymore. I don't want anything or person that reminds me of him and you work just like he did."

I said, "Yes sir, he told me how he wanted things done and I have sure tried to do it and I thought I was pleasing you also." He gave me a very good letter of recommendation to the King Ranch in Texas. I still have the letter but I never did look into it. He told me he was going to San Antonio and that I could stay on the job for another thirty days. I gave about twenty of them back to him. He sent the money he still owed me and in the letter he asked why I had left so soon. He had decided to keep me on. We were saving money but it wasn't a good life for Mart and the kids. We had saved enough money that we could try to make it in Dublan again.

I had some friends, named Jarvis, who owned a ranch close to Bell's. I knew that he went to Dublan once in a while. I phoned him and he was getting ready to go right then to Casas Grandes. I asked him if he would please swing by Atotonilco and pull my trailer with him. He was driving an army commando type truck. He told me what day to be ready and for sure we had all our things on that no--spring trailer once more.

Mart wouldn't let me put my saddle on top of her machine that time. Mart and I rode in the cab with Joe, and Floyde and Sid and their dog, Shorty rode in the truck with a canvas for shade. Mart reminds me that she also rode in back with the kids most of the way. I have never seen Joe Jarvis since but wherever he is, he is one of my very memorable good friends. He was the same fellow who helped us find Shorty when we were on our way to Atotonilco. We stopped for a couple of hours in Durango City and then we were in the right gear for home to Dublan once more. We traveled all day and the next night and arrived in Dublan the next evening. Sure enough tired and dirty but happy, as young folks should be. We had saved our money so we were in good shape financially.

At the border between Durango and Chihuahua was a check station. The fellows looked us over and were just ready to tell us to go on when Shorty decided he better bite one of them. The kids were under the canvas and had the dog under there also but he smelled something that made him mad and he came out from under that canvas with his teeth sticking out. They looked at Shorty and told us we would have to leave the perrito. I tried to talk to them but they wanted the little dog. The kids started getting off the truck. They would just stay with the dog. I think the guys thought they would get only the little dog but when they found out they would have to take the kids also, that was more than they had bargained for. They let us keep the dog. We drove straight through and arrived home the next night.

While we were at the Bell Ranch, Ernestine Hatch went to see us. She arrived on some santo day. The ranch workers had bought a lot of fireworks and she thought they were sure glad to see her. I had told her that we were going to celebrate her arrival. They really put on a show. She was there about a week and we enjoyed her. She has been our very dear friend for all our years.

19

Dublan Fourth Time

We were in Dublan for the fourth time and our ambition was to try to get into some kind of business besides our few cattle, so we could live there and make it our home. We liked it there. We had some survival money in the bank. Mart got a job teaching school and her dad loaned me $5000.00 (pesos) to buy an automotive repair shop in the Station (Nuevo Casas Grandes) from Jesus Acosta. I got a five year lease on the building and bought all his tools for the $5000.00 (pesos). Harve loaned me the money for one year at 12% interest. I asked him what kind of papers he wanted me to sign, or what he wanted for collateral. He said, "Your word and a handshake." He got it. He wrote me a check right there. I handed it to Jesus, and I went to work. I hired three mechanics and a tool man. I made a room for my office and a tool room. I put numbers on washers and gave each man six, with his number. As he checked out a tool his washer was hung in its place, so I knew where my tools were at all times. It worked well. I learned the washer number system in Morenci. The boys had their own hand tools, but that was the way I handled the special tools. The shop had a large yard in back with a high adobe wall. The front was on the sidewalk. To get a car into the shop you went through the alley in back and then a large wooden gate into the yard. I had lots of business. The shop held two cars inside, then I put the large lumber trucks in the yard corral. The big thing in those days was hauling lumber from the sawmills in the mountains. There were lots of bobtail trucks hauling lumber. The lumber was going to the US. Much of my business was stretching the frames of the lumber trucks.

We worked on cars in front of the building faced right up to the sidewalk. I had too much business to put inside. We did the small jobs on the sidewalk. We would have a car jacked up with a mechanic under it and a "travieso" kid would let the jack down and run. We knew the kids and when they would come around again the boys would catch them and dust their pants a little. It was a game they liked to play with us and no one ever got hurt.

We didn't have any nice scooters to get under the cars with. We used cardboard boxes flattened out. When it wore out or got too dirty, we would get a new one. They were hard to come by, so care was taken, and each mechanic had his own. We did engine overhauls, or whatever was needed.

While we were living in Dublan that time, Memmott wanted Dad to finish paying him for the ranch. He and Dad bought the ranch as partners in the first place. Then Joe changed his mind and wanted out. Dad was paying him as he sold cattle but still owed about $12,000.00 (pesos), according to Dad's numbers, but Joe had a different set of figures. He thought Dad owed him $16,000.00. By then I had about as many cattle as Dad did. I was paying Dad pasture for them. I said, "Dad I believe I can pay the ranch off." He told me that if I could pay it off he would make me half owner. I told him my plans. Together we had enough cattle to sell and pay Mr. Memmott.

I went to Casas Grandes and found a buyer. Francisco Anchondo. I told him to come and ride with me over the ranch and give me a price. He did. I put the numbers together and came up with a surplus of money after paying Joe. We rounded up all the cattle and counted the ones that belonged to Tio and Raymon, so I could send them their money.

Memmott got word that we were selling all the cattle and there he came. I mean he was making the dust fly. He jumped out of his car and got hold of Dad and said, "I hear you are selling your cattle, and I want my money right now." Dad tried to explain to him what we were doing and that we were selling in order to pay him. He was so excited he couldn't hear. I finally got his attention and told him that he was now dealing with me and not Dad. I told him to go back to Dublan. At three o'clock I would meet him at Julio Gonzalez's office and pay him in full. He had made such a fuss that I was afraid to trust him by myself with no witness. He was on time and we told Julio what was up. I told Julio why I felt I needed a witness. Dad had recorded payments he had made to him that Memmott didn't record because Dad would just give him money with no receipt, and hope he would put it down in his book. Sure enough, we went round and round there before Julio. I was first prepared to pay him what he wanted, and Dad was also, but when he got so nasty, Dad told me to have at him, and I did. I finally told him that I would not give in because I felt I was right and I was sure he must feel the same way. I said, "Let Julio flip a Peso. Joe, you call it. Julio is our witness."

Joe thought a minute and said, "I never won a toss in my life, but let,s get it over with." He called heads. When he saw those tails, I thought he was going to pass out. Was I glad for Mr. Julio Gonzalez. Mom had told Dad many times that he wasn't getting credit for his payments, but he thought Joe was the kind you could shake hands with. He was, and I think he honestly forgot to give credit. I feel sure he thought he was right. However, Dad had recorded dates and amounts and some of them Joe would remember and admit to, so I stood my ground.

I did lots of welding. At that time the sawmills were going strong in the mountains, and everyone was hauling lumber. Lots of it was being sent to the US. Those haulers liked long trucks but they couldn't buy them. I did lots of frame lengthening, mostly four feet. There were very few welders so I had all I could do. I also had to lengthen the drive shaft, and get it straight enough so it didn't jump around. One thing I learned was to put the U--joints pointing parallel to each other.

I also repaired lots of fuel tanks of cars and trucks. Mostly from gravel and rocks making holes in them. I had one boy that was pretty good at brazing them with the acetylene torch. I let him do it his way. I sure didn't know how to handle them. He would drain all the fuel out, then sit the tank outside a window of the adobe wall and play the torch on it. It would jump and he would bring it back up to the window. When it quit jumping he would take it inside the shop and sit close to it and put the brass weld on it. He was inside the wall, so he was safe. One day he thought he had made a fuel tank gentle and took it inside to weld its holes. We used brass because even though solder was safer it would not hold. The rafters, or beams in my shop were 2x12 that spanned the shop. He was sitting with the tank between his legs, as he had done many times, and was welding the first hole. The filler neck was turned down. We heard a swish and a bang. That tank took off like a rocket. I had learned something about rockets when I was at Fort Bliss. It went away from him at about a 30--degree angle up. Hit a rafter and broke it. He sat there so scared he couldn't turn his torch off. After that we decided to not only gentle those tanks outside the window but to weld them there also. We found out they are very untrustworthy.

I bought a Model A Roadster which had a rumble seat. I put my gas welding bottles in the rumble seat and went around town where ever there was work. I always thought those were the neatest seats that were ever put on a car. When Casas Grandes put in the first city water lines, they bought used pipe and it had lots of holes in it. It was four inch pipe. They would get the ditch dug and the pipe laid out with the holes marked then I would take my little A car to the site and weld them. I was the only one who did that. Maybe because it was summer and sure hot. The money looked good to me. One thing I had done was saved enough money that I could buy the tools I needed for the job.

A lumber yard burned there in Casas grandes. What a fire. They had three train cars loaded to ship to the US. They melted into various shapes. A fellow bought them for the iron but couldn't move them without cutting them into smaller pieces. I bid to do the cutting and got the contract. I had some good experience with a torch in Morenci. That was a good time to find out if I could put it to work. I bought a heavy cutting--torch and me and my little A car with the rumble seat full of cutting equipment, got right in the middle of the burned and twisted rail cars. They were all metal cars, so just think how hot it was up on the side of them in the hot summer with a hot cutting torch. I was about two weeks cutting them into pieces that could be moved. I made good money.

About a month later, Mart and I were home, when we noticed a light in the sky towards the Station. It had to be a fire. We jumped in our little A Roadster and went up there. Would you believe what it was? That same lumberyard was burning again. That time there were four cars of lumber. The same fellow bought them and came to me with the same deal but wanted me to cut my bid. I told him no way. He said he had a fellow that would do it cheaper and left. I knew the fellow had to be a good burner, or he would blow out more gas than he could afford. It took the fellow three days to learn that he was not winning. He didn't know how to cut sheet metal for the amount of gas he was using. I went to the yard and watched him cutting and I knew he couldn't last long.

Sure enough, the buyer came back to me and he was very friendly. He would let me have the job and pay me the same. I told him, "No, I can't do that. I made very little profit on the other job, and I really don't want it anyhow."

My bluff worked because then he was begging me to do it for him. I knew he only had so many days to get it moved. I doubled my price. He reminded me of a chicken who had just had its head removed. He got his breath and told me to go ahead with the job. Then I told him, "Payment in advance, todo." He went into his chicken act again, but he paid me and I went to work. That time things went very well because I had the equipment already bought, and knew just where to cut for best results. I cut up the four cars quicker than the three before. The main problem the other fellow had was cutting the axles. About eight inch solid steel.

I have told that when I was growing up on the Corralitos, we had a neighbor to the west, named Jeffery. Otis Jeffery still had that ranch and was a big operator. He would buy a car or a truck and use it until it quit, then put it in his junk pile and buy another. During rainy season, he would get stuck in the mud some where on his ranch. He would just leave the vehicle there and go get another one. All his cars and trucks were used up and he never traded one in. I bought his iron pile. I sold it to Jesus Acosta, the fellow I was leasing my shop from. There were pump--jacks and windmills of all kinds from years of collection. In the junk was two cars, a 1942 Plymouth, and a 1941 Olds. The Olds was gone but the Plymouth was worth fixing. All that was wrong with it was the motor was shot, the front end was worn out, the U--joints were gone, no tires, but the wheels were all there. The doors would open and close. The windshield and other glasses were OK. The upholstery was in good shape. I kept the Plymouth and put it in my shop. We dismantled it and then rebuilt it. I got new front end bushings and welded the worn holes in the A frames to fit them. He had worn the bushings out and right on into the A frames. I measured its negative camber by the inches.

There were three army commandos in the deal. I used one for parts, and made two good ones. I kept one and sold the other to a fellow who worked for me. Manny Anderson. I cut mine down and put a flatbed on it, sure was handy. I made a real nice car out of the Plymouth.

I sold the Plymouth to a taxi driver there in the Station. He was making a run to Ciudad Juarez with three passengers. One of the fellows in the back seat was doing something with his pistol when it fired. The slug went through the back of the front seat and killed the passenger sitting there.

My business was so good that I couldn't get the parts I needed at local parts stores. After work on a Friday, Mart and I would get in the Plymouth and go to El Paso. Pick up all the parts I needed for jobs in the shop, and be back for work Monday morning.

I had a charge account with a place in Ciudad Juarez called Millon De Refacciones. They would ship me parts on the plane. LAMSA DC 3 daily flight. Jimmy Gratton, a rancher from one of the Corralitos ranches, needed a motor in his 1 1/2--ton truck. I called my source, Millon De Refacciones in Juarez. I told him to send me a complete motor on the plane. The plane got in at my shop quitting time, and Jimmy needed his truck by morning. My men went to supper while I went to the airfield and picked up the motor. They already had the old motor out. That night while we were putting in the motor, and it took us all night, Jimmy was at the hotel across the street playing poker. The next morning as we were finishing the installation, Jimmy came into my shop all starry eyed. He told me he had played poker all night and won enough money to pay me. He did, in cash. Lots of pesos. When the Corralitos was sold, Mr. Gratton, from El Paso bought the part that had joined us on the north when we were on the Corralitos.

Jimmy was younger than I. We became good friends. He invited me to go deer hunting with him on their ranch. I spent two days at the ranch. We drove his truck with the new motor up the ridges to the foot of the high mountain. No road. He sent a cowboy with our horses to the spot where we couldn't drive any farther. We took one man with us in the truck just in case. Always good to have a spare. On the way up the ridges we jumped several antelope. It is hard to hit a running target from the back of a truck at full speed. One of them went down but he jumped up and caught the herd and got back in line. They went over the ridge and out of sight. Antelope always run single file.

The cowboy was where he was told to be and waiting with our horses. He had left the ranch very early. The cowboy we took along with us to take care of the kill and carry it back to the truck. The spare man we left with the truck with a .30--30 and one bullet. He was not a hunter, just a watchman.

We mounted the ponies and up the mountain we went. Our eyes seeing everything that looks like a deer. There was a large boulder on top of the ridge we were climbing. We saw a deer with big antlers watching us from either side. Two big bucks. We leaped smoothly from our horses and each got a good knee rest shot. Jimmy shot at the left one and I shot at the one on the right. We could only see their heads. We shot at the same time and those deer both disappeared behind the boulder, but came out jumping and dancing. One had a broken hind leg. We never knew which one of us hit him. We could only see the heads when we shot, so maybe he broke his leg when they bumped into each other behind the large bolder. They went down the mountain and we were shooting, but the more we shot the faster and farther they ran. We sent the cowboy to get the wounded one and bring him back. We were sitting on top of a high steep ridge that went down to the valley.

The deer got away, but while Jimmy and I were watching the race of the two deer and the cowboy, we saw a bunch of javelinas coming up the ridge from below us. We couldn't wait for them to get closer so we got excited and started shooting. I got one, but he was far down and it was so steep I waited for the cowboy to come back. I motioned to him where the pig was and for him to bring it up, then I turned my attention to Jimmy. Those pigs came up the mountain and right to us. Jimmy put his gun down and was going to get a pig with his hunting knife. As they topped the ridge he took after them. They outran him and I think he was lucky. When the cowboy got to us again, he did not have my pig. He didn't understand that I wanted it. They were no good to eat, but I wanted the hide to tan for Mom, (my mother) to make gloves with. Javelina hides made very tough gloves.

The show was finally over and we had nothing, just like when it started. We rode on up the mountain and came to a very high bluff. We were on top of it. We dismounted and went quietly to look over and down into the brush below, just in case there might be something down there. Exactly under us at about a hundred feet were two very large Black--tail bucks. They were so straight down we had trouble getting a bead on them, in fact we didn't, because when the shooting was over the deer were gone. Those deer were so scared they just jumped and danced. They couldn't tell where the shooting was coming from. They jumped up and down right there under us until we emptied our guns. They were in an open spot, but when the shooting stopped they hit the brush, and even from our vantage spot, we never saw them again. Of course we jumped on our horses and tried to hurry down there to try and find them. We knew they were hiding in that thicket.

In our rush to get down to them we slid our horses down a place where we couldn't go any farther down and we couldn't go back up. The cowboy hadn't followed us down yet so he was still free. He took more time and found a better way down. It was late evening by the time we finally got our horses out of that mess. We did get them down from there, however. We turned them loose and let them find their own way down. It was like swimming a horse, you must turn him loose, or you will turn him upside down. We had a lot of fun and a good hunt but no deer we thought. When we got back where we could see the truck, we looked at each other and started to laugh. Do we see what we think we see? The man we left with the truck, a .30--30 and one bullet, was skinning out a big black--tail buck.

After I got the Plymouth I sold my little Ford A model. Floyde learned to drive it. Sometimes he would drive it from home to the shop if I had an extra car to take along. He was eight years grande.

On one of my trips to the US for parts, we went out by Antelope Wells. It was rainy season. We came to a wash that was about a hundred yards wide and full of water. In those days, the gals wore dresses, so I told Mart, "Honey, how about you pull your dress up and wade across and see if it is too deep to drive across." She did. We had left our camera home. The water was fine and I followed her across in the car. She still gives me some bad words about that when she thinks about it. It still seems to me it was a good idea. She could pull her dress up easier that I could take off my pants and she was a whole lot cuter.

In January 1950, things were going well for us, but I was starting to think. Maybe I could make dollars as easy as I could make pesos. Besides the US was where all the parts were anyhow. I was working away in my shop when in came Jesus Acosta. He asked me to go across the street to the hotel and have some coffee. We had done that before so I wasn't ready for his proposition. He wanted to buy the place back. He offered me $11,000.00 (pesos). I had paid him $5,000.00 (pesos) and used it a year. He would pay me $2,000.00 down and $1,000.00 per month at 12% interest. We agreed and wrote it on a table napkin. I went home and asked Mart if she would like to move to El Paso. When she could stop hugging and kissing me she said, "Yes." Jesus and I wrote up the notes and he gave me a check. I sold my Plymouth and Commando. Since Mart was teaching school she couldn't go with me. I got Dad to go to El Paso with me to buy a pickup. I bought a 1950 Ford 1/2 ton. I spent a few days at home and then I went to El Paso to find a job. Mart had to finish her school contract.

All the time since I borrowed the $5,000.00 (pesos) from Mart's dad I had been doing lots of work for Harve on his well drilling rig and his ranch and farm trucks and cars. Instead of paying me, I kept track of his account, and I kept all the tickets, because mostly one of his men brought the jobs to me. When I sold out, I added them up and I had almost exactly $5,000.00 (pesos) worth, so I owed him the interest. I went to him with my tickets and my check book to settle up with him, as per our agreement. It had also almost been a year, so it all came together at the same time. He took the tickets and told me he would not count them, and that he would give me the interest. He shook my hand and told me that he was proud of me, and that he hadn't thought I could do it. I always had the most respect for him. He was a very high quality man in every way. He told me that was the first time he had known what his equipment cost him for repairs.

Domer, my sister, lived in El Paso, and I went to live with her and Dick while I was looking for work. She and I have had our differences over the years but I want to say here that I appreciated it then and I still do, how well she treated me. I love her for it. I would look for work during the week then go to Dublan on the weekends.

I had a standing invitation to go back to the mines in Mexico with AS&RCO but that just had to be my last choice. After about three weeks of looking for a job in El Paso I finally got so restless that one day I went up the elevator in the Mills Building to the top floor where the AS&RCO offices were to put in my application. Walking down the hall, I told myself, "Don't do it. SPETY,SPETY. There has got to be a place out there somewhere for me."

I was sitting at Domer's when there was a phone call for me. It was Annie Walser. A very good friend from Colonia Juarez. Her husband, Floyd, was my coach at the JSA. She asked if I was going home to Dublan and could she ride with me. The first thing I thought of was the danger. I knew she was at her sister's place and taking treatments for cancer, and it was terminal. How could she stand to ride a pickup over those rough roads? She wasn't concerned so I was glad to have her company.

20

El Paso Second Time

Mart and I spent 1949 in Dublan, then in about February of 1950 I sold my shop in the Station and went to El Paso to find work. Mart couldn't go with me because she was teaching school. I lived with Domer, my sister. She really treated me good. I have told that I took Annie Walser to Dublan with me on one of my trips home. I went about every weekend, while I was looking for a job. Mart had to stay there and finish her teaching contract. That trip was the last time I saw Annie, but it was one of the most memorable times, and the most turning points in my life. She had terminal cancer and I sure hoped I could drive smooth enough so she would not be hurt. As we traveled, we talked about things in general. I told her how I was looking for a job to get established in El Paso. Also that Mart and I planned to never try to make it in Dublan again.

Her sister, Sarah, was married to Orie Pernell, who had the service station where I bought tires for my pickup when I first came home from the Navy. She told me what a fine fellow Orie was and she was sure he needed a good man. For me to go talk to him when I returned to El Paso. I did, with my boots and big hat on, and while I was asking him for a job, I had one foot resting on the bumper of a car sitting there. Just plain old western comfort. We talked a little and I could see that I didn't impress him at all. I wasn't sure if I wanted to pump gas anyhow, but in the conversation I told him about selling my shop in the Station and that I had a few tools. Then he got a little more friendly, mostly because of Annie, and asked me a few more questions. He told me I sure didn't look like a mechanic, but he needed someone to run the shop. I could come to work the next morning, but to leave the boots home. He would pay me $50.00 per week. When I got my feet on the ground he raised me to $75.00 and when I left there after four years I was drawing $100.00 per week and owned half interest in his station. That wasn't what I had in mind of getting into, but I needed some thing to get me started. I worked for him four years and learned a lot. He was a good boss, a good friend, and most of all a good teacher. He taught me how to make money, and I soon found out that service station dealers make good money. I worked hard for him, and learned the trade. I wanted to be a dealer some day.

After I went to work I didn't have time to go back to Dublan on weekends because I worked six days. Mart would fly out on Friday evening and go back on Sunday. At that time the Lamsa Airline made a round trip from Ciudad Juarez to Casas Grandes every evening. They were DC 3 planes. I would meet her at the Juarez airfield. One day I played a little joke on her. I have always liked to tease her, anyhow. A fellow I worked with got a pair of those funny glasses with the eyebrows and big nose and mustache. He put them on with an old army jacket and an old hat then went into the shop where I was. I didn't recognize him for a minute. Ideas came to me right away. Mart was coming in that day on the plane to Juarez. I decided to get over there a little early. I told the folks at the airfield office what I was up to or they would have had me arrested, I think, because they thought I was real. My pickup was parked in front in plain sight. The plane arrived on time and people were filing off and there was Mart coming in the crowd and looking everyplace. Those folks looked at me then turned their heads to keep from staring. Mart looked and went right on by, real close, like about three or four feet. She had looked me over and was aware of the odd person. While she was getting her luggage I went around the building and got inside my truck to wait for her. She looked around and saw my pickup but couldn't see me. She walked up to the truck and opened the door to get in and there sat that ugly man she had noticed when she got off the plane. She threw down her luggage and ran for the office. I was calling to her and trying to catch her, "Honey, it's me, I'm Bill." She ran clear to the building and there was a crowd watching the show. By that time I knew my joke was out of hand and I was taking off the garb so she would let me catch her. In her mind she thought that terrible looking guy had done something to her Bill and then he was after her. I had only wanted to play, not scare her to death. We still get some good laughs about that day. I bought a new house on Keltner that was still under construction, but was ready by the time school was out. We were very proud of it for sure.

Now the story of how come I got half interest in Pernell's station. I have told about the Bell Ranch and how Raymon Bell paid off his son and daughter. It made them each rich. Mundito, the son, bought a service station on the corner of Cotton and Montana in El Paso. When he found out where I was he went to see me and wanted me to run his station for him. He had a three--bay garage he wanted me to take over. He offered me double what I was making. I gave Pernell two weeks notice, but in about three days he couldn't stand it any longer. He took me to the corner coffee shop and told me what a good job I had done and he just couldn't afford to lose me, and what would it take for me to stay. Was I happy with him? I told him I was very happy with him, and would rather stay. He asked what Bell had offered. He then told me he would leave me on $100.00 per week draw. He priced the station at some thousands of dollars. When my half would pay him back that much I would be his half partner. My foot was in the door. Now I had something to build to. We kept books on my payments and a little over a year I about had it paid off. The Chevron reps at that time were Gene Byce and E Y Beaver. Gene went to Pernell with a deal. They had an empty station on Piedras and Fort Blvd. and they needed a dealer that day. Would Orie work out a deal with me to take it. He did. Orie and Byce went over there and checked it out. They ordered it filled with gasoline, and put in all the merchandise it would hold. Then went back to Pernell's and handed me the keys. Pernell gave me the station pickup and helped me put my tools and such in it and told me to go get it. They told me to be careful about getting rich too quick. That was what broke most new dealers. I had $35.00 to put in my cash box. The first month I cleared $750.00 and I knew there was some thing wrong with my numbers. I took them to Pernell to look them over and see where I had miss figured. He looked them over and said they sure looked good to him. He told me he knew I could do it.

Things went from there to better. That was in February of 1954. In a few months I bought a new 1954 Chevy. We sold our home on Keltner and bought a new one on Mt. Rushmore in June 1955. I had already put a good cushion account in the bank. About the time I got my own station Mart's sister, Ethel, and her baby, Rhonda, came to live with us. We enjoyed them and especially the baby. We had two boys, so that little girl was special. We all spoiled her for sure. Floyde and Sid would make some money setting bowling pins and shining shoes then come home and get Rhonda and take her for some treats. They were with us about a year and we love them special. There was a bowling alley near our house and the army base was only a short distance away. That was where Floyde and Sid made their spending money.

Things were going good and quite often we would go to Mexico to see our folks. I have told that I own half interest in the ranch with dad. He was buying and selling cattle. Mainly big steers. As we drove up to the ranch on one of our trips, there was Dad and Lorin Taylor, Mart's uncle, branding some steers Dad had just bought. Now they were not doing it the normal way. They were playing, and calling it work. Dad had made a chute where he could load and unload cattle. They had a branding fire on the outside of the corral. They had the hired man turn out one steer at a time and one of them would catch it by the head and the other one would get the heels. The man would run over and put the scorch on him. Dad didn't know we were coming, but he had my horse, Penny, in the corral. He told me to saddle up and join the fun. Now Penny was good to rope on. He would follow perfect, and give me a perfect shot every time. The man turned a steer out for me. Penny put me just right and I put my loop on his horns. We always roped with the rope tied to the saddlehorn. As I caught the steer and threw my coils, there was a strong gust of wind and those coils floated up and came down over my head. Now that was not a guillotine but the results are the same. Off comes the head. I threw my reins down and with both hands I grabbed those coils and put them back over my head just as they tightened. It skinned my forehead. All that time Penny was following that old steer just as I had taught him to do. Don't stop until I pull on the reins or jump off. I didn't do either one that day. My reins were on the ground and my rope was around my neck. With my head cleared of rope coils I stepped off. I had to get him stopped because the next real danger was for Penny to get a front foot over my rope and get jerked down an top of me. I stepped off, picked up my reins and petted him on the neck as I remounted. He had sure saved my life.

Floyde was working with me at the station and I could see he was taking to those monkey wrenches and learning how to use them. When I was with Pernell, I had gone to several schools that came to town. They were sponsored by some of the large companies. General Motors had a carburetor school they sent around the country. I had gone to the first one, and carburetor repairs in those days was good business, and still is. A mechanic could go only by a sponsor, and Pernell sent me. The school was usually for about two weeks. My parts rep. told me the school was in town and asking for pupils. I asked Floyde if he would like to go and he would. I called and asked permission to send him. When I told them he was fourteen they said he was just too young to understand carburetors. What they didn't know was that he was already into carburetors. I asked them to give him a try and after the first night, they could make a better decision. One of the teachers was a very good friend of mine. He had taught the school when I went. I knew he would give Floyde a fair shake. After that first night he was the class mascot. The class took him in hand and he made some real friends. Frank Murphy was the teacher. It was a good school and Floyde did real good with carburetors.

He had to get to work after school the best way he could. Mostly walk from the Austin High which was close by. I was cleaning my driveway and I saw a fellow coming my way with one foot walking on the sidewalk and the other one walking in the street. I sort of shuffled my broom until he got to me, thinking maybe I should sort of help him to cross the street, if I could find out which way he wanted to go. When he got to me, the only thing he was sure of was that he needed some more money to get drunker. He could still walk. There was no way I was going to loan him money. "NO NO NO, not a loan, I sell you my car. They take my license, and if I drive they put me in jail." He told me he had a 1947 Chevy 4 door and he would take $75.00 for it. He convinced me to take him to his house, which I had decided to do, anyhow.

Sure enough there sat the car. It had been sitting there in his yard for some time, and was being used for a chicken house. I won't tell you what a chicken does in his house, but that little chevy was full of it. I bought the car range delivery, I mean where is and as is. He gave me the title. I took him back to my station and gave him the money and never saw him again. When Floyde came to work that evening I asked him if he would like to have a car of his own. That was another time that I said the right thing. He could hardly wait for the rest of the story, but what I didn't tell him was what was in it, and I was waiting for his reaction when he saw it. When he saw it he looked at it like I did. It could be cleaned up, and his smile got bigger. We took it to the station and he went to work on it. The interior was in fine shape and cleaned up beautiful. It had a warp in one fender. We had that repaired and a new paint job. It was really a very good little car. Now let me tell you about that kid. I knew he was going over it mechanically, and I knew he had the carburetor off. He called me to see what he had done. He had modified a FORD see--through carburetor and installed it on his Chevy. It worked perfect. I couldn't believe he would mess up a Chevy that way.

When Mountain View housing area was built we moved to Mt. Rushmore which was in 1954. That whole area was a flood plain. No drainage had been put in when they built those houses. During the first summer we lived there the rain man decided to give the east side of the mountain a good wash down. The only place for the wash water to go was out in the flat area where they had built Mountain View housing addition. That whole housing area was under water. Mart called me and told me about the water. I jumped in my truck and headed home. The water was so deep in the street I couldn't make it. I jumped my truck up on the sidewalk to try and keep the water out of the oil, and walked or waded to our house, about eight blocks. Where I left my truck the water was in the houses, so I knew what I would find when I got home. It turned out that a few houses where we were was on a little higher ground and the water only got onto our lawns. It ruined most of the houses in that addition. Later that same summer, Mart and I had gone to Phoenix. We heard on the radio that Mountain View was flooding again. We called home and talked to Floyde. He told us it wasn't as bad as before and that we were OK. They made some large drain ditches so it couldn't happen again.

My station was on the east side of the mountain and the wind came over it in one big reversed roll. My station faced the mountain, or west and those winds would blow my Coke box over and out into the driveway. I had to tie it to the building. I kept my cash box on a stand at the pumps. I was making change one day when a gust hit and sucked all the bills out of the box before I could get the lid closed. I saw my money going over the roof and I never did find it. A large cardboard box blew in from someplace and fixed itself on the windshield of a car passing. It covered the windshield completely and about caused a pile up. That same day the wind was so hard that it started the power lines to dancing and one of them broke. That was the first time I had ever seen a live electric wire. I do mean alive. The end of it ran around my driveway, I was inside the office, no customers, and it whipped into my shop and was acting like a snake. Sparks going all over the place. I called the electric company and they shut it off. I stayed in my office until someone came and took it out of there. A short while before I sold that place and moved to Las Cruces, there was a car wreck on my corner. It was a four--way stop. Some stopped, some almost stopped, and some just went on. A car was stopped going uphill, or west, and another car hit him in the rear. The rear--ender moved his car to try to make it look like it was the other fellow's fault. The cops came and made a report but didn't ask me any questions. I was standing in the drive and saw it happen. After I moved to Las Cruces I was called to El Paso to be a witness. The rear--ender was suing the other fellow. The two lawyers poked me around quite a bit, and I wasn't giving them the answers they were looking for. Instead of describing the cars as traveling west, I said they were going uphill. The lawyer got smart and asked how I could tell they were going or facing uphill. I told him, because I have seen the water run there and the wind blow there and they both went the same direction, downhill. I was the fellow's only witness and I caused him to lose. His lawyer sure tried to mess me up, but I was determined not to get into his noose. It was sort of like playing checkers with a good checker player. You give him jumps so fast you mess up his plays then you can probably beat him.

I decided I wanted a car with air conditioning. I went to the Lone Star and there they had just taken in a '53 Cadillac. Low mileage and like new. I traded my '54 Chevy on it. That was really uptown. By that time, Floyde and Sid were big enough to help in the station. I bought a thirteen--ft. travel trailer. We headed for a fishing vacation at Big Lake, AZ. We went by way of Phoenix, and that was when I learned how much I didn't like vapor lock. Our first fishing stop was at Sedona. We camped near the river. We had Bob by then, he was born September 28, 1951. He was just big enough to be into everything, and especially the water. He fell in that river, and it was so cold he about froze before we could get him to the trailer and get his wet clothes off and into some warm quilts.

We went to some of the lakes that Floyde had been to the summer before with his scout troop. Bob caught a fish in one of those little lakes. Instead of reeling it in like a fisherman, he put the pole over his shoulder and walked away from the lake until he drug his fish upon the shore. It was a small lake near Alpine. From there we went on up to Big Lake. We got on a wrong road going up a hill and had to unhook the trailer and back it down by hand. When we got out of the car to inspect the situation, we found the trailer door was locked on the inside and we couldn't open it. It had a small storage door on the outside that looked in under the bed. We poked Bob in there and boosted the bed up so he could get into the trailer and he was smart enough to open the door. We finally got it turned around without losing it down the hill. We went to the other side of the lake and found a nice campground.

Benny and Wanda Henry and girls, Sue and Ann were to meet us there and we would do some fishing in Big Lake. We were there a week, and a very memorable one. We rented a rowboat and fished a lot and caught lots of fish and ate lots of fish. It was such a good place that we spent several vacations up there.

A short while before I left Pernell, Floyde was on a Scout hike in the Ruidoso area. Chuck Romney was in charge. The morning they were about to break camp, some of the boys were sliding down a hill on a piece of tin they had found and were sure having a time. It was Floyde's turn to ride and he was in front. They were about to run into a tree. He stuck his foot out to catch the tree and change course, but the impact folded his foot under the tin. It cut the leader in the back of his foot. The achilles tendon. They quickly loaded the camp and kids and Chuck took him to the hospital in Ruidoso. The doctor bandaged him up and sent him on his way. Chuck was smart enough to call me. I called Mart and she called Ernestine, our most precious friend and nurse, who called a doctor who told her that time was the element if they could save the foot. It all happened so fast I didn't have time to plan on what to do. When Ernie told us to hurry, I jumped in my car, a '50 Chevy coupe, picked up Mart and we put the peddle to the metal. When we reached Alamogordo we found them stopped at a drive in to get some goodies. Chuck had not been told of the danger Floyde was in. When we got back to El Paso, Ernestine had everything arranged for him to go directly to the operating room. The time element was marginal but we made it because of Ernestine. So she claims one foot of Floyde. He loved to work with me at the station and of course I loved to have him, but after this foot cut, he walked on it crooked, and that bothered me. I checked with Ernie to see what to expect. She told me that it should be used straight, or it would develop crooked. I told him that if he was going to work with me he would have to walk straight on his foot, or I just couldn't bring him to work. I watched him, and it hurt me to see how hard he worked at walking straight, but he did. It heeled up in fine shape and he played basketball in high school. There is a little scar there and that is how he can tell which foot it was. Bob learned to skate about the time he learned to walk. He carried a little pillow that cured all his hurts, but he also used it to hit people over the head with. Mostly Floyde and Sid. He lost his skate key and we couldn't find it at all. Mart had told him and told him to put it in a certain place when he wasn't using it. So he not only lost his key but he was in trouble with his mama. Days went by and still no key. Sid was playing with him and grabbed his little pillow and hit him over the head with it. He fell on the floor, bleeding with a gash in the top of his head. Mart gave Sid a good thrashing for trying to kill him, and wanted to know just what did he hit him with. Sid said, "Mama, I just hit him with his little pillow." With closer inspection of the pillow, out popped the lost skate key.

My folks came to visit us regular. Mart's folks stayed with Roy and Della when in El Paso, but mine stayed with us. Dad was a tall thin man, about 6 ft. 6 in. In Dublan there was another tall thin man named

Hawkins. Now Dad didn't want to be called Hawkins, and I'm sure Hawkins didn't want to be called Adams. Dad was at the train in Ciudad Juarez on his way returning to Dublan when a stranger came up and asked if he was Brother Hawkins. "Hell no," and Dad got on the train. Another day in Casa Grandes a fellow walked up to Dad and asked, "Are you Brother Hawkins?" "Hell no," and dad was gone again. Now Dad was sitting on the couch at our home in El Paso, and we were having a nice conversation when the phone rang. It was near Dad so I told him to go ahead and answer it. He did and then he started to cuss like maybe a horse had stepped on his foot. When he hung the phone up I asked just what was said. He said, and I quote, "I was getting on the train in Ciudad Juarez and someone asked if I was Brother Hawkins. I was in a store at Casas Grandes and someone wanted to know if I was brother Hawkins. By hell, when they asked me over the phone, that is just too damn much." We found out later that our phone number had belonged to a someone Hawkins, and his name was still in the phone book.

It was getting about time for Marty to join our little family. Mart was miserable and didn't like to cook and I didn't think she liked me very much anymore besides. Our neighbor gals wanted to give her a surprise shower and asked if I could get her away from home for a while in the evening. Sure, I could handle a little thing like that. I called her and invited her out to supper. She went to my station. They wanted her at the Henry house at about 5:00 PM. I was busy and she could see I wasn't in a hurry to take her, but she waited with very little patience. I finally got loose and she told me where she wanted to go, but I didn't like that place, so she chose another, and that didn't suit me either. By that time she was getting hard to handle, and all the time I was heading towards home. She got very out of control, and said I had invited her out and I was darn sure going to take her someplace. She would not cook, period. We got home and she wouldn't get out of the car. I finally convinced her to let's go to the Henry's and see if they would feed us. I was about half dragging and carrying her. When Wanda came to the door she turned loose about how I was treating her. About that time she saw all those ladies. They were calling surprise. I winked at Wanda and left while I was still in one piece. Marty was born September 9, 1956.

Those neighbors liked to baby sit Marty, and some times when Mart didn't know they had him.

When we moved to Mt. Rushmore, we were among all new people. They seemed to be a very friendly bunch. We had met the close neighbor folks and they seemed nice but we hadn't done any partying with them. I was home one evening after work and there came a bunch of the ladies, about five and they wanted to know if I would go to the dance with them. Of course that included Mart. I knew that all their husbands had gone fishing, and I was getting messages like, Bill, you don't want no part of this. While Mart and I were trying to explain why we couldn't go, they started to laugh. They had done it on purpose to see what I would say. The men had returned from fishing and we all went dancing. That evening was the beginning of a life--long friendship with the Henrys. We have taken several vacations with them, the first being at Big Lake. They will come into my story from here on because we still get together every chance we get. So you think Benny taught me how to fish? Wrong, he showed me how to fish.

I was not too busy at my station when a friend drove in. Jack Krause. We chatted some and I told him let's take a run to Mexico and spend the night with my folks at the ranch and come back the next day. I took Bob with me. He was like Floyde and Sid, no problem to take with me. By then the road had been oiled from Casas Grandes to meet the highway from Ciudad Juarez to Chihuahua. It was about twice as far but worth it. We entered Mexico at Juarez, then south to Sueco, and there we got the road to Casas Grandes. We went to El Carmen, then El Valle, then Galeana, and next to Casas Grandes, then just a few miles on to the ranch. Our ranch joined the Casas Grandes city limits. The Mexican highways were not fenced in those days and many of them still are not. We were in the '53 Cadillac. I had been driving about sixty MPH. It was night by the time we turned onto the Casas Grandes highway. We had gone through the other towns and were at Galeana. I slowed down to go through there. I was just about back up to speed when my headlights showed some horses crossing the road. I knew those things would be hazardous to my health, so I had to do some fast thinking. Hit the brakes and slide. I couldn't quit the road because it was about six feet above the level ground. I knew it was safer to get two horses than just one. I went between two horses and got some of each one. The first thing they knocked out was my headlights, then a horse head came through my windshield on Jack's side, and I saw a horses tail on my side of the windshield. The noise was terrible. Bob fell down in between the seats. Jack and I didn't bump our heads or get any of the flying glass. I learned some years later that the same maneuver is also recommended to flyers who have to land in trees. Go between two trees, clip off the wings to cushion the forward speed. Those two horses spun around and got all four of my doors and then slid off the tail fins. When we got stopped and inspected the damage, there was a horse down the dump on each side, one dead and one wished he was dead. Both head lights were gone, the windshield busted, and all four doors caved in. A scratch on each tail fin and that was my damage. The hood wasn't even scratched. The park lights were good enough to drive by, so we went on to the ranch, about twenty miles. The next morning I taped some cardboard over the hole in the windshield and we went the same road back to El Paso. My insurance was no good in Mexico. I had the car repaired but it was never right. It had electric windows and those body folks sure messed them up. I went to Phoenix soon after and traded it for a new '57 Chevy station wagon.

Benny Henry's folks lived in Corpus Christy. He had a vacation and asked us to go with them and do some fishing in the ocean. I had installed air conditioning in the '57 Chevy, because by then I had learned to like it. I went to a school on installation of air conditioners and they sold me a unit wholesale. I hooked onto our little thirteen--foot RV trailer and we headed to Corpus with the Henrys. We left Marty with Domer. We were to be gone about two weeks. I got one of life's lessons on that trip. Floyde was driving and doing a good job. About noon time I decided that Mart and I would go back in the trailer. While she put dinner together, I would take myself a nap. I told Floyde about how far up the road to stop, and dinner would be ready. If you have never tried it, then you should. You will never do it twice. Not only Mart didn't fix lunch, I didn't lay on the bed. We both rattled all over that trailer. Of all my rough rides, that was the most memorable. It had a window in front, and I made all kinds of signals, but do you think those damn kids would ever look back? Floyde went to where I told him, stopped and came back to the trailer with a big grin. He soon noticed that his mom and dad had no smiles at all. We didn't eat that day.

Somewhere south or east of Del Rio, as we were rolling along it sounded like things were getting mixed up under the hood of my car. When I installed the frig, I noticed that the belt had a slight crook in it, but that was what they sent and it had to be OK. Not so. The frig belt jumped off and then proceeded to dismantle everything else under the hood.

Benny had a Plymouth S/W and I had the Chevy S/W and of course we argued all the time about which one was better. We were just outside of some little town, maybe two miles. While I was trying to get my belts off to take to town for size, Benny was putting a tow line on my car and was trying to get his Plymouth hooked to it. Wanda was ready with her camera. I didn't let him tow it but he sure tried.

At Corpus, we had some real good fishing. We went out in the ocean on a charter boat one day and that was something. Everyone caught lots of fish but Granny. Benny's Grandmother. She was trying so hard and everyone was pulling them in on each side of her. I wanted her to get a fish so I sneaked her line down the side of the boat and put a fish on it that I had just caught and threw it back into the ocean. Then I went over and was fishing by her side. Pretty soon I told her to snap her line a time or two, looks like she might have one. She did and it wiggled. She reeled it some and that old fish tried to run away and she got excited. She stole the show then and there. We all quit fishing to watch her bring in her fish, and of course we were all giving her instructions. She never caught another fish but that made her day.

Tio lived in Las Cruces. He worked for the state of N.M. as brand inspector. He started in Albuquerque, then was transferred there. He worked Dona Ana County, and so got to know what was going on and who was doing it. One Sunday we were visiting he and Helen in Las Cruces. He told me about a ranch that was for sale, about twenty--five miles west, towards Deming. We talked some about it and the more he told me the more I wanted to know about it. It belonged to Mrs. Mims. We went to her house and found out she wanted $20,000.00 for it. $5,000.00 down and ten years on the balance at six--percent interest.

We got permission to go look at it. That was in June 1956. The place was dry and no grass, and the cattle were poor. There was about eighty head. We came back to town and again went to see Mrs. Mims. I wanted the ranch and I offered her $18,000.00 for it. She stood up and said, "We have talked long enough. I can pick up the phone and get that. I have a standing offer."

I said, "I will give you the $20,000.00 you are asking." She had Ed Meechem draw up the contract, and the next week I had me a ranch. Twelve sections. A hundred cow unit. One cow would have starved on it. She told me it hadn't rained enough to make grass for seven years, and the range looked like it. Tio told me I was too easy to trade with. When I took my good friend, Jack Krause, to see it, he said, "Bill, you been falling in holes and come out smelling good, but this time you have made a mistake." In the deal there was to be sixty head of cattle. Robert Mims, her son, went to the ranch and closed the corral gate to the water so the cattle would stay there to be counted the next day. We counted out the sixty head and there were two or three extras. I knew all the cattle were not there, so I offered him $100.00 for the remnants. He took it. I wound up with over eighty head. When we shook hands and he was ready to return to town, he said, "Bill if it goes to raining I'm sure going to wish I hadn't sold it." We were still shaking hands when a little shower fell. It didn't get us wet. I bought the brand also, so I didn't have to brand them. Lazy K L.

I started a program of feeding those poor cows. At the Taylor Feed Mill in Las Cruces I bought cotton seed meal and salt. Now there was where Floyde and Sid started to learn what it was like to work all day and most of the night. Even Bob had his private stir shovel. We mixed the feed one--third salt. We cut some fifty--gallon drums for feed troughs and put in two sacks of meal and one of salt. It had to be mixed good or the cows would eat too much of it. That, I couldn't afford. That was why the salt. It controlled their appetite. At least now instead of laying around the water, those cows would eat some salt and meal, then drink some water, then eat and more water, then head for the range to find just anything to go with that meal and salt and water. We spent the summer feeding cows. Every time we went to the ranch and got the feed mixed and were ready to start home, back to El Paso, I did a rain dance, in fact Floyde and Sid learned to do a rain dance. That was an every Saturday job. By the first of September, I thought I was going to lose the cattle because I couldn't afford to feed them any longer. I still felt like the ranch was worth the price, but if I could save the cattle they would pay for the ranch. I was told at the feed mill, that it was too late to talk about grass now even if it started to rain. I was raised on a ranch and I could remember some of our best producing rains came in September and October. Well sir, in September it began raining, and there is never a more beautiful rain than on your own ranch. It rained so much I would get my truck stuck in the mud. The best rain dances I did were in the mud. The grass grew and the cattle got fat, and I was in the clouds.

Dad came out from Mexico to see what I had done, and he was pleased. He had trouble understanding how in such a short time, I had a new home, Mart had a new car, I had a new pickup, and a twelve--section ranch. And it all had to come from just a little old gas station. I told him that Floyde and Sid and Mart could help me tell him how we were doing it. We all worked. Floyde and Sid worked with me at the station and Mart sat baby kids. At first Floyde and Sid set bowling pins and shined soldiers' shoes.

I got a paint horse with the ranch deal but he was old and untrained and I wanted my horse from Mexico, anyhow. I asked Dad if he would send Penny and Grasshopper to me when a trainload of cattle was coming to Juarez. Those were the horses I had left in Mexico. He sent them right away and it was a mistake. I hadn't thought about, when I turned them on my ranch I wouldn't be able to catch them when I wanted. They had never been taught to come to me for feed on the open range, and try as I did they refused to learn. They were in the way and I finally gave both of them to friends in town where they would be in a corral all the time.

My friend, Benny Henry, came to our house one evening and invited me to go fishing. I listened to him and it sounded like fun. His boss had a boat, and a fellow he worked with wanted to go also. I would take my truck to pull it with. I told him I had sold my truck but I had bought a new Chevy but it was still in Anthony. It would be ready to pick up the next day. It was a 1956 half--ton Chevy. We were going to Boquilla,

Mexico, south of Chihuahua City. The next day, Benny picked me up at my station and we headed for Anthony. On the way he was in such a hurry that he got a speeding ticket. To this day he thinks I should have paid it. We have had our rounds over that ticket. It was evening by the time we were ready to leave for Boquilla. We drove all night and arrived at Boquilla after daybreak the next morning. We found a place for breakfast then found a guide and into the water with the boat. I think the boat was maybe twelve feet with about a ten--horse outboard. This was all new to me but I could see this could be something I should look into. It was an open aluminum boat with a small kicker controlled by a handle. Like I say, that was alright. Fishing was good. We caught a large ice chest full. One time I cast my line, but being new at this fishing thing, it caught on a reed and my worm didn't get to the water, about six inches hanging in the air. Before I could get it shook down into the water, a fish jumped up there and got hold of it. He was sure worm--hungry. We fished two days, then back home. We had one of the best fish fries I have been to. We had enough fish for the whole neighborhood.

Tio was brand inspector for a while and then he got a job at WSMR as range rider. There were still lots of wild cattle, horses and burros on the range that needed to be caught and moved off. The range had been closed to deer hunting since the government took it over. There were so many deer that a hunter was allowed either sex. The tag percentage was very high. I enjoyed hunting there, and so did Floyde, Sid, and Bob. I had killed a deer and had it hanging in a tree, and Bob had been inspecting it. He called out, "Hey Dad, this deer has a price tag on it." How right he was. It cost $50.00 for an out--of--state permit, besides the license. We all thought it was worth it. When we moved to Las Cruces we made the hunt on the range every year, and enjoyed being out there with Tio.

I think after I bought the ranch was when the wind started to blow. We had a couple of winds that made me afraid to go see if my windmill was still standing. It was and I still don't know how. It wasn't even tied to the ground. It was just sitting there. I kept it tied off as much as I could so the wheel would feather if the wind should get bad. I was doing the best I could to get things going at the ranch and still keep my station un--neglected. It was about a hundred and fifty miles every time I went to the ranch, and I couldn't keep that up. I talked to my Chevron reps about buying a station in Las Cruces. By then my good friend, Gene Byce, was in charge of the Las Cruces office. It just happened they had a dealer who wanted to sell. When I went to see it and talk to Gene and Tommy Thompson. I asked if there was any chance he would back out on me, and I was assured he wouldn't. Now all I had to do was sell my Fort Blvd. station and move to Las Cruces. In a few days the El Paso rep. had a buyer for my place. I was ready to move to Las Cruces.

21

Las Cruces

630 MONTE VISTA

While I have been writing my book I have had a birthday. December 18, 1989, I became 70 years old. I have lived half of that time in Las Cruces, NM. We moved here in June 1957. The last thirty--three years have been so good and so exciting, I don't know if I should start from now and go backwards, at the move to Las Cruces and go forwards or start in the middle and go both directions, or just call it quits here and let my kids write the rest of my life story.

Floyde had a chance to sell his first little Chevy car and make a little money. Then he bought an Olds 88. It was a good car but sure used lots of gas. He sold it and took in a Buick with a bad engine. It had a bad rod. We filed the rod cap to take the slack out of it, but knew it wasn't very good. By then he had money in all his pockets. When we moved to Las Cruces I walked north on Main Street with my money bag to find a bank. The first one I came to was the First National of Dona Ana. I walked in and the first person I met was Jack Campbell. I told him my story and he asked me to change my checking account from El Paso and put it in this bank. I did and it has been there ever since. In our conversation he told me he had a 1950 Buick he had bought new, but he had bought a new car and his Buick was for sale. Floyde and I looked at it and it was like new. He would finance it with no down, and small payments. Floyde made a good buy, and started his credit reputation that day. When school started, it was his senior year, so he stayed with Roy and Della in El Paso. He wanted to finish high school in El Paso at Austin. He came home on weekends, so he needed a good car.

The winter of 1957--58, we had a snowstorm that closed the schools. There was no traffic to Las Cruces, almost. It was Friday. I called Floyde and told him not to try to come home, but I would go to El Paso. We would take his car and go to the ranch in Mexico. We went into Mexico at Ciudad Juarez in order to have the oiled road all the way to Casas Grandes. When we got to Villa Ahumada we were frozen because his Buick's heater didn't get hot. We stopped at a little store and bought a cardboard box. We fixed a cover over the radiator so the water would get hot, and then we were warm again. That was where we should have done a 180--degree turn and returned home. We kept going. There was lots of snow everyplace, and sure cold. A few more miles south and there was a Mexican Greyhound on its side. It had skidded and was about a hundred feet off the road. We continued in the same direction and the snow was getting more and colder. At Sueco we turned west on the Casas Grandes highway. There was still lots of snow. We arrived at El Carmen and went right on through it.

In my story of our trip to the Bell Ranch, I told about a very high mountain we went down. We were approaching that same mountain, but from the bottom. We were going to climb it and the road was iced over. There again we should have done a 180. Nope not us, in fact we didn't know very much about a 180 at that time. We hadn't started flying yet. Up the mountain we went, Floyde driving. He needed to learn to drive on ice and that would be good practice. That was in the days of the old slush--o--matic transmissions. No gear shifting, just give it some more gas and spin the oil a little faster in the torque box. The transmission made the car great on ice or in the mud, because it would not spin the wheels. We were slowly making our way up the mountain and around the curves. We were getting about to the top, when we found the reason we hadn't met any traffic. At first we thought it was because we were the only ones so stupid to be out in the snow and cold. The traffic was all stopped in the road and facing every direction but the right one. There was a wide place there and it was full of cars. There we met Scott Bluth. He had a little Toyota type car with chains on it. He was trying to get people headed in the right direction. Some down hill and some up hill. No one was being foolish with the space because a mistake would send him about a thousand feet almost straight down. We pulled off the road in the only place available and helped Scott help those folks. We couldn't go by anyhow, but no one leaves someone in trouble there in Mexico. When we got things and people going again, Scott gave us a little push and helped us back onto the road. There again Floyde, was still practicing on the ice. He took it easy and we topped out. We went down the west side that was not so steep and the snow was mostly gone. We went on to El Valle, Galeana, Casa Grandes, and then a short distance to the ranch. Dad was surprised to see us. He had heard that there was so much snow no one could travel. The snow had melted when we returned so we had no trouble returning home the next day.

In the spring of 1958, Dad and I decided to sell the ranch in Mexico. Mom was already living with my sister, Ada Beth, here in Las Cruces. Dad's health was bad so he came to live with Mart and me. He had arthritis in the worst way. His driving was muy malo so I would not help him get a driver's license. I wanted him to stay close to home where we could help him. One day he was gone and we had no idea where he was. In a few days he drove into my station with a big grin on his face. I knew he had been up to something but I wasn't ready for what it was. He had a nice new driver's license. I knew right then he was going to keep me worried a lot, and he did, but he enjoyed it. Not worrying me, but the fact that he could go when he felt like it, or even if he thought he felt like it.

I'll explain the driver's license. Back in the Barranca story I told about Jack Wright riding up one day on my horse, Nestegg. Then later that same Jack Wright showed up again and traded his used up horse for my Nestegg horse I had learned to love. I hoped I had seen the last of him, then one day he showed up again with a horse called Toothpick from the Klondyke era. Dad gave him a nice fat horse to leave on. Those horses had been left in Arizona when we moved to Mexico. Again I hoped I had seen the last of him. I looked at the license and YEP you guessed it. I didn't. I had to read it. Jack Wright. He was the judge in Duncan, Arizona and he sure fixed Dad up real legal like. I'm sure that Jack Wright was an alright man, but he was sure a nuisance to me.

When Floyde bought the Buick from Campbell he gave the other one to Sid. We knew it wasn't very good but it was better than what Sid had. None. We had it running good and it sounded good. We opened the station for work one morning and there sat a red Ford coupe in front of the station at 302 South Main. In those days there was a hotel across the street from us. The owner of the red Ford came from the hotel to see if we could get it started for him. In the talking we traded him Sid's Buick and took the Ford as part payment. The little Ford had just been too long without a tune up. They were from California. Sid made a nice little car out of the Ford. Before long he sold it, and bought a 1950 Studebaker. It was a good little car. Each time he traded he made a little money. I have lost track of all the cars he and Floyde have owned.

All our friends were left in El Paso, especially Benny and Wanda Henry. We went to see them often, or they would come to see us. On one of our trips to see them we went to dinner in their car and as we drove down the street we passed a service station where Benny traded. The fellow had a boat for sale. I had been in a boat once already. That was when I went with Benny to Boquilla in Chihuahua. Benny told me the guy wanted $300.00 for it. I said, "Let's take a look at it." The fellow let me take it home. We hooked onto it then and there. That was Saturday, and Benny would come to Las Cruces on Sunday. We would go to the Caballo Lake, and if we liked the boat he would take the man's money to him. If not, then he would take the boat back to him. It was a fourteen foot fishing boat that had been modified. An aluminum cover had been put on the bow. They had put a steering wheel on it to be driven from the middle of the front seat. It had a twenty--five--horse Johnson fastened to the end behind the bow. The motor was so old it was the old green color. I have only seen one since. When I pulled into our home yard with that little boat, and the kids, Floyde, Sid, Bob, and Marty, saw it, Santa couldn't have been more welcome. Marty was too little to drive it but he was excited anyhow.

That was Saturday evening when I pulled into the yard with it and it was a very long night waiting for Sunday to arrive so we could take it to the lake. We went to Caballo Lake. It was quite a trick to get into the water with the little boat. There were no boat ramps in those days. Just find a place to put it into the water. I'm good with ropes, and that was how we let it down the bank to the water. The lake was very low in those days. I'm an old Navy man, so I sure didn't see any problem with that little thing. Since I was the buyer, I was the one to take it for a dash in the water to see if I liked it. I already knew that with the kids excitement, my only choice was to like it.

I pulled the rope crank a few times and the little green motor started to purr. I put it in reverse to get out in the water from the bank, full throttle. I almost swamped it, but as I say, I had been in a boat once. I didn't drive it but I sure paid close attention to Benny. I changed to full forward and planned to jump it out there and run it about some. That little green motor was sure wound up but the boat just sat there. I looked on the bank and Benny was sure laughing, but Floyde and Sid were serious. I think, "Who wants a boat that backs up so good and won't go forward." They tossed me a line and pulled me back to the shore. Benny explained that when I changed directions at full throttle, I had sheared the prop pin. In those days there were two levers, one to shift gears, and the other was the throttle. There was an extra pin in the boat. He showed us how to change it. Then a lesson on how to not make pieces of the sheer pin. The little boat ran fine and I gave Benny the money to take to the fellow in El Paso.

We enjoyed it so much we called Lawrence and Ethel, Mart's sister and husband, in Salt Lake City, Utah, to meet us at Kanab, Utah. From there we went to Lake Mead for a vacation. They brought their daughter, Rhonda, with them. In a couple of days they returned home but we stayed on for two more days. We took a picnic lunch and went about a mile out to an island for the day. I'm almost afraid to tell what we did. I put us all in that little fourteen--foot boat, with the worn--out little green Johnson motor. Floyde, Sid, Bob, Marty, Rhonda, Mart, and I. It might have been safe for two if the weather was calm. The wind came up and we had to stay on the island all day. Floyde and Sid learned to ski that day. With several tries, Floyde was finally able to make it all the way around the island without falling. We ran out of drinking water so Floyde and I went to shore at the marina and filled our jug. It was evening before the wind let us return to the marina with all the family.

That was the only thing I did right that day was wait for the wind to stop, almost. There were no trees so we crawled under some bushes to get a little shade.

We all learned to ski and liked boating so well, I traded it in for a new Lonestar eighteen--foot boat with a cabin over the front seats, with a V4 Johnson fifty horse. We were then into boating with the best of equipment, and we spent all our spare time at Caballo or Elephant Butte Lake. Floyde and Sid took friends and we taught many kids to ski. It would pull four skiers at a time. We had some great parties.

Sid took a friend, Larry Parker, a good kid but not used to that sort of playing. He didn't realize some of the dangers. One of them being a turning prop. I had been towing skiers and was near the bank waiting for someone to get hold of the ski rope when I heard a scream. The boat was in about three feet of water. Larry had come out to the boat and walked into the prop. I'll tell you for sure, that prop only had one thing in mind and that was to cut his leg off, and about got it done. We took him out of the water and filled the cuts with salt, then back into the boat and we headed for the Dam Marina. It was the only one on the lake in those days. That was where our car was. We took him to the hospital in T or C. They fixed him up, and told us how smart to salt the cuts, and asked how we knew to do that. I told the doctor that salt was the only medicine we kept on the ranch when I was a kid. I told him that if we were going to fix it we salted it, and if we were going to eat it we salted it. It scared me so much I was going to get rid of the boat, but Floyde and Sid made me see that it wasn't my fault. I'm sure they were right, I was just driving the boat, actually just sitting with the motor idling in gear to keep off the bank.

I decided we need a smaller boat and one without a cabin so visibility would be better. I traded boats but kept the motor. We still had lots of fun at the lake. After Sid got married, and then Floyde, our boating slowed down. I traded the boat on my first airplane. Sid got married Sept. 7, 1960, and Floyde got married April 1, 1961. I bought the airplane in about June 1961. It was a Cessna 170.

The Mangum families went fishing in Mexico at Angostura and invited us to go along. The roads were very bad. The first time we went with them I had a new 1960 Chevy truck six cylinder, three speed. That almost wasn't enough to pull my boat up the mountain roads. It was strictly camp out at the lake. Fishing was good and boating was fun. Owen and Ralph each took a boat. It was so much fun that I got myself ready for the next trip. Floyde took his Jeep, and girlfriend, Connie, and a friend, Bob Parker, and his girlfriend. I made a shell camper for my truck so Mart and I would not have to sleep on the ground. No windows, and the rear door hinged on top to swing up. I made fasteners on the door for the outside for traveling but no way to fasten it from the inside. I had planned to sleep with the door propped open. We had a good camp. The Mangums had tents and the girls had a tent. Floyde and Bob slept in the Jeep. Mr. and Mrs. Mangum had a large tent. They had all the little kids in there with them. By the second night there, we had settled in and had a nice camp. During the night, it started to rain, then blow. It blew the tent down on the girls. I think the only tent that stayed put was the big one. Mart and I were in our truck and holding onto that back door. The wind was trying to tear it off. We didn't know all that had happened until the next morning. We could hear some of them shouting and running around in the wind and rain, but we stayed put. It rained all night so we had to hold the door all night. I held my side and Mart held her side. I would slack of on my side to see if she was holding on. If the door flopped I would tell her to hold on tight, and she would. Then I would go to sleep and let her hold it. She would doze off and it would get away from her. I would tell her again, she must hold her side. When it got daylight so she could see, she saw me asleep. I thought she was going to kick me out of there without my clothes. She had held that door all night long, and thought I was holding my side. She was a good sport though, she didn't kill me.

When we got camp sort of organized again we walked down to the Angostura Lake to check our boats. Mine was gone. We had a large rubber raft that Mr. Mangum had brought along, and my boat was tied to it. The raft was gone also. We got in Owen's and Ralph's boats and started to look for the runaways. We went up the lake to where the river came in. Across the lake the way the wind was blowing. We looked up all the canyons across the lake and no boats. They must be on the bottom. Must have punctured the raft on a stub of a tree. There were plenty around. We had given up when someone suggested we look on the upwind side of the lake. It didn't make sense but we had searched out the downwind side with no luck. There was a bluffy canyon up lake and upwind from where the boats had been tied. We went into it, maybe two hundred yards, and there they were, still tied together and as far up the canyon as they could go, with not a scratch. The wind must have been whirling to send them in there.

Another thing that slowed down our boating was a little girl that joined us Feb. 20, 1961. The sixties were great years for me and my family. Many changes and for the better. We were working and growing and looking straight forward. The only time we looked back was for a lesson we could use to make the front a little better.

Now about the little girl. We picked her up in El Paso. I figured Mart had gone in to get us another little boy and I knew what they looked like, so I went to the airfield and looked at an airplane that was for sale. While I was there a friend took me for a little flight. He had been trying to sell me a plane, and had flown me to my ranch a few times to show me how I could use an airplane. That was before I bought the 170 airplane. When I returned to the hospital there was a little red--headed girl. Mart has never forgiven me for not being there, and I'm sure never will. We named her Bonnie, and what a joy she was and is in our lives. She is my favorite daughter and she knows it.

Sid was working with me and the Christmas of 1963 we decided to go to Disneyland. Our first time, so it was an adventure. He had a GMC pickup with a camper for his kids and I had a 63 Chevy. We went by way of San Diego. Went to the zoo, and it was very interesting. We were driving on up to L.A. at night. Sid was following my tail--lights because they were different from most. We didn't have CB radios in those days. I got stopped by the Highway Patrol and almost got a ticket for holding up traffic. Mart was driving. She was going too slow. That was a new twist to me. She was being careful not to speed. We were barely out of San Diego. I took over and spent the rest of the trip to L.A. trying to catch the fellow in front of me. Sid lost me and had no idea which car was me. I sure didn't know where he was. When I arrived in Anaheim I pulled into the first service station to fill up and get some directions to a motel. While I was filling up with gas, Sid drove up. We found a motel close to Disneyland and that was a trip that caused us to spend many Christmases that way. All the kids were of an age to really enjoy it. My three little ones, Bob, Marty, and Bonnie, and the grandkids.

The Christmas vacation was catching on. In 1965, we all planned to spend it in Memphis, Tennessee. Floyde was in the Army by then and stationed in Maryland. He had a new Chevy wagon. We still didn't have CBs so Sid and I sure had to be careful in order to stay together that far. Sid was driving a new 1965 Chevy Suburban and I was driving a 1961 Cadillac I had bought for my carlot. He told me later that his Chevy six sure huffed and puffed to keep that Cadillac in sight. In those days the speed limit was seventy MPH, and I used it all the way.

Floyde had taken flying lessons and had his license. He was anxious to take me for a ride, and so was I to ride with him. By that time I had my second airplane and quite a few hours flying time. It was a Cessna 180. The Memphis Airfield is an island in the Mississippi River. We took a small boat out to it. Floyde rented a Cessna 150 and we got some very good views of the city and the river. His flying was great.

On our return trip we stopped in Fort Worth for supper. I had coffee and Marty always liked a little sip. I would give it to him. Something must have been wrong with that coffee, because a few miles down the road, Marty and I got very sick. We stopped at a truck stop and got some baking soda. We drank some soda water, and it helped us get rid of what ever was doing us in. Sid didn't see us turn into the truck stop and he went flying by. No problem, we would see him at the motel in Odessa where we stayed on the way to Memphis. He tried to catch us all the way home to Las Cruces. Mart and I stayed in Odessa. We sure could have used CBs. Actually we had CBs on the trip but they were good at about yelling distance.

A short time before Floyde was to get out of the Army, he came to Albuquerque for an interview at Sandia. When he returned to Maryland, he and Connie took Bonnie with them. I had planned to fly up there and bring her back but I didn't get it done. She was with them until they returned here.

When they were ready to leave Maryland and return to our part of the country we stayed in touch. When they reached Fort Worth they called us. We set up a time schedule to meet them in Van Horn at the Ramada Inn and restaurant. Sid and family were in his car. Bob, Marty, and Mom were with Mart and me. We had breakfast in Van Horn, and we knew we were early so we decided to drive on down the highway towards Dallas until we would meet them. At the junction of I--10 and I--20, we still hadn't met them. Possibly they got by us but not likely. In the afternoon we gave up and went back to Van Horn and ordered a late noon meal. When we were eating a fellow came to our table and asked if we were Adams. He had a message from a Floyde Adams. He had the message when we were there in the morning but didn't give it to us. The message was that Floyde had a bad wreck and Connie was in the hospital in Weatherford. Floyde was in a motel with four little kids, and sure needed some help, like Mom and Dad. I called him. He had sat by that phone all day, it was then late evening.

He was towing his Jeep, and had totaled both cars. The kids were banged around, but OK. I told him we would drive into the night and be in Weatherford early the next morning. Sid took our kids and my mother and returned to Las Cruces. Mart and I spent the night in Big Spring, then on to Weatherford, early. Floyde was glad to see us. We went to the hospital to see Connie. She was glad to see us also. She was released to go with us. We took her with us. She and Mart took the kids so Floyde and I could go check out the damage to his station wagon and Jeep. The tow folks had tried to buy the Jeep for a few dollars. We looked the cars over. I told Floyde, "Let's take these cars home and then decide how to handle the salvage part." They were sure beat all to hell body--wise but were driveable. We hooked them together and headed for home. We drove straight through. We were afraid to stop at a motel for fear someone would steal his things, because the windows were gone from his car. We took turns driving and sleeping. Sure was a long night but we made it.

Bob was married November 19, 1970. Bonnie was married August 9, 1980. Our home seemed empty with all our kids married and on their own. They all lived in Las Cruces at the time Bonnie was married, so we saw all of them often.

We called my mother MOM. She was Mom to everyone, especially my kids. She lived here in Las Cruces with Ada, my sister. I saw and enjoyed her for several years since she was here close. Mart and I took her with us on some of our trips. I think she enjoyed them. She liked to fly with us, and in those years that was the way we mostly traveled. Cancer took her October 31, 1974. She was seventy three years old. She was a precious Mother, and I loved her dearly, and I told her so.

302 SOUTH MAIN

I found a Chevron service station I could buy in Las Cruces at 302 South Main. A date was set for delivery, and I was assured by the Chevron reps of the deal. The place would be inventoried when I received it. All I had to do was get my Chevron station in El Paso sold and our home sold so we could move by the date we had set. Things really fell into place for me. I got my home and station in El Paso sold and delivered at about the same time. We loaded our tools on our pickup late one evening. Floyde, Sid, and I headed for Las Cruces. That meant we were inventorying the new place at night. I was not arguing prices with the guy until he threw in a worn out broom, a bunch of used and no good inner tubes and also some used tire skins. I told him he could just throw them in the garbage so I wouldn't have to, or take them with him. He blew his fuse and decided he wouldn't sell to me. I called Tommy and Gene, who were the Chevron reps, and told them what I was up against. They both arrived about the same time. They had anticipated that very thing and they each figured I wouldn't want his junk. They took him around the corner for a cup of coffee. When they came back he was mad but mancito. He took my check and left. I never saw him again.

He did get the last laugh however. I had been there about two months when a Police Officer handed me a letter. It turned out the guy had never paid any city tax on his tools and business. The letter was a Court Order for me to pay the bill in thirty days or they would auction off my tools and merchandise until the sum was satisfied. I think it was about $500.00. I got hold of my Chevron reps and told them. The City Drug and Restaurant was on Main Street on the same block and south of my new station. We went there to talk and have coffee. They told me they couldn't pay it, but for me to pay it. When they got that far I was already sliding down in my seat, sort of disappearing, when I heard them continue with some more words. I stopped sliding long enough to catch their last words. They said, "We will ship you merchandise to cover it."

I climbed back up to my cup of coffee and it sure tasted good. They sent some extra merchandise, and at the wholesale price, so when I retailed it I came out very good. I must mention here that there was a third man in the Chevron office. His name was Bill Russell. Bill and I became good friends also. I hadn't known him in El Paso but I had known Gene and Tommy when I was with Pernell. They were the reps who put me in the Fort Blvd. station. They had been transferred to Las Cruces and were the top men. I had known them for several years.

I took Floyde and Sid to Las Cruces and put them on what they called an expense account. I gave them the keys to the station and told them to run it until we could get moved from El Paso to Las Cruces. They had a room at the Kilby Motel on Main Street. Let me say here, those two boys did one fine job. At that time all the east and west traffic was on Main Street. There was no freeway or bypass around the town. Main Street was the through--town artery. The new station was overstocked with fan belts, and those kids sold them all.

It took the whole summer of 1957 to get things going our way at the station and take care of the ranch also. There was lots to do to bring them both up to our standards. The station was rundown and the ranch was worse. Floyde and Sid worked hard with me that summer. We had things fairly well shaped up by the time for them to go to school. Floyde went to El Paso to finish at Austin High and Sid went to Las Cruces High. Bob started first grade at Mesilla Park. Marty was just one year old.

In the summer of 1959, Floyde had a job with the El Paso Natural Gas Co. and went to Santa Fe. Sid ran the station while Mart and I went on a trip to Salt Lake. We Returned by way of Raton and then to Eagle's Nest to do some trout fishing there. We chose a weekend when Floyde could meet us there and we caught some nice trout. They charged by the inch so we couldn't afford to catch many. I must mention here how responsible those two boys were, and at that young age.

Marty was a lively little guy and Mart would sometimes leave him with me when she went shopping or on church work. He ran out in the drive and a customer ran into him and knocked him down. The tire just touched his leg. It was a very close call. I had a stack of tires in the office. I put him inside of them and told him to stay there until I could go in the shop for a few minutes and then come back to get him out. In those days all tires were wrapped in paper for protection from sunlight. When I came back to the office I couldn't see him until I got right over the tires, and there he was having a big time. He had torn all the paper off those tires. I had trouble getting it off with my pocketknife when I sold one. He wanted to stay in there and finish what he started and I let him.

I soon made a very good friend here in Las Cruces. His name was Kenneth Munn. His business was behind my place on Water Street. He had the Culligan Soft Water business. He would walk through my place on his way to the City Drug for coffee, and sometimes I would go with him. That was also when and where I got to know Grayson Meerscheidt. He worked for Munn. Grayson and I still drink coffee regular, he is a special friend. The City Drug was owned by the Gutierez's, and run by the son, Eduardo. He also was a good friend. He traded with me and charged his account. At the end of the month he would sign a check and tell me to put in the amount and let him know. Our doctor was Dr. Goosen, and we liked him very much. He had an airplane. A 180 Comanche. Ken and I talked flying often. I wanted to learn to fly but the time wasn't right yet. Goosen was going pheasant hunting in Nebraska and invited Ken, Ed, and me to go along. We had been planning for a couple of weeks, but when the time came to go I just couldn't get away, and Ed couldn't go either. Goosen and Munn left in the wee hours of the morning in his Comanche and were never seen again, alive. That was in October 1960. They were found in November by deer hunters in the Sacramentos, completely off course. Ed and I still wonder what really kept us from going.

By 1960, things were looking good financially. One day I was at the Jeep agency, where I also had a good friend. When I left there I was driving a new yellow Jeep. When I drove into the shop, Floyde and Sid acted about like when I came home with the first boat. We all tried it out and liked it so much that they each bought one. By then Floyde had a new 1960 Chevy, but he sold it and went for the Jeep. Sid had a little Studebaker which he sold and got a Jeep. Floyde's was white and Sid's was red. Floyde turned mine over on a deer hunt. Sid turned his over when we were all being silly running around bushes. Floyde turned his over in front of the girl's dorm at the college. By then he was trying to convince Connie Stevens how smart and dependable he was, and also what a good driver he was. He rolled it down a high bank right there in front of all her friends. The Jeep was on its side down in the arroyo. Floyde climbed out to call me but Connie was too embarrassed to get out with all her friends watching. She was very calm, and stayed in there until I arrived. We tipped it back onto the wheels. I called Grayson and he came out with his winch and pulled it up onto the road. Grayson was the one that got us started with Jeeps, anyhow. His first one was an army surplus. He would take us hunting rabbits at night. The Jeeps were great sport.

One day, Floyde and I heard a loud grunt and a sort of help sound in the shop. We were at our station. Floyde and I went running from the office to the shop and found Sid flat on the floor under some tire racks. We asked him what happened and he told us he bumped his head. I said, "Just how in the hell did you do that?" He said, "I was cleaning here and when I stood up I hit my head," and down he went again. He showed us how he did it.

A fellow came in for a tire switch on some kind of foreign car. I had just bought an electric torque--wrench for just such things. He got his book out to tell us how to do it but he couldn't keep up with us. Floyde was running around zipping the nuts off and Sid and I were shifting the wheels and then Floyde was putting the nuts back on. By the time he found the instructions we had him ready to go. He didn't understand. He wasn't sure we had done it right, or if we had really changed his wheels at all.

We always looked for a customer's needs, and especially bad tires. In those days bubbled, tires were quite common. The bubbles were caused from cord separation. We had lots of California trade. By the time they hit Las Cruces, if there was a problem it would show, and we looked for it. The fellow had a bad tire. A large bubble, and Floyde showed it to him. Floyde put the car on the hoist and raised it up to show the man better. It was a big obvious bubble. The man looked at it and felt it and still didn't believe he had a problem. The fellow was very suspicious, and even though he could see the large bubble on his tire he thought we were trying to sell him something he may not need, so he didn't buy. As Floyde was letting the car down so the fellow could go on his way he said, "Mister, you haven't got a Chinaman's chance." Floyde has never had a look like that fellow gave him, before or since. He didn't say one word, just got in his car and drove off. The guy was a Chinaman.

When I bought the station it had two built--in problems that had worried the previous owner to his selling out to me. One was a bowling alley across the street. Those people liked to park their cars at my place and none of them traded with me. I had the only good parking space in the area. The other was a garage that did mostly front--end work. He had no parking at all for his customers, so they used my parking space. I had to figure how to join them. The bowling folks would barely get parked when we were trying to sell them something. They got the message and some of them did become good customers. When they traded with me I was glad for them to park at my place.

I watched the garage operation for a while then decided I had a bird nest on the ground. I would get into the front--end business, and divide his customers with him. I had done front--ends when I worked for Pernell. I bought a pit type front--end machine and wheel balancer. When we got them installed, I sent Jim Parrish to school in El Paso to a friend in the business, Everett Adler. Jim Parrish was a good man and worked for me for several years. We went to work on the next door customers. When they drove up, we greeted them. When they told us they had an appointment, which most of them did, we said, "Yes sir," and took their keys and car. All he could do was look out his shop window and see me getting his customers, and get mad. I had tried to reason with him before and he didn't hear, so I decided to give him some competition. He lasted about a year and moved to a new location, but by that time I was well--established. We are still in the front--end business. Floyde has the best equipment in town, computerized. He still has the original equipment, however.

In 1960, Mart's youngest brother, Claudius, was trying to get his papers in order so he could come from Mexico to the US and become a US citizen. He wanted to move to Los Angeles. I told him to come and work for me while he was waiting for his papers, and he did. I had been wanting to take flying lessons and buy an airplane to use on the ranch. While I had Sid and Cotchy, (Claudiuis) was the chance for me to do just that, and I did. About the time I was ready to solo I bought a Cessna 170, July 13, 1961. I traded my boat and $3000.00 for it. I had been learning to fly in a Cessna 150, but when I got the tail--dragger I had to start all over. About sixty hours of lessons and I had my license.

When we moved to New Mexico we could better afford to go deer hunting and not feel like we were spending our last dollar. Tio was chief range rider on the WSMR (White Sands Missile Range) and we went every year where he was. It was great. In those days we could drive our Jeeps anyplace we were brave enough, and that was a lot. We could cover lots of country, and easily hunt out the headers, and we always filled out.

We went antelope hunting at Engle, but for them we had to stay on the roads, except to pick up a kill. Floyde and I sat on a small rise near the road and waited. There were hunters everywhere so sooner or later someone would chase a herd our way. We were carrying 243 rifles. They are very fast and flat shooting, but small bullets. They are suppose to mushroom on impact, but don't always. We spotted a buck coming our way so we sat still. He changed directions before he was within shooting range, and would soon be gone, so nothing to lose by dropping a shot over his direction. I told Floyde to watch with his binoculars and see where I hit. I pointed my 243 up in the air and fired. Nothing happened. He couldn't see where the bullet fell and it didn't bother the antelope. I told him to watch my next shot and I pointed the gun in the air again in the general direction of the antelope, thinking maybe I could turn him back in our direction. Floyde told me he saw him flinch that time but there was still no dust to show where I was shooting. I said, "If he flinched I must have hit him, so let's sit here and watch for a minute." He walked a little farther and laid down, and pretty soon he laid over on his side. We walked over to him and just as we approached him, a herd of about six skylined on the ridge about a hundred and fifty yards distance. I told Floyde to get behind one of those soapweeds and make it count. He did, and got one. He went after his antelope while I was cleaning mine and about the time he got to it, another hunter ran up and claimed it. Floyde had no doubt that it was his and neither did I. I watched to see if I was needed but I wasn't. They turned the antelope to show where the bullet came out and that proved it was Floyde's. The other hunter was on the other side of the ridge. As we walked back to our Jeep we stepped off the distance I had shot my antelope and it was seven hundred and fifty yards. The bullet had gone through his heart. Floyde gave his to Connie and her dorm friends.

In 1960, a young boy started to work for me. He was crippled in one foot, but seemed to get around OK. I hired him to do clean up. I never had to show him the same thing twice and never had to tell him to not be holding down chairs. I had him a few days when a fellow came along that was a mechanic and had lots of experience. I had lots of shop work. I couldn't afford two men so I let the crippled boy go. The look on his face when I told him I didn't need him anymore kept me from sleeping at night. I just kept thinking of how hard he had tried, even though he didn't know anything, he wanted to learn. I called his mother and asked her to tell him to come back to work. He did and was with me for ten years. He was the best man I ever had, besides my kids. His name was, and is, Andy Perez. I sent him and Sid to the Bear front--end school in Chicago at different times, and they were good front end men.

LAZY K L RANCH

The house we bought in Las Cruces was being built, so we rented a place on Lee's Drive. We moved into our new home in September 1957. We all worked hard that summer trying to get organized in our new surroundings and still make a living. The ranch was very rundown and took lots of work. I knew I had to get some water in the north end of the ranch because that was where the only feed was and the cattle were not going to it. There was a mud hole type of tank in a tabosa draw. Dick Olsen, Domer's husband, worked for the El Paso Gas Co. He got one of the men to drop a D12 Cat off at my ranch on a Friday, and to pick it up again on Monday. Dick and I spent two of the dirtiest and dustiest days of our lives enlarging that mud hole. It wasn't a mud hole, it was a dry hole. We dug a tank about six feet deep and about seventy--five feet across. In a few days a big rain hit and filled it to the top. I moved all the cattle up there and some blocks of salt so they would locate. I fed them meal a few days until the grass could get started, and I never had to feed them meal again in the ten years I had the ranch. The ranch was twelve sections.

The one thing I must have was water at the north part of the ranch. There was one windmill in the south end with a large storage tank, and plenty of wind to keep it full, if the mill was kept working. The tower was only standing on the ground. Not anchored at all. Some of the X braces were gone, and it was pumping a very small stream of water. I hoped it was because of worn out leathers. Our priority was to get the windmill in good shape. I made some channel irons to bury in the ground in cement to bolt the legs to and I sure slept better when the wind was blowing. The wind blew most of the time and sometimes pretty hard. With the tower fastened solid to the ground our next job was to pull the sucker rods and replace the leathers. The leathers were worn out all right, but close inspection told me, so was the cylinder. To change the cylinder meant pulling all the pipe. It had three and a half inch pipe, and I didn't have the tools to pull it. We put new leathers on the piston then back into the well with the sucker rods. The well was over three hundred feet deep and the cylinder was near the bottom. I changed the stroke from the bottom to the top of the cylinder, but it was worn out there also. In a few months it was only pumping a small stream of water again. When Floyde, Sid, and I pulled the sucker rods, we found one of them rubbed almost in two about halfway down. I replaced the bad rod. The well was crooked, and I found that rod had to be replaced often, or it would wear in two and then the whole enchilada had to come out of the well, which was a big job.

I hired a windmiller, named Ligon, to go to the ranch and pull everything from the well. When he got all the pipe out we measured the distance to the water and it was only seventy--five feet. The well was straight, down to a hundred feet, so I told him to put the new cylinder at about a hundred feet. He did, and it never pumped out and never gave me anymore trouble. We left two joints of pipe standing in the tower that we didn't need. Ten years later and it was still OK.

I fenced the ranch into three pastures. A section on the south end at the windmill, and two sections on the north end with the fence running through the center of the dirt tank I dug with that D12 Cat. The cattle from either side could water. The rest of the ranch was left in one large pasture. That way, I could control those old cows eating habits. I had a well drilled near the tank on the north end. Over three hundred feet and it was drier at the bottom than it was at the top. Now here is the rest of the story of my well. I learned it a few years after I had sold the ranch. The well did have water in it. There was a gravel strata about thirty feet down and the driller sealed it off and kept on drilling until I told him to quit. When the mud seal finally wouldn't hold the water back, it came in and filled the well to about fifteen feet from the top. After all these years I finally went to see for myself and sure enough there was the water. I was totally depending on the expert driller and he fooled me.

After I had wasted money on the dry hole I started thinking of how to use what I had. At first I bought a couple of old discarded underground gas tanks from the Chevron Distributor, Ray Burk. I put one on a trailer to haul water and the other one I put at the dirt tank. The dirt tank would dry up in the spring when I needed it the most. Those old cows drank more water than I had planned on. After one summer of hauling water to the north tank I put my thoughts to work on a better way.

There was a hill about three--quarters of a mile from the windmill. I thought I would build a water tank on top of it and pump from the windmill to it then gravity flow from the hill on up to the dirt tank. I had found a place in Phoenix that made plastic pipe. Two things were going for plastic were the price and very little friction to overcome. I took my transit to the ranch and spent a whole day checking directions and elevations. I found out that the top of my hill was the same altitude as the steel tank I would put at the dirt tank. I went back to the drawing--board and started figuring friction and pressure to pump water the four miles. I came up with about three gallons a minute by laying a one and a quarter inch plastic line with, as I remember, about eighty--five psi of pressure. I think the pipe was rated at one hundred psi.

I laid a plastic pipeline from the windmill to the tank north, about four miles of pipe. I put a ten thousand gallon storage tank in the middle of the ranch and a ten thousand gallon tank at the north dirt tank. I used one and a quarter inch plastic pipe. I bought it in Phoenix at the factory, and since I bought so much, they set me up as a dealer for this area. Once I had mine in and working, I sold pipe to other ranchers. I got good at figuring friction and pressures, and gallons squirting out the far end.

To lay the pipe I used a three point hookup ripper blade on a small tractor. The ripper blade was turned forward and plowed a ditch but left the ditch covered up. I welded a ninety--degree two--inch L of heavy conduit pipe to the ripper. The conduit was looking backwards where the ripper had been. The bottom of the conduit was even with the bottom of the ripper, and the top was well above the ground. I set the tool to run about one foot into the ground. By feeding the plastic pipe into the conduit and moving forward, it was buried and covered up in one operation. The pipe came in three hundred foot rolls. To brake the ground I ran the tool to the north end and back. That made it easy to plow the pipe into the ground. We rolled the pipe out along the route and spliced it together after it was in the ground. The pipe was put on the shoulder of the tractor driver as he drove under it then feeding it into the ground. Sure worked good.

Floyde helped build the pasture fences, and that was quite a job. Part of it was in a snowstorm which I'm sure he will verify, but he was in school in New York when Sid and I put in the water and pipeline. Tio helped me on weekends. Sid and I built the steel water--storage tanks. I'll tell a little more about before we installed the pipeline. Sid and I put a one thousand gallon ex--underground gasoline tank at the dirt tank. We raised it up on railroad ties about four feet to give it a gravity flow to the water trough. Then I put another tank on a trailer with a little pump on it to pump the water from the windmill tank then pump it into the tank at the north pasture. These were abandoned tanks I got from the Chevron people. With the trailer we hauled water to the north end, and those old cows drank it about as fast as we could haul it to them, thus the thinking of the pipeline. Transferring water from one tank to an other was very slow.

I have told how I plowed the pipe into the ground as I went. I sold several miles of pipe to Buck Greer for his ranch at Engle. I told him how I plowed it in and offered to loan him my tool, but he had an old road grader. He angled the blade and dug his ditch then unrolled the pipe in it and spliced it together the full distance then the next day he was to come along and cover it up with the grader. The pipe was laying in a ditch full of sun all day. When he arrived with his grader to cover it up he found the plastic pipe had crawled out of the ditch and was everyplace it didn't belong. It was looped all over the place. After some thinking he knew what had happened. It got so hot in the summer sun that it expanded and literally formed loops and crawled out of the ditch. The only thing to do was get out the old pocketknife. He cut out the loops and put that thing back in the ditch and got it covered up before it did something silly again. He got it covered and smoothed the ground and the next day he turned the water into it. He was running water down hill so all he had to do was open the gate and let it go. Buck went to the discharge end and had some coffee while he waited for the water to come gushing out. Lots of coffee later and he still had no water. He thought there must be a plug someplace. Maybe a rock got in there with all the cutting and splicing. Up the line he went, thinking of how to find where the plug might be, and then he spotted it. Not a plug but a broken pipeline. When he cut the loops out of the line in the heat of the day, then covered it up, it cooled down and went back to its original length, which means it was too short for the ditch. It pulled apart at the splices. He had to dig it up and put all those pieces back in. He finally got the pipe and the ditch the same length, and the water ran fine.

When I was having the well drilled on the ranch I assumed I would get water so I ordered a five stage deep well pump. It was the pump I used to push the water to the storage tanks. It was about four miles with about a hundred feet lift. My calculation was about three gallons per minute and it was almost exactly that. When the water line was set and ready to go, I started the pump then patiently waited for some sign of water at the north end. I ran the pump for hours, but no water, and it appeared there wouldn't be any. I would hold my hand over the end of the pipe at the tank to see if it was building pressure. I couldn't feel any. As the line left the windmill, it went over a hill then down the other side. The hill was the same altitude as the north tank. I finally decided maybe there was an airlock at the top of the hill. I knew about airlocks but I didn't think it could hold back the pressure the pump was putting out. I drilled a one--sixteenth hole at the highest point. The air was there alright. I let it out and wrapped the pipe with inner tube and then I could sure tell that the water was traveling. It still took all the next day before it reached the north tank.

The five stage pump I had bought for the dry hole I had drilled was put to good use and worked fine. I put a ten gallon gas tank and a one gallon oil tank on it. It would run for over twenty-four hours, so it was easy to keep the water tanks full. It seems it took about eighty-five lbs. pressure to pump water to the last tank. I did get about three and a half gallons per minute and that pleased me very much.

We tore down the old corrals, actually, they were down already, we just drug them off into the grease wood and made a garbage dump. I don't know how anyone could run a ranch in the condition that one was. We built new corrals out of lumber and with a branding chute. The house, or barn, was such a mess we threw some gasoline on it and then a match. Floyde and I sat to one side and shot rats as they came out. We built a little barn to keep feed and things we wanted to leave there. Mostly feed because tourists felt free to help themselves. I felt very lucky, however, because the tourists never shot my windmill or my water tanks. For some reason they are a great target temptation to people with guns. Also interesting was a pair of eagles nesting on the platform of the windmill.

The old cows were all colors and a bunch of misfits, but when I got them trimmed up with a dehorn-saw they looked pretty good. The State had me round them up for a bangs-test, so I trimmed their heads at the same time. A wonder I didn't kill all of them, they were so poor. Then I had to hurry and brand those poor little calves. I still thought like ranching in Mexico. "If I don't brand them, someone will eat them." We were still in El Paso and I invited our friends, the Henrys and also the Parkers, to go along for the big roundup. We had a big cookout, Floyde threw Murphy, Henry's dog into the water tank. The dumb little dog couldn't swim. Guess who jumped in to get him out. Floyde got all wet. After we were finished branding, we took a drive around the ranch and Horace Parker shot a jackrabbit. I think his first.

It was great having my own place to hunt. I took friends out there. Dove season was fantastic. Rabbits were so plentiful, we hunted them at night from our Jeeps. Floyde's college friends liked to go with us. They worked with us but they also played with us. Also there were many coyotes. Floyde, Grayson, and I were hunting in the north end. We were using a rabbit squeal. We spotted a couple of coyotes coming towards us, then one changed his mind and ran away. The second one was so excited he ran right among us. We were all three shooting and he was missed entirely. We were looking at each other and trying to figure him out, when there he came back, and again ran right among us. He committed suicide, however, when he made second charge. That time as he went by, one of us got him. We were all smoking him. We couldn't shoot when he was among us for fear of hitting one of us. There were also many rattlesnakes. We had to watch very close for them.

I was trying to teach my horses, Penny and Grasshopper, to come to me for food when I was at the ranch. I carried morrals (nose bags) and grain in my truck so I could feed them wherever I found them. Penny would not let me put the morral on him unless he was captured in the corral, so I fed him from a pan. Grasshopper would take the morral, and when he was finished he would come to me to get it off. One day he was silly and ran away with it on. Now realize the morral covered his face almost to his eyes so he couldn't eat or drink. I went back to town and two days later I went to the ranch, hoping I wouldn't find him drowned. When he tried to drink, he didn't get water in the morral. He was OK, but thirsty and hungry, and for sure looking for a friend. He came running to me with his head down and promised never to do that again. I gave both of them away because when I needed them I couldn't catch them.

Before I got rid of them, I was on Penny, putting some cows in the corral and one broke back. Those cattle had been badly handled and some of them were almost impossible to pen. That old cow was one of those that was spoiled but Penny and I would sure put her in the corral. I had broken him from a colt so I knew him well, I thought. He turned after the cow but she kept going and Penny kept turning, I mean spinning. I don't know if he was mad at me or the cow, but he sure popped me on the ground. He walked up to me as I was getting up and I climbed on him trying to figure what went wrong. I think when he turned back with the cow I leaned over his neck so far that he just couldn't resist the temptation to play. He had never bucked before, or since.

An old paint horse came with the ranch, but he was spoiled, and a little silly, and too old to try to train. I sold him for $100.00. Then I bought a palomino horse from Oklahoma. He was a big horse and gentle. He would come to me anyplace on the ranch and I liked that. When I tried to use him I found out that he was very spoiled, and big enough to prove it. He was nice to ride if I didn't go very far, then he would turn and try to go back to the corral. With some coaxing, I could get him to carry me over the ranch. He would not work cattle, and he was silly and dangerous to rope on. He was young, like six years old, so I thought I could teach him to behave.

One day, I was in no mood for his silliness so I decided to give him a cowboy lesson. I had my rope in my right hand waiting for him to turn back towards the corral. When he tried to turn back to the corral with me I would use that rope on his head until he changed his mind. The plan would have worked, but the first time I hit him he put his head down between his front legs where I couldn't reach it. No matter, because by then I was too busy trying to stay on him. That old buckskin horse went crazy. He bellered and bucked and I traded my rope for the saddlehorn and I dug my spurs in, to hold on. I couldn't quit spurring until he quit bucking and he wouldn't quit bucking until I quit spurring. We sure knocked down a lot of good grass while we were testing each other. He finally gave up and I never told him how close he was to winning. We were friends after that and he seemed to enjoy carrying me over the range. Whatever direction I pointed him, he gave it his best gait. He never would consent to being a good cow horse or rope horse, so I sold him to the forest service.

August 19, 1961 I got my pilot's license. I had already bought a Cessna 170 and I needed an airfield on the ranch. There was a good place to make one right in front of the corrals, and windmill.

I had about a mile of fence covered up with sand between me and the Corralitos. That would be my east fence line. Tumbleweeds had rolled against the fence, then the wind blew sand and covered them up fence and all. It was so bad, my cattle could walk over it. I looked at it every time I went to the ranch and I tried to figure out how to uncover my fence. We had burned and fought tumbleweeds since the day I bought the place, but that time the wind came and rolled them to the fence and covered them in the same operation.

I had a friend with a grader who volunteered to clean the sand and tumbleweeds from the fence and while he was at it he also made me an airfield right in front of the windmill.

I didn't land my plane on it until it rained and settled the loose ground. I used it for many years. It is listed on the New Mexico air--maps. The landing strip sure made it easy for me to check the ranch. Many times I would get up early and fly to the ranch, then back to town in time to open my gas station.

When Uncle Bill was running the Canannea Ranch in Mexico, he rode a mare that he said was one of the best that ever looked through a bridle. While he was there she had a colt and it was given to him. He brought it to his place in El Paso. He had a boy riding him and teaching him and of course gentling him. He called him Lucky. The horse was too smart for his trainer. Bill soon saw that Lucky was going to get out of hand. He gave him to Tio who took him to Columbus to use in his border--crossing stockyards. Tio didn't need him so he gave him to me.

He was some kind of pet and about too much horse for me. When I worked cattle on him and a cow would turn back, I had to hold the horn with both hands to stay on him he was so fast, and quick. He was a quarter horse. When I went to the ranch with my trailer and wanted to take another horse someplace, I had to tie Lucky to keep him out of the trailer.

I was moving some cattle from the north pasture to the south pasture. They were silly and didn't want to go through the gate, so I was moving them slow and easy. The cattle were not wild, they were hard to handle Mexican roping steers. I didn't ride Lucky that day but he followed me and helped me round up the herd. He worked those cattle as if he had a rider on him. I had left the gate open to put the cattle through. As we were getting close with the herd, Lucky went on ahead, got behind the gate and pushed it closed, then he came back to help me with the herd. I thought it was sort of clever, so I didn't say too much to him. That time I tied the gate open. I had to put those ornery steers back together again. They were big Mexican roping steers that I was pasturing for Buck Greer from Truth or Consequences. We were approaching the gate again. Like I said the steers were not wild, they just didn't give a damn. I had them about to the gate again and Lucky was helping me some more. That time he went in front of the herd and stood in the gate and wouldn't let them go by. That was enough and I became very unhappy with him. I put him in the corral, shut the gate and tied it with a rope. Before he could get the rope untied and get out to help me some more, I got those steers through to the other pasture.

He was very bad to open gates. When I sold the ranch I gave him back to Tio, and back to Columbus. Tio had his gates fastened with a horse shoe. Lucky was trying to open one of the gates and got the horse shoe hung in his lip and panicked. He tore his face open and it sure left him messed up.

I got the great idea to raise some shetland ponies and some burros. I would go for the little horses first. When I started to look for some breeding stock I found them hard to find and the ones I could find weren't for sale. I made a trip to Roswell to look at some shetlands I heard about. I found the little horses but I couldn't buy any. I went to Safford, Az. because I remembered little horses there when I was living at Klondyke. I found some, but not for sale. By then I was becoming enthused about my idea. Those little horses are sure enough hard to find, so they had to be a good thing to raise. I put out lots of effort and followed all the leads. I finally bought a shetland mare and a stud. I gave $500.00 for the mare and $350.00 for the stud. In due time, the mare had a very cute spotted colt. They were all paints, and very pretty. I was sure proud of my first little colt. I already had a sale for him when he was old enough to wean. One day when my little colt was about ready to deliver, I was at the ranch and I found his mama but no colt. I figured someone had stolen him. Not long after that I found the little mare dead. I tried to find bullet holes to see if she had been shot. I found a swelling on her nose and decided a rattlesnake had bitten her. They usually bite on the nose and the swelling cuts off the breathing. Several months later I found the colt. Just the skin was left, and I feel sure a snake got him also. I was through with shetlands. I took the little stud to town and sold him.

I was smarter and not ready to give up. I would get some burros because I knew they are tough. A burro would probably kill the rattlesnake. I bought a jack and about ten jennies. Before I knew it, I had burros all over the ranch. Tio caught a couple of wild ones on the WSMR and gave them to me. We tied a chain to a front foot of the wild burros until they settled down enough to run with the herd.

A fellow in Arizona heard about my burros and called to see if I would sell him a little one. I would. He came after it in a station wagon. We poked that little burro in there and shut the tailgate. He thought that little burro would just stand there and ride like a dog and behave himself. I heard from him later, or actually I heard of him. A few miles down the road after he left my ranch, his little burro tried to take the wagon apart. It rearranged the inside, and of course it wanted in the driver's seat. I guess they sure had a time keeping it from the front seat. There were two men.

After a few months I saw that the burro thing had to go, but I couldn't find a buyer. I was the only burro buyer in the country. A friend, Earl Stull Sr. had also bought a few burros and was ready to sell them. We had talked about how smart we were to be raising the things and what a good market we would have. Sears even advertised little donkeys in their catalog. One day Earl came to me and said, "Bill, I have a buyer from Texas for our burros. He wants a bobtail load so he can send his truck after them." We took the Texas man to my ranch to show him my stock. He had already seen Earl's burros and liked them. Some of mine were a little spooky, especially those two from WSMR. I had taken the chains off of their front feet so our buyer couldn't tell them from a standard donkey. One of my young ones had a broken back, and walked funny and ran even funnier. Tio had roped it one day and jerked it over backwards and about ruined it. The Texas man noticed it and said, "What is the matter with that one, he runs funny."

I said, "Tex, that one is a pacer."

"So he is," he said. Earl looked way off and finally had to get out of the truck and walk around some to get his face straight. Tex bought the burros, and Earl and I laughed about the pacer every time we met. We sure sold those burros for a good price. We had cornered the burro market and were sure glad to let it be uncornered.

Floyde and I were doing some work on the ranch. The wind blew most of the time, but that day it was rolling tumbleweeds over the speed limit. My hat blew off. It stood up on the brim and wheeled eastbound. It was headed back to town without me and was passing those tumbleweeds. I ran after it and I was thinking of a story I read when I was in the first grade about a fellow who chased a little gingerman. He got away and so did my hat. After about a half mile, I turned back expecting to see Floyde coming after me in the truck. He was just wandering around the corrals and windmill, so I walked back and sure enough tired. I asked him why the hell he didn't come after me. He said, "Dad, you disappeared and I was looking everyplace for you, sure never thought about you running off out in the pasture." We went to look for my hat and found it bushed up about a mile away. It taught him a lesson, however.

Floyde, Tio, and I were at the ranch. We sent Floyde in Tio's pickup to the north tank to wait for us. Tio and I went around the fence in my Jeep to see that it was not down someplace. We were buying cattle from the Deming Cattle Auction and some of them always tried to go somewhere else, instead of locate. Tio and I were crossing the hills at the north end when I drove into a deep ditch and got one wheel off the ground. I had crossed at an angle. That killed the Jeep entirely. We could see Floyde at the tank with Tio's truck. Tio wanted to walk on down there, about one mile. I told him, "Let's wait a few minutes because Floyde is real good to look around. After my hat chase I knew he would look harder. He will spot us and be up here before long." Sure enough, Floyde climbed on top of the truck and we could tell he was looking hard at the fence line where he knew we would be going. He had Tio's field glasses. Our Jeep was in the brush and down in the ditch. We would be hard to spot but Floyde kept looking.

When I saw him get into the truck I told Tio, "He has spotted us," and sure enough there he came. I still don't know why he couldn't spot me when I chased my hat. I was out in the wide open. I wanted to improve the quality of my herd. In the fall of 1957, Mart and I went to Chickasha, Oklahoma, to pick up a two--horse trailer at the factory. Bill Crabtree, Mom's youngest brother, came by from Phoenix on his way to pick up one and asked me to go along. Tio wanted a trailer, so we took

Mom and went by Vernon, Texas to see Mom's sister, Clara. I bought a couple of hereford yearling bulls from a fellow in Quanah, Texas. I turned them on my ranch. They looked good compared to those all colored cows I had.

I loaded the two bulls into the trailer early one morning and we drove straight home from Quanah. If we stopped for a night I would have to unload the bulls someplace. It was in the winter. We returned home by way of Cloudcroft, N M. I was towing the trailer with a 1957 Chevy station wagon. It was night as we started off the mountain at Cloudcroft. As I went around the first curve it was iced over. I was going slow but, all of a sudden, I had bulls pulling me instead of me pulling them. My quick wishes were that those bulls were still in Quanah and that the trailer was never heard of. It was too late for that so I held on and got things lined up back in order and very carefully came off the mountain to Alamogordo. We arrived home about midnight, and after unloading our things and stretching a little we got in my car and headed to the ranch to unload the little animals. I knew they were as tired as I was. Now here is the part that still makes me shiver. When I went around the corner of the street, here at my house, the trailer came off the ball and stopped in a few feet. To this day I can't figure how I pulled it about six hundred miles, jockeyed the ice at Cloudcroft, and it waited for a nice slow home--street curve to come off the hitch. The only thing I can figure is that the bulls rode forward all the way home, then tried to get in the back seat as I left my house and lifted the hitch off the ball.

I bought three head of registered hereford cows from Mr. Brown in Las Cruces. He had a large farm out on the Jornada. We took a stock--trailer and went to his farm to get them. I took my saddle and rode one of his horses. We had to drive those three cows about a mile to corrals and a loading chute. I have lived my life on, under, and around cows, but I have never been put to such a test as that one. The cows were gentle but spoiled, and could not be driven. I won't try to describe what I was riding. That old pony didn't know about being a cow horse and his ambition to learn was NADA. We finally decided to drive all the cows, because we absolutely could not drive the three. There were about fifteen head. In about three hours we moved them the one mile to the chute and cut out my three cows. The chute was in some corrals on the

Jornada Ranch. We would put one cow in the trailer by pushing and pulling, then go for another. The one in the trailer would get out. We played yo--yo with those cows until I wished I had never heard of them. I was not used to handling cows by pushing and pulling. I thought they should walk on their own.

I took them to the ranch and I was trying to think of how I could show those cows that things were different now. The first thing I would teach them was to be driven. I put them in my branding chute, branded them, then to be sure to change their attitude, I cut their horns off slick to their head. I left them in the corral overnight so they would be sure and locate the water. The next day I went to the ranch to check on them and I turned them into the section pasture at the windmill. On a Friday morning I flew out to the ranch. I circled to look things over and see how the cows were doing. They were on the fence as far towards town as they could get and just standing there. I could tell from my plane that they had not been to water and had no intention of going.

I called Tio and told him about my cows. We went to the ranch to check on the cows. I had told him how ornery they were to handle. We got on horses, he got on Lucky, and we went after them. Sure enough, they hadn't been to water since I turned them loose. We drove them back to the corral but they refused to go in, and that was where the water was. Tio told me to get out of the way and he and Lucky would show me how to put those cows through the gate. Tio decided to put the cows in the corral one at a time. That old cow would not turn. She was pushing and bawling. She was so mad she was crazy. She had never been contested before. She would lean on Lucky and keep running. Tio took his rope down and was whipping her but good. She was sure crowding him, and Lucky was crowding her right back. He was good, and no cow was going to mess with him. I was backed off and watching the show. When the whipping started the old cow got mad. She started to bawl and decided to run away. Lucky was determined she wouldn't, and they were by then at full speed. All of a sudden Lucky's feet got mixed in with the cow's feet. I had heard of someone hitting a buzz saw. That looked like they had hit an eggbeater. They rolled and tumbled and feet were flying in the air, but I couldn't see Tio. I knew he was in the wreck someplace. When they stopped rolling, the cow got up and went into the corral and started drinking. Lucky got up and checked his legs to see which ones he wound up with, his or the cows', and Tio just laid there. I ran over to him. He was knocked out for a few minutes. I dusted him off and he was OK. It is amazing what a cowboy can go through and come out unhurt. He was sore for a while. I had enough of those fine quality cows and looked for a buyer. I sold them to Woodward of Woodward Lumber Co. and he had nothing but trouble with them. He bought them because he knew Brownie, like I did. He still didn't know Brownie's cattle, however, and I did.

In 1966, I sold all the cattle from the ranch. Tio and I went together as partners to buy and sell cattle. He would buy the cattle and I would furnish the pasture. We would split the profit, if we made any. We loaded the ranch with young steers. We had a good summer and they were fat and big but the market was down. We couldn't make any money if we sold them. Smith and Morris had brought in a hundred head of little Florida brahma calves and they couldn't give them away. We are both in trouble as far as making any money. They needed to sell their little calves and pay their bank, and we needed to have collateral for our bank or sell our big cattle. Our steers had to go because they were at a point where they would start to loose pounds rather than gain. We all four met and drank a lot of coffee and came up with a solution. We would trade cattle pound--for--pound and the one with the most pounds would get paid thirty cents per pound for the extra pounds. Tio and I looked over their little cattle, then took Smith and Morris to the ranch and let them look over our big cattle. We all did some range weight guessing, and concluded that Tio and I would owe them some money. They were planning on a shrink because we had to round up ours and ship them to Las Cruces to the scales. What they didn't know was how Tio and I could move cattle and gain weight at the same time. We were sure they would owe us money, and quite a bit. We didn't tell them because they guessed the way we wanted them to. Their calves were in the Black corrals on Picacho Street in Las Cruces. Morris had his own cattle truck. Tio and I rounded ours up and had them in the corrals at the ranch, ready to ship. We tossed them a few bales of hay, put some blocks of salt in there with them, and so all they did was eat hay, lick salt, and drink water. They were full and settled down. We took the first load of their calves to the ranch, then a load of ours to town. Black had scales at his corrals. We loaded our steers light so they wouldn't squeeze out those pounds. It took three truck--loads each way to complete the trade. By the time we were loading the last load of their little cattle, they knew they would owe us a bunch of dollars. As we were trying to get their little cattle to go up the chute into the truck, Smith called to Morris, "Hand me another one of them little SOBs." When they took the fat cattle to El Paso, they really learned about shrinkage. They hauled them all in two trips rather than three as we did.

After we had our little cattle branded, vaccinated, and turned into the small pasture until they would locate, Tio and I were returning to town and he said, "Bill, I have always wanted to own a hundred head of cattle, why don't you sell me your half interest and lease me the ranch?" I did. That night it was cold and snowed and those little cattle cuddled up in a fence corner driven by the snow. The ones on the outside kept pushing, and the ones next to the fence couldn't move. When we went to check on them the next day there were about twelve dead calves that had been smothered.

We went often to check on them. After a few days we put them in the big pasture so they could roam the entire ranch. Brahma cattle are crazy to handle, so we started to train them for roundup time. We carried a bale of hay in the pickup. We would toss a chip to them and before long they would come to us when we drove through the ranch, and would follow the truck. When it came time to sell them we just drove into the corral and every one of them followed us in. There again, the only thing a cow man can sell is pounds.

On one of our trips to see how those little steer's health was, we jumped a coyote near the north tank. Tio always had the sawed off .30.30 and he was a good shot with it. The coyote was running straight away from us, and Tio pulled off as pretty a shot as I had ever seen him do. That coyote literally stood on his head as he went over, his tail standing up. He was off about a hundred yards. That was almost out of sight for that short gun. We went over to him and Tio gave him a kick to turn him over to see where his good shot had hit him. The coyote was lying there with his eyes open and a grin on his face. As Tio kicked him he grabbed hold of Tio's foot and held on. Tio handed me the rifle and told me to shoot him but not in the head. It reminded me of the time the mouse had Bounce by the nose when we were kids at Barranca. Tio and the coyote were looking eye to eye. The coyote knew that if he turned loose and ran, it would be suicide, just like that mouse, but his choices were few, and decreasing. He turned loose and ran and I got him. We looked him over and found a very small crease in the top of his head right between his ears. Barely cut the skin.

I have mentioned Grayson Meerscheidt. Our ranch, at one time, belonged to his dad. He ran sheep on it. He has an older brother named Stuart. I got acquainted with this family when I first came to Las Cruces and we have been close friends ever since. They like to hunt and fish and we have done a lot of it together and still do. This is one of the families that came here in the early days and helped put the Las Cruces valley on the map.

I bought the ranch in 1957. I sold it in 1967. I had it a little over ten years. I got it with eighty--five head of cattle. In a few years I sold the cattle and paid off the notes I had signed for it.

1805 WEST PICACHO

Changes were happening in the little town of Las Cruces, and I could see that I needed to make a change also. Valley Drive had been opened to traffic and the tourist business was passing me by. My place was scheduled to be torn down in the not too far future, so a move I had to make. I was offered the Chevron station at 1805 West Picacho. I went with E.Y. Beaver to look it over and see what I needed to lease it. I got along good with the Chevron people so it was mine right then. With Floyde, Sid, and Andy, we made short work of transferring our tools and merchandise. I didn't sell anything because no one moved into 302 S. Main. We had a very close call while moving the quart cans of oil. We were unloading it, one can at a time. I backed the pickup into the bay and was tossing the cans to Floyde. He was catching them and sitting them on the shelf. We were tossing them about twelve feet. We got into a rhythm and we were sure moving the cans, when he stopped to adjust one he had just put on the shelf. I had already tossed the next can. He turned around just in time to catch it in the face. We were very lucky it didn't do much damage, but for sure it scared us and we have never done that again.

When E.Y. offered me the station, I had one stipulation. That I could put in my front--end machine. He said, "That will be no problem at all. I will get permission for you." It was a pit type machine and took a hole in the floor about ten by ten, by three feet deep. I was barely moved in when I hired a contractor and put my machine in the wash bay. I didn't like to wash cars, anyhow. The men were just finishing up the hole in the ground when E Y came by to see how I was getting along in my new place. When he saw what I had done, he fell out of his car and cried, and rolled on the ground and cursed, and I thought the man had gone crazy. I told him I thought he said he would get me permission, so I went on with it.

He said, "Yes, but that takes time." I learned early in the game that when you have a sale made, shut up. I had my hole ready for my machine, so all I had to do was let him get over the shock and I was sure he could handle it, and he did. I knew it would take time to get a permit, in fact I didn't think Chevron would give me one. I also knew that the most they could do was make me put it back, so it was worth the chance, and it turned out just right. That decision made me lots of money.

Mart and I flew to Dublan, Mexico, in my Cessna 170 and when I was tying my plane down a fellow at the field helped me. He pushed the stabilizer over a pipe sticking out of the ground and creased it some. I flew it home and asked my instructor, Bob Crawford, who or where I could get it repaired. He told me that Harry Burrell was the best, if I could get him to work on it. Harry worked for Stahman Farms. I called Harry, and he did work on it. Harry maintained my 170 until I sold it. That was the start of a long--lasting friendship. When he did the first annual, I thought he had destroyed my 170. He had been working on it, I should say taking it apart. I went to the hanger to see how he was doing. As I walked up, and he did it on purpose, he took hold of the seat belts and with his bare hands twisted and pulled and broke both of them. I had never seen machinery tested that way. He told me that if he could break them, I needed new ones. He was right, but he sure took my breath for his trouble to show me. I sold the 170, February 15, 1965. I was a few months without a plane. Harry didn't care for it anyhow. It was too marginal for a four place. A friend flew to the ranch with me one morning and he liked my plane so much I sold it to him with the hanger.

Harry heard of a plane in El Paso that he might buy to fix up and sell. The price sounded good. He asked me to go with him. I did, just for the ride. He looked at the plane and it wasn't what he had in mind, but tied there on the field was a Cessna 180 with a for--sale sign in the window. We took the phone number. Harry told me that it was the type of plane I needed for the ranch or anything else I should want to do with an airplane. It sure looked big and mean to me, but he said he would teach me to fly it. He had worked with me in the 170, so I knew that he was a good flyer and a good instructor. I called the fellow and we set up an evening to look at it.

The fellow flew it from El Paso to the Crawford Airfield east of town in Las Cruces. Harry showed up with Bob Chamberlain in tow, and with books. Harry told me he had one question. He said, "Bill, if we inspect this plane and OK it, are you ready to buy it or are you just looking and thinking." I told him I had already been to the bank and had permission to write him a check. They looked it over like an inspection and pronounced it a good airplane. The seats were ragged and the guy had an army blanket over them. It looked terrible. I bought the plane that evening and the fellow had to walk home. I mean he didn't fly. After the inspection, Harry took it up for a spin. The fellow was sure nervous and asked me if he could fly a 180. I told him, "It is too late to worry, let's just wait and see." Sure enough he could. April 15, 1965.

Harry told me to get Bob Crawford to check me out in it, then to fly it some to get the feel of it then he would get with me and teach me how to fly a real airplane. I did and he did. Let me give credit right here where it belongs. Harry maintained my 170 and flew with me some but didn't really take me in tow until I bought the 180. He said he would help me learn to fly it and he did. I spent many very nervous hours with him sitting in the right seat. Harry was good. He didn't make me nervous but that damned 180 sure did. Evenings after work he would stop by my place for coffee then to the flying yard we would go. Harry made it possible for me to be able to fly with confidence that I could handle the 180. Harry was right about what a great airplane it was. Only those who have flown one, can know what I mean. After Harry had taught me to fly it with some confidence, he brought Brad Blake into the game. They relayed me. I mean when one of them got tired of me the other one took me on. We flew together a lot and often. During those training flights, no matter which one of them was with me, I noticed he would touch my elbow ever once in a while. I never learned why until years later. They were checking for sweat. Not if, but how much. Harry and Brad are my very special friends.

To get me started with the 180, Bob Crawford had me fly to the municipal field and shoot some landings. I did and they were good. Bob never talked much. He said, "Let's go home. Tie the plane down and we'll try it again tomorrow." The next day he had me shooting landings again on the municipal field and they were good. We went around for another landing and he told me to do a full--flap landing. On short final, I reached down there and pulled the flap handle all the way up. Now that is a bunch of flaps on a 180 and that old airplane changed its disposition right there and then. I didn't make a three--point and I sure didn't make a wheel landing. I landed on both wheels, but jumped into the air. I was trying to land it and was getting the wheel back as I should, I thought, and down we came again. That time on one wheel, a bounce up in the air again and down on the other wheel. By that time my air speed was gone. Bob took over the controls and with full throttle we made a go--around, and headed for home to the Crawford field. My thought was that I knew it was a very mean airplane. Bob asked me what I was going to do. I said, "I thought," and that was all I got to tell him. He cut me off right there. He said, "Bill, you do your thinking with the throttle all the way in." I heard him good and never forgot it. We landed at his field and he told me to take it up and practice and never forget to use the throttle. Then I started flying it with Harry and he taught me to love that throttle.

My business was good and Sid was doing a good job running it with Andy's help. Mart and I decided to go to the world fair in New York. Floyde and Connie were there. He was going to the University of New York for his Master's. I had just bought a new Chevy wagon, a 1964. We were about two weeks on the trip. We really enjoyed New York with Floyde and Connie to show us around, and that they sure did. I had spent some time there during the war so it wasn't all new to me. Of course the high light was the fair. It was very exciting. We went up there by way of Dallas, Arkansas, Tennessee, Virginia, Washington DC, Maryland, New Jersey, Philadelphia, and finally, to New York City.

On our return trip we went through Pennsylvania to Niagara Falls. What a sight to see so much water falling. We spent the night in Canada then crossed back to the US at Buffalo. We followed the lake drive to Chicago, then turned south. We hit St. Louis, then Oklahoma City. We stopped at Raydon Oklahoma to see Bill Parks, then Amarillo and home. A very nice and memorable trip and Floyde and Connie made it special.

In 1964, I was working my Chevron station and happy with what I was doing and how I was doing it. A fellow drove into my drive, hopped out of his car and introduced himself. "I'm Jim Shelton and I own this place. Would you like to buy it?" I told him yes. Then he told me the story. His lease with Chevron was almost up and he wanted to sell the property, and since I was on it, he would give me first chance. Tony Parker wanted to buy it and turn it over to Don Nichols. Both of them were my good friends. I learned I was close to no place to go.

When I had the papers all signed I started looking at how to deal with Chevron. They would lease it from me for ten years and pay me two cents per gallon, then lease it back to me for one and a half cents per gallon. I would be in the same control position as before which was none. Chevron would be in charge and I liked to do things they didn't like. Tony was deformed because I got it instead of him, and wouldn't give me a good deal at all. He was a distributor for one of the gas companies, I think Sinclair. I went to the Mobil office. I walked in and asked to see the boss. "I'm the boss." It was Thelma Flowers. She was reared back in her chair with her feet on the desk and smoking a cigar. I told her I had bought my station and thought maybe she would be interested in leasing it from me. She said she would pay me two cents per gallon and paint the station the Mobil colors and put up a sign. I was with them for eight years and enjoyed it very much. They were good people and we were very good friends.

Now that I owned the place, I didn't have to ask anyone what I could do with it. I had wanted to expand for some time.

I had Sid and Andy with me and I needed something for them to do when we didn't have a customer in the drive. I kept thinking of the car business. One day a customer drove up in a new Studebaker. There was not a dealer in town, and I asked him some questions of how I could contact, and who, to get a dealership. That was one of those days. He told me he was looking for places to put in dealers. That was his job. He had me sign some forms that he would take to the office in South Bend, Indiana. Before long they had me set up as a dealer and set me up with a floor plan with CIT. I got boxes of books and forms of how to order cars. My cars came from Canada. They were shipped by train to Belen, then by truck to my place. I had a good parts business because there hadn't been a dealer in Las Cruces for some time and all the Studebaker cars needed something. I collected for orders in advance because all orders were special. I didn't stock anything. In 1966, the Studebaker Co. shut its doors. I only stocked about six cars at a time so I was in good shape. They were good little cars and I was just about to get the hang of it.

Since I had gotten a feel for the car business, I would like to stay in it. I went to my bank, the First National and talked to Mr. Baker. He set me up with a floor plan to buy used cars. Sid and I went to Phoenix to see what we could find. Mart's cousin, Ab Taylor, who went to school with us at the JSA in Mexico, was my very good friend. He was the Used Car Manager for Rudolph Chevrolet. I bought two cars from him and took them home to see what we could do with them. I made some money and went back for more. That time he wanted to sell me something I didn't like, so I went to Courtesy Chevrolet on Camelback. I met the Used Car Manager. He made me feel welcome and explained how they sold used cars wholesale to dealers. I bought cars from Courtesy for about twelve years. One of their managers called me cousin. His mother was an Adams. He took me to the Southwest Auto Auction and helped me get set up there and I still buy at the auction. So I have been buying cars in Phoenix for about twenty--five years. It is now 1990.

Back to my Cessna 180. It was sure handy for the ranch, but when I got into used car buying I really put it to good use. I would fly to Phoenix and buy some cars. Mart would drive one home and then on the weekend I would fly three drivers over there and they would drive some more home. We had two tow bars and so towed many of them. It was slow because we were buying so many. I found a place in LaFayette, Georgia, that sold auto transports. I called and talked to the man. He had all kinds and sizes to choose from and he said he would put them together any way we wanted. I put Sid on an airline plane and told him to go see what he could do. If he didn't find something that looked good to come on home. He called me and told me that he found what looked good and was on his way home. I think he was about three days hurrying home with it. It would haul five cars, two on the bottom and three on top. He drove it home with my dealer license.

As soon as I had the insurance and title registered on the transport, Sid and I went to San Angelo for a load of cars. I bought five very worn-out cars. It was our first time to load a transport and Sid was the driver. Room for a mistake when driving a car up those ramps was very POQUITO. We loaded the bottom first. The cars were so bad they didn't even have enough power to pull up the low ramp without a run at it. It took Sid several tries before he let the car go into the cage. When he did get a car in there he couldn't get out of it. He had to crawl out the window. We had the bottom loaded and that made the top sure enough look spooky. He would back way down the street to get up speed to try and go up the runners to the top. He wouldn't hold the gas down when all he could see was blue sky. He knew he would go on over and off the front end. I was on top to guide him, but when he couldn't see me as he was climbing up he would stop. I decided he couldn't run over me if he tried so I told him to keep coming and I would get out of the way. I told him to go around the block and get all the speed he could. Watch me and if I was still telling him to come on, then let her fly. He did and that time he topped out with no power left. I had paid $75.00 and $100.00 for those old cars and they sure made some money when we got them home.

I would go to Phoenix and buy a load of cars and call Sid. He would take the transport and get them. Sid and I went to Dallas and Fort Worth but didn't find anything we could use at what we wanted to pay. I went to Denver to look for some old cars, and on the way Mart and I stopped at Pueblo for the night. I went looking around the car agencies there and bought eight cars. I called Sid to bring the transport. They were all old cars and cheap. One was an old International pickup. I put one on my car for Mart to tow and I tied two together for me to tow. Sid hauled the rest. We were two days coming home. We called Floyde as we came through Albuquerque and he and Connie met us for coffee. We enjoyed those get--togethers. I sold the old International while we were still unloading it. Sid went into business for himself so I sold the transport. I sure didn't need it without Sid to drive it.

In 1968, I bought a new Chevy and with Marty, Bonnie, and Mart, I headed for Florida. Maybe I could buy cars there and have them shipped to Las Cruces worth the money. I couldn't but we had a nice trip. Marty and Bonnie enjoyed swimming in the ocean. We took the coastal route going down, and I--10 returning. In Orlando, we stayed at a Johnson Motel. The kids enjoyed the swimming pool. There was a high slide to drop into the pool and Marty was having a time on it. Bonnie couldn't quite get herself talked into going down it, but she couldn't let Marty have all the fun either. She finally decided she would go down it if I would be ready to get her if she had trouble. I was at the edge of the pool just in case, but that wasn't enough. She said, "Daddy, get all the things out of your pockets so you can get me." She wanted me to be ready. She went down the first time, and then she never quit. The reason I went to Florida was that the State had passed a law that all cars had to pass a smog test, and the older cars would be too expensive to modify, which would make them cheap. By the time I got there, the State had rescinded the law on older cars.

In November 1971, I made Floyde an offer to quit his very good job at Sandia and join me in my business. I offered him half interest. We knew that it was only a short time when I--10 would open and my highway trade would be gone. He and Connie went back to Albuquerque and talked and thought. I'm sure it was a hard decision, but they called me in about a week and told me they had decided to take me up on the offer. Then was when I hoped with all my heart that it was the right thing for them to do, and someday we would know. They moved to Las Cruces in the latter part of December, just in time for the Christmas rush. We named our business, ADAMS AUTO CENTER, Floyde's idea. We opened our bank account as BF 72. My idea. Bill and Floyde 1972.

The ribbon--cutting to open I--10 was about April 1972, and for sure our traffic was gone. We were adjusting to the change. Our business was good except for gasoline. Used cars and shop work. Bill Russell showed up and wanted to buy my dinner. He was with Chevron when we moved to Las Cruces. He left and I hadn't seen him for years. After some talk, I asked him what was his reason for buying me dinner. He was the Dunlop tire rep. for this area. Dunlop was going to put a tire store in Las Cruces. They were interviewing several prospects and would like to include us, Floyde and me. A night meeting was set up at one of the motels. At the meeting was St. John and his two top salesmen, Bill Russell, a Dunlop rep. from Denver, and Floyde and me. St. John had the Dunlop warehouse in El Paso. Those fellows all knew what the meeting was for. Floyde and I didn't yet. St. John wanted to set up a dealer in Las Cruces to sell tires from his warehouse, and he would take all the year--end bonus. We soon caught onto what they were trying to do to us. We told them we had a better deal than they were offering, and we own our property at 1805 West Picacho. Then they got down to doing business. Bill had already checked our credit--rating and knew we could handle the finances.

We finally settled for a distributorship. Our tires would be purchased combined with St. John and the total would be the bonus percentage. That would raise his take and we would get the amount that our purchase created. We would get the same percent, but only on our purchase. It sounded good for us because we would have to buy $100,000.00 to qualify for a bonus, and we knew we couldn't do that, at first anyhow. The first year, St. John took all the money. We didn't like that, so we read our contract some more and decided that wouldn't happen again. It didn't but he sure got unhappy with us. He got a lawyer and sicked him on us but when we talked to the lawyer, he went back to St. John and told him he had better behave while he didn't have much trouble. The whole thing they had set up with us was not legal. We were in the driver's seat. This area was later put in the Dallas region, rather than the Denver, and the Dallas office didn't go along with the deal that had been put on us. We had a new rep. shortly, and St. John has been gone for years. Nineteen years later and we are still selling Dunlop tires.

Bob and Marty both worked for me there on Picacho, but Bonnie didn't get to work for me until we got the tire store on North Main. She worked for me until she got married. She detailed cars, and kept my books, and was learning to sell cars when she flew the coop.

FARMS

I sold the ranch and had some cash to do something with. My neighbor, Dave Steinborn, was in the motel business and also was getting into the real estate business. He came to me one day with a deal. There were some farms for sale at Vado, NM. About eighty--five acres. I still held mortgage notes on the ranch. I traded them for the farms. I had already bought a sixteen acre farm from Mrs. Mims in Fairacres. She is the same person I bought the ranch from. I sold that farm to Sid and sold Floyde a thirteen--acre farm at Vado. Bob didn't want to farm. He was the only smart one of us. The Vado farm on the west side of the river had a good well and pump on it. Sid put a well and pump on his and Floyde put a well and pump on his. I put a well and pump on the ten acres I offered to Bob. They were east of the river. Floyde's farm was east of the river. The Vado farms all adjoined the river. The wells were because those were years of very little lake water.

I sold my cotton allotment and we all planted pecan trees. That was sure the way to get rich, was with pecans. Stahman had already proved it could be done. We went to Stahman for the information we needed and bought our trees from him.

All we had to do was plant the trees, half inch for size. There was more of it under ground than on top. Water them once a week, and keep the weeds from taking over. Floyde and Connie spent weekends from Albuquerque, on the farm. Mart watered them while I flew to Phoenix to buy cars. We all had blisters from wearing out hoes and shovels, and the weeds still covered up our little trees. One thing we did right was buy a new tractor and tools. It was because of our hard work and long hours on weekends trying to get the weeds controlled that we lost Marty. We were working late and were all tired, when Marty fell into the rototiller and was killed. Floyde and Sid were there with me. If I had been alone I couldn't have stood it. That was a tragedy I will never get over. He was buried on his thirteenth birthday, September 9, 1969.

Sid lived on his farm and when Floyde moved to Las Cruces he lived on his also. We got the idea of putting sheep in there to eat the weeds and grass. We fenced the farms on both sides of the river. That was another blister project. We made a good fence to keep the sheep in and the dogs out. We were putting the finishing touch on it and talking about what a good job we had done when we looked up and saw a big runaway steer coming our way, and inside our field. He was wet so we knew he had come through the Del Rio Drain. But when he got to our fence he went through it as if it wasn't there. While we are still in shock, there came a man from Vado after his wild steer. We told him, "Yes, he just went by us. He went over the levee and he is down there in the river some place." He told us his steer was bad to go through fences. We believed him.

The fence did keep the sheep in, but the dogs were some kind of trouble. It sure didn't keep them out. We found out that the valley is full of wild dogs and they loved sheep meat. We bought the sheep in Roswell at the auction, and hauled them home in a stock trailer. All the long hours and hard work on the farms gave us the collateral to buy the property at 2001 South Valley Drive. When we look back and think of the blisters then look at our business on Valley Drive, we don't feel so bad. My blisters are sort of like my saddle sores, I still remember where they were and how they got there.

2223 NORTH MAIN

In May 1972, we moved to our new place on North Main. St John had a ten year lease on the place and signed it over to us. Us being Adams Auto Center. The property belonged to P.T. Gonzalez. We were well stocked with used cars, but the Dunlop people didn't want us to have them, so we sold them to Sid. We were then neighbors to him, and he was also selling used cars. In November 15, 1972, I sold the 180 airplane. Since we were not going to Phoenix for cars we didn't need it and we did need the money.

December 19, 1972, Adams Auto Center had a chance to buy a third interest in a 250 Comanche airplane. I told the two partners that we would buy them out if and when they wanted to sell. Even though Floyde and I owned a third of the airplane, the other two partners wouldn't let Floyde fly it. He had instructor's rating but one of them didn't like him, and that was it. We just bided our time.

Harry was flying with me at night to get me some night experience. When we would go out to fly, the right seat would be shoved all the way forward. Harry kept telling me, "Bill, don't shove it forward, just leave it back." One evening we flew into the night and when we put it in the hanger, he told me again, "Here is the way to put this plane into the hanger, straight, and leave the seat back, like so." We closed the hanger and went home.

I was going to Arizona the next morning. When I opened the hanger door, the plane was in there at an angle. I opened the airplane door and the seat was all the way forward. I called Harry to come and help me look at the situation. The fuel tanks had been topped also. Harry was soon there and we found damage on the bottom of the right wing, and a little damage on top of the left wing. Then we knew why the seat was pushed forward. Someone was using it at night. They disconnected the tack cable for their drug run then connected it when they put it back in the hanger. To do, that the seat was pushed forward to lay on, to get under the instrument panel. It was all so clever that the three partners had never suspicioned their long--range Comanche was running drugs (it had tip tanks).

We called the Narcos to come out and give it a very close inspection for drugs because there was no doubt it was being used at night and had been for some time. The two partners thought I had wrecked it and was trying to pass it off. When they were convinced that they had been furnishing a plane for the drug runners they were very unhappy. In a few days one of them came to me and asked if I still wanted to buy him out. I did, and wrote him a check then and there. That gave Floyde a third owner, and I was a third owner. The partner we still had was the one who wouldn't let Floyde fly it. His say was gone, and he was not happy about it. He would sell his third, but he wanted more money than we paid the other fellow. We told him we would give him the same price or we would sell him the whole thing. I was pushing, because I knew he didn't fly it very much and I also was quite sure he didn't have the money. He phoned, and called me some names, then his wife called me some names that he forgot, then he said he would take my check. It was a good airplane and we used it a lot. Since we knew there were many hours on the engine that were not recorded, Harry did a major on it. He found most of the rings broken. It was time for the major.

July 1, 1976, Mart and I drove to Alaska. We were back in the car business again. I had picked up a couple of 1973 Blazers in Phoenix. We had heard that four--wheel--drives sold good up there. We would tow one of them and sell it at Fairbanks to pay for our trip. We thought it was a good idea. We drove a Ford three--quarter ton with a camper, and planned to sell it also and fly back. When we got to Fairbanks, the pipeline was winding down and there were 4x4 pickups on every carlot. Those guys wouldn't even look at my Blazer for no price. I started looking to sell my pickup camper, and there was one on every corner. I had a cousin there in Fairbanks, Pearl Kenemore. She is Tom Crabtree's oldest, and about my age. I had known her when we were little kids in Arizona. She and her husband, Buck, treated us great. At the museum was the airplane that killed Wiley Post and Will Rogers. I sold the Blazer to Pearl and Buck. We drove the Alcan both ways. We were on the trip about five weeks.

One of the highlights of the trip was the day and night we spent at Whitehorse. It is on the Yukon river. We took a tour--boat ride up the river which was very interesting. The entire river squirts through a narrow gorge. The boat was about a sixty footer. The captain had no trouble going upstream, but to shoot that fast water going downstream was sure enough tricky. It was so tricky that in the old days there was a little railroad that went around the gorge to haul the cargo. The boats would not chance shooting it. It was a very interesting trip, but enough of Alaska. I still flinch when I think of the mosquitoes.

Our business was good and we had many service calls. Floyde and I decided we should get a wrecker of our own. That was in the spring of 1977. Sid had one he bought when he was in Nebraska. We called the same place where Sid had bought his. The fellow had what he thought we wanted. Floyde would go up there and buy it if he liked it. By that time, Connie was working for us at the store. Our secretary. Temporary, to help us out, she said. We sure needed someone to handle the money for us. Connie and I went to town to get Floyde a ticket for the airline. On our way to the travel agency, I asked her if she could keep a secret. If so, we would have some fun with Floyde. She wasn't sure. I told her, "Let's get two tickets, but not let Floyde know." She liked the idea, but how would she ever fool Floyde. Someway she packed his clothes and got hers in there without him knowing it. Mart and I took them to El Paso. Floyde thought she was following him to the plane steps to tell him goodbye. She got him a good one and we still laugh about it, and especially Floyde. The wrecker was good. He bought it and drove it home. That made a fun trip for them. The wrecker was bought in Kansas.

Towards the end of the summer of 1977, we could see our business was growing and we had used up half of our lease. We needed to start thinking of buying a place. We started to pay attention to what was available around town, and noticed the Ford Tractor Agency building was for sale. The tractors had been gone for some time. Haynes was using it for a warehouse. It belonged to Grindell and Rawlins, the insurance people. They had tried the Chrysler Agency there, but it didn't work like they wanted.

2001 SOUTH VALLEY DRIVE

We bought the place at 2001 South Valley drive and moved there in October 1977. The place was badly rundown but with lots of work, and since Connie and I liked to paint, we got it in good shape. The story of our purchasing it should be told here. Floyde and I looked it over and stepped and measured and did lots of thinking and it looked like we could make a good auto repair shop out of it. It belonged to Grindell and Rawlins and they wanted cash only, no financing. I knew Bob Rawlins real well from our flying days, so I went to see him. He had a buyer on it and had to hold it for a week more. If he didn't get the money Bob would deal with me. The fellow didn't get his money so Bob called me. I went to see him and we agreed on thirty days for me to raise the cash. We shook hands and I felt good. When he told Grindell, he said let's make Adams honest. Draw up a contract and have him pay $1000.00 earnest money. So we did. Floyde and I went to the First National Bank and borrowed the money. It was a very good purchase for us and it gave us a home for our business. The earnest money and contract was what saved the deal, but that would be the rest of the story.

Our business took off as if we had not moved across town. We had spent five years building our business on North Main. When we moved across town we were afraid maybe we would have to start over. The shop was good and the used cars were good. We bought the vacant lot north of us also from Grindell and Rawlins, and made a carlot there to separate the shop and used cars.

We started looking for an auto transport and found one in Los Angeles. It was the Hadley people who do all of Ford's hauling. They sell the older trucks. Floyde, Connie, Mart, and I went to L.A. to see what they had that we could use. They had what we wanted and at a price we liked. It was a seven car hauler. The salesman thought the engine was bad so he gave us a good price. We listened and decided it was worth a chance. We thought it was OK.

We had taken our checkbook, but they wouldn't even look at it. No problem. We went to a bank near by and planned to bring back the cash. That was the day we got a California lesson. We walked into the bank and were greeted nicely until we told the lady what we wanted. No way. We just stood there and asked to talk to someone else. She called another lady over to explain, for us to leave. We didn't. By then we had drawn some attention and people were looking at us as if we had asked for the impossible. We asked to talk to whomever was in charge of the bank. A fellow came out of his office to give us a NO WAY that we could understand. The girls had filled him in on what we wanted so he was ready for us. We told him that all we asked was for him to do us the courtesy of calling our bank and then go from there. I had one of Dell Avant's cards in my pocket which I presented to him. He was gone to his office for a few minutes then came back out where we were, still being stared at by those two important ladies. He said, "How much was it you fellows need?" He told one of the ladies to cut us a check for whatever we asked for. When we took the cashier's check to pay for the truck, the salesman was very surprised also. The banker didn't tell us what Dell had told him but it must have been good.

Floyde bought a new Honda G L 1000 and I bought a Honda 400 for Bonnie. We tied them on our truck and headed home. Floyde and Connie driving the truck and Mart and I following. Climbing out of Indio, and as Floyde was going to shift gears, something broke in the clutch linkage. He was able to put it in the lowest gear, then start the motor and get it to the rest stop at the top of the hill. I went back to Indio and was able to get a part, and Floyde put it in there in the hot sun and grease. The engine was OK and we got a lot of use out of the transport.

We had so much business, we got Sid to come and run the shop, and I ran the cars. Floyde was able to be where he was needed, and that was all the places. Sid did a good job for us and was with us for about a year. After he left we built an office on the carlot and I moved over there to run it.

When the Columbia landed at White Sands, Bob was working for the radio station KGRT. He went for the radio station. He got passes for Floyde and me. We had a front--line flatbed trailer to stand on to watch history in the making. It was very interesting and of course very special to get to see it from such a vantage point.

In January 1980, Floyde and I were having coffee in El Paso. We were down there trying to collect on a car we had sold. I told him I thought it was time for me to retire. I would like to turn things over to him. I felt he should be free to make decisions without my interference. I could see that we were in a position to really go forward if things worked out. I felt maybe I was holding him back on things he would do if I was out of the way. I was right, and he has made it into a first--class, and well--organized business. A far cry from what he came from Albuquerque to join me in. I am very proud of it and glad I was part of the original. I should give Connie the most credit however, because she has stayed in there and done a fine job with the finances. That has given Floyde complete freedom to run and develop the business.

We agreed to each write down a proposal of how to divide our assets, and liabilities. We looked at Floyde's first and I accepted it. It was very near the same as what I had in mind and what I had written down. I knew we were both trying to be fair. Basically, he took the shop and I took the carlot. We stayed partners on a few things like trailers, airplane, and he gave me an office and a little shop in the back that we had used to paint cars in. I now use it to repair boat props. I later sold the farms and the carlot.

I went to St. Louis and learned to repair boat propellers. I enjoy that. It leaves me time for things Mart and I enjoy. We travel a lot and of course I like to go fishing.

When I was doing so much flying to Phoenix I always passed over a volcanic mesa on the Indian reservation at San Carlos. It is a high volcanic flow mesa and completely bluffed in on all sides. The only way up or down is by trails and not many of them. I know this because Dad had told me how he once caught wild horses on the mesa before they could get to a trail to go down. My life has been working and climbing to the top of this mesa and I am there. I'm enjoying being there, and I know that someday I will travel one of those trails back down off this mesa. I can see now, it doesn't take very long to live seventy years.

22

Fannie Ada Crabtree Adams

I must dedicate this part of my book to my mother. The last and best. She came from a large family and was raised in Texas in the Crowell and Vernon area. Her dad worked on the Wagner Ranch when she was a young girl. She was noticing boys yet, because I have heard her talk about Guy Wagner. He was about her age. Then her dad went to share cropping on farms so there would be away for all the family to pitch in. I have heard her tell of the cotton she picked, and I thought, "I would make sure I kept my life away from those cotton patches." I did chop cotton one day. I was given a hoe and a row and told to chop cotton. I did. I left the weeds, and all the time thinking there was something about cotton chopping I just didn't savvy. I got fired.

After her dad died, her mother moved to Duncan, Arizona. They moved to Duncan because her uncles, Bud and Hyrum Nunn, were already there and farming. I thought they were rich folks when I was a little kid and we went to visit them. They were her mother's brothers. Mom was working in the only restaurant at the Carlyle Mines near Duncan when she met Dad. I think she was sixteen. They were married in 1917, and about two years later I got acquainted with her. I stayed in close touch with her for fifty--five years and got to know here real well. The longer I knew her the more I loved her. I think of how she worked so hard and raised seven clean and fat little kids. I have told about so much of my time spent with Dad, and of course that was the way we worked, but Mom made the home, and we had a good one.

As I was getting older and dating girls, she always waited up for me and wanted to know if I had a good time. She knew I would be hungry so she had something good to eat and we would sit and talk. While she was waiting for me she would make pies, and that was the special treat. Sometimes I would even cut my date short so I could hurry home to chat with Mom and eat some of her good pie. (that line is for my then girlfriend if she happens to see it) Mart liked Mom so much, is the reason she married me, and Mom loved her.

Mom was very disconfiado when we moved to Mexico in 1927, but she found some wonderful and life--long friends there in the Mormon colonies, and so did I. Our church overflowed at her funeral.

When Domer was born at Klondyke, Az., Dad bought Mom a new Singer sewing machine. Her machine was to her as water is to a duck. It was her life. She learned to use it and became an expert at making most anything. I was the best dressed kid in school. She made all my clothes, even my suits. When I graduated from the eighth grade, she made my shirt from a flour sack. We bought our flour in one hundred pound sacks. I had the nicest shirt of the class. When I was in high school, Dad bought a cloth called mole skin, by the bolt. I think it came from England. She made our pants from it. I have never had clothes that fit me so good since. Mexican--made clothes were not so good and we couldn't afford to go to the US to buy them. When I graduated from the JSA she made my suit.

She learned to work leather and made jackets and gloves. She had all the business she could do. She made gloves for lots of folks. Ranchers came to her from miles away. They would usually bring their own hide. Lots of buckskin. She liked to work with buckskin because it was soft, but she had trouble with the fingers twisting. She judged a buckskin glove by how straight the fingers were. The gloves were made wrong side out, and I was one of her glove turners. The glove turning was a tough little job, but if she could make them, the rest of the family sure learned to turn them. After some years of the glove turning, she handed me a pair of gloves to turn and I noticed a string hanging from each finger. She told me to pull the string and see how that would work. It took all the fun out of turning gloves. As she sewed the end of the finger she attached a leather string, and when the finger was turned, we just cut off the little string. How simple, but I have always thought, how clever.

Mom did so many things I thought were clever, or you might say just using her head and working with the tools she had, which were few. I have told how she made candy at Klondyke and how she made cookies at Columbus. The thing she did that I remember so clearly is how she made the first donuts that I had ever seen. Her wedding ring was one of those wide gold bands and that was how she cut the holes. That was at Klondyke. She didn't make them very often because it took too much grease. She also cooked those little holes.

Mom was very good at doing and making things. She was good with a hammer and saw, and a few sticks of wood. She built many things around the house, and I helped her. I learned from her, and I think I inherited my abilities from her. When I am making something in my wood shop, I always think how she would enjoy the tools I have to work with. I think those abilities run in the Crabtree family because I have seen cousins who are very good with their hands.

It is hard to put in writing all the things my mother did to make me love her so much, but right now I'm thinking of how she made it possible for Mart to be with me during World War II. While I was stationed in California, Mom took care of our little boys, Floyde and Sid. Those boys sure did love her.

In later years when she was a widow, we both lived in Las Cruces, N M. She made her home with Ada Beth, (my sister) and helped to raise Ada's two boys, and of course they loved her. In fact, they thought she belonged to them only. I was able to spend lots of time with her in those years, and I did lots of things for her, but could never make up for all she had done for me. We just ran out of time. Mart and I traveled a lot and we took her with us many places when she could go. She always told me she really didn't like to fly, but when I said let's go, she soon got ready. I guess the longest trip we took her on was to Salt Lake City. Mart's three sisters in Salt Lake took her in tow and sure made her feel welcome. On part of that trip, Mart let her ride in the front seat, and I got her to do some of the flying. She was amazed that we didn't fall out of the sky with her at the controls.

In Las Cruces, she quit making gloves. There really wasn't a demand and her hands couldn't work the leather anymore anyhow, but she did lots of sewing, mostly things she enjoyed. She made pillows with western scenes. When we opened our tire store, she made me a pillow top for the grand opening, and I have it on the wall of my office. I look at it and think of her often. I also have the last pair of gloves she made. They were for me.

Her resting place is next to mine and Mart's, and so some day we will join her there. I told how she loved her machine and how she made so many things. When she moved to Las Cruces, to live with Ada, she bought a Pfaff and enjoyed it for many years. When she knew she had terminal cancer I went to see her one day and she was putting her machine away for the last time. She cleaned it so gently and folded it in it's cabinet. I watched her and as we were talking I was thinking to myself, "I hope when my time comes I can be as much a man as she was a lady." I can't write down all the credit she deserves because I just don't know how.

I used to think of things I knew that no one else knew about me. Now I think of things that I know that everyone else knows about me if they have read my book. I have sure laid my life into an open book. I hope as my autobiography is read, it will be enjoyed as much as I have enjoyed writing it.

Siempre Agradecido

Bill Adams

www.ingramcontent.com/pod-product-compliance
Lightning Source LLC
Chambersburg PA
CBHW060513230426
43665CB00013B/1497